Making Meaning

Harvard Film Studies

WITHDRAWN

1 1 JUN 2024

College of Ripon & York St. John

3 8025 00321146 6

Making Meaning

Inference and Rhetoric in the
Interpretation of Cinema

LIBRARY, UNIVERSITY COLLEGE
OF RIPON & YORK ST. JOHN
RIPON HG4 2QX

David Bordwell

Harvard University Press

Cambridge, Massachusetts
London, England

Copyright © 1989 by the President and Fellows of Harvard College
All rights reserved
Printed in the United States of America
THIRD PRINTING, 1994

First Harvard University Press paperback edition, 1991

Library of Congress Cataloging-in-Publication Data
Bordwell, David.
   Making meaning : inference and rhetoric in the interpretation of
cinema / David Bordwell.
      p.   cm.
   Bibliography: p.
   Includes index.
   ISBN 0-674-54335-1 (alk. paper) (cloth)
   ISBN 0-674-54336-X (paper)
   1. Film criticism. 2. Motion pictures. I. Title.
PN1995.B6172   1989
791.43'01'5—dc19   89-30324
                                                          CIP

For
Samuel Becker
Angelo Bertocci
Richard Goldman
Fred Silva
Patricia Ward

Contents

Preface

Viktor Shklovsky began his 1923 book *The Knight's Move* by announcing that his subject was the conventionality of art. It is probably a measure of the difference between his epoch and ours that I take as my subject the conventionality of criticism.

Shklovsky could hardly have anticipated that criticism would become rationalized on the scale it is today. Interpretation has become a significant American industry, sustaining many thousands of journalists, intellectuals, and academics, and consuming even more thousands of pages of print. A college graduate risks less ignominy and hardship by following a career in Criticism, Inc., than by trying to write novels, paint pictures, or make films. We are well along in Randall Jarrell's Age of Criticism, and there is no sign that it is on the wane. Nevertheless, despite recent conceptions of "institution" and "discourse," demands that critics acknowledge their theoretical assumptions, and severe attacks upon earlier critical traditions, one set of practices remains almost wholly taken for granted. Put aside the schools, doctrines, nomenclature, and agendas; ignore the official histories that show one critical theory crowned, only to be neatly overthrown by another that fortunately answers just those questions that its predecessor ignored; above all, pay less attention to what critics say they do and more attention to their actual procedures of thinking and writing—do all this, and you will be led to nothing but a body of conventions no less powerful than the premises of an academic style in painting or music. Shklovsky might well conclude that this body of conventions, like any familiar style, needs to be roughened, put at arm's length, "made strange."

This is the task that I pursue in the pages that follow. This book is at once a history of film criticism, an analysis of how critics interpret films, and a suggestion for some alternative research programs. Except for a few polemical stretches, the book seeks to survey interpretive practice with the ethnographer's calm curiosity. I have tried to take nothing for granted and have hoped to be surprised. I want to describe how an institution constructs and constrains what is thought and said by its members, and how the members solve routine problems by producing acceptable discourse.

Criticism is neither a science nor a fine art, but it resembles both. Like them, it depends upon cognitive skills; it requires imagination and taste; and it consists of institutionally sanctioned problem-solving activities. Criticism is, I think, best considered a practical art, somewhat like quilting or furniture-making. Because its primary product is a piece of language, it is also a rhetorical art.

The chapters that follow will not treat interpretation from the standpoint of philosophy or linguistics. Debates within hermeneutics or Wittgensteinian ruminations on the concept of reading lie only on the fringes of this book. Nor am I concerned primarily to summarize developments in criticism as following from changes in film theory. Plenty of such expositions are available; synopsizing contemporary film theory has become a minor genre of academic writing. More to the point, my argument will suggest that the influence of film theory upon practical criticism has been generally misunderstood.

Nor is this book principally concerned with particular interpretations. In order to study critical practice as such, we must pretend that all theories are correct, all methods are valid, and all critics are right. Holding partisan debates in abeyance helps us trace out underlying norms. We can study how film critics build up interpretations and try to convince others that those interpretations warrant attention. Because of my argument's generality, the book has implications for critical argument in all the arts, so readers outside cinema studies may find some pages of interest.

If criticism is cognitive and rhetorical, metacriticism is too. It would be disingenuous to pretend that I am neutrally surveying critical activities, in fee to no goal of my own. For one thing, I cannot fully play the ethnographer. I am a member of the group I am studying, my categories come to a large extent from that group, and I use examples drawn from my own writing. By acknowledging my place within this institution, I hope to draw on my sense of the conventions while gaining empathy with other participants' actions.

More broadly, my own concerns show in a three-point argument. First, I characterize the short history of film criticism by surveying two approaches to interpretation: thematic explication and symptomatic reading. Both have existed in one form or another since the Second World War, but the former dominates the 1950s and 1960s, while the latter, emerging during the 1940s, gained prominence at the beginning of the 1970s. Both currently coexist, although the symptomatic approach is today widely believed to be at the cutting edge.

Probably most practitioners of film criticism will find this dichotomy fairly uncontroversial. My second argument is more contentious. I want to show that, as practiced, both the explicatory and the symptomatic modes share a fundamental interpretive logic and rhetoric. Although their theoretical commitments differ, the two approaches utilize similar inferential moves and persuasive devices. This ought not to surprise us; criticism is shaped by the institutions that house it, and the practices by which institutions guide the act of interpretation are constant across critical schools. Nonetheless, I do not expect to win the reader's assent easily on this point. The bulk of the book is devoted to proving it.

Finally, I want to suggest some problems with giving interpretation a starring role in criticism. This book was written out of a belief that the great days of interpretation-centered criticism are over; that the basic strategies and tactics have all been tried; and that this book itself, by laying out a logic of interpretive practice, will have suggested what a routine activity criticism has come to be. (Indeed, in some sense I will probably be the last to grasp, the book is itself a symptom of the lassitude of the interpretive tradition.) I could certainly be wrong on all these counts. Nonetheless, if this book has a sting, it is in the tail. The last chapter tries to remind the reader of alternatives to an interpretation-driven criticism. One can do other things with films besides "reading" them.

I have called this project ethnographic, but it is fundamentally an exercise in practical poetics. From one angle, analyzing critical norms is a natural step beyond studying the conventions underpinning various sorts of filmmaking. Moreover, in the course of my research I have been trying to construct a historical poetics of cinema, an account of how, at various times, films have been put together and have elicited particular effects. Again and again I have encountered the issue of meaning, and the ways its definition, function, and importance vary within various filmmaking practices. I have also been challenged, on more than one occasion, to show how my own critical practice engaged with the "semantic" dimension of films. I had always found this request puzzling, since I thought that I was addressing problems of meaning at many points. Yet my ideas were not explicit enough to my questioners, chiefly because they were not clear enough to me. With *Narration in the Fiction Film* (1985), I started to treat meaning as one effect of a film, and in the revision of the textbook *Film Art: An Introduction* (1985), I tried to distinguish different kinds of meaning. I began to understand why I had fallen afoul of certain presumptions. The types of meaning I was interested in were taken as unproblematic and uninteresting by most film scholars, while the sorts of meaning I was expected to discuss were considered absolutely central to the institution of film criticism.

This disparity excited me. It encouraged me to pursue my hunch that various types of meaning constitute part of a film's effects, and that one could study how certain viewers—for instance, critics—register those effects. I began to suspect that principles of cognitive psychology and rational-agent social theory could cooperate to produce a constructivist theory of interpretation. The result has been an argument that may contribute something to the theory of the reception of films, and that should demonstrate that metacriticism can be an integral part of a poetics. I would hope, then, that apart from serving as a report on how a certain tribe thinks and talks, this book shows that a historical poetics of film can illuminate the problem of how, when, and to what extent films mean.

In writing this book, I have faced a hard choice about how to handle the pieces of critical writing I discuss. I considered concentrating on a few influential exemplars, but I rejected this possibility. Comprehensively describing an activity requires one to look at "ordinary" as well as "extraordinary" examples. The book thus offers a wide range of evidence developed at varying lengths. This tactic has required short quotations from many works; I have sought to be sensitive to the peril of pulling things out of context.

In an institution that puts a premium on novelty, members do not like to be told that they significantly resemble their predecessors and adversaries. Critics who think of themselves as predominantly theorists do not welcome arguments that theory is not essential to their enterprise. Yet as one who has learned most of what he knows about criticism during that turbulent period 1963–1976, I should point out that this book comes from the tradition that holds that critical discourse is a mode of practice, that institutions maintain themselves by means of representational conventions, and that the concepts, discourse, and history of any intellectual activity should be subject to analysis. Critics who want to denaturalize a society's taken-for-granted activities should not reject an attempt to do the same to their work.

While writing this book, I became aware of many studies of institutional and inferential conventions in scientific and humanistic inquiry. Like the new parents who discover that the world is suddenly full of babies, I have come to realize that I am not alone. The works of R. S. Crane, Richard Levin, Jonathan Culler, Tzvetan Todorov, Michel Charles, Ellen Schauber and Ellen Spolsky, Bruno Latour, and others have helped me pursue my inquiry. Up to the very last stages of revision, publications such as J. C. Nyíri and Barry Smith's *Practical Knowledge: Outline of a Theory of Traditions and Skills*, Paul Thagard's *Computational Philosophy of Science*, and Ronald N. Giere's *Explaining Science: A Cognitive Approach* sustained my hope that the "cognitive revolution" offers a useful framework for understanding sophisticated and specialized problem-solving practices.

Other debts remain. My research and writing were supported by a summer grant from the University of Wisconsin–Madison Graduate School and by a fellowship during the fall of 1987 in the University of Wisconsin–Madison Institute for Research in the Humanities. I have come to depend upon the Seminary Book Cooperative (5757 University Avenue, Chicago IL 60637) as much as on our fine campus library. Diagrams were provided by the University of Wisconsin–Madison Cartographic Laboratory; I am especially grateful to Onno Brouwer there. Lloyd Bitzer and Michael Leff answered my questions about classical rhetoric. Kevin Hagopian and Donald Crawford lent me useful articles. Edward Branigan, Mike Budd, Francesco Casetti, Don Crafton, Thomas Elsaesser, Lea Jacobs, Henry Jenkins, Richard Maltby, Kevin Sweeney, and Charles Wolfe offered sharp commentary on my ideas. Noël Carroll provided virtual line-by-line commentary. As usual, Kristin Thompson loyally struggled to make meaning out of my prose, and then she helped me rewrite it.

I have realized, in the course of the book, what critical thinking has meant to me, and especially how its less conventional possibilities were incarnated in five splendid teachers. Their names are found on the dedication page.

Making Meaning

1
Making Films Mean

For better or worse, it is the commentator who has the last word.
—Vladimir Nabokov, *Pale Fire*

"I do not know," remarks Roland Barthes, "if reading is not, constitutively, a plural field of scattered practices, of irreducible effects, and if, consequently, the reading of reading, meta-reading, is not itself merely a burst of ideas, of fears, of desires, of delights, of oppressions."[1] Barthes's doubt seems to me too strong; a systematic metacriticism of interpretation is a plausible project. Nonetheless, the task does require some ground-clearing.

Interpretation as Construction

To speak of "interpretation" invites misunderstanding from the outset. The Latin *interpretatio* means "explanation" and derives from *interpres,* a negotiator or translator or go-between. Interpretation is then a kind of explanation inserted between one text or agent and another. Originally, interpretation was conceived as wholly a verbal process, but in current usage the term can denote just about any act that makes or transmits meaning. A computer interprets instructions, a conductor interprets a score. A divinator interprets the will of the gods, while at the United Nations an interpreter translates between languages. In the criticism of the arts, interpretation may be counterposed to description or analysis; alternatively, criticism as a whole is sometimes identified with interpretation. A perceptual psychologist may describe the simplest act of hearing or seeing as an interpretation of sensory data, while a philosopher may speak of interpretation as a high-level act of judgment. Our first problem, then, is to interpret "interpretation."

I start by stipulating some exclusions. Some writers take "interpretation" to be synonymous with all production of meaning.[2] The chief notion behind this broad usage is that any act of understanding is mediated; even the simplest act of perceptual recognition is "interpretive" in that it is more than a simple recording of sensory data. If no knowledge is direct, all knowledge derives from "interpretation." I agree with the premise but see no reason to advance the conclusion. Psychologically and socially, knowledge involves *inferences*. In the chapters that follow I shall use the term *interpretation* to denote only certain kinds of inferences about meaning. For much the same reason, I shall not be using *reading* as a synonym for all inferences about meaning, or even for those interpretive inferences about films' meanings. I reserve the term *reading* for interpretation of literary texts.[3]

Introducing the concept of inference enables us to flesh out a common conceptual distinction. Most critics distinguish between *comprehending* a film and *interpreting* it, though they would often disagree about where the boundary line is to be drawn. This distinction follows the classic hermeneutic division between *ars intelligendi*, the art of understanding, and *ars explicandi*, the art of explaining.[4] Roughly speaking, one can understand the plot of a James Bond film while remaining wholly oblivious to its more abstract mythic, religious, ideological, or psychosexual significance. On the basis of the comprehension/interpretation distinction, tradition identifies two sorts of meaning, summed up in Paul Ricoeur's definition of interpretation: "the work of thought which consists in deciphering the hidden meaning in the apparent meaning, in unfolding the levels of meaning implied in the literal meaning."[5] Thus comprehension is concerned with apparent, manifest, or direct meanings, while interpretation is concerned with revealing hidden, nonobvious meanings.[6]

To speak of *hidden* meanings, *levels* of meaning, and *revealing* meanings evokes the dominant framework within which critics understand interpretation. The artwork or text is taken to be a container into which the artist has stuffed meanings for the perceiver to pull out. Alternatively, an archaeological analogy treats the text as having strata, with layers or deposits of meaning that must be excavated. In either case, comprehension and interpretation are assumed to open up the text, penetrate its surfaces, and bring meanings to light. As Frank Kermode puts it: "The modern critical tradition, for all its variety, has one continuous element, the search for occulted sense in texts of whatever period."[7]

Yet to assume that sense is "in" the text is to reify what can only be the result of a process. Comprehending and interpreting a literary text, a painting, a play, or a film constitutes an activity in which the perceiver plays a central role. The text is inert until a reader or listener or spectator does something to and with it. Moreover, in any act of perception, the effects are "underdetermined" by the data: what E. H. Gombrich calls "the beholder's share" consists in selecting and structuring the perceptual field. Understanding is mediated by transformative acts, both "bottom-up"—mandatory, automatic psychological processes—and "top-down"—conceptual, strategic ones. The sensory data of the film at hand furnish the materials out of which inferential processes of perception and cognition build meanings. Meanings are not found but made.[8]

Comprehension and interpretation thus involve the *construction* of meaning out of textual cues. In this respect, meaning-making is a psychological and social activity fundamentally akin to other cognitive processes. The perceiver is not a passive receiver of data but an active mobilizer of structures and processes (either "hard-wired" or learned) which enable her to search for information relevant to the task and data at hand. In watching a film, the perceiver identifies certain cues which prompt her to execute many inferential activities—ranging from the mandatory and very fast activity of perceiving apparent motion, through the more "cognitively penetrable" process of constructing, say, links between scenes, to the still more open process of ascribing abstract meanings to the film. In most cases, the spectator applies knowledge structures to cues which she identifies within the film.

Taking meaning-making to be a constructive process does not entail sheer relativism or an infinite diversity of interpretation. I take the informing metaphor seriously. Construction is not ex nihilo creation; there must be prior materials which undergo transformation.[9] Those materials include not only the perceptual output furnished by mandatory and universal bottom-up processes but also the higher-level textual data upon which various interpreters base their inferences.[10] A composition, a camera movement, or a line of dialogue may be ignored by one critic and highlighted by another, but each datum remains an intersubjectively discriminable aspect of the film. While critics build up meanings by applying institutional protocols and normalized psychological strategies, we shall see that they typically agree upon what textual cues are "there," even if they interpret the cues in differing ways. Indeed, in Chapter 11 I shall argue that one virtue of a poetics of cinema is that it offers middle-level theoretical concepts that capture intersubjectively significant cues.

Both comprehension and interpretation, then, require the spectator to apply conceptual schemes to data picked out in the film. What sorts of conceptual schemes might be used?

The first candidate might be a *theory*. A film theory consists of a system of propositions that claims to explain the nature and functions of cinema. Many critics today would assert that, consciously or unconsciously, the interpreter employs some theory in order to pick out relevant cues in the film, organize them into significant patterns, and arrive at an interpretation. For example, to execute a Freudian interpretation of a film is to utilize a theory about, say, how cinema channels desire, and this will affect the selection of data and the inferences which the critic draws from them. Less obviously, many critics would go on to assert that even the critic who claims to subscribe to no theory but seeks only to understand the film "in itself" can be shown to have a tacit theory (humanist, organicist, or whatever) that shapes the interpretive act.

In several respects, I think, theories do play a role in conceptual schemes, particularly in contemporary criticism. There seems little doubt, for instance, that psychoanalytic theories of cinema do assist many critics in making meaning. But we must ask how this assistance takes place. In what sense does the interpretation *follow from* the theory?

Perhaps the critic's interpretation *tests* a theory. That is, a critical exegesis, judged acceptable on grounds of interpretive propriety, functions to confirm, revise, or reject a theoretical argument. This makes the interpretation roughly analogous to the scientific experiment that tests a hypothesis, while the conventional procedures across theoretical schools become something like an accepted scientific method.

In the course of this book I shall be trying to show that no such pure separation of theory and method obtains within film criticism. For now, I simply suggest that film interpretations do not conform to the "testing" model. Unlike a scientific experiment, no interpretation can fail to confirm the theory, at least in the hands of the practiced critic. Criticism uses ordinary (that is, nonformalized) language, encourages metaphorical and punning redescription, emphasizes rhetorical appeals, and refuses to set definite bounds on relevant data—all in the name of novelty and imaginative insight. These protocols give the critic enough leeway to claim any master theory as proven by the case at hand.

Merely finding confirming instances does not suffice as a rigorous

test of a theory in any event. This is the error of "enumerative inductivism." A confirmed scientific hypothesis must also pass the test of
"eliminative inductivism": it must be a better candidate than its rivals.[11]
At any given time, a scientific claim is tested against a background of
alternative theoretical explanations. But this condition is usually not
met within the interpretive institution. Even interpretations which
tacitly claim to be the most adequate do not characteristically present
themselves as confirming one theory at the expense of others.

Instead of positing an inductivist separation of theory and criticism,
perhaps we should think of the critic's interpretation as *deductively*
deriving from the theory. According to this line of argument, no
description of anything is conceptually innocent; it is shot through
with presuppositions and received categories. Therefore every critical
interpretation presupposes a theory of film, of art, of society, of gender,
and so on. Stanley Fish pushes this notion toward a thoroughgoing
"coherentist" account, whereby every interpretation necessarily confirms some underlying theory; there is no Archimedean point outside
the theory on which the interpreter can stand.[12]

On conceptual grounds, the deductivist conception is far from co-
gent. A theory has conceptual coherence, and it is designed to analyze
or explain some particular phenomenon. Assumptions, presuppositions, opinions, and half-baked beliefs do not add up to a theory. My
conviction that credit sequences come at the beginning and end of
movies, that the film's star is likely to portray the protagonist, and
that Technicolor is aesthetically superior to Eastmancolor does not
constitute a theory of film. Nor can a theory be inferred from my
entire (very large) stock of such beliefs—a stock which, incidentally,
contains fuzzy, slack, and contradictory formulations.

Even if every interpreter tacitly harbored a full-blown theory of film,
it would not necessarily determine the details of any given interpretive
outcome. Two psychoanalytic critics might agree on every tenet of
abstract doctrine and still produce disparate interpretations. In any
event, no critic acts as if every theory automatically extruded an interpretation that is challengeable only in terms of that theory. Critic B
can agree with Critic A's putative theory but suggest that certain
aspects of the film still need explaining. Or Critic B can accept the
interpretation as valuable and enlightening while proceeding to dispute the theory. Neither critic assumes that the theory dictates the
interpretation.

So might we simply say that the critic's interpretation *illustrates* a theory? Jacques Lacan opens his seminar on Poe's "Purloined Letter" by announcing: "We have decided to illustrate for you today the truth which may be drawn from that moment in Freud's thought under study—namely, that it is the symbolic order which is constitutive for the subject—by demonstrating in a story the decisive orientation which the subject receives from the itinerary of the signifier."[13] In a similar fashion, some theoretically inflected criticism has used films to illustrate the theories proposed.[14]

This is a much weaker claim than the inductive and deductive conceptions. To make an interpretation a parable of a theory is not to undertake to establish the truth of the theory. Any doctrine, be it psychoanalysis or Scientology, can be illustrated by artworks. Moreover, this proposition runs into a problem already mentioned. If not every set of beliefs relevant to the interpretive act counts as a theory of cinema, then the interpretation may illustrate the beliefs but will not illustrate a theory.

Perhaps, then, a theory merely offers *insights* which can guide the critic's interpretation. This formulation sounds appealing, and many practicing critics would probably accept it. Once again, though, this makes the relation of theory to the work only contingent. An unusually wise critic, wholly innocent of theory, might be brimful of insights which could yield intriguing interpretations. And once again, this view surrenders any concern for the theory's claims to truth. From this perspective, a critic could use the I Ching, numerology, astrology, or any fanciful system as long as it generated hunches that led to acceptable interpretations. In fact, the critical institution does not permit such wide-ranging research methods. Only certain theories count as worth mining, and those are assumed to be valid or accurate on grounds other than their applicability to the film at hand. (Psychoanalytic theory furnishes obvious examples.) "Insight" does not suffice as a criterion to guide critics' choice and use of theories.

I have tried to show that the critic's interpretation does not follow from a theory in any strong sense. Some other sort of conceptual scheme must play a role. Since Jonathan Culler's pathbreaking *Structuralist Poetics,* several theorists have proposed that critics produce interpretations by following *rules.*[15] Despite the significant results of this line of research, the concept of rules upon which it rests remains somewhat vague.[16] In most cases, the term *rule* is largely synonymous with "norm" or "convention."

Being a little fussy here will help clarify the argument to come.

Critics arrive at interpretations, I suggest, by using certain conventions of reasoning and language. Criticism is conventional in that broad sense identified by David Lewis: it creates regularities in behavior by coordinating the actions of agents who have expectations that common goals will be met.[17] But critics do not obey stringent rules, like the one that directs drivers to stop for a red light. Critical interpretation, it seems to me, chiefly consists of a "covert" or tacit conventionality. In such cases people are largely unaware of the conventions they obey. Imitation and habit lead agents to expect coordinated action from others but without any particular awareness of an underlying rule.[18]

The concept of tacit convention seeks to capture both psychological and social dimensions of the interpretive activity. Psychologically, interpretive conventions rely upon reasoning practices. Most generally, human beings possess broad inductive skills which govern everyday sense-making, and these play a large role in interpreting artworks. Critics also possess skills which are attuned to specialized domains. Together, all such reasoning practices constitute interpretive expertise. The rules involved are primarily rules of thumb. Like an artisan using strategies derived from experience, the critic draws upon a repertory of options and adjusts them to the particular task. And this skill no more constitutes a theory of cinema than a good bicyclist's know-how amounts to a physics of moving bodies or a sociology of recreation.

From a social perspective, conventions can be seen as coordinating agents' patterns of action for the benefit of the goals of a group. To perform the role of film interpreter is to accept certain aims of the interpretive institution and to act in accordance with norms that enable those aims to be reached. Here again, goal-achieving strategies need not consist of theories in any rigorous sense. Indeed, if the critic is like an artisan, she will tend to "dwell within" the standard practices: abstract theoretical knowledge will fade into the background, tacit procedures will govern her inferences, and attention will focus on the minutiae of the task at hand.[19]

A constructivist account of "the beholder's share," then, has the task of explaining how pragmatic reasoning practices guide the critic's act of assumption, expectation, and exploration; how cues are highlighted, arranged, and worked into the basis of critical inferences; how the film flashing on the screen is reconstructed into a meaningful whole by the perceiver's perceptual and cognitive activity. Chapter 2 will seek to show how institutional norms and reasoning strategies shape the conventions of critical interpretation. Before we consider them, though, I want to introduce some distinctions that are fundamental to this book's argument. It is time to say more about meaning.

Meaning Made

I suggest that when spectators or critics make sense of a film, the meanings they construct are of only four possible types.

1. The perceiver may construct a concrete "world," be it avowedly fictional or putatively real. In making sense of a narrative film, the spectator builds up some version of the *diegesis,* or spatio-temporal world, and creates an ongoing story *(fabula)* occurring within it.[20] The spectator may construe nonnarrative forms, such as rhetorical or taxonomic ones, as proposing a world that manifests structures of an argumentative or categorical nature.[21] In constructing the film's world, the spectator draws not only on knowledge of filmic and extrafilmic conventions but also on conceptions of causality, space, and time and on concrete items of information (for example, what the Empire State Building looks like). This very extensive process eventuates in what I shall call *referential* meaning, with the referents taken as either imaginary or real. We can speak of both Oz and Kansas as aspects of referential meaning in *The Wizard of Oz:* Oz is an intratextual referent, Kansas an extratextual one.[22]

2. The perceiver may move up a level of abstraction and assign a conceptual meaning or "point" to the fabula and diegesis she constructs. She may seek out explicit cues of various sorts for this, assuming that the film "intentionally" indicates how it is to be taken. The film is assumed to "speak directly." A verbal indication such as the line "There's no place like home" at the end of *The Wizard of Oz,* or a stereotyped visual image such as the scales of Justice, could be said to furnish such cues. When the viewer or critic takes the film to be, in one way or another, "stating" abstract meanings, he is constructing what I shall call *explicit* meaning.[23] Referential and explicit meaning make up what are usually considered "literal" meanings.

3. The perceiver may also construct covert, symbolic, or *implicit* meanings. The film is now assumed to "speak indirectly."[24] For example, you might assume that *Psycho*'s referential meaning consists of its fabula and diegesis (the trip of Marion Crane from Phoenix to Fairvale, and what happens there), and you might take its explicit

meaning to be the idea that madness can overcome sanity. You might then go on to argue that *Psycho*'s implicit meaning is that sanity and madness cannot be easily distinguished. Units of implicit meaning are commonly called "themes," though they may also be identified as "problems," "issues," or "questions."[25]

The spectator may seek to construct implicit meanings when she cannot find a way to reconcile an anomalous element with a referential or explicit aspect of the work; or the "symbolic impulse" may be brought in to warrant the hypothesis that any element, anomalous or not, may serve as the basis of implicit meanings. Furthermore, the critic may take implicit meanings to be consistent, at some level, with the referential and explicit meanings assigned to the work. Or, as in the process of irony, implicit meanings may be posited as contradicting other sorts. For example, if you posit that the psychiatrist's final speech in *Psycho* explicitly draws a line between sanity and madness, you might see the film's implicit denial of such a demarcation as creating an ironic effect.

4. In constructing meanings of types 1–3, the viewer assumes that the film "knows" more or less what it is doing. But the perceiver may also construct *repressed* or *symptomatic* meanings that the work divulges "involuntarily." Moreover, such meanings are assumed to be at odds with referential, explicit, or implicit ones. If explicit meaning is like a transparent garment, and implicit meaning is like a semiopaque veil, symptomatic meaning is like a disguise. Taken as individual expression, symptomatic meaning may be treated as the consequence of the artist's obsessions (for example, *Psycho* as a worked-over version of a fantasy of Hitchcock's). Taken as part of a social dynamic, it may be traced to economic, political, or ideological processes (for example, *Psycho* as concealing the male fear of woman's sexuality).

In what follows, I shall assume that the activity of comprehension constructs referential and explicit meanings, while the process of interpretation constructs implicit and symptomatic meanings. But I do not intend the comprehension/interpretation couplet to correspond to a distinction between the naive viewer's "innocent viewing" and the trained viewer's "active" or "creative" reading. A first-time viewer of a film under "normal" conditions may well seek to construct implicit and symptomatic meanings, while the interpretive critic reflecting on the film after the fact will still find referential and explicit meanings relevant. Still, in this book I will not be much concerned with comprehension.[26] My stress here falls on interpretation, conceived as a cognitive activity taking place within particular institutions.[27]

Barthes's pessimism about a metacriticism of reading is probably based on the fact that interpreters can ascribe an indefinitely large range of meanings to a textual element. If I am right, however, each such meaning will function as one of the four sorts I have indicated. The taxonomy makes it possible to study—socially, psychologically, rhetorically—the principles and procedures of meaning-making, independent of the particular meanings that are made.

What must be stressed is that these four categories of meaning-construction are *functional* and *heuristic,* not substantive. Used in the processes of comprehension and interpretation, they constitute distinctions with which perceivers approach films; they are assumptions which can generate hypotheses about particular meanings. To the same textual element, different critics assign not only different meanings but also different *sorts* of meaning. The sexual meaning of the skyscrapers and drills in *The Fountainhead* may be considered explicit or implicit or symptomatic, depending on the rationale of the critic's argument.

This is one reason why interpretation can generate a cycle of meaning-production. Critic A can take certain referential and explicit meanings as literal and seek to interpret the film as having other, implicit meanings. Critic B can take the same implicit meanings as a point of departure and build a symptomatic interpretation of what they, and the referential and explicit meanings, repress. But the next interpretation can swallow up Critic B's. Critic C may offer a new set of symptomatic meanings, perhaps by treating Critic B's interpretation as repressing the real dynamic of the text. Or Critic C may treat the entire configuration of meanings as implicit, so that the work deliberately symbolizes the relation of the repressed to the manifest content.[28]

Consider a controversy that arose in 1955 around Lindsay Anderson's critique of the ending of *On the Waterfront.* Although the opening title announces the film as showing how a "vital democracy" can defeat "self-appointed tyrants," Anderson contends that the film actually celebrates undemocratic action. He suggests that throughout the movie Terry acts wholly on his own, spurred on by selfishness and revenge. Anderson also proposes that the final scene of the beaten Terry leading the dockmen back to work harbors a fascist meaning, that of the need to follow a strong leader. Anderson is constructing an explicit meaning (the democratic moral), which he attributes to the film's "consciousness," and a repressed meaning (the totalitarian faith in a superman) that works against this. The latter meaning emerges in the final image of the lowering portcullis shutting the men off from the mob. "Whether intentional or not," Anderson notes, "the symbolism is unmistakable": the men are locked in a dark world of toil, and Terry's sacrifice has won them no real liberation.[29]

Several *Sight and Sound* readers wrote in to dispute Anderson's symptomatic interpretation. Some recast his data in referential terms: the workers follow Terry because they recognize his right to a job; they acknowledge him to be their surrogate and let him go forward as "a matter of courtesy and respect." Others proposed implicit meanings: Terry's walk symbolizes his moral rebirth or recalls Christ's Via Dolorosa.[30] The most extensive rebuttal was offered by Robert Hughes, who posits a psychological development in Terry that leads him to cut himself off from both Johnny Friendly's gang and his fellow workers. Hughes points out that before the climactic fight Terry replies to the gang's taunts with: "I'm standin' over here right now." Hughes adds: "His standpoint has changed." That is, Hughes puns on the word *standpoint* to make Terry's physical separation imply psychological independence.[31] Thus Terry's final walk becomes not the march of a herd's leader but a signal that he has repudiated the gang, a decision that impels the dockers to cluster around him. Hughes counters Anderson's symptomatic interpretation with one that relies on implicit meanings. We have long known that critics can shift their interpretive focus from datum to datum (here, from the portcullis image to a significant line of dialogue); we ought to recognize that they can also shift among types of meaning.

Nor should we assume that the four sorts of meanings constitute levels which the critic must traverse in a given sequence. The interpreter need not analyze referential or explicit meaning in detail. There is evidence that whereas beginning interpreters of poetry do read referentially and have trouble making the thematic leap, skilled interpreters try out implicit meanings from the start and often neglect the "literal" level, or summon it up only to help the interpretation along.[32] Teaching cinema in college furnishes plenty of occasions to watch people plunge into interpretations of shots whose diegetic status has not yet been established. I once attended a conference at which a British film theorist confidently offered symbolic interpretations of frame enlargements from movies which he had never seen.

At times, of course, a critic can try to halt the play of meaning by dismissing implicit or symptomatic possibilities and tying the film more closely to the referential and explicit levels. This is what some of the *Sight and Sound* readers tried to do with Anderson's symptomatic interpretation. Another example would be Dwight MacDonald's claim that Fellini's *8½* expresses its theme of aging "not in Bergman-esque symbols or narcissistic musings but in episodes that arise naturally out of the drama." The film is "nothing but a pleasurable work of art . . . a worldly film, all on the surface . . . delightfully obvious."[33] Yet another critic can always claim that sticking to the literal level ignores the intriguing possibilities of meaning offered by the text, and that one is entitled, perhaps compelled, to look more closely.

Furthermore, as the *On the Waterfront* instance suggests, there is not always a consensus about the film's explicit and referential meanings. Most viewers seem to agree that *Invasion of the Body Snatchers* offers a "message," but there is considerable dispute about exactly whether it is anticommunist, anti-American, or anticonformist. Worse, viewers may also disagree about "what happens" in the diegesis—about the concrete actions, the characters' motives, the definiteness of the resolution, and many other aspects. The critic can back up his construal either by seeking out extratextual information, such as interviews with the director, or by looking for more evidence at the referential level. Neither course will inevitably yield firm results. A moviegoer writes in to a columnist:

> Dear Pat: I almost had a heart attack when the writer in the movie *Stand by Me,* played by Richard Dreyfuss, turned off his word processor without pushing the key to "save" the story. Now a friend insists this was meant to be symbolic, that he was putting the past behind him. What are the facts?
>
> —Hacker, Marina del Rey, California

> Dear Hacker: It was ignorance, not philosophical. Neither director Rob Reiner nor Dreyfuss uses home computers—nor apparently did anyone else connected with the picture.[34]

Hacker's friend follows the critic's rule of thumb that referential anomalies furnish good cues for implicit meaning. In an equally common countermove, Pat looks for extratextual sources to explain the referential uncertainty. The first tactic encourages the critic to ask, "What does the referential anomaly *contribute* to the text?" (Is it, for instance, inviting "symbolic" or "philosophical" reflection? Does it create an ambiguity?) The second tactic invites the critic to ask, "How did this anomaly *get in* the text?" (Did the artist make a mistake? Did censors interfere?) The disparity is that between functionalist and causal explanations and, more notoriously, between a "formalist" criticism and a "historical" one.

Taking meaning-making as a constructive activity leads us to a fresh model of interpreting films. The critic does not burrow into the text, probe it, get behind its facade, dig to reveal its hidden meanings; the surface/depth metaphor does not capture the inferential process of interpretation. On the constructivist account, the critic starts with aspects of the film ("cues") to which certain meanings are ascribed. An interpretation is built upward, as it were, gaining solidity and scale as other textual materials and appropriate supports (analogies, extrinsic evidence, theoretical doctrines) are introduced. Another critic may come along and add a wing or story to the interpretation, or detach portions for use in a different project, or build a larger edifice that aims to include the earlier one, or knock the first one down and start again. Yet every critic, as I shall try to show, draws on craft traditions that dictate how proper interpretations are built.

Interpretive Doctrines

The types of meaning-making I have described are clearly discernible across many centuries of literary interpretation. A thumbnail history, however schematic, can usefully remind us that film criticism carries on the routines of a remarkably coherent tradition.

In antiquity, pre-Socratic writers made Homer the vehicle of symbolic meanings. Anaxagoras identified Penelope's web with the process of the syllogism, while the Sophists and the Stoics interpreted Homer's gods as representing natural cosmic forces. Such significance, often labeled "allegory" or *hyponoia* ("under-meanings"), is a clear instance of implicit meaning. For Plato, however, implicit meanings could not redeem poetry: "A child is not able to judge which [works] have hidden meanings and which do not."[35] Therefore, Plato argued, only those works with accurate and morally correct meanings (specifically, of referential and explicit sorts) ought to be produced in the Republic. For Aristotle, however, poetry necessarily treats the universal qualities of human behavior.[36] Although the *Poetics* notably avoids discussing interpretation, the claim that poetry is "more philosophical and serious" than history furnished Renaissance writers with a rationale for disclosing implicit meanings in a literary work. Similar possibilities were opened to eighteenth-century thinkers by Longinus' remark that in a great passage of literature, "more is meant than meets the ear."[37]

By the second century A.D., the Bible had replaced Homer as the chief spur to interpretive activity. In the Roman period, the Hellenistic Jew Philo of Alexandria borrowed the Stoics' allegorical method in order to produce implicit meanings, as in this account of Samuel: "Probably there was an actual man called Samuel, but we conceive of the Samuel of the scripture not as a living compound of soul and body but as a mind which rejoices in the service and worship of God and that only."[38] In rabbinical commentaries on the Bible, *peshat* ("plain sense") focused on explicit meanings, while *midrash* consisted of filling in referential gaps (for example, what Cain said to Abel) and producing symbolic interpretations (for example, in planting a seed a biblical personage is imitating God, who created Eden).[39] With the spread of Christianity, the church fathers needed to make the Gospel coherent and comprehensive for the sake of winning converts and combatting heresy. Pauline exegesis developed the doctrine of typological meaning, whereby a person or event in the Old Testament was said to prefigure one in the New. This required an implicit analogy, or what Paul, borrowing from the Greeks, called "allegory."[40] Now explicit meanings in one portion of Scripture could furnish the basis for discovering implicit meaning in another.

The Alexandrian interpreter Origen, who was the first person to teach theology under church auspices, devised an interpretive method that eventually became Augustine's famous doctrine of the four senses of biblical texts. According to this, any passage could be read historically, allegorically (or typologically), morally (that is, as presenting how we should live now), and anagogically (as prophesying the heavenly glory to come). In our jargon, the historical meaning is referential, while the other three may be either explicit or implicit, depending on the passage. The doctrine of the four senses was imported into the reading of secular works as well, as can be seen in the celebrated 1319 letter, possibly by Dante, that suggests that *The Divine Comedy* is "polysemous, that is, having many meanings."[41] Such operations of meaning-making were not confined to texts. The twelfth-century Abbot Suger described his bejeweled altar panels as shining "with the radiance of delightful allegories" and leading the mind to heaven "in an anagogical manner."[42]

Interpretive thought in the Renaissance continued to appeal to the sorts of meanings I have described. With pagan mythology and the

Bible as their basis, commentators and historians assigned referentially based historical and cosmological meanings to obscure passages, ascribed explicit morals to fables, and explicated tales and icons as edifying allegories of the moral life.[43] Renaissance mythographers produced detailed symbolic readings of Homer, Virgil, Ovid, and even ancient Egyptian texts.[44] A dance could be taken as an allegory of the planets' celestial course.[45] The northern humanists of the sixteenth century composed emblem books and mythographic encyclopedias aiding the public in deciphering symbolic images and serving as manuals for practicing artists.[46] Within a century, Vermeer's paintings of everyday interiors could bear implicit meanings.[47] Literary theory had arrived at the formulation that poetry both teaches and pleases, and Renaissance theorists linked poetry's didactic function to its power to deliver knowledge of ethical activity. In the hands of humanists like Sidney, verbal art became an allegory of right conduct.

While such pragmatic interpretive activities continued in various arts over the next several centuries, a new theory of interpretation was emerging that promised, in contrast to church exegesis, a "scientific" basis for assigning meaning. This can be traced to Spinoza's *Tractatus theologico-politicus* of 1670. Spinoza insisted, against patristic exegesis, that hermeneutics must be concerned wholly with meaning, not with truth. He proposed that the interpreter's construction of meaning be constrained by the grammatical rules of the text's language, by the coherence of its parts, and by the historical context of its epoch.[48] Spinoza's tenets came to inform what has been called the "philological" tradition of hermeneutics in the nineteenth century. According to F. A. Wolf, the interpreter must grasp the author's thoughts, and this can be done by filling in referential background.[49] Friedrich Ast took a more comprehensive view, arguing that the interpreter must grasp not only the letter (that is, the referential meaning) and the "sense" (what is assumed to be the explicit meaning) but also the "spirit" (the implicit meaning).[50] F. D. E. Schleiermacher revised the philological tradition by shifting the emphasis from textual features to the psychological process of comprehension, conceived as an identification with the author.[51] In founding hermeneutics as "the art of understanding," Schliermacher took it out of the provinces of law, linguistics, and religion and made it a central domain of the human sciences—a project which Wilhelm Dilthey was to continue in his development of hermeneutics as a psychological, comparative, and historical discipline.[52]

The philological tradition resurfaced in literary studies at the end of the nineteenth century under the aegis of Gustave Lanson, the founder of literary *explication de texte*. Like the hermeneutic thinkers, Lanson sought to interpret the text historically. The interpreter starts with the text's literal or *grammatical* sense and supplements that with social and biographical background. Both activities involve what I have called the construction of referential meaning. Then the interpreter explicates the *literary* sources of the text, as determined by contemporary models of language or genre. Finally the interpreter moves to the *moral* meaning of the text.[53] Since the latter two stages reveal what Lanson called the text's "secret,"[54] they produce what I have called implicit meanings. Like other philologists, Lanson constrained his interpretation by a principle of fidelity to authorial intention, arrived at through scrupulous positivist research.[55]

Lanson's Viennese contemporary Sigmund Freud proposed a far more radical conception of interpretive activity. Some historians hold that psychoanalytic interpretation derives from the rhetorical, ecclesiastical, and philological traditions.[56] Others consider psychoanalysis to be allied with that "hermeneutics of suspicion" practiced by Marx and Nietzsche.[57] Michel Foucault sees psychoanalysis as providing "a perpetual principle of dissatisfaction" in that it points "not toward that which must be rendered gradually more explicit by the progressive illumination of the implicit but towards what is there and yet is hidden."[58] Certainly, in many respects Freud did not go beyond revealing what I have called implicit meanings. (His later approach to symbolism supplies the most obvious examples.) Yet he also made an original contribution to the interpretive tradition by demonstrating the force of *repressed* meaning. Explicit or implicit meaning could be a decoy. Freudian psychoanalysis posits not discrete layers to be peeled away but a dynamic struggle between "rational" pressures and the upswellings of more primal forces. Worked on by the unconscious, repressed wishes and memories return in cryptic and highly mediated forms, drawing on all the resources of figurative language and visual symbolism in order to find a compromised, and compromising, expression.[59]

By and large, twentieth-century interpretive activity has refined all these conceptions. In art-historical research, Erwin Panofsky sought to synthesize the description of subject matter (referential and explicit meanings), the analysis of "images, stories, allegories" (explicit meanings), and the interpretation of a culture's symbolic values (implicit and symptomatic meanings).[60] Anglo-American New Criticism reacted against the philological tradition by emphasizing intratextual unity, rejecting authorial intention as a guide to exegesis, and concentrating on implicit meanings. Northrop Frye's archetypal criticism can be seen as reviving allegorical translation, while the Geneva school of phenomenological criticism constitutes a new version of the philologists' reconstruction of authorial vision. Although it is common to set contemporary hermeneutics in opposition to structuralism, in fact structuralist theory has a strong interpretive bent. Claude Lévi-Strauss, for instance, ascribes implicit or symptomatic significance to customs and myths. More recently, a Marxist critic has recast Augustine's doctrine of four senses.[61] Lacan, Althusser, and Derrida have charted new domains of symptomatic reading: what is repressed becomes desire, ideological contradiction, or the subversive force of writing. Now more than ever, scholars take the construction of implicit and symptomatic meanings to be central to understanding the arts and the human sciences.

This search has shaped the history of film theory and criticism in important ways. When film study broke away from journalism on the one side and fandom on the other—when, that is, it became academic—it could have become a subdivision of sociology or mass communication studies. It was instead ushered into the academy by humanists, chiefly teachers of literature, drama, and art. As a result, cinema was naturally subsumed within the interpretive frames of reference that rule those disciplines.

More specifically, the growth of film studies attests to the powerful role of literature departments in transmitting interpretive values and skills. Academic humanism's omnivorous appetite for interpretation rendered cinema a plausible "text." (Advertising and television would later become texts too.) Moreover, literary criticism continued its expansionist phase in the 1960s, when—New Criticism and its derivatives having become solidly entrenched—the popularity of film courses made cinema a prime candidate for inclusion in a critical-skills curriculum. By this time, literary studies had embraced the ideology of multiple "approaches"—intrinsic, myth-centered, psychoanalytic, cultural-contextual, and so on. Film could be studied from all the critical perspectives that could be mobilized around a poem. The liberal pluralism that absorbed film studies (admittedly not without friction) would also eventually accommodate black and ethnic studies, women's studies, and literary theory by adding departmental units— areas, programs, courses—that brought in new interpretation-based subjects and methodologies.[62] Film also proved highly assimilable to the existing schedule of teaching novels and plays: a film or two per week, lectures and discussions interpreting the film, assigned papers to probe further. These concrete historical factors led film studies to follow the interpretive path, constructing implicit or symptomatic meanings along lines already laid down in other humanistic disciplines.

Such historical forces cast doubt on any hypothesis that interpretation is merely an assortment of diverse practices. Throughout its history, interpretation has been a social activity, a process of thinking, writing, and speaking within institutions governed by norms. Biblical interpretation was overseen by Jewish and Christian communities. Philology developed largely out of a pressure to reconcile academic and religious approaches to Scripture. Psychoanalytical interpretation was conducted within the confines of a movement characterized by a firm hierarchical structure of master, disciples, and excommunicants. Studies in art history, literature, and allied fields are conducted according to protocols of academic inquiry. Interpreters may celebrate the unique insights of particular interpretations (the "humanistic" move) or gain comfort from the way practice appears to confirm theory (the "scientific" approach). Yet both attitudes usually ignore the extent to which social factors shape not only the interpretive outcome but the very notion of what shall count as an illuminating essay or a powerful theoretical demonstration. The institution sets the goals. The next chapter suggests some ways in which it does so, and what the consequences are for making films mean.

2

Routines and Practices

Interpret and receive reward!

—*The Aggadah*

The concept of convention implies that a social group—broadly speaking, an institution—has an interest in defining common goals and regulating members' actions accordingly. As a convention-bound activity, making films mean can be treated as an institutional process. I will consider film criticism, like criticism of other arts or media in this century, to be carried on within three "macroinstitutions": journalism, essayistic writing, and academic scholarship.[1] Each one has its own characteristic "subinstitutions," both formal and informal. Table 1 gives a simplified outline.

A sociological study is beyond my abilities, but it should be clear that each of the factors noted has, at one time or another, shaped the development of film criticism. For instance, formal institutions such as Columbia University in the 1940s or the British Film Institute (BFI) since the 1960s have served to initiate or disseminate important critical ideas. Circles of collaborators, such as those around *Cahiers du cinéma, Screen,* and *Jump Cut,* have sustained interpretive projects. "Invisible colleges" have also played a large role: here friends, students, and acquaintances are linked in a circuit that need not respect geographical, theoretical, or methodological boundaries. Particularly in the academic sphere, however, utter strangers may belong to the same "school" by virtue of sharing a critical theory or method. The concept of a "school" usefully indicates that certain implicit or symptomatic meanings are valuable, vivid, or visible only to certain interpreters.

The different degrees of coherence one finds among subinstitutions should remind us that a macroinstitution may house groups pursuing significantly different interests. The medieval Christian church was riven by disputes between the schools of the monks and those of the

Table 1.   Interpretive Institutions

	Publishing format	Formal institutions	Informal institutions
Journalistic criticism	Newspapers and popular weeklies (e.g., *New York Times, Village Voice*) Television and radio programs	Employment by periodical Professional associations (e.g., New York Film Critics' Circle)	Invisible colleges (network of acquaintances, mentors, disciples, etc.)
Essayistic criticism	Specialized or intellectual monthlies or quarterlies (e.g., *Cahiers du cinéma, Artforum, Partisan Review*)	Employment by periodical Galleries, museums, etc. Colleges or universities	Circles and salons around periodical Invisible colleges
Academic criticism	Scholarly journals (e.g., *Cinema Journal*)	Colleges or universities Centers and government agencies Academic associations (e.g., Society for Cinema Studies) Conferences and conventions	Invisible colleges "Schools" (groups of practitioners of a particular theory or method; e.g., auteur criticism, feminist criticism)

friars. A more self-consciously "democratic" institution, such as modern literary criticism, assumes that the intrinsic complexity of the material under study and the impossibility of definitively assigning meaning to it permit a wide range of interpretations. Moreover, since "schools" compete in producing interpretations, what binds them into one institution are not rigid and explicit rules but rather tacit, pragmatic principles. (If the rules were explicit, somebody would be sure to found a new school based on violating them.) Critics who differ in theory or method remain consanguine by virtue of the concrete routines they employ.

Interpretation, Inc.

Film criticism was born from reviewing, and the earliest prototypes of the "film critic" were journalists charged with discussing, on a daily or weekly basis, the current output of the film industry. The reviewer might be a professional journalist or a freelancing intellectual like Louis Delluc, Riccioto Canudo, Siegfried Kracauer, Otis Ferguson, James Agee, Parker Tyler, or Graham Greene. During the 1910s and 1920s, there also appeared film journals addressed to a cinephiliac public and publishing belletristic essays. After the Second World War, most significant new schools of theory and interpretation emerged from such coterie journals: *L'Ecran français, La Revue du cinéma, Raccords, Cahiers du cinéma, Positif,* and *Cinéthique* in France; *Sequence, Sight and Sound,* and *Movie* in England; *Film Quarterly, Film Culture, Cahiers du cinéma in English,* and *Artforum* in America. Before 1970 or so, despite the importance of the education department of the British Film Institute in London during the late 1960s, most trends in film interpretation began outside the academy.

Soon, however, as film courses began to appear in upper-level school curricula, there emerged professional associations of film educators such as the Society for Education in Film and Television (SEFT) in England and the Society for Cinema Studies (SCS) in the United States. During the 1970s, educational and academic journals like the British *Screen* (published by SEFT) and the American *Cinema Journal* (published by SCS) and *The Journal of the University Film Association* came to focus more and more on theory and criticism. In 1973 the Arno Press launched a series of reprints of American Ph.D. dissertations in cinema, and when that series lapsed, the UMI Research Press continued the project, thus assuring a steady flow of scholarly monographs. At about the same time, American university presses took more interest in cinema, not least because a film book promised to sell more copies than the ordinary academic title. Now the author of a film book was apt to be an academic, whose professional career required publications bearing a scholarly imprimatur. In sum, the academicization of film publishing created an expanding institutional base for interpretive criticism.

As long as film criticism was tied to mass journalism, interpretation in the sense in which I am using the term could not flourish. Newspapers and popular magazines were impatient with exegeses. But in the pages of journals such as *Cahiers du cinéma* or *Movie* or *Film Culture*, the critic could play the role of interpreter. By and large the writing models were two: the reflective belletristic essay (cultivated chiefly in French journals) and the "close reading" (as in the work of the *Movie* group). And just as literary reviews like *La Nouvelle revue française, The Criterion, Scrutiny, The Sewanee Review,* and *Partisan Review* played host to essays by academics and provoked the growth of new schools of criticism within the academy, so film journals at once selectively imitated academic discourse and influenced the emergence of academic schools of interpretation.

That emergence was fostered by many material conditions, such as the expansion of academic publishing after the Second World War, the growth in size and prestige enjoyed by universities in western Europe and North America, and the wider accessibility of media technology, such as 16mm film projection in the 1950s, Steenbeck editing tables in the 1960s, and videocassettes in the 1970s. More specifically, certain aspects of the academic institution pushed film criticism toward concentrating upon interpretation. As I suggested at the end of the last chapter, university film studies arose within departments of literature, drama, and art history—disciplines already committed to explication and commentary. Over the same period, there also emerged a canon that could serve as a reference point for academic discourse.[2] The growing availability of 16mm prints of classic films, distributed by the Museum of Modern Art and such private firms as Audio-Brandon, made classroom study more feasible. Textbooks teaching interpretive techniques began to appear, one of the most successful being frankly titled *How to Read a Film*.[3] The film professor, constrained by course budgets and screening time, soon settled into the pattern of teaching one or two films per week. Once the single film became the unit of study, interpretation became the most convenient activity. With luck, the professor could try out some ideas in class meetings, get student reaction, and go on to make the single film the focus of a critical essay of his or her own. Like New Criticism, academic film criticism has proven easily assimilable to the university's demand for teachable techniques, professional specialization, and rapid publication output.[4]

Any institution, Mary Douglas reminds us, must create a stable context for the beliefs of its members. It must ground those beliefs in nature and reason; it must provide solid categories; it must generate a selective public memory; and it must guide its members toward routine analogies.[5] The historical situation of Anglo-American New Criticism provided such a context for film interpretation. To say as much is to do more than trace an obvious doctrinal affiliation, for in an important way New Criticism was not simply one "approach" to criticism. As a theory, it defined literature as neither scientific nor philosophical discourse, effectively creating a specialized domain of professional knowledge. Historically, New Criticism reconstituted the field of literary study and virtually created the academic institution of criticism as we know it. Whatever school, trend, or movement to which a critic pledges allegiance, the practice of interpreting a text proceeds along lines laid down by New Criticism.[6]

Several recent studies have traced how this practice works.[7] For the academic working in the shadow of New Criticism, as for the film analyst, the object of study is a text or group of texts possessing veiled meanings. In these meanings lies the significance of the work or works. The interpretation aims to be novel and to exhibit the critic's mastery of the skills of attentive, usually "close" examination.[8] To interpret a work is to produce a "reading" that justifies the work's interest for us now as well as vindicates the critic's overall claims about it. The best evidence that everyone, from myth critics to deconstructionists, accepts these premises as natural and reasonable is that virtually no one argues with them. They have become the foundation for literary criticism as such.[9] These assumptions shape the arrangement of specialties in the field, the nature of departments, the patterns of academic conferences, the sorts of books and journals that are published, the way people find jobs and get grants and promotions. All proportions kept, the same premises and institutional forces are at work in academic film criticism.

Every institution writes its own history, and here too academic film criticism models itself on its literary counterpart. Overlooking the extent to which New Criticism has become, simply, criticism, literary studies constructs a history of "approaches"—more or less elaborated theoretical doctrines about what texts may mean and how one may talk about them. The currently dominant version runs this way: First there was New Criticism (in the narrow sense), followed by myth criticism, psychoanalytic criticism, Marxist criticism, feminist criticism, reader-response criticism, deconstruction, postmodernist criticism, and so on. Every approach is assumed to create a "school," a community within the critical institution, possessing its own journals, specialized conferences, and social networks.

On the whole, the scheme is well adapted to ongoing institutional activities. A book or conference can be assembled around a single text "approached" from different angles, or critical papers can be brought together that apply the same approach to different texts. Either alternative displays the richness of literature and of literary criticism. If you believe the diversity of approaches to be salutary, you will tend to see the history of criticism as the devising of various, equally useful tools for jimmying open texts. Or you may take a partisan stance, declaring pluralism an act of intellectual evasion and asserting the superiority of one approach. This position will make you either hark back to a golden age or look forward to an era of permanent possibility (fueled by what are usually called "recent developments"). Whether you take the pluralist or partisan position, you will likely forget important things which do not fit into the reigning historical scheme— the way in which Russian Formalist criticism sought to integrate criticism with literary history, or the arguments flung at the New Critics by the Chicago Neo-Aristotelians, or the important contributions of Continental stylistics before the Second World War. Like military history, literary history is mostly written by winners. As Douglas puts it, any institution makes its members "forget experiences incompatible with its righteous image."[10] At several points in this book, we shall trace a comparable process at work in film interpretation, whereby the institution constructs a usable past for its members out of a tidy, selective chronicle of "approaches."

The legitimation of an institution, Douglas also suggests, requires the use of analogy.[11] At the level of literary schools, this is easy to see: the "intrinsic" critic compares the poem to an organism, the myth critic treats it as a piece of folklore, the Freudian likens it to a patient's recounted dream. But the more basic analogies are not often recognized. Literary interpretation seldom acknowledges the degree to which it models itself, as my thumbnail history in Chapter 1 has shown, upon mythological and scriptural exegesis. It is in many ways a secular version of biblical criticism.[12] In similar fashion, film interpretation freely confesses borrowing from this or that literary approach, but it ignores the extent to which its premises derive from the fundamental analogies laid down in postwar literary criticism.

An institution must stabilize its members' belief day in and day out, and this is accomplished less through sworn adherence to an abstract body of doctrine than by more concrete factors. The interpreter's exemplar[13] is a canonical study—an essay or book which influentially crystallizes an approach or argumentative strategy. In literary criticism, works such as Ian Watt's essay "The First Paragraph of *The Ambassadors*" or Jacques Lacan's "Seminar on 'The Purloined Letter'" or Barthes's *S/Z* are exemplars. Other exemplars will reappear throughout the pages that follow: Kracauer on German film, Bazin on Renoir and Welles, Wood on Hitchcock, Wollen on the auteur theory, the *Cahiers* editors on *Young Mr. Lincoln,* and Mulvey on gendered representation. The exemplary essay is frequently anthologized, widely taught, and constantly cited. If an exemplary book goes out of print, it leads an underground life, jealously guarded in faculty offices and photocopied by eager graduate students. The exemplar instantiates "what the field is about": if it is progressive, it shapes future work; if it has been superseded, it still must be acknowledged, attacked, quarreled with. Essayistic and academic critics write in the shadow of exemplars.

Most critics do not produce exemplars. They practice what we can call "ordinary criticism." Like T. S. Kuhn's "normal science," this is the ongoing program of a group of researchers using approved problem/solution routines to expand and fill out the realm of the known.[14] Ordinary criticism is not brainless drudgery. In science, good puzzle-solving requires the ability to spot relevant resemblances between a new problem and the paradigmatic case given by scientific training. Similarly, the watchword of ordinary criticism is analogy, often called "application." Within film studies, explicating the Western by means of a Lévi-Straussian dialectic of nature and culture or assimilating Douglas Sirk's films to a version of Brecht's "distancing" effect exemplifies how analogies drawn from other fields can be successful in the terms defined by the institution. A powerful semantic field, such as that of reflexivity, can generate a wide range of analogies (looking equals filming, mirrors equal framing, and so on) that can be endlessly projected onto films. The more recalcitrant the film, the greater the triumph when it is subsumed to a familiar interpretive scheme. Whatever the critic's school or approach, the protocols of interpretive activity are reaffirmed when a new case is accounted for, and the interpreter's membership in the community of researchers is reconfirmed by a display of interpretive ingenuity.

Exemplars and routine procedures are transmitted through education. New Criticism won its victory through being eminently teachable, and here again we find academic film studies shaped by its literary analogue.[15] The American or British film critic is likely to have had a literary education. In secondary school, he learned that disclosing implicit meanings was the central activity in understanding literature. College education reinforced and refined interpretive skills. "Reading English" at a British university often involved learning to imitate Richards, Empson, and Leavis. During the 1950s an American fresh-man encountered this passage:

> The student will do well in reading any story to ask himself such questions as the following:
>   1. What are the characters like?
>   2. Are they "real"?
>   3. What do they want?
>   4. Why do they do what they do?
>   5. Do their actions logically follow from their natures?
>   6. What do their actions tell about their characters?
>   7. How are the individual pieces of action—the special incidents—related to each other?
>   8. How are the characters related to each other?
>   9. What is the theme?
>   10. How are the characters and incidents related to the theme?[16]

Even without such explicit instruction, students could gradually master interpretive skills by writing critical papers and adjusting their efforts to the standards of reading laid down by teachers and textbooks.[17] As Barry Barnes points out, institutional training relies heavily on osten-sive definition and exposure to nonverbal, even inexplicable behav-iors.[18] In literary studies, the student learns tacit routines. Whatever critical "schools" the student encounters, she or he acquires an under-lying logic of critical practice. Historically it has proven no great difficulty to transfer such interpretive skills to cinema. Today, tens of thousands of high school and undergraduate students are learning "how to read a film" from textbooks, lectures, and writing assign-ments.

The workaday, highly structured nature of all these activities, both essayistic and academic, makes it tempting to recall John Crowe Ran-som's description of literary study as "Criticism, Inc."[19] Interpretation has become a going concern to be maintained at all costs. Conse-quently, shifts in ruling film theories do not profoundly alter the logic of interpretive practice. Most critics are "practical critics," which is to say "pragmatic critics." This should not surprise us: scientists neglect theories that may be true but leave the community little to do, and they may pursue implications of theories that they do not consciously embrace.[20] In film interpretation, as in other domains, theory is rarely constructed for its own sake. Theoretical doctrines are instantiated in exemplars, and they are then absorbed and revised in ways that sustain ordinary criticism. As a result, various schools of criticism, each with its own interests and purposes, can arrive at fresh critical interpretations but cannot reject the basic mental or rhetorical processes that produce them. Barnes points out that any conceptual judgment

> can only be made if *other* concepts are assumed to have a routine usage which others will continue to follow, and which can accordingly be taken for granted as a stable feature when the judgment is made. There is no way of judging the pragmatic value of continuing to use "goose" as a term denoting a species, if in the meantime usage of the term "species" is developing rapidly and unpredictably. Hence goals and interests, considered in the context of an over-all, coherent, verbal culture, must, for the most part, act upon judgments so that concepts are applied in the expected way, the predicted way, the way that is called "routine."[21]

As we shall see, even the most putatively radical theories of film leave the conventions of film interpretation untouched. The construction of implicit or symptomatic meanings is a routine institutional activity, a body of ongoing craft practices that draws upon abstract doctrines in an ad hoc, utilitarian, and "opportunistic" fashion.

My use of the last adjective is not meant to impugn practitioners' motives. The argument so far, and much of that to come, might lead the reader to think that individuals participate in these routines cynically. Far from it: most consider it a worthwhile, even noble endeavor. They are probably not motivated solely by external rewards such as promotions and salary raises. Many critics are in the business largely to achieve what two sociologists of science call "credibility"—a position of recognized expertise that is continually renewed through the redeployment of accumulated resources (money, grants, facilities, publications).[22] The desire for credibility may in turn be based on a host of individual desires (ambition, service to a purpose, conviction that the truth should be spread). The interpretive institution can accommodate them all.

You may retort that emphasizing routine procedures overlooks the discontinuities riddling the history of film studies. Is not the shift from explicatory criticism to symptomatic cultural analysis proof of a sharp division in the critical institution? I shall argue in the rest of this book that it is not; here I can only propose that the shifts in critical theory follow a pattern familiar in the sciences. A fresh approach (authorship, or semiotic-structuralist analysis) attracts young workers to a field. They wager their time and energy that the new trend will pay off. At first there is a wide tolerance of exploratory work, seen in brief, informal, and horizon-setting essays (often simply called "notes" on this or that). Although this work will appear loose, eclectic, and superficial by later standards, it is arresting not only because of its promise but because of its hortatory, often uncompromising rhetoric. Then, as the contours of the school emerge more clearly, normal criticism sets in. Many scholars, along with new generations of students, flock to the field and set about refining, revising, and applying the core ideas. Now essays are narrowly focused, packed with details and distinctions, perhaps also dotted with footnotes. Now entire books are devoted to what first-phase theory handled in four paragraphs. There is no longer a need for grand rhetorical gestures; basic assumptions can be taken for granted. Auteurs exist. Genres reflect culture. Texts seek to repress contradictions. If the institution routinizes everyday critical work, it also shapes the production of even those striking novelties that appear at the moment, or in official histories, to be revolutionary changes.

Here, however, film studies diverges from the natural sciences, for in the second phase of development of explicatory and symptomatic criticism there is a slackening of constraints on what will count as acceptable argument within the paradigm. Instead we find a continuing process of spreading, overlapping, and recasting of concepts, a diffuse "application" that appropriates whatever can be made compatible, however forcibly, with the production of proper interpretations. Theoretical claims are renegotiated for the sake of practical criticism, even if the revisions in the claims are never acknowledged.[23]

Such processes of assimilation bring criticism into contact with other institutions, most proximately filmmaking itself. Perhaps the first academic film critic was Eisenstein. In his classes at the Soviet All-Union State Institute of Cinematography and in his voluminous writings he "read" films (sometimes his own), scanning them for implicit meanings—how the staging of Clyde's murder of Roberta in *An American Tragedy* symbolizes his tragic fate; or how the arrangement of Madame Vauquer's table reflects a social hierarchy; or how conventional color symbolism is reversed in *Alexander Nevsky*, in which the sturdy Russians are clothed in black while the Teutonic knights wear white, the color of "cruelty, oppression, and death."[24] He also comes near to constructing symptomatic meanings when he comments on the disparity between subject matter and treatment in Chaplin's *Modern Times,* and when he interprets Griffith's parallel montage as revealing a dualistic bourgeois world view.[25] In later years, less intellectual filmmakers learned how to make movies that squared with critics' interpretive categories. Would the director of *Stranger than Paradise* claim to be fascinated by the problem of communication if he had not gone to film school and encountered discourse about Antonioni, Ray, Rivette, Pasolini, Sirk, and others?[26] All of the critical trends I shall survey in the next two chapters, from the *politique des auteurs* to feminism, have in one way or another "fed back" into filmmaking, so that, at various points, this book will consider how canonized cues and meanings find their way into films as well, there to be discovered by critics using the same interpretive frameworks that the filmmakers originally borrowed from them.

The Logic of Discovery, or, Problem-Solving

Ordinary criticism, like Kuhn's "normal science," can be considered a process of puzzle-solving. This is especially evident in the oldest interpretive traditions, such as *midrash,* which concentrates on biblical "problem points" to be explicated.[27] Christian interpreters were required to reconcile disparities between church doctrine and the words of Scripture. The Freudian psychoanalyst has the problem of constructing the latent dream-thoughts by linking free associations with material in the manifest dream.[28] As rational agents, interpreters seek out strategies for correctly performing the tasks set by their institutions. Thus my study of the logic of critical interpretation can fruitfully ground itself in the cognitive psychology of problem-solving.

Put generally, the goal which the institution of criticism sets the film interpreter is this: Produce a novel and persuasive interpretation of one or more appropriate films. This goal will shape the mental set, the assumptions, and the expectations with which the critic approaches the task. More specifically, four problems confront the critic:

1. How is the critic to make the chosen film a proper specimen for critical interpretation? Few critics analyze trailers, home movies, or industrial documentaries; when they do so, they must construct arguments for their significance. Let us call this the problem of *appropriateness.*

2. How is the critic to adjust her critical concepts and methods to specific features of the film? Does the film "fit the approach"? How will aspects of the film, not at first interpretable in an acceptable way, be rendered interpretable? Call this the problem of *recalcitrant data*.

3. How is the critic to give the interpretation sufficient *novelty?* The institution discourages critics from replicating one another's readings (although students may be permitted to do so as a learning exercise). The interpreter is expected either to (a) initiate a new critical theory or method; (b) revise or refine an existing theory or method; (c) "apply" an existing theory or method to a fresh instance; or (d) if the film is familiar, point out significant aspects which previous commentators have ignored or minimized.

4. How is the critic to make the interpretation sufficiently persuasive? Although all three other problems have rhetorical dimensions, this is preeminently rhetorical in nature. Call it the problem of *plausibility*.

These problems are even more daunting than they might appear. What cognitive psychologists call "well-defined" or "definite" problems specify an initial problem state, a desired goal state, and a theoretically determined method for linking the two. A chess problem affords a good instance. The diagram of the position presents the initial state, the instruction provides the goal state ("Mate in two moves"), and the method for arriving at a solution consists of following the rules of chess. But the four interpretive problems I have just reviewed are indefinite. The critic must establish the initial state (by picking a film or an approach). The desired goal state is vague: the institution does not specify exactly *how* the interpretation should be novel or persuasive. And there is no theoretically determined means of linking the problem state to the goal state, since there are, strictly speaking, no rules for film interpretation. Yet interpreters solve such indefinite problems daily. What enables them to do it?

Without entering into the intricacies of what has been one of the most exciting areas of debate in contemporary cognitive psychology, we can say this: Interpreters, like most everyday problem-solvers, construct a problem in keeping with the norms of the institution they inhabit.[29] They go on to employ pragmatic strategies that allow them to produce appropriate critical inferences.[30] These strategies consist of some general inductive propensities and principles and some strategies specific to the domain of interpretation. Let me sketch out how these might work in a single act of interpretation.

I decide, for whatever reason, to produce an interpretation of a film. I must construct my own initial problem state. This can be done in only two ways. I might notice the *compatibilities* that the film affords with respect to concepts currently in circulation in criticism. I might, for instance, find that it illustrates or confirms other critics' accounts of analogous films. I could then frame the hypothesis that my film exemplifies general properties which are already accepted as relevant within the interpretive institution. Alternatively, I might attune myself to *anomalies*. Within the film, perhaps a scene or bit of behavior does not initially seem to fit with others; or perhaps previous critical interpretations have ignored or overlooked something I can pick out; or perhaps the film as a whole does not square with some current conception of genre or style or mode.[31] I can then hypothesize that the film will somehow justify its difference by virtue of certain other properties that are institutionally acceptable (for example, internal plot logic, thematic coherence, or ideological aspects). The anomaly strategy faces the *recalcitrant-data* problem (4) straight on, while the compatibility approach will encounter it sooner or later; but either approach gives the critic a more or less definite initial problem state from which to build an interpretive solution.

Constructing the interpretation involves the fundamental cognitive process of hypothesis-testing; for example, if this scene means such and such, then wouldn't this item in the scene take on a symbolic function? At any point I may confront the recalcitrant-data problem. To solve it, I can call on a range of empirical knowledge—other films that may be compared to the target film, critical writings that may function as exemplars for my interpretation, more abstract conceptions of genre or mode or narrative structure, still more abstract theoretical doctrines (feminism, psychoanalysis), and themes or semantic fields (active/passive, powerful/powerless) that have saliency for the audience which I am addressing.

In drawing on these data, I also make use of various sorts of skills. For instance, if I am to compare the film with another in the same genre, I will need to employ the basic cognitive capacity to draw analogies. I also approach the film with skills of a more specialized sort. I have been trained to look for *significance*—that is, I assume that any film worth interpreting has something consequential to "say." I further assume that what the film says is not "literally" on the surface but is instead meaning of an implicit or symptomatic kind; that is, I look for *interpretability*. I have also learned to look for *unity*, not simply of surface features (such as the plot) but also of occulted meanings. Even if my critical approach valorizes disunity and symptomatic meanings, I can grasp such qualities only if I am attuned to noticing unity. As an interpreter I also pick out *patterns*—repetitions, variations, inversions—which can be invested with significance. And I should be skilled at selecting *salient passages*—the "key portions" that most clearly or vividly instantiate the meanings I ascribe to the film. A domain-specific assumption, for example, is that beginnings and endings are salient segments for interpretation. By using such skills, I can make stubborn data meaningful. I can posit that such data function implicitly or symptomatically, and I can show how they participate in unified patterns or how they operate at privileged moments.

All these are interpretive skills which the institution has passed on to me, chiefly through ostension and imitation. They are not, of course, specific to film criticism. They derive from twentieth-century criticism generally, and especially literary interpretation—which is probably why most film critics have literary training, and why students of literature can so quickly learn to produce acceptable interpretations of films.[32]

In the course of my explorations of the film's "problem space," I will shape my thinking so as to maximize the possibilities of attaining appropriate degrees of novelty and plausibility. Thus, if previous critics have ignored a scene I think significant, I can chastise them (mildly or severely), highlight that passage, and connect it to other aspects of the film, thus creating grounds for a novel interpretation. If I can seek out continuity between my interpretive enterprise and values or ideas held by my presumed audience, I will be closer to a persuasive interpretation (a solution to problem 4). In sum, even if my problem is indefinite, I can formulate an initial state, generate hypotheses from it, tap pertinent empirical knowledge, and mobilize domain-specific skills in order to mount a novel and convincing interpretation.

A psychological explanation of how all this works would require a book in itself, but a summary might run as follows. Critical logic is predominantly inductive because it is probabilistic. Interpreters work with pragmatic reasoning strategies that "characterize relations over general classes of object kinds, event relationships, and problem goals."[33] These lie between the ultragenerality of deductive logic and the comparatively atomistic features of this or that content domain.[34] Such reasoning procedures are not rules in the strict sense; they are rather probabilities arranged in default hierarchies, in which expectations hold good only if not disconfirmed by data.[35] As with any inductive system, the perceiver is "set" for data that confirm rather than falsify the initial hypothesis.[36] (Hence critics' assiduity in seeking out evidence for an interpretive claim and their reluctance to find evidence that would disconfirm it.) Analogy-making is central here: the critic compares the film to others, likens his or her analytical process to that of other critics, and models the final form of the argument upon prototypes supplied by the institution. By finding a pertinent analogy, the critic can move closer to solving the interpretive problems posed by recalcitrant data.[37] Since the problem-solving process works with stored memory schemata, the interpreter must draw upon prototypical cases (for example, a key film or exemplary critical essay), template schemata (for example, an anatomy of narrative structure or stylistic options), and procedural schemata (for example, knowledge of how to segment a film or assign significance or unity).[38] And since interpretation is generally unconstrained by rules of formal demonstration, its inductive processes frequently rely upon "quick and dirty" corner-cutting rules of thumb, such as the *vividness* heuristic, which makes the most concrete and unusual data most salient.[39] In all, the skills of critical interpretation derive from general human inferential abilities.

I have sought to keep the social nature of interpretation at the forefront of even so "individual" a process as problem-solving because the two aspects are inseparable. The psychological account, indispensable as it is, provides only the "hollow forms" of critical reasoning. My construal of this or that film is a product of my problem-solving skills applied to a task largely defined by forces lying outside my personal history, according to norms of thought and writing established long before I came on the scene. "No account of inductive logic, or of an individual agent as an inductive learning machine, suffices to identify the 'best' way of applying a specific concept."[40] The critical institution—journalistic reviewing, essayistic writing, or academic criticism—defines the grounds and bounds of interpretive activity, the direction of analogical thinking, the proper goals, the permissible solutions, and the authority that can validate the interpretations produced by ordinary criticism.

The Logic of Justification, or, Rhetoric

"In what way," writes one literary theorist, "is a critic, producing interpretations, different from a reader, who, in reading a text, is under no obligation to explain it or comment upon it, does not have to make clear what is important and significant about it, and generally satisfies himself with a modest, unassuming comprehension, for his own use and in his own measure?"[41] My answers so far should be evident. A critic, unlike the common "reader," acts according to conventions laid down by an interpretive institution, and she employs skills of problem-solving in order to arrive at an interpretation. One more stage of the critic's activity remains to be sketched in: the mounting of interpretive arguments.

For the practicing critic, it is not enough to discover—that is, construct—implicit or symptomatic meanings; one must justify them by means of public discourse. All the problems set by the institution have a rhetorical dimension, the demand for a persuasive interpretation being the most obvious instance. It is, moreover, chiefly through rhetoric that critics learn inferential processes and encounter exemplars, analogies, and schemata. Rhetoric also constructs a critical persona and an implied audience.

Through all these channels critical rhetoric helps maintain institutional coherence. Ordinary criticism, making its tacit appeals to deeply held beliefs about the problem-solving procedures proper to criticism, gives its practitioners and audiences the communal satisfaction of a church ceremony or a parade. Disputes among interpretive "approaches" renew the institution's group dynamics; heterodox interpretations remain interpretations, and as their conclusions become less shocking, a new rhetoric of recantation, conciliation, and assimilation will absorb their insights. The abstract tenets of "theory" or "method" and the evolving and differing schools of criticism become superstructural phenomena. Interpretive rhetoric, as a vehicle of the reasoning process characteristic of interpretation, forms the permanent basis of public critical activity.

Rhetoric, classically conceived, is concerned only with persuasion, not truth. More modern adherents argue (rhetorically) that in our age we cannot so easily consign the establishment of truth to the exact sciences, and that the process of arriving at consensual agreement is at least a worthwhile, and possibly the only, path to such truth as is allotted to humankind.[42] Since my own view lies closer to the first conception, I shall treat critical rhetoric as an instrument for rendering the conclusions of critical reasoning attractive to the interpreter's audience. This is not to say that rhetorical conditions and conventions do not also inform the very process of critical reasoning, such as when the interpreter keeps an eye peeled for what can be profitably written up. But such cases are covered by what I have taken to be the prior demands of novelty and plausibility. Rhetoric, for my purposes here, is primarily the domain of language, the structure and style of critical discourse.

Film interpretation can be analyzed into distinct processes characteristic of all rhetorical activity: *inventio, dispositio,* and *elocutio.* As a way of introducing these ancient categories and their constituents, and as a means of illustrating how a critical rhetoric works, I will draw my examples from a mode of writing that will play almost no role in the rest of this book but which bulks large in the discourse around cinema. This mode is that of the journalistic reviewing of current films.

The conventionality of film reviewing has long been apparent, and many aspects of it are nicely laid bare in Matt Groening's accompanying cartoon. All I aim to show here is that several aspects of this conventionality constitute an institutional rhetoric. Reviewing is part of the mass media, and it functions as an offshoot of the film industry's advertising: reviews publicize the film and sustain the habit of moviegoing. As a piece of journalism, the review operates in the discursive category of "news"; as a branch of advertising, it draws on material from the film industry's discourses; as a type of criticism, it draws on certain linguistic and conceptual forms, especially those involving description and evaluation. And as rhetoric, it clearly utilizes traditional strategies and tactics.

What the ancients called *inventio,* or the devising of substantive arguments, includes three particular sorts of proofs. *Ethical* proofs appeal to the virtues of the speaker. In film reviewing, ethical proofs serve to create an attractive role that will warrant the critic's opinions. The reviewer may present himself or herself as a solicitous consumer guide, advising the reader or viewer of the best and worst on offer (for example, Gene Siskel and Roger Ebert, two nationally televised reviewers). Or the reviewer's ethos may be that of the passionate advocate for the bizarre or overlooked film (for example, J. Hoberman of *The Village Voice*). The reviewer may present the image of the vulgar but righteous film fan (Pauline Kael) or the cultural pundit

Figure 1. Copyright © 1985 Matt Groening. Used by permission of Acme Features Syndicate.

with stringent standards (John Simon). Minimally, the reviewer must play the role of either the well-informed expert or the committed amateur, each of which offers an idealized surrogate for the reader. In any event, the attractive aspects of the reviewer's ethos act as warrant for his or her judgments.

Pathetic proofs rely on emotional appeals to the audience. Eager to present the film as "news," the reviewer will play up the qualities that he assumes will strike his audience. A film centering on recent headlines or contemporary problems; a high-priced purchase of an original source; an old star's return to the screen or a new star's blazing debut—all these qualities and others may arouse interest. In addition, the reviewer will frame his or her descriptions and judgments so as to arouse emotions, sympathetically bringing out emotional qualities of the film or dramatically demonstrating the film's shoddiness, absurdity, or pretensions.

Classical rhetoric called arguments directed to the nature of the case itself "logical" or "artistic" proofs. For the sake of simplicity, we can divide logical proofs into *examples* and *enthymemes*. Examples are inductive or pseudoinductive arguments which back up a claim. The film reviewer may select a passage of the film (either through verbal description or, on television reviewing shows, by running an excerpt supplied by the producers) and claim that this sample is typical of the whole. Similarly, if the reviewer judges a performance to be bad, the claim can be supported by a contrasting example of a good performance from another film. In film reviewing, such evidence tends not to be organized as a coherent body of knowledge; it functions in the mode of connoisseurship, in that the reviewer's taste and experience guide him or her intuitively to the proper examples.

Enthymemes are deductive or pseudodeductive arguments. In film reviewing, the canonical enthymeme runs this way:

A good film has property p.
This film has (or lacks) property p.
This is a good (or bad) film.

There are only a few properties that can fill the p slot: important subject matter, realistic treatment of the subject, a logical story line, spectacle, intriguing characters, a valid message, and novelty within sameness (for example, revamped remakes, significant sequels).

Within the realm of the enthymeme, Aristotle singles out *topoi* as particular stereotyped arguments that the audience will grant without question. Some reviewers' topoi take the form of evaluative maxims: "If you spend the money, put it on the screen." "We ought to care about the characters." "Good acting looks natural." "Some films are only entertainment, but others offer food for thought." Of course, like all rhetors, reviewers may appeal, on different occasions, to logically contradictory examples, enthymemes, or topoi.

Inventio, or the crafting of critical arguments, then, relies on rhetor-centered (ethical) appeals, audience-centered (emotional) appeals, and case-centered (logical or pseudological) appeals. *Dispositio* consists of arranging these arguments into an appealing order. The film review is built out of four components: a condensed plot synopsis, with particular emphasis on big moments but with no revelation of the ending; a body of background information about the film (its genre, its source, its director or stars, anecdotes about production or reception); a set of abbreviated arguments; and a summary judgment (good/bad, nice try/pretentious disaster, one to four stars, a scale of one to ten) or a recommendation (thumbs up/thumbs down, see it/don't). The reviewer can arrange these components in any order, but the most common structure seems to be this: Open with a summary judgment; synopsize the plot; then supply a string of condensed arguments about the acting, story logic, sets, spectacle, or other case-centered points; lace it all with background information; and cap the review by reiterating the judgment. The organizational options are in fact so few that it is hard for the reviewer to create a distinct identity on this basis.

Much more promising is the third realm of rhetoric, that of *elocutio,* or style. While the academic critic's style often verges on the anonymous, the great reviewers—Baudelaire, Shaw, Virgil Thomson—endure chiefly through it. Style is what encourages the reviewer to use time-honored gimmicks, such as writing the review in the form of a letter, or recounting the film in the argot of a character. Along with a skill in argument and a range of knowledge, style is the film reviewer's chief means of constructing a persona—amateur or expert, elitist or democratic—and a personality—sardonic (Rex Reed), commonsensically wry (Siskel and Ebert), waspish (Simon), tempestuous (Kael), and so on. For the daily newspaper audience, the writer can cultivate a brisk, telegraphic style,[43] but for a weekly publication, one must display greater verbal dexterity, since here the review is read more for its intrinsic interest as a piece of language. The reviewer must swing from puns and epigrams to purple patches, from metaphorical fancies to metaphysical affirmations, from savage denunciation to lyrical praise. If a reviewer comes to seem, over the years, a "character" or even a celebrity to be interviewed, that is the reward accorded someone whom an impersonal institution has allowed to cultivate a colorful style.

Although most essayistic and academic writers are at pains to distinguish themselves from reviewers, all critics are rhetorical creatures. Reviewers' arguments, organizational structures, and stylistic flourishes may look simple, but that is chiefly because their rhetoric need not deal with interpretation and all its problems. (Of course, evaluation is no simple matter either, and most academic critics have defined it out of existence or left it to the reviewers.) In any event, as we shall see in Chapters 9 and 10, interpretive film criticism has its own characteristic *inventio, dispositio,* and *elocutio.*

Defining critical rhetoric as the persuasive use of discourse has the advantage of recognizing the comparatively small role that rigorous logic and systematic knowledge play in film interpretation. For one thing, film study has not evolved through the clash of tidily presented opposing views. The history of film criticism is largely that of predecessors ignored or forgotten, ships passing in the night, people talking at cross-purposes, wholesale dismissals of prior writers' work, and periodic cycles of taste. Obliviousness is of course common in other fields of inquiry, but more than most of his peers in philosophy or psychology or art history, the academic film interpreter avoids dialectical confrontation with alternative positions. At a scholarly conference in film studies, a paper devoted wholly to scrutinizing another critic's interpretation will be taken as a sterile exercise. Instead, the interpreter practices a strategy of exclusion (no mention of other interpretations) or one of supersession, declaring an earlier interpretation fine as far as it goes (which is never far enough). Furthermore, an attention to specialized topoi and recurrent enthymemes shows how film criticism, especially in the last fifteen years, relies heavily on appeals to authority—either previous writers or some theoretical doctrine. (The canonical statement of this tendency might be the catchphrase "Psychoanalysis teaches us that . . .") And we must be prepared to recognize even the *absence* of traditional rhetorical devices as having a belief-inducing effect. Donald McCloskey finds this to hold across a range of academic discourse. Since long and complex arguments foster the suspicion that the writer is putting something over on us, "the Announcement, the more bald, unargued, and authoritarian the better, is the favored form of scholarly communication."[44] In film studies the parallel is the sheer general assertion ("Art illuminates the human condition," "Cinematic pleasure depends upon voyeurism"). The general assertion is typically linked to a network of in-house beliefs that go without saying.

Studying critical rhetoric, then, requires us to analyze interpretations for their characteristic argumentative, organizational, and stylistic maneuvers. It requires not a hermeneutics of interpretation—though we should be sensitive to what critics imply, and what they seem to repress—but rather what I shall call, at the end of this book, a poetics of practical interpretive reason.

An Anatomy of Interpretation

The notion of interpretation as an inferential and rhetorical practice should, by now, have suggested why I do not share Barthes's suspicion that "reading" is an irreducibly heterogeneous activity. Interpretation is one of the most conventional things that film critics do. Even when a critic purports to produce an "unconstrained" interpretation, he or she will not only use standard strategies but will very likely generate a highly routinized reading, rather as the improvising pianist will often fall back into the most banal tunes and chord progressions.

I do not say, however, that the *desire* to interpret does not have diverse temperamental sources. Criticism certainly gives pleasure to its practitioners. It yields the intellectual satisfaction of problem-solving, the delight of coming to know a loved artwork more fully, the mastery of a skill, the security of belonging to a community. Less innocent interpretations of interpretation are suggested by Susan Sontag's charge that the interpreter is something of a sadist: "Interpretation is the revenge of the intellect upon art . . . the compliment that mediocrity pays to genius."[45] Or the interpreter may appear somewhat masochistic, using the critical institution to confirm that interpretive inadequacy evoked by Frank Kermode: "World and book . . . are hopelessly plural, endlessly disappointing."[46] It seems evident, though, that the critic's darker drives remain largely sublimated in all institutionally acceptable interpretive activity.

This is not to disparage critics for obeying norms. Whatever creativity is, puzzle-solving and persuasion would seem to partake of it. No interpretation is produced by rote. The apprentice learns to construct an institutionally significant problem. The skilled critic finds a fresh analogy, produces an exemplar, or pulls off a powerful rhetorical effect. In all such cases, we see how creativity is *enabled,* not constrained, by institutional practices of language and reasoning. The comparison to which I shall often revert is that of the artisan. There are inept electricians, passable potters, and highly creative cooks. Like them, the critic practices a craft, and there is nothing inherently ignoble in that.

The interpreter's craft consists centrally of ascribing implicit and symptomatic meanings to films. *Ascribing* here captures several important senses: inferred meanings are *imputed* to a film, but they are also (and principally) "scribed," written up, articulated in language. The ascriptive acts take place within an institutional frame of reference, which defines, usually tacitly, how the writer is to proceed. The goal assigned to the interpreter is to produce a persuasive and novel interpretation, in a process that is at once psychological, social, and discursive.

We can conceive this process as involving four activities. Once the film has been selected:

1. *Assume the most pertinent meanings to be either implicit or symptomatic or both.* In the next two chapters, I will survey the principal trends in the history of film criticism and show how each has subscribed to particular assumptions about these two sorts of meaning.

2. *Make salient one or more semantic fields.* In ascribing meanings the interpreter must mobilize semantic fields (for example, thematic clusters, binary oppositions). Chapter 5 examines how this occurs within film criticism, considering the various principles of semantic discrimination and the particular domains most frequently drawn upon.

3. *Map the semantic fields onto the film at several levels by correlating textual units with semantic features.* The cognitive skills of interpretation—building analogies, mental modeling, the hypothesizing of unity and pattern, picking out relevant passages—all come into play here. At any moment, the problem of recalcitrant data may emerge. Chapters 6–8 study how interpreters use concrete strategies to make films able to bear semantic fields.

4. *Articulate an argument that demonstrates the novelty and validity of the interpretation.* Chapters 9 and 10 survey critical rhetoric as a distinct aspect of the interpretive act, tracing how the arguments, organizational structures, and styles of discourse operate within an institutional framework, in order to persuade the critic's audience.

These activities do not necessarily take place in the sequence I have outlined; each one can accompany, inform, or interrupt the others. You might be struck by an anomalous textual feature (3) and then seek out a semantic category that would explain it (2). Trying to cast your idea into acceptable critical prose (4) might force you back to

other aspects of the semantic field (2) and then back to the text (3)—
all the while assuming a certain kind of meaning to be present (1).
Or, more likely, these activities occur "in parallel." In any event, what
the outline and the following chapters provide is neither a phenomenological, step-by-step description, nor a psychological or sociological
flowchart, but rather an analysis of the logic underlying the interpretive activity. What follows seeks to show that, whatever the vicissitudes
of the critical instincts, interpretation answers to the reality principle
often enough to constitute no less a craft than land-surveying or wine-
making or parlor magic.

3

Interpretation as Explication

If we examine this more closely, and I think close examination is
the least tribute that this play deserves, I think we will find that
within the austere framework of what is seen to be on one level a
country-house week-end, and what a useful symbol that is, the author has given us—yes, I will go so far—he has given us the human
condition.

—Tom Stoppard, *The Real Inspector Hound*

On a summer day, a suburban father looks out at the family lawn and
says to his teen-aged son: "The grass is so tall I can hardly see the cat
walking through it." The son construes this to mean: "Mow the lawn."
This is an *implicit* meaning. In a similar way, the interpreter of a film
may take referential or explicit meaning as only the point of departure
for inferences about implicit meanings. In constructing those meanings, the critic makes them apparent. That is, she or he *explicates* the
film, just as the son might turn to his pal and explain, "That means
Dad wants me to mow the lawn."

Explicatory criticism rests upon the belief that the principal goal of
critical activity is to ascribe implicit meanings to films. In this chapter,
I will consider how this belief has emerged historically within criticism
of mainstream and experimental cinema. The next chapter surveys a
significantly different conception of the interpreter's goal. Both chapters aim to describe the first area of critical practice outlined at the
close of the last chapter—the conceptions of meaning that underlie
interpretive conventions.

The French Connection

Shortly after the Second World War, explicatory criticism emerged as
a distinct trend. In France, England, and the United States there

appeared writing that, despite its frequent connection with journalism and reviewing, sought to produce genuine interpretations, and to make them persuasive and novel.

Two factors were crucial to this process. First, certain new films compelled interpretation. Successive waves of the European "art cinema" encouraged film critics to apply techniques of exegesis already common in the interpretation of literature and the visual arts. Italian Neorealism raised questions of realism, characterization, and narrative construction, while the 1950s work of Kurosawa, Rossellini, Bergman, Fellini, and others presented ambiguities that invited interpretation. American experimentalists such as Maya Deren, Kenneth Anger, Gregory Markopoulos, and Stan Brakhage made films that sought to be construed on the models of poetry and myth. A second, related influence on explicatory criticism was the growing power of the idea of individual authorship. The art cinema and the 16mm "personal" cinema celebrated the director as the creative source of meaning; it became natural to think of the director's output as an oeuvre, a repetition and enrichment of characteristic themes and stylistic choices. At the same time, critics began to apply a comparable concept of authorship to the popular, mass-production cinema of Hollywood. Before the 1950s only a few directors had been singled out as individualists, but soon the mantle of the auteur was bestowed on such men as Hitchcock, Hawks, Minnelli, Aldrich, and Jerry Lewis. Like Antonioni or Buñuel, these directors also had recurrent concerns and "personal visions"; they too created their own "worlds." "Once the principle of directorial continuity is accepted even in Hollywood," wrote Andrew Sarris, "films can never look the same again."[1] Time has proven him right.

This story is so well known that there would be no point in telling it again if my purpose were not somewhat unusual.[2] For one thing, the historical connection of author-centered criticism with the rise of the art cinema is still played down in orthodox histories. More important, my concern is less with the history of taste or film theory than with the rise of an interpretive practice. Thus a film like *Rashomon* could inspire a critic like Parker Tyler to claim that its ambiguity makes it an instance of modern art.[3] And auteurism—which, as Peter Wollen put it, requires "an operation of decipherment"[4]—is significant here not as a theory to be evaluated for its logical rigor but as a cluster of assumptions and hypotheses that permit particular interpretations to come into being. Not only did auteur criticism, the avant-garde, and the art cinema push film writing toward explication; but also, particular interpretations could appeal to these filmmaking practices as sources of persuasiveness and novelty.

Immediately after the war, Parisian cinéphiles were visited by major revelations. The second half of 1946 witnessed an American invasion: Paris hosted premieres of *Citizen Kane, Double Indemnity, Murder My Sweet, The Maltese Falcon, Phantom Lady, How Green Was My Valley, The Little Foxes, The Westerner, The Magnificent Ambersons,* and many other films. This sudden access to the accumulated wealth of Hollywood's 1940s output had a far-reaching impact on French criticism. Then, during 1947-1949 came the revelation of Neorealism in such works as *Shoeshine, Paisan, Germany Year Zero,* and *The Bicycle Thief.* The newly revived film weeklies such as *L'Ecran français* had plenty of movies to discuss, and intellectual journals such as *Esprit* began to take notice of the cinema. In 1946 there appeared a more "serious" monthly, *La Revue du cinéma,* edited by Jean-Georges Auriol.

Contributing to several of these journals was the young André Bazin. Like most of his colleagues, he was drawn to the cinema of France, America, and Italy. Yet he did more than simply review films: between 1945 and 1950, he changed the face of film criticism.

To a remarkable extent Bazin's essays anticipated arguments that would preoccupy critics over succeeding decades. As early as 1943 he had called for a cinema of authorship. "A film's worth stems from its auteurs . . . It is much safer to put one's faith in the director than in the leading man."[5] Which directors? Bazin's 1946 list reads like a 1955 auteurist pantheon: Welles, Sturges, Wilder, Hitchcock, Preminger, Siodmak, Ford, Capra.[6] His claim that modern film technique enables the director to practice a kind of *écriture* (writing) in film was picked up by Alexandre Astruc some years later as the idea of the *caméra-stylo.*[7] In the late 1940s Bazin also developed his "dialectical" history of film style, in which the classical decoupage of Hollywood was absorbed by the deep-focus long takes of Welles and Wyler.[8]

Apart from these substantive points, Bazin's work constituted a model of critical method. He committed himself to explicating the films he discussed. Others had occasionally done this in the pages of *Revue du cinéma,* but not with Bazin's concern for nuances of meaning and his attempt to link thematic richness to stylistic complexity. His early explorations climaxed in his 1950 book on Welles, a virtual prototype of explicatory criticism for the next several decades.

Here Bazin assumes that Welles is the creator ("auteur") of the films and that they project his personality. *Citizen Kane* and *The Magnificent Ambersons* are obviously autobiographical and can be taken as reflecting an unsatisfied childhood. More equivocally, the basic theme of a long-ing for childhood emerges through elusive symbols: snow, statuary, the figure of the mother. Yet the films go beyond simply expressing Welles's ambivalent nostalgia. They grant their characters a realistic ambiguity of motive and reaction typical of the classic novel. Bazin goes on to show that the ambiguity of theme and characterization is embodied in a specific style. (He sums up the movement in the chapter title "De la profondeur du sujet à la profondeur du champ.") Welles uses lengthy shots to present multiple points of interest, either diag-onally in depth or strung along a horizon line. He thus compels the spectator "to feel the ambivalence of reality."[9] In *Citizen Kane,* the elliptical construction and the deep-focus long takes face the spectator with the same puzzle about the meaning of Kane's life that confronts the reporters. In the kitchen scene of *The Magnificent Ambersons,* Welles's long take creates "pretext actions" that distract the spectator from Aunt Fanny's reactions until the moment when her outburst startles us as it would in life.[10] Thus the central implicit meaning of Welles's work—the ambiguity of reality—is carried at the levels of theme, character delineation, and cinematic style.

It is not much of an exaggeration to see Bazin as the focal point of *Cahiers du cinéma,* which commenced publication in 1951. True, his name was not on the first issue's masthead, and he did not assume the main editorship until 1954. But from the start *Cahiers du cinéma* relied upon those postwar critical ideas which Bazin had most clearly enun-ciated. The journal's principal subjects were Neorealism, Hollywood, stylistics, realism, and certain French directors like Renoir and Bres-son. The early issues offered a mixture of news, journalism, interviews, reviews, and interpretive analysis. To the inaugural number Bazin contributed a fresh, more complete version of his account of the evolution of film style.[11] In this first issue, the director-as-author was already central to *Cahiers*'s project: there were essays on Dmytryk, Bazin's discussion of Welles and others, and reviews of films by Wilder, Bresson, and Rossellini. The same number also included a study by Astruc which interpreted *Under Capricorn* as a Protestant film and *Stromboli* as a Catholic one. This essay can stand as an early instance of the sort of explication for which *Cahiers* would become notorious. It seeks to be persuasive by appealing to commonplaces of religious and cultural belief, but it achieves (outrageous) novelty by putting Hitchcock on a par with Milton, Meredith, and James.[12]

It was thus not authorship as such that *Cahiers*'s Young Turks introduced in the early 1950s, only a *politique des auteurs,* a policy of favoring particular directors. Truffaut's 1954 attack on the cinema of quality, Rohmer's admiration for Hitchcock, Rivette's celebration of Hawks and Lang and Preminger—all seemed excessive to Bazin, who criticized the extremes of the new auteurism.[13] Yet the magazine's younger generation based its criticism firmly on principles he had been the first to enunciate. Bazin had followed Sartre's maxim that every technique reveals a metaphysics, and his younger colleagues took their masters at their word. *Cahiers*'s critics dedicated themselves principally to showing how a director's characteristic stylistic and dramatic patterns reflect underlying themes.

Because France had nothing equivalent to Anglo-American New Criticism, the *Cahiers* essays did not usually practice "close reading"; instead the essays favored broad pronouncements laced with citations from philosophy, literature, painting, or music. But explications these writings certainly were, seeking to gain assent through appeal to cultural assumptions about artistry in other media. After 1956, *Cahiers*'s Young Turks began to reflect more explicitly on their critical practice, answering objections from readers and engaging in internal discussions. A growing self-consciousness about the journal's interpretive practices also emerges from the numerous roundtable conversations on particular films and from the occasional exercise of letting two or more critics review the same film.

In these years, *Cahiers* fulfilled the classic function of an intellectual review—proposing and promulgating opinions too "serious" for journalistic reviewing but more speculative and idiosyncratic than academic research would tolerate. In 1957 Rohmer declared that the magazine's goal was not to advise its readers which films to avoid (that was a job for journalism) but rather to "enrich" the readers' reflections on the films they saw.[14] *Cahiers* quickly became the most influential film journal in the world, a position it was not to lose until the 1970s. It created a canon of great directors that remains with us. It promoted the idea that cinema could sustain writing of intellectual depth. Not least, it encouraged the idea that films, like novels and plays, harbor layers of meaning, and that the sensitive and trained critic should be prepared to reveal them. If this enterprise was encouraged by the artistic ambitions of a film by Bergman or Resnais, it was most revelatory when exercised on the masters of the American cinema. *Cahiers*'s willingness to turn its exegetical lens to the most overlooked products of the Hollywood industry marked a significant point in cultural criticism generally.[15]

In 1952, scarcely a year after *Cahiers* began publication, the first issue of *Positif* appeared in Lyon. From the start it established a sharp alternative. It was surrealist and explicitly political, taking an anticlerical and pro-Soviet stance.[16] *Positif* was committed to a director's cinema, but it attacked such *Cahiers* idols as Hawks, Cukor, Ray, Preminger, and Bresson while praising Huston, Vigo, Fellini, Biberman, Losey, prewar Renoir, and above all Buñuel. Always more outrageous than *Cahiers*, *Positif* gave a home to the surrealist Ado Kyrou, to Robert Benayoun (expert on Jerry Lewis and postwar animation), and to Raymond Borde, who with Etienne Chaumeton wrote the first book on film noir. While *Cahiers*'s special Hollywood issue (December 1963) contained filmographies, interviews, and essays, *Positif*'s parallel number (December 1963) consisted wholly of Benayoun's chatty account of his trip by Greyhound bus from Manhattan to Los Angeles and of his stay in Hollywood, which included visits to Disneyland, Tex Avery's home, and Jerry Lewis's television show.

Despite its genuine eccentricities, *Positif*'s criticism was fully in the explicatory tradition. An essay on Minnelli starts with the claim that his work is reducible to a single theme, that of the problems of dream and reality confronting the creative artist.[17] Like their *Cahiers* confrères, *Positif*'s critics took up the challenge of the art cinema, producing exegeses of the symbols in Buñuel and Antonioni. One critic interprets Losey's film *The Servant* in a mythical perspective, comparing the central couple to Don Juan and Leporello as well as Faust and Mephistopheles.[18] Until the 1970s, *Positif* lived in the shadow of *Cahiers*, but both journals were committed to revealing implicit meanings in the films their writers judged valuable.

Explication Academicized

During the 1950s, an exegetical film criticism also emerged in the United States. The pivotal figure here is clearly Andrew Sarris, and the exemplary essay his 1956 *Film Culture* piece "*Citizen Kane*—The American Baroque." It is a paradigm of explication, all the more significant in that it precedes Sarris' conversion to throroughgoing auteurism.

"To believe, as some do, that *Citizen Kane* is the great American film, it is necessary to produce an interpretation that answers some of the more serious objections to this film."[19] With this sentence Sarris bases evaluation squarely upon interpretation. He will counter attacks on *Kane* by a "closer examination" which reveals "an inner consistency of theme, structure, and technique."[20] Concentrating on two themes—the debasement of a public figure and "the crushing weight of materialism"—he traces their development through the film's mystery-story structure and reveals their embodiment in images and sounds. He defends "Rosebud" as a symbolic summation of Kane's nostalgia and justifies the film's stylistic exhibitionism as a reflection of Kane's personality. He also connects visual motifs to thematic concerns; the low-angle shots, for example, reinforce the materialist theme by making Kane "the prisoner of his possessions."[21]

In its explicatory project, the essay conforms to the sort of "practical criticism" that then dominated literature departments of American universities. (Sarris has recalled that he was "meandering through graduate English" when he started to write about film.[22]) As a result, the essay emerges as much more precise, detailed, and comprehensive than almost any other American film criticism of its time. Significantly, Sarris ignores the canonized Bazin line, making no mention of deep focus, the long take, or the ambiguity surrounding Kane's character. Apparently all Sarris needed was a conviction that the film was sufficiently rich to justify explication.

The art cinema could also supply such a conviction. In the later 1950s Sarris went on to produce interpretations of *The Seventh Seal* and *A Man Escaped,* while his colleague Eugene Archer mounted an explication of Bergman's work revolving around "man's search for knowledge in a hostile universe."[23] Soon, however, the importation of *Cahiers*'s auteur policy provided another ground for Anglo-American interpretive criticism. At the very start of the 1960s, New York film critics began to embrace auteurism. The *New York Film Bulletin* (founded in 1961) was an important vehicle, as was *Film Culture.* Sarris, who spent "a long sojourn" in Paris in 1961, returned a confirmed *Cahiers* admirer.[24] His essay "Notes on the Auteur Theory in 1962" pledged the critic not only to a director's cinema but also to explication, or the search for "interior meaning."[25] Yet after a few essays, Sarris left interpretive criticism to writers like James Stoller and Roger Greenspun. He took the role of provocateur, guiding spirit, and tastemaker. His replies to polemical attacks on auteurism revealed a calm reasonableness that made his opponents' outrage look deranged in its excess. His catalogue raisonné of Hollywood directors (published in *Film Culture* in 1963) became enormously influential in mapping out the thematic and stylistic issues that would occupy critics for decades.[26] He also laid out particular assumptions—some derived from

Cahiers, others of his own devising—that were central to the development of an interpretive method. Since a film was the vehicle for a director's vision of the world, one could study the biographical individual behind the film. (In 1967 Sarris edited the first collection of interviews with film directors.[27]) Yet the film was also self-sufficient and could be studied independently of its social and historical surroundings: the proper context was the director's other work.

In America, Sarris could fight isolated skirmishes with individuals. In England, however, the critical orthodoxy occupied a stronger institutional position. There stood the British Film Institute, a tradition of quality if ever there was one, sustaining the world's most widely read film magazine, *Sight and Sound.* In its pages Lindsay Anderson had as early as 1954 charged the *Cahiers* Hitchcocko-Hawksians with "a perverse cultivation of the meretricious."[28] Although *Sight and Sound* was often accused of a bland uniformity, it contained at least three strains—a belletristic connoisseurship (for example, the essays of Penelope Houston), a more exacting critical journalism (for example, that of Gavin Lambert), and a leftist humanism (seen most clearly in Anderson's contributions).[29] By the beginning of the 1960s, none of these seemed persuasive or fresh to a younger generation of writers. New, more provocative journals emerged, such as *Definition* (founded in 1960), which featured articles by Alan Lovell and David Thomson, and *Motion* (founded in 1961), which published essays by Raymond Durgnat, Peter Cowie, and Charles Barr. Both journals were self-consciously "serious" (*Motion* called itself "The University Film Magazine") and highly critical of *Sight and Sound.* The most eye-catching and influential new publication of this era was *Movie,* which grew out of film articles in the student journal *Oxford Opinion.* As undergraduates, Ian Cameron, V. F. Perkins, and Mark Shivas had already imported *Cahiers*'s taste in filmmakers, but they were also far more analytically inclined. For Sarris, the survey of a director's career was the favored format, but the Oxford critics launched a magazine that, for the first time, devoted most of its pages to in-depth articles on single films.

A 1960 article by Houston in *Sight and Sound* had already linked the Oxford group to *Cahiers* and chastised them for their commitment to technical analysis: "Cinema is about the human situation, not about spatial relationships."[30] As if in defiance, the very first article in *Movie* (June 1962) lambasted not only British directors but critics who lacked awareness of technique. Now, it seemed, the entire future of the British cinema hinged on spatial relationships: "Until it is accepted that style is worthy of passionate feeling and detailed analysis, there will be no change."[31]

From the start, the central *Movie* critics—Cameron, Perkins, Shivas, Paul Mayersberg, and Robin Wood—displayed an unprecedented attention to a film's thematic range and formal texture. Their pantheon of authors derived from Sarris and *Cahiers,* but they pushed further in showing, in a meticulous detail that owed something to Cambridge "practical criticism," how a film achieves a coherence of theme, subject, narrative, and style. Recall William Empson's celebrated gloss on the exfoliating implications of Shakespeare's line "Bare ruined choirs, where late the sweet birds sang,"[32] and compare Ian Cameron and Richard Jeffrey's unpacking of the first shot of *Marnie.* After describing this shot, in which an unknown woman, clutching a bright yellow purse, walks away from the camera down a railway platform, the authors go on at length:

> It is a shot of enormous complexity. From one point of view it is a single shot montage of bulging handbag, Marnie, and empty station, telling us quite clearly that she is traveling some distance at an unusual hour with this bag and its contents. The end of the shot has the chilly symmetry of a street or corridor, seen down its length, an image Hitchcock uses in *The Birds* (for example, where Mrs. Brenner starts down the corridor towards Dan Fawcett's bedroom) and more in *Marnie* where it fits more closely into the design. Its function is often to make us wonder what we may find at the other end. In this particular shot, the symmetry is broken slightly, obviously from choice, by the unassimilated cylindrical shape of a gas-holder in the distance.
>
> Again, the composition of the image—Marnie walking directly away from the camera down the straight line on the platform, which bisects the image, with the great slanting planes of the platform roof flying out at us on either side—is of the character having chosen a course and holding to it, threatened by the potential schizophrenia of the split, symmetrical picture.
>
> Finally, the shot is a very direct image of Marnie's life, of getting away, with the camera in pursuit flagging and finally grinding to a halt, while Marnie doesn't stop until she is at a good distance and in her own world, suggested by the slanted perspectives of the platform roof above her. This interpretation of pursuer and pursued is encouraged by the next shot, which shows Strutt staring out of the screen, as if the first shot had been a Hitchcock subjective shot from

which he would cut to the person whose viewpoint he had been showing.[33]

It proved easier for *Sight and Sound* to adopt *Movie*'s canon of directors than to undertake such precise and intricate construction of implicit meanings.

Many commentators have considered *Movie* a kind of cinematic *Scrutiny*. In the journal's commitment to "close reading," the analogy is fair; but if it suggests an aesthetic derived from F. R. Leavis, it is not. *Movie* lacked Leavis' concern to extend literary study to a broader cultural critique. *Movie* practiced a purely aesthetic, more "American" intrinsic criticism that merged the analysis of technique with the delineation of themes. *What* themes were identified might be those dear to Leavis (truth to "life," moral awareness, the balance of the physical and the mental), but they also might not. Robin Wood was by 1965 explicitly linking films' thematic concerns to those of Leavis' Great Tradition, but Wood was exceptional in this respect. Other writers, such as Perkins, rejected attempts to model *Movie*'s work on Leavis'.[34]

It should by now be evident that the institutional factors mentioned in Chapter 2 strongly shaped the development of interpretive criticism. In the 1950s and early 1960s, such criticism found its principal home in essayistic revues, not academic journals, and positions emerged from internecine battles. *Positif* could attack *Cahiers*'s Bazinian legacy. *Sight and Sound* could cluck its tongue over the excesses of *Cahiers* and *Oxford Opinion; Movie* would in turn castigate *Sight and Sound* for contributing to the cheerful vacuity of British film culture. *Film Quarterly* could question auteurism and publish Pauline Kael's 1963 broadside against Sarris and *Movie*. The pressures of regular journal publication meant that hasty polemic often replaced considered debate, but the excitement of the fresh critical approaches spurred the development of new magazines. In France, there was *Présence du cinéma* (founded 1959), *Etudes cinématographiques* (1960), *Jeune Cinéma* (1964), and others; in America, *The Seventh Art* (1963), *Moviegoer* (1964), and *Cahiers du cinéma in English* (1966).

In the same period, publishers began to bring out series of monographs on directors, providing at once a venue for auteurist explication and an encouragement of it. The earliest series were, predictably, French: the Editions universitaires series (started in 1954), the "Premier Plan" series (1959), and Seghers's "Cinéastes d'aujourd'hui" (1961). The monthly *L'Avant-scène du théâtre* created *L'Avant-scène du cinéma* in 1961, then initiated a monograph series, "Anthologie du cinéma." In 1962, *Motion* published a pair of monographs which became initiatory titles in the Tantivy Press series two years later. In 1963, *Movie* launched a series that included monographs, anthologies, and interview books. American trade publishers copublished the British series and brought out an occasional study translated from the French. Outside the series format, books such as Eric Rhode's *Tower of Babel* (1966), David Thomson's *Movie Man* (1967), and Raymond Durgnat's *Films and Feelings* (1967) further disseminated the new explicatory criticism. By 1970, there could be no doubt that the antiauteurist forces had lost: the boom in film criticism was built solidly upon the study of individual directors.

So were the academic fortunes of film study. Art cinema and auteurism, discussed in quasiacademic terms by the writers on *Cahiers* and *Movie,* helped cinema enter universities. If Bergman, Fellini, Kurosawa, and Hitchcock were great artists, should not scholars be studying them? Philosophy departments used films by Godard and Antonioni to illustrate existentialism; teachers of literature studied *Throne of Blood* as an adaptation of *Macbeth*. Soon whole courses were devoted to a single director's work. As film courses slipped into the curriculum, publication patterns changed. Academic periodicals like *Cinema Journal* focused more intently upon interpretive practice. By the mid-1970s, when director monographs proved insufficiently profitable for commercial publishing, educational institutions stepped into the breach. The British Film Institute began a vigorous publishing program based largely upon the director monograph. The long-lived Twayne's "Authors" series began a subseries featuring film directors. American scholarly publishers started to follow the lead of Indiana University Press, MIT Press, and the University of California Press, all of which had been committed to film studies since the mid-1960s. On the whole, the institutional context of academic film studies has been the result of explicatory, chiefly auteur-centered criticism.

Picture Planes

All in all, the creative act is not performed by the artist alone; the spectator brings the work in contact with the external world by deciphering and interpreting its inner qualifications.

—Marcel Duchamp

The concept of an avant-garde or experimental cinema often implies outright hostility to mainstream fiction film. Yet Anglo-American critics of avant-garde cinema have been no less committed to explication than their peers who address the work of Welles or Bergman. This should not surprise us, since historically the critical schools are linked. It was in *Film Culture* that Sarris published his most influential auteurist work, that many critics discussed European art cinema, and that the writings around the American avant-garde crystallized. In 1960, the journal's editor, Jonas Mekas, compared the New American cinema movement with the French *nouvelle vague* and British Free Cinema.[35] Some critics were led to study the avant-garde by their interest in art cinema,[36] while others, such as P. Adams Sitney, wrote on both Brakhage and Bresson without changing interpretive strategies. It would not be difficult to show how the pertinence and richness of implicit meanings prized by critics of narrative cinema operate as criteria for the explicator of experimental films. According to David Curtis, for instance, Steve Dwoskin's films study "human isolation and the gestures we make towards communication."[37] Another critic finds Bruce Conner's *Report* to harbor "an evocative ambiguity and painful irony."[38]

Not only the particular meanings constructed but the conception of implicit meaning itself is central to criticism in the avant-garde tradition.[39] Writing on the avant-garde relies on widely held assumptions about aesthetic practice. For the avant-garde explicator, as for critics of other stripes, the artist stands as creator or transmitter of meaning. The artist draws upon personal experience (here autobiography enters), or upon a private mythology (for example, Kenneth Anger's predilection for Aleister Crowley), or upon the art world, which passes along inherited "problems" to be solved. The critic will use the artist's writings, interviews, and recollections to support ascribed meanings. And just as Ford's or Antonioni's films add up to a unified oeuvre, so do the films of Robert Breer, Maya Deren, or Dore O. The experimental filmmaker's output must also be studied in relation to work in other media—Conner's assemblages, Michael Snow's painting and music. In Western culture, critical interpretation in any medium has long assumed that a psychological unity binds the artist's thought and behavior to the finished work. Asking Hollis Frampton to explain what he meant is not different in principle from asking Hitchcock, or the suburban father in my opening scenario.

The affinities of American avant-garde criticism with its mainstream counterparts is most evident in its treatment of those experimental works now seen as dominating the 1950s and early 1960s. The prevailing tendency was to interpret the films of Deren, Stan Brakhage, James Broughton, and Sidney Peterson on the analogy of narrative or poetry. Parker Tyler considered that dream, myth, and ritual provided the best models for understanding such works.[40] Insisting particularly upon symbolic meanings which "represent the fictions of the imagination,"[41] Tyler asserts that the mythic film need not be like a novel, since it can build itself shot by shot, as a poem is made word by word.[42] P. Adams Sitney, the 1960s' most influential interpreter of experimental film, likewise emphasized literary analogues, revealing "imagism" in the theme and form of *Dog Star Man* and treating *Anticipation of the Night* as a narrative possessing a protagonist, a first-person point of view, and a "language of visual metaphor" that presents "the ritual of an artist's quest for untampered vision."[43]

Such interpretive tactics, close to those which other critics applied to the European art cinema, bear the traces of a period when avant-garde filmmaking was starting to become somewhat respectable. The Filmmakers Cooperative, founded in 1962, and the Canyon Cooperative, created in 1966, were making films available. Filmmakers were beginning to receive foundation grants, and the Filmmakers Cinémathèque received a large Ford Foundation subsidy in 1968.[44] Departments of art and literature came more and more to include experimental film in their curricula. However antiacademic the motives of Mekas, Tyler, Sitney, and others might have been, treating the films as personal poetic testaments along the lines of conceptions of the art-film director's "vision" had the effect of making avant-garde films acceptable objects of study.

At the same time, critics began to position the experimental film within the fine-arts tradition. A main impetus for this maneuver came from the hyperbolic publicity attending Andy Warhol's entry into filmmaking. In 1963, just as he was becoming a successful Pop artist, Warhol made his first films, and soon critics were ascribing implicit meanings to them on the basis of concepts drawn from the modernist tradition in painting. Since these ideas became important to the history of film interpretation, I will trace them very briefly and roughly.[45]

1. *The modernist artwork courts chance.* Duchamp's willingness to embrace accident inspired John Cage, who conceived works based on the contingent and unstructured. The artist could set up a situation

but need not seek complete control over what transpired. Abstract Expressionism and Happenings were only the most obvious manifestations of the principle. Warhol films such as *Sleep, Eat,* and *Empire,* all records of an object or process, could easily be subsumed under this schema. In Warhol's narrative films, non-professional actors, sketchy scripts, long takes, and the fixed camera could all be interpreted as tactics allowing chance to play a dominant role.[46] *The Chelsea Girls,* with its randomly arranged reels projected two at a time, also seemed highly Cagean.

2. *The modernist work seeks a formal and substantive purity.* The Symbolist sources of modernism linger on in this supposition, a key premise for traditions stressing abstraction and integrity of materials. Within this frame of reference, Warhol became a minimalist: his "content-less" early films appeared "to examine cinema at its roots."[47] Shorn of plot (as in *Eat* or *Sleep*), emptied of human presence (as in *Empire,* an eight-hour film recording the Empire State Building while sunset becomes night), his films presented cinema as a medium "for experiencing time, rather than movement or event."[48] Along with presupposition 1, this "purist" schema shaped "ontological" conceptions of the modernist work.

3. *The modernist work retains overt traces of the process of its making.* This idea can be traced back to Duchamp and Cage, but the most proximate source in the American art world is the criticism arising around postwar "action painting" and Abstract Expressionism. The main concern of this art, according to one critic, was "the registration of the act of creation as a unique and dramatic event ... All the exhibited marks of freedom, in handling and execution, were left in visible evidence in the finished work to document the artist's dilemmas of choice and decision: whipped lines, torn shapes, emendations and erasures, and smeared color."[49] In Warhol's films, the critic could point to the inclusion of light-struck footage and flash frames, the awkwardness of performers reading their lines for the first time, and the impromptu, almost willful zoom-ins and -outs—all choices recorded ineluctably in the time-bound medium of cinema.

4. *In the modernist artwork, formal properties or specific aspects of the medium become the focus of the perceiver's experience.* For critics of the time, this commonplace was most powerfully articulated in Clement Greenberg's 1961 essay "Modernist Painting," in which he claims that

unique properties of the medium become "positive factors that are to be acknowledged openly."[50] Thus modernist painting stresses the two-dimensionality of the surface, flaunting three-dimensional effects as purely optical phenomena. The perceiver becomes aware of the work in all its specificity, a process which was often seen to entail an "anti-illusionist" attitude. It was not difficult to apply this schema to such Warhol films as *Empire,* which could be said to display cinema's essential ability to record time or to present shifting gradations of black and white.[51] The film portraits, in their contrasty photography, could be said to "demand a consideration of the flat negative-positive values of the surface."[52] Even Warhol's scripted psychodramas include the reel ends and light-struck footage, while the performances and camera handling can be seen, in one of the most used phrases of the period, as making you aware you're watching a film. In this version of reflexivity lies one epistemological tenet of the modernist work.

5. *The modernist work criticizes dominant theories and practices of art-making.* This presupposition gives avant-garde film criticism a historical, contextualizing dimension which auteur studies lacked. Again Greenberg articulated the issue most forcefully: since Kant, the essence of modernism has been "the use of the characteristic methods of a discipline to criticize the discipline itself."[53] Here is reflexivity in another sense. Now a painting is not only "about" paint, color, line, and flat surfaces; it is, more negatively, "about" other paintings, styles, and traditions. Thus Warhol's "static" films could be seen as denouncing narrative cinema; his sexual spectacles as unmasking Hollywood's hypocritical concupiscence; his "superstars" as parodying the star system. *Lonesome Cowboys* becomes an "anti-Western,"[54] while *Kitchen* undermines the representation of space in Renaissance art.[55]

6. *The modernist work encourages aesthetic distance.* Kant's concept of aesthetic contemplation was transformed by the Symbolists into a dispassionate conception of art which, in the twentieth century, had diverse offshoots, from the transcendent visions of Kandinsky to the parodic detachment of Joyce and Stravinsky. Likewise, Viktor Shklovsky's concept of *ostranenie* ("making-strange") and Bertolt Brecht's *Verfremdungeffekt* ("estrangement-effect") stressed the alienating, non-empathic qualities of art. Greenberg implies something comparable when he claims that in modernist painting one cannot really imagine entering the depicted space.[56] The use of this concept constitutes an important break with the poetic-mythic tradition of avant-garde film

criticism, since critics like Sitney had stressed the viewer's intense emotional involvement with, say, Brakhage's work.[57] Now there was Warhol's cool reticence. The fact that his silent films were slowed in projection could be said to create an annoying flicker and an uninvolving sense of time, while the refusal of his camera to enter the action could bespeak an alienated voyeurism; indifference entails distance. Here is a second sort of "anti-illusionism": a refusal to be "taken in" by the spectacle.

Framed within these presuppositions, avant-garde films were newly "readable"—and writable. Anti-illusionism and reflexivity became commonplaces of film interpretation, while Greenbergian conceptions of flatness, framing, and the act of looking set a fresh critical agenda. The force of the change is evident from Sitney's controversial 1969 discussion "Structural Film," an essay which differs significantly from his prior work. Gone are the appeals to narrative, poetic, and mythic form. A structural film, Sitney explains, is essentially about the potential of cinema. Brakhage's *Song 27* "reaffirms the space of the film frame."[58] George Landow is devoted to "the flat screen cinema, the moving-grain painting."[59] *The Film That Rises to the Surface of Clarified Butter,* in its tension of surface and depth, yields "a metaphor for the relation of film itself (a two-dimensional field of illusion) and actuality."[60] Sitney's essay is typical of the period in showing how the critic could combine several modernist assumptions in order to construct implicit meaning. Now a critic could argue that Bruce Conner's attack on illusionism (the "art-is-critical" concept) depends upon using flicker to treat the screen as a physical thing (the "purism" concept) and results in a refusal to get the spectator absorbed (the "aesthetic distance" concept).[61]

It fell to another critic to propose a seventh schema that, while related to these, manifested a unique authority. In June 1971 Annette Michelson published in *Artforum* one of the most powerful exemplars within the explicatory tradition, an essay called simply "Toward Snow." Michelson rests her argument on many traditional grounds. She portrays Michael Snow's films and fine-arts work as revealing an overall unity and a logical development. She quotes his description of *Wavelength* in order to demonstrate his awareness of his goals and methods. She describes his project in Greenbergian terms: Snow transforms depth into flatness, figuration into abstraction, "illusion" into "fact." The halting zoom in *Wavelength* can be seen as criticizing at least two traditions: that of the Hollywood narrative and that of the American avant-garde's disjunctions and hypnagogic vision. Snow's films also embody the viewer's awareness of the medium; echoing many writers on Warhol, Michelson claims that *One Second in Montreal* forces upon the viewer "the consciousness of time as duration."[62] This in turn promotes a kind of reflexive aesthetic distance in which we become aware of our own awareness. But Michelson goes beyond such commonplaces to propose a new interpretive tactic for avant-garde film, the creation of an epistemological thematics.

Critical writing on the avant-garde had long invoked categories of perceptual activity. To *Film Culture*, Warhol's work had seemed to cleanse vision: "We have cut our hair, we have eaten, but we have never really seen those actions."[63] With the rise of modernist interpretive schemata, a film became characterized as at once a perceptual object (for example, involving a play of flatness and depth or stasis and movement) and a cognitive enterprise. If the modernist work was self-conscious and critical, it was not anomalous to describe a film as conducting an inquiry or taking a step in a larger research program. Thus *Empire* could be an "investigation of the presence and character of film," and *Kitchen* could make the star system "the subject of scrutiny."[64] As early as 1966 Michelson had raised the issue of cinema's epistemological resources, and in a 1969 essay she suggested that *2001* offers a "discourse on knowledge through perception as action, and ultimately, on the nature of the medium as 'action film,' as mode and model of cognition."[65] This concept became her major methodological contribution to avant-garde film interpretation. "Toward Snow" opens with the definitive statement of it:

> There is a metaphor recurrent in contemporary discourse on the nature of consciousness: that of cinema. And there are cinematic works which present themselves as analogues of consciousness in its constitutive and reflexive modes, as though inquiry into the nature and processes of experience had found in this century's art form, a striking, a uniquely direct presentational mode. The illusionism of the new, temporal art reflects and occasions reflection upon, the conditions of knowledge; it facilitates a critical focus upon the immediacy of experience in the flow of time.[66]

Michelson goes on to interpret *Wavelength* as being centrally about human perception and cognition. The film's shape parallels the psychological process of expectation; the trip across the room is a metaphor for the "horizon of expectation" subtending every subjective process.[67] The structure is a "grand metaphor" for narrative: "Its 'plot' is the tracing of spatio-temporal *données,* its 'action' the movement of the camera as the movement of consciousness."[68] If Brakhage represents closed-eye vision and Warhol offers a stare, Snow opens our eyes to the role of intentionality and temporality in experience. By finding that the unique features of the medium are not simply self-referential, Michelson makes the work reflexive in a new, "phenomenological" sense. She produces a seventh presupposition: *The modernist artwork takes as its theme some aspect of human perception or cognition.*

The move proved fruitful. This assumption could interlock with other modernist tenets, as Michelson's essay shows. It could move the critic away from Greenberg's more object-centered notion of the work toward a conception of the beholder's participation in a developing transaction. Above all, it allowed the critic to explicate a film as thematizing some aspect of human cognition. Over the next decade, Michelson and others filled in different patches of the phenomenological canvas. *Zorns Lemma,* according to Wanda Bershen, traces a development of knowledge from linguistic symbols to visual perception.[69] Ken Jacobs' *Tom Tom the Piper's Son* was seen to be "didactic" in its demonstration of the role of memory in all film viewing.[70] Brakhage's *Scenes from under Childhood* could be interpreted as capturing a child's visual perception.[71] Now Warhol could be discussed as presenting a drama of self-conscious attention and apprehension.[72] The schema was extended to Soviet modernism by showing that Eisenstein's and Vertov's styles incarnate dialectical modes of thought.[73] Sitney offered a romanticist version of this schema in his monumental *Visionary Film,* which plotted how various dimensions of subjective experience—dream, ritual, imagination, memory, vision—are manifested and examined in the works of the American avant-garde.[74] A major by-product of all this activity was writing of considerable precision; the phenomenological premise generated critical descriptions at least as minute as those seen in the best *Movie* essays.

Just as important as Michelson's insight was her institutional situation. Teaching film at New York University put her in contact with an avant-garde film community, the Manhattan art world, major publishers, and eager students. The phenomenological thematics of avant-garde film played an important role in a stream of publications: an avant-garde film number of *Artforum* (September 1971), an Eisenstein/Brakhage issue of the same journal (January 1973), Stephen Koch's book on Warhol (1973), Sitney's *Visionary Film* (1974), Michelson's exhibit program *New Forms in Film* (1974), Sitney's collection *The Essential Cinema* (1975), the American Federation of the Arts volume *A History of the American Avant-Garde Film* (1976), the first issue of *Millennium Film Journal* (founded in 1977), Sitney's anthology *The Avant-Garde Film* (1978), and an updated edition of *Visionary Film* (1979). Many contributors to these publications were, in one way or another, affiliated with NYU.

Michelson's impact was comparable to that of Sarris and *Movie:* she showed that a serious explicatory criticism could be attractive to an intellectual public. Her contribution came as film studies was entrenching itself in the academy. Thus her philosophically informed essays helped make the study of avant-garde film part of modern art criticism and history.[75] Although experimental film was never absorbed into the fine-arts market,[76] avant-garde film criticism could be assimilated into the academic institution. As the 1970s writings entered the critical canon, and as NYU graduates moved into positions of college teaching and arts administration, the work of Sitney, Michelson, and others became established as the most sophisticated explications of experimental cinema.

Disputes still rage about the degree of influence of the American avant-garde upon British filmmaking, but there was in any event a considerable lag in the critical study of British avant-garde cinema. The London Film-Makers Co-op was founded in 1966, four years after its New York counterpart, and British journals devoted to experimental film tended to be even more marginal and sporadic than *Film Culture.*[77] Not until the early 1970s did well-financed arts organizations begin to support experimental cinema. The British Arts Council and the British Film Institute started to subsidize film projects and programs. In 1970 the National Film Theatre (NFT) held its first International Underground Film Festival, and followed with a 1972 program on English independent cinema and a 1973 program of films from the Co-op. In 1972, *Studio International,* the British counterpart of *Artforum,* began coverage of independent cinema, and in the same year *Art and Artists* published a special number on experimental film. It was 1975 by the time a major museum, the Tate Gallery, initiated its own program of experimental British films.[78] In 1976, the NFT presented an eighteen-program season devoted solely to "Structural/Materialist" cinema. Such exhibitions generated a considerable amount of critical writing: a special number of *Studio International* (1975), the BFI *Structural Film Anthology* (1976), Malcolm Le Grice's *Abstract Film and Beyond* (1977), the British Arts Council catalogue *A Perspective on the English Avant-Garde Film* (1978), and the Arts Council–Hayward Gallery catalogue for the *Film as Film* retrospective (1979).

In the English critical discourse, American writing often served as a target.[79] Sitney's Romanticism was often attacked as outmoded (a "theology of art," Peter Sainsbury called it).[80] Peter Gidal upbraided Michelson for her claim that Warhol's cinema was predicated upon a "stare."[81] Political critiques appeared as well: Sainsbury suggested that the American avant-garde's attention to perception and structure kept it locked within asocial aesthetic categories.[82] Yet English critical writing owed a considerable debt to American film analyses and articulations of modernist theory. Despite complaints about Sitney's essay "Structuralist Film," Gidal's "structuralist/materialist" genre owes more than its name to Sitney, and is considerably influenced by Greenberg. Throughout the British writing of the period one finds nearly all the modernist schemata in place. In 1972, one critic could praise *Zorns Lemma* for its calculated integration of chance, while another could find that David Larcher's *Mare's Tail* reveals basic elements of film—grain, frame, strip, projector, and light.[83] Le Grice congratulates Warhol for presenting the processes that compose the work, and he celebrates the capacity of "systemic" film to make the physical properties of the materials counteract the illusionistic image.[84] Writing about Kurt Kren, Le Grice composes a straightforward art-historical essay consisting of biographical information, apt quotations from the artist, mentions of Kren's affiliations with other artists, a list of recurrent thematic concerns, and a discussion of changes in form and style across his career.[85] Deke Dusinberre remains within a Greenbergian frame of reference when he claims that emphasizing the process of projection challenges illusionism by displaying the literal three dimensions of the viewing space.[86] Even in their most severe political assaults, the English avant-garde critics tacitly accept many of the cognitive assumptions of NYU criticism, as when Sainsbury asserts that the new political cinema of Frampton and Godard "does not seek to portray, reflect, interpret, symbolise, or allegorise—but to enquire. The new cinema is an epistemological one."[87]

The disputes between the English and their New York peers thus came to typify certain family quarrels within modernism itself. In rejecting Michelson's phenomenological thematics, English critics tried a deflationary tactic I examined in Chapter 1: turn an implicit meaning into a referential one. Thus *Central Region*, according to Gidal, "is not a metaphor for consciousness. It is a form of such."[88] The film does not imply; it refers, though only to itself. This move is part of a suspicion of representation in general. Le Grice in effect returns to a Greenbergian purism in demanding that the image never become overwhelmed by illusionism, and he can denounce even *Wavelength* because the manipulation of the time of the profilmic event is never explicitly stated in the film.[89] Gidal remarks that a purist return to materials is always at risk—"'Empty screen' is no less significatory than 'happy carefree smile'"[90]—unless it constitutes *presentation*, not representation.

The return to referential and explicit meaning—what Dusinberre calls "structural asceticism"[91]—did not stop avant-garde critics from interpreting films. We have already seen that Le Grice could ascribe meaning to Kren's protostructuralist work. Gidal is no less orthodox in suggesting that art is full of "images of silence" (rocking chairs, blindness), or in proposing that Snow's ⟷ (known as *Back and Forth*) shows people making metaphor in order *itself* to make a metaphor for the inadequacy of language.[92] Gidal also finds his own preoccupation with the tyranny of ordinary cinema thematized in *Zorns Lemma*'s use of the Bay State Primer.[93] The humanist themes of auteur and art-cinema explication and the epistemological themes of Michelson's work are supplanted by art-world themes derived from avant-garde criticism itself. A film can become a demonstration of a precept already formulated by Greenberg or Beckett. No matter how "literally" ascetic structuralism sought to present the processes and materials of cinema ("In this film, grain destroys illusion"), the critic could turn them into themes ("This film is *about* grain's role in destroying illusion").

The English avant-garde's appeal to politics can also be seen as a return to a contested issue within modernism generally. Gidal, as usual, is most blunt: "The attempt at clarification of material objectivity, the *process* of awareness (of consciousness of actuality), the *attempt* to deal with the given in a dialectic manner rather than a model-oriented one, belies the tradition of romanticism to the core. If anything, a marxist aesthetic lies behind these films, whether the film-makers know it or not."[94] Mike Dunford links film-as-film cinema to the creation of a new consciousness: "Breaking down the illusion of transparent naturalism is an important first step, extending the critique of bourgeois imagery and the creation of a truly antagonistic film practice, a film practice that helps the people to perceive their situation and to destroy the ideological chains that bind them."[95] The Marxist recasting of formal film might seem to take a long step beyond conventional modernism, but in fact the language of revolution (materiality, critique, subversion, radicality) was part of modernist discourse. Greenberg had stressed the critical function of contemporary painting, and Michelson herself had linked experimental film to radical political aspirations. In any event, such assertions as Gidal's and Dunford's did not become the basis of critical interpretation until the late 1970s, when the notion of the "contradictory text" provided a way to link signification to Freudian/Lacanian conceptions of the "split" human subject. The avant-garde's promise of political efficacy was underwritten by a theoretical discourse that saw experimental film as acknowledging contradictions (in the text, in the unconscious) which mainstream cinema repressed. I shall consider this attempt "to combine New York modernism with Parisian ('68) theory"[96] in the next chapter.

Meaning and Unity

The 1960s boom in explicatory interpretation was not accompanied by many debates that critics today would consider "theoretical." Still, the trend was undergirded by particular assumptions about form and meaning. A film was presumed to be a composite of implicit meanings given material embodiment in formal patterns and technical devices.[97] That is, "beneath" the referential meaning of the film and any explicit point or message, there lay significant themes, issues, or problems. The critic might choose to emphasize the meanings, as did Sarris and most *Cahiers* writers in their attempt to distinguish each director's underlying vision or metaphysic. Alternatively, the critic could take the themes as given and go on to study how form and style make them concrete and vivid.[98] This trend has always been salient in avant-garde criticism and was an important feature of most *Movie* critics' approach to narrative and technique. Some critics, such as Bazin, Wood, and Michelson, are significant for their attempt to balance the concerns of theme and style. Apart from this methodological choice, however, there was a more important disparity within the explicatory movement.

Any interpretive practice seeks to show that texts mean more than they seem to say. But, one might ask, why does a text not say what it means? The symptomatic approach has a straightforward answer: the text *cannot* say what it means; it tries to disguise its actual meaning. The principal analogy here, as we shall see in the next chapter, is to the discourse of the psychoanalytic patient. The explicatory account presumes a different sort of process to be at work. There are actually two tacit models within the explicatory trend: that of "transmission" and that of the autonomous object.

The transmission model suggests that the text acquires meaning much as a conversational utterance does. The text passes from a sender to a receiver, who decodes it according to syntactic and semantic rules and according to assumptions about the speaker's intent in this context. In our hypothetical opening example, the father's remark about the length of the grass is tested by the son for its relevance to the situation. The implicit meaning of the statement is a product of the son's pragmatic inferences, involving implicatures, presuppositions, or speech-act rules.[99] Likewise, the explicatory critic can infer communicative purposes and assume that the filmmaker, like ordinary speakers, uses indirect meaning to achieve effects not available in "speaking directly." The text does not say outright what it means because implicit meaning, in art or in life, can produce greater economy, subtlety, or force. This account does not require that the speaker be wholly aware of his or her intentions. The assumption is only that the public context of reception will impute appropriate contextual intentions to any utterance.

The transmission model thus leads to an *artist-centered* conception of meaning. According to this view, the film is a vehicle for meanings "put there" by the filmmaker—either as an act of deliberate *communication* or as an act of only partially self-aware *expression*. The father who obliquely asks his son to mow the lawn may be seen as craftily hinting at his point or as spontaneously expressing his devious personality ("That's the way my dad talks all the time").

Auteur criticism and the art cinema evidently encouraged both communicative and expressive assumptions. Astruc saw the *caméra-stylo* as a means by which the artist could convey his ideas: "The fundamental problem of the cinema is how to express thought."[100] To treat the modern cinema as one which lets the director have the freedom to say "what he wants" is to take the communicative or expressive dimension for granted.[101] Rivette wrote in 1954 that to study Preminger was to reveal "the obsessions of an author who knows what themes suit him best."[102] Discussing Antonioni eight years later, Cameron claimed that any film by a good director becomes "an experiment in expressing whatever is important to its author."[103] As in the writings of Richards, Empson, and Leavis, there is a belief that the artwork evokes a "mental condition" that echoes that achieved by the creator in completing the work.[104] By concentrating upon the artist, the critic could assume that the implicit meanings found in the work were, calculatedly or spontaneously, put there.

Most historians have pointed to the strong Romantic basis of auteur theory, and certainly the notion of self-expression provides some evidence for it.[105] Yet if we look at auteur criticism as one brand of explication, we see that the artist-centered model has far deeper roots. Almost from the start of the Western hermeneutic tradition, exegesis took the author as a salient category. By Spinoza's day this assumption was self-evident.[106] Even an anti-Romantic positivist like Gustave Lanson could confidently assert that textual interpretation requires knowledge of the writer's life and personality.

We have already seen the extent to which the explication of avant-garde cinema also presupposes a bond between the artist and the oeuvre. In the 1950s and 1960s, criticism often appealed to an expression model in discussing the work of Brakhage or Markopoulos. Steve Dwoskin could describe *Mare's Tail* as a film that "explores the subjective responses of Larcher himself to his own life and to his personal visual experiences."[107] Even those filmmakers who utilized chance could be seen as deliberately making a point, creating an effect, inquiring into a problem.[108] The language of intention is everywhere: Warhol "coyly refers" to Hollywood[109]; a work's style is, according to Michelson, "the structural and sensuous incarnation of the artist's will."[110] Avant-garde criticism has in fact been the last stronghold of intentionality in film interpretation. While Hollywood films can often be rendered interpretable only by positing unintentional and spontaneous artists behind them, the experimental filmmaker, supposedly free of commercial constraints, has usually been assigned more responsibility for the effects the film creates. Divergences in viewers' responses can be credited to an artist who deliberately seeks a range of implicit meanings or who frees the spectator from the tyranny of pat messages.

Furthermore, explicatory criticism has always relied to some degree on filmmakers' statements. It is likely that Bazin's account of deep-focus realism was influenced by Gregg Toland's explanations of his technique.[111] Sarris' 1963 mention of Hawks's eye-level camera seems to pick up a hint dropped by the director a year earlier.[112] Michelson's phenomenological interpretation of *Wavelength* may be considered a fleshing-out of Snow's note that his films try "to suggest the mind in a certain state or certain states of consciousness."[113] Indeed, often the experimental film cannot be interpreted without seeking out the artist's notes, plans, or recollections. Like Stuart Gilbert receiving the blueprint of *Ulysses* from Joyce himself, Sitney writes of *Dog Star Man:* "Brakhage once outlined the plot of the entire epic to me, and a synopsis will clear this and many other problems."[114]

Within avant-garde circles, where critical writing often directly influences filmmakers, one finds extensive feedback loops. In 1967, Paul Sharits submitted a "statement of intentions" to a film competition. Four years later a critic's article on Sharits cited passages from it.[115] In 1975, Sharits could cite that article in another statement of intentions.[116] Reigning interpretive strategies can shape the artist's entire project, as in this statement by filmmaker Tim Bruce:

> One of the most important points of intervention is to challenge the system of film codes which have developed . . . , to make them visible, to show how they work and so to subvert them.
>
> *Visit* challenges editing codes, that are the fulcrum of time/space distortions. Two separate events are edited together. The action and the editing intimate that they are taking place at the same time and in a particular spatial relationship to one another. However, the film goes on to contradict this illusion by showing that the two events have been shot in a completely different spatial relationship to one another and as one continuous take.[117]

Here the artist becomes a critic by providing a conventionally acceptable explication of his film.

In such ways, explicatory criticism subscribes to the transmission model.   But, like New Criticism, this approach harbors a more *object-centered* theory of meaning as well. Here, according to widely accepted assumptions in post-Kantian aesthetics, the artwork presents itself as an autonomous whole cut off from the maker's intentions. The work's "formally controlled complexity" creates the determining context for all meanings.[118]

Insofar as avant-garde cinema has identified itself with modernism, such an insistence on the self-sustaining object has been an important premise. Michelson points out that modernism developed out of the Symbolist conception of an "autonomous, self-justifying and reflexive order."[119] Within avant-garde criticism, the issue often revolves around the extent to which the film can be interpreted independently of the artist's personal life. A recent writer complains that the unity of Yvonne Rainer's *Journeys from Berlin* suffers because "it is highly unlikely that any spectator could come up with any rationale for linking all these concerns meaningfully without the figure and biography of Rainer herself."[120]

This is, of course, to raise the New Critical issue of the irrelevance of "extrinsic" information. Eliot's conception of poetic "impersonality," Richards' proof that undergraduates presented with unsigned poems were incapable of saying anything pertinent about the work "in itself," Empson's dazzling display of the productivity of the words assembled on the page, the American critics' attack on authorial intention, and the growing centrality of linguistic devices such as metaphor, irony, and paradox—all these developments in literary theory shaped a more "immanent" or "intrinsic" criticism. University-trained film critics inherited this objectivist strain. Sarris' landmark essay on *Citizen Kane* stands as an early articulation of the assumption that a film's meaning is not what the author probably put in but what the critic can plausibly get out. Years later, in explaining why the filmmaker and the critic may disagree, Sarris cited *Cahiers:* "An objective criticism, methodically ignoring 'intentions,' is as applicable to the most personal work imaginable, like a poem or a painting."[121] Despite the *Movie* writers' proclivity for interviewing their preferred auteurs, they used their skills in close reading to push objectivism to new limits.[122] In his 1972 *Film as Film*, Perkins formulated an objectivist credo:

> If the relationships established in a film are significant, it makes no difference to the spectator how they came, or were brought about, or to what extent their significance was intended. A movie has a meaning for the spectator when he is able to interpret its pattern of actions and images. Provided that its relationships are coherently shaped, the film embodies—and can be shown to embody—a consistent meaning which may or may not have been sought, or sincerely felt, by the director.[123]

Perkins' emphasis on pattern, coherence, and consistency points to the central attribute of meaning in both the transmission model and the objectivist model: unity. "What matters in a film is the will toward order, harmony, composition," wrote *Cahiers*'s Fereydoun Hoveyda in 1960, adding that the critic's task was to reveal, behind each filmmaker's characteristic ordering principles, the work's hidden meaning.[124] Jonas Mekas could claim that the good experimental film has its own "plot": "These events are as tightly knit and proceed with as much inevitability and time-place-character unity as on the other, outer level (circle) of being (art)."[125] In all these critical idioms, unity can be attributed to a single film or to an entire career. "There's not content on the one hand and technique on the other," observes Jacques Rivette; "there's 'expression' and, if the film succeeds, this expression forms a whole."[126] According to Sarris, the auteur critic "looks at a film as a whole, a director as a whole. The parts, however entertaining individually, must cohere meaningfully."[127]

In general, the *Cahiers* critics gravitated toward an extrinsic, "citational" conception of implicit meaning, whereby iconography found its way into films. (Christian symbolism furnished favorite instances.) Similar atomistic tactics dominated much of the explicatory criticism around the New American Cinema of the 1950s and early 1960s. The *Movie* critics, however, insisted more upon the intrinsic, "contextual" significance created within the work. Thus in a 1962 roundtable, Cameron praises a motif in *Barabbas* for furnishing the sort of symbolism that "links back to something else within the picture, rather than annexing a meaning from elsewhere."[128] Similarly, with the rise of "structural film," avant-garde explication became more holistic and contextual, assuming that the film's underlying concept yielded a clear shape that at least partly modified whatever symbols might be present. (Ironically, in their refusal of the morphological premises of American structural film, many English avant-garde critics returned to atomistic theme-spotting.) And in its occasional insistence on a dialectics of form, avant-garde criticism came close to *Movie*'s tendency to treat the film as having a dynamic structure, like that which many New Critics found in a poem: bristling with internal thematic tensions that are checked, if not resolved, by an overall form.[129] Despite such local differences, however, explicatory criticism treated formal unity primarily as a manifestation of a unity of meaning.

Like the art cinema and avant-garde filmmaking, explicatory criticism sought to demonstrate that film was a worthy cultural enterprise. Cinema produced rich, complex experiences that could form the occasion for intellectual reflection and debate. So powerful and pervasive were the effects of this critical trend that not only its methods but its underlying notions of meaning provided the basis of film interpretation. Probably most teachers and critics still practice explication, assuming some version of the communication-based, expression-based, or objectivist conceptions of implicit meaning, and seeking to reveal the film's thematic unity. Since the late 1960s, however, a second critical trend has become steadily more influential, and it has based its approach to interpretation on significantly different conceptions of meaning.

4

Symptomatic
Interpretation

Freud in his analysis provides explanations which many people are
inclined to accept. He emphasizes that people are *dis*-inclined to
accept them. But if the explanation is one which people are dis-
inclined to accept, it is highly probable that it is also one which
they are *inclined* to accept. And this is what Freud has actually
brought out.

—Ludwig Wittgenstein

On a summer day, a father looks out at the family lawn and says to
his teen-aged son: "The grass is so tall I can hardly see the cat walking
through it." The son slopes off to mow the lawn, but the interchange
has been witnessed by a team of live-in social scientists, and they
interpret the father's remark in various ways. One sees it as typical of
an American household's rituals of power and negotiation. Another
observer construes the remark as revealing a characteristic bourgeois
concern for appearances and a pride in private property. Yet another,
perhaps having had some training in the humanities, insists that the
father envies the son's sexual proficiency and that the feline image
constitutes a fantasy that unwittingly symbolizes (a) the father's identification with a predator; (b) his desire for liberation from his stifling
life; (c) his fears of castration (the cat in question has been neutered);
or (d) all of the above.

Now if these observers were to propose their interpretations to the
father, he might deny them with great vehemence, but this would not
persuade the social scientists to repudiate their conclusions. They
would reply that the meanings they ascribed to the remark were
involuntary, concealed by a referential meaning (a report on the height
of the grass) and an implicit meaning (the order to mow the lawn).
The social scientists have constructed a set of *symptomatic* meanings,
and these cannot be demolished by the father's protest. Whether the

sources of meaning are intrapsychic or broadly cultural, they lie outside the conscious control of the individual who produces the utterance. We are now practicing a "hermeneutics of suspicion," a scholarly debunking, a strategy that sees apparently innocent interactions as masking unflattering impulses. Nietzsche set out the catechism of symptomatic interpretation in all the human sciences: "When we are confronted with any manifestation which someone has permitted us to see, we may ask: what is it meant to conceal? what is it meant to draw our attention from? what prejudice does it seek to raise? and again, how far does the subtlety of the dissimulation go? and in what respect is the man mistaken?"[1] Repressed meaning is what no speaker will own up to.

At least as far back as Kant, the hermeneutic tradition was willing to grant that an interpreter might understand the author better than he has understood himself.[2] But this activity was concerned with clearing away logical confusions in the author's project, the better to clarify his true intention. What Freud and his followers brought to the interpretation of human behavior, including artistic creativity, was the dynamic conception of the unconscious, whereby deeper meanings were systematically concealed by a process of resourceful repression. For example, Freud was intrigued by Leonardo da Vinci's fantasy of a vulture settling down at his cradle and striking him on the lips with its tail. According to Freud, this fantasy conceals Leonardo's reminiscence of suckling at the maternal breast; the unconscious has transformed this infantile memory into a homosexual fantasy.[3] In a similar fashion, Ernest Jones traces Hamlet's vacillation back to his erotic attraction to his mother, which emerges in the distorted form of manic-depressive symptoms.[4] "His emotions are inexplicable . . . because there are thoughts and wishes that no one dares to express even to himself."[5] Marie Bonaparte finds Poe's "Tell-Tale Heart" a drama of parricide, and urges us to treat all his tales as analogous to dreams, in which unconscious material that can never be brought to the surface is represented in symbolic but displaced, condensed, and censored images.[6]

It is impossible to exaggerate the impact which the concept of repressed meaning has had on artistic theory and practice in our century. Within film studies, virtually every brand of "symptomatic reading" has been explored. Nevertheless, only certain versions have proven central to academic film criticism. Psychobiographical study has won relatively few adherents in film studies. By the time the study of cinema arrived at the university—that is, the late 1960s—the psychoanalysis of the artist was already being criticized as either irrelevant to the work's aesthetic effect or blind to the sociopolitical context of individual action. (Such critiques seem to have developed out of the cultural-studies tradition consolidated in comparative literature and American studies, and they were probably strengthened by the 1960s' countercultural attack on orthodox psychoanalysis.) Nor did the surrealists' "irrational enlargement" of scenes from favorite films attract many imitators, perhaps because Western university life, especially since New Criticism, rewards the interpreter who seems to analyze a publicly accessible "work" or "text" rather than the critic who reflects on her or his idiosyncratic associations. By and large, symptomatic interpretation in film studies has preferred to show how repressed material has social sources and consequences. An "objectively" analyzable film secreting something significant about the culture which produces or consumes it: since the 1940s, this has been the text constructed by the most influential versions of symptomatic criticism.

Culture, Dream, and Lauren Bacall

Hollywood is the mass unconscious—scooped up as crudely as a steam shovel scoops up the depths of a hill, and served on a helplessly empty screen.

—Parker Tyler

While Bazin was marking out his critical position in France, alternative trends were arising in the United States. At Columbia University, home of the anthropologists Ruth Benedict and Margaret Mead, there emerged an attempt to study film as part of what Benedict had called "patterns of culture." The most visible results of this tendency were Gregory Bateson's 1943 monograph on German propaganda, Martha Wolfenstein and Nathan Leites' *Movies: A Psychological Study* (1950), and essays in Margaret Mead and Rhoda Métraux's *Study of Culture at a Distance* (1953). The exiled Frankfurt Institute for Social Research, also attached to Columbia, produced its own analysis of cinema in the "Culture Industry" chapter of T. W. Adorno and Max Horkheimer's *Dialectic of Enlightenment,* published in 1947. In the same year, Siegfried Kracauer's *From Caligari to Hitler* appeared. Shortly thereafter, in *The Lonely Crowd* (1950), the sociologist David Riesman used current films to support his arguments about American mass society. At this time Robert Warshow, one of the group around *Partisan Review,* was writing a series of essays that displayed many assumptions held by the more academic analysts. Similar beliefs were held by Barbara Deming, who in the late 1940s drew up a batch of interpretive synopses that did not see print until 1969.[7] And from a still different perspective came Parker Tyler, homespun American surrealist, who composed a string of lyrical books—*The Hollywood Hallucination* (1944), *The Magic and Myth of the Movies* (1947), and *Chaplin: The Last of the Clowns* (1948).

A typical specimen of this approach is a 1950 article by Wolfenstein and Leites on *No Way Out* (1950), a liberal social-problem film. A black doctor is accused of malpractice when his white patient dies. The patient's brother, a psychopathic racist, persecutes the doctor, who is eventually proven innocent by an autopsy. Wolfenstein and Leites start by constructing the film's explicit meaning: that racial prejudice is repugnant to decent-thinking people. "On the *conscious* level—the level of argument—it is likely that any but violent Negro-haters will be moved by this film in the direction that the film-makers desire them to go."[8] But Wolfenstein and Leites go on to suggest that certain scenes tend to contradict the film's message. The authors emphasize the doctor's lack of confidence, the extent to which he imposes on the whites who come to his defense, and the sacrilege associated with the autopsy of a white man. In addition, a pattern of iconography associates blacks with comedy, and a climactic scene of violence includes the image of a screaming woman confronted by a band of black men. Wolfenstein and Leites conclude:

> There is of course no doubt of the good intentions of the makers of this film. But in order to show how wrong race hatred is, the film-makers had to create a plot and characters, and elaborate them in detailed images; here their fantasies from a less conscious level come to the surface: the Negro becomes a terrible burden that we must carry on our backs; a sacrifice of white corpses is required for his preservation; the image of the violated white woman forces its way to the screen; and so on. There is an effort to deny these unacknowledged nightmares about the Negro by locating them in an exceptional, pathological character, but this attempt at denial remains, at bottom, ineffectual. The very title of the film, extremely puzzling in terms of the plot, expresses the basic ambiguity; though the Negro-

hater is supposed to be defeated and the falsely accused Negro saved
and vindicated, the title seems to state a deeper belief and draw a
contrary "moral": there is no way out.[9]

Like many interpreters of their period, Wolfenstein and Leites disclose
an incompatibility between the film's explicit moral and what emerges
as a cultural symptom.

To a great extent, the search for repressed meanings developed in
response to wartime cinema. German and Japanese films offered cultural anthropologists a chance to test their theories of "national character" and the symbolic dimensions of culture.[10] Benedict drew on
Japanese films for evidence in *The Chrysanthemum and the Sword*
(1946), but she used them wholly referentially, as a way of explaining
oddities of Japanese personality. More probing was Bateson's 1943
analysis of *Hitlerjunge Quex* (1933). Here he carefully distinguished
between explicit propaganda and implicit themes, and then went on
to suggest that the film also betrayed "unconscious" meanings related
to the Oedipus complex. The film pointed to a "split in the Nazi
personality."[11] Kracauer's *From Caligari to Hitler* responded to Nazi
cinema with a more historical argument about a collective German
disposition to submit to tyranny. Like Bateson, Kracauer posited at
once an explicit meaning, an implicit one, and a symptomatic one
disrupting the implicit one. The "adolescent" films of 1924–1928, for
instance, display a discontent with the democratic regime, and this
implies a revolt against all authority; but according to Kracauer, this
rebellion actually betrays an abiding desire to be ruled.[12] The popular
conception of Nazism and Japanese militarism as "collective madness"
doubtless hastened the importation of psychoanalytic concepts into
the study of film's cultural functions.

The same interpretive strategy was applied to American cinema.
While Bateson and Kracauer were scrutinizing Nazi footage at the
Museum of Modern Art, the twenty-five-year-old Barbara Deming
was there as well, selecting films for the Library of Congress. In 1950
she completed the manuscript of what would be published, two decades later, as *Running Away from Myself*. Here she treats even the
most apparently optimistic Hollywood film as offering images of loss
and futility at odds with official American values. In the same period,
Wolfenstein and Leites recast symbolic anthropology along psychoanalytic lines, borrowing from American ego psychology and emphasizing Oedipal identity conflicts. Adorno and Horkheimer used a more

"European" Freudianism to suggest the sadomasochistic appeal of American comedy. Without benefit of such explicit theories, Warshow's postwar essays on American popular culture pointed out social meanings that lie "in the deeper layers of the modern consciousness"[13] and that undergo denial and distortion.

Projection, defense, distortion, symbolism, trauma, obsession, fixation, regression, the Oedipal crisis, persecution delusion, the inferiority complex—the psychoanalytic vocabulary that entered American cinema in the late 1930s emerges no less vividly in writings about cinema. The master metaphor is the dream. For Kracauer, the Weimar "street" films produce a "dreamlike complex of images constituting a sort of secret code."[14] Deming, in a 1944 article, posits that "a film is multivocal"[15] and urges that the analyst treat films as both syndromes—that is, significant constellations of symptoms—and dreams "censored" by the overt morality of the producers and their public.[16] In *Running Away from Myself,* she asserts that the Hollywood film presents, in veiled form, what the audience wants to escape from, in the manner of a dream.[17] Warshow appeals tacitly to the metaphor in discussing how oppositional social impulses must be "disguised" and "distorted" before the plot can accommodate them.[18] The more academic Wolfenstein and Leites revise the metaphor to compare films to daydreams, but they continue to insist on the unpredictable eruption of unconscious impulses.[19] The anthropologist-psychotherapist Bateson pushes the comparison squarely into the social sphere: "The film has [here] been treated not merely as an individual's dream or as a work of art, but also as a myth."[20] Most writers of the period assume that the methods of contemporary sociology, anthropology, or cultural criticism could trace how the Freudian dream work was writ large in a society's films.

Undoubtedly the most original of these writers was Parker Tyler. Neglected in the 1940s and generally ignored by critics today, his three major books of the period constitute symptomatic interpretations that remain powerful and (to use one of his own favorite words) piquant. Tyler starts from the premise that the Hollywood film offers at once stereotyped meaning and a rich but fragmentary batch of personal and collective fantasies. Drawing on Sir James Frazer's symbolic anthropology and Freudian conceptions of fantasy and dream, Tyler looks for traces of popular myth and repressed symbolism in order "to reveal a weightier entertainment value in films than Hollywood itself is aware of."[21] Unlike many of his contemporaries, he is usually not moralistic, confessing himself frankly entertained by movieland's dream logic. He sniffs out Hollywood's "displacements," concentrating on the innumerable substitutes for the sexual act (elision, metaphor, suggestive dialogue, costume, skin, voice, and the "somnambulistic" woman).[22] He delightedly discloses homosexual attraction at the root of *Double Indemnity* and castration anxiety in *Arsenic and Old Lace*.[23] He declares *Suspicion* "a mesh of fictional incongruities" and traces its disparities to the absence of sexual satisfaction in the couple's marriage, which the script tries to conceal with a bogus happy ending.[24] In his book on Chaplin, Tyler portrays his hero as embodying the archetypal clown and carrying within himself narcissistic and schizophrenic tendencies.

All this is set forth in a style sharply different from the beige academic prose of Wolfenstein and Leites or the earnest skepticism of Warshow. It was perhaps Tyler's style, by turns precious and slangy, that made him insufficiently appreciated at the time. One reviewer remarked that *Magic and Myth of the Movies* "reads like a message from a hashish dream, still to be translated."[25] A fair sampling of Tylerese can be found in his description of Lauren Bacall's path to androgyny:

> That she approached Hollywood with a certain Machiavellianism, I think, is shown by the mild Mephistophelian peaks of her eyebrows. Yet all of us are human; the most sensational military plans, even if the army wins, sometimes go kerflooey. Miss Bacall had evidently intended her voice to give notice that she was a Garbo to the gizzard, hard to get, and not going to let Humphrey triumph at the first shot.[26]

Yet Bacall could not sustain this pose because in *To Have and Have Not,* her first scene with Bogie symbolized her role as the young actress asking the big star for a part in his next picture. A page later, Tyler happily discovers that Bacall's song was dubbed by a young man: "I would say now that Miss Bacall's analytical equation balances even better, with Cow Cow Boogie the power of every integer on both sides. Her Hepburnesque Garbotoon, clearly confirmed in her subsequent pictures, equals Dietrich travestied by a boyish voice."[27] Tyler's writing creates a phantasmagoria of blurring and merging movie images—a "Hollywood hallucination" not unlike that produced by *Rose Hobart,* the collage film made by his friend Joseph Cornell.

Tyler was as fecund a critic as Bazin, but possessed of a wildness that looked ahead to contemporary criticism. His interpretation of

Citizen Kane reveals layers of verbal acknowledgement—the religious confessional, the psychoanalytic clinic, the legal third degree—that resemble the dynamic of law and desire that would inform 1970s critical theory.[28] His chapter on voices in movies uncannily anticipates Barthes's discussion of the pleasure in "the grain of the voice,"[29] and he later recalled his 1940s work in terms that suggest a "post-structuralist" notion of critical pleasure: "The only *indubitable* reading of a given movie, therefore, was its value as a charade, a fluid guessing game where all meanings made an open quantity, where the only 'winning answer' was not *the* right one but *any* amusingly relevant and suggestive one: an answer which led to interesting speculations about society, about mankind's perennial, profuse and typically serio-comic ability to deceive itself."[30] In *Magic and Myth,* Tyler, like Barthes in *L'Empire des signes,* confesses that he has created his own myth. And no one can deny the serious playfulness of the surrealist who, sensitive to the infantile fixations in films, dedicates his first book "to the memory of my mother, that golden nature whose image so often illuminated with me this side of the movie screen."[31]

It was probably not Tyler whom Andrew Sarris had in mind when he launched his attack on those "forest critics" who condemned Hollywood for mass-producing fantasies. Nonetheless, Sarris' assault on the New York literary intelligentsia and academic social scientists did turn younger readers away from the character typology and myth analysis promoted in 1940s symptomatic criticism. Instead, the auteurists' reinterpretation of American cinema emphasized individual artistry and implicit meaning. Only with the mutation of auteurism, as initially conceived, did mainstream film criticism reconsider the issue of symptomatic meaning; and this decline was, significantly, the result of a certain dialectical tension within the concept of authorship itself. Repressed meaning, itself repressed in auteur accounts, returned.

Myth as Antinomy

There can only be a science of what is hidden.

—Gaston Bachelard

The 1960s saw the triumph of auteur and genre studies. Both had firm roots in an explicatory conception of meaning, but because of the influence of Continental structuralist theory and method, both grew into a shape that made the critical institution more hospitable to symptomatic interpretation.[32]

Midway through the decade, a circle of young intellectuals around the British Film Institute initiated a more rigorous study of a film author's themes. Under the pseudonym Lee Russell, Peter Wollen wrote several auteur pieces for *New Left Review* between 1964 and 1968. These essays, often directly responding to Sarris' 1963 *Film Culture* issue on American directors, pursued the explicatory line, often by seeking out thematic dualities.[33] In 1967, Geoffrey Nowell-Smith published *Visconti,* a landmark attempt to study the "hidden structural connections which bind his work together."[34] This is explained in a famous passage: "The purpose of criticism becomes therefore to uncover behind the superficial contrasts of subject and treatment a structural hard core of basic and recondite motifs. The pattern formed by these motifs, which may be stylistic or thematic, is what gives an author's work its particular structure, both defining it internally and distinguishing one body of work from another."[35] Nowell-Smith treats Visconti's structures as either abstract character roles and relations (husband/wife, lover/mistress) or overarching thematic oppositions (for example, actual world/ideal world).[36] Although Nowell-Smith declares that a completely structuralist study of a director is probably unfeasible, his attempt to disclose implicit narrative or semantic structures led to a more systematic and dynamic notion of authorial unity. Auteur structuralism would reveal how the structures "are formed, within the film, into an autonomous and equilibrated whole."[37]

During the same period, BFI-based writers were exploring the concept of genre as a correlative to authorship. Both *Cahiers* and *Positif* had pioneered a genre-oriented study of Hollywood, and the early 1960s saw the publication of several French books on the Western.[38] Taking his lead from these works, Alan Lovell argued that genre study could set director studies in a solid context that would nuance thematic readings.[39] Like most auteur studies, genre criticism played down visual style in favor of recurrent themes. And critics found that seeking the thematic base of a genre led inevitably to broader social meanings. The Western became nothing less than an American myth, and as Lovell put it in 1968, "to make sense out of our use of 'myth' seems to me a crucial problem for mass culture studies."[40]

Structuralist analysis of authorship and genre was consolidated by the publication, in 1969, of Peter Wollen's *Signs and Meaning in the Cinema* and Jim Kitses' *Horizons West*. The former, the most influential book in English-language film studies of the period, proposes a theoretically grounded structuralism. Like Nowell-Smith, Wollen organizes his material into "a system of differences and oppositions."[41] He picks two contrasting auteurs, Hawks and Ford, to illustrate his method. He divides Hawks's work into two genres, the adventure drama and the screwball comedy; he then adduces such oppositions as professional/unprofessional, male/female, elite group/outsider, and so on. He goes on to assign positive and negative value to each, asserting that the self-reliant male group celebrated in the dramas is ridiculed in the comedies' themes of regression and sex-reversal.[42] When Wollen turns to Ford, he finds a "master antinomy" between the desert and the garden that organizes a range of contrasting meanings (nomad/settler, Indian/European, gun/book, West/East). He argues that Ford's work is richer than Hawks's in that the antinomies shift across the career, often reversing the values ascribed to them in earlier films.

Wollen insistently pushes the concept of authorship into a cultural domain. He draws explicitly on the folklore and myth studies of Vladimir Propp and Lévi-Strauss. He derives Ford's master antinomy from Henry Nash Smith's *Virgin Land,* wherein the desert/garden contrast is shown to be, in Wollen's words, "one which has dominated American thought and literature, recurring in countless novels, tracts, political speeches and magazine stories."[43] By treating the auteur's themes as myths, the critic opens up the work to a new kind of interpretation, in which the "Ford film" may be seen as a *symptomatic* expression of cultural ideology.

Thematic dualism also plays a major role in Kitses' *Horizons West*. Here the garden/desert antinomy is said to be the core structure of the Western genre. "What we are dealing with here, of course," Kitses writes, "is no less than a national world-view."[44] The genre is thus not a mass of inert material but a historically, ideologically structured set of subjects, themes, and values. Like an auteur's oeuvre, the genre needs interpretation, and the critic looking at, say, a film by Anthony Mann must plot out how he treats inherited conventions. In the genre studies contemporaneous with or subsequent to Kitses' work, critics were eager to follow the Antinomy Trail, finding in the Western the tension between an agrarian ideal and an industrial reality, or the opposition of man and nature.[45] By and large, genre criticism was content to operate as a complement to authorial analysis, although both Ed Buscombe in England and John Cawelti in the United States suggested studying a genre for its own sake.[46] Colin McArthur summarized the détente neatly: "Each genre has developed its own recurrent images and its own themes against which individual artists have counterpointed their personal vision."[47]

The British work owed a good deal to the emerging cultural studies movement descended from Richard Hoggart and Raymond Williams and to the political theories of culture explored in journals like *New Left Review*.[48] For my purposes here, however, it is the impact of structuralism that sheds most light on the British critics' search for a rigorous interpretive method. The most significant source is Claude Lévi-Strauss, whose work was being steadily translated into English between 1963 and 1969. That remarkable research itself hovers in a fascinating way between a conception of implicit meaning and a commitment to symptomatic meaning. Lévi-Strauss's mentors are Durkheim and Freud, Jakobson and Marx. He asserts that cultural activities have "unconscious" foundations, yet he compares them to phonological features of language (which are not repressed or censored in any psychoanalytical sense). He claims that the structure of the human mind is a purely formal one, a view quite different from Freud's emphasis on particular psychic contents. Thus when Lévi-Strauss interprets a cultural system, he may be considered to have constructed the implicit meanings of which the social actors are unaware. Yet at the same time, Lévi-Strauss's analyses of myth move toward a notion of symptomatic meaning. According to him, myth works to represent the overcoming of a social contradiction.[49] His binary oppositions point to realms of cultural contestation, which the tale seeks to mediate and transcend. Thus a tension within society can be seen as *present in but repressed by* the overall structures of the myth.[50]

Many BFI structuralists relied upon Lévi-Strauss at one point or another.[51] Most often, the nature/culture antinomy (of which the vaunted desert/garden couplet seems but a variant) was used to interpret a single film, an author's work, or a genre.[52] By 1970, the practice had become so common that Nowell-Smith criticized it as superficial and whimsical.[53] Some years later Charles Eckert raised similar objections to straightforward "applications" of Lévi-Strauss.[54] Such criticisms are just, but the significance of structuralist interpretation lay not in its rigorous employment of theoretical concepts (never a strong suit of film criticism) but rather in its ambivalence. Like Lévi-Strauss's work, this critical practice oscillated between a conception of implicit meaning and a conception of symptomatic meaning.

We must also remember that the movement did not trigger a radical turnabout in critical practice. Structuralism in the hands of the BFI writers remained resolutely thematic. Although Wollen distinguishes between a style-centered auteur criticism and one devoted to revealing a core of "thematic motifs,"[55] he puts the former aside. Indeed, in quoting Nowell-Smith on deep structures, he omits the remark that the work's motifs "may be stylistic or thematic."[56] (Wollen justifies his thematic emphasis by citing Lévi-Strauss's claim that "myths exist independently of style."[57]) Even structuralist auteurism's most "scientistic" moments, such as Alan Lovell's 1969–1970 critique of Robin Wood's work, did not break with the commitment to theme. Indeed, it is chiefly because both Wood and Lovell were committed to explication that they were able to disagree about method.[58]

Yet despite their adherence to explication, structuralist auteur critics occasionally gravitated toward self-consciously symptomatic accounts, chiefly by seeking out what were called "ambiguities" and "contradictions." Wollen's New Left Review essays contrast "coherent" directors (for example, Renoir and Hitchcock) and "incoherent" ones. One of the latter, Samuel Fuller, is said to represent "a far point of bourgeois romantic-nationalist consciousness, in which its contradictions are clearly exposed."[59] Nowell-Smith likewise locates areas of "complication and contradiction" in Visconti.[60] The idea of involuntary symptomatic expression emerges when Nowell-Smith claims that the tension between "drama" and "epic" in Rocco and His Brothers is not under Visconti's control, reflecting an ambivalence in his personal social status.[61] In Signs and Meaning, Wollen treats the auteur text as arising from the introduction of the script's incidents into the author's conscious or unconscious mind, where they react with his characteristic themes. The critic must then play psychoanalyst, reconstructing the latent text that is concealed by the manifest film.[62] Genre criticism was also sensitive to the symptomatic dimension of Lévi-Straussian antinomies, as when Colin McArthur interprets a shot in The Covered Wagon as presenting "a major split in the American psyche."[63] Novelty is perceptible only to those primed to look for it, and although most auteur and genre critics subscribed to a notion of the unified work, the routine of ascribing antinomies to films prepared them to embrace that 1970s doctrine of the "contradictory" text and the construction of symptomatic meaning.

Système à la Mode

From the perspective of this book, we can see many French theorists of the 1960s as attempting to demonstrate the power of symptomatic interpretation. Besides Lévi-Strauss, whose claims for a cultural "unconscious" we have already encountered, there were many thinkers who argued along symptomatic lines. Roland Barthes's analysis of bourgeois "mythologies" was frankly derived from Lévi-Straussian and Marxist tenets concerning the social construction of a culture/nature opposition. Jacques Lacan's "return to Freud" consisted at least partly in asserting the centrality of repression to psychic and linguistic phenomena. Under Lacan's influence, Louis Althusser undertook a "symptomatic reading" of Marx, aiming to reveal a text "present as a necessary absence in the first."[64] For Jacques Derrida, Western thought was haunted by its repression of writing.[65] Michel Foucault took Freudian interpretation as a paradigm of the skeptical role of the human sciences, a principle of perpetual suspicion.[66] Within literary theory and criticism, the *Tel quel* group drew upon Lacanian psychoanalytic concepts to elaborate a conception of the "speaking subject," and used Marx to theorize a critique of literary ideology, while Pierre Macherey suggested how literary texts might be read as built around concealed absences.[67]

All these theories were provocative and powerful, but they might not have won so many adherents had they not been accompanied by authoritative interpretations of particular texts. Ordinary criticism could take these readings as exemplars for ongoing practice. For every reader who has worked through the entirety of *Mythologiques* or *For Marx* or Lacan's *Ecrits* or *The Order of Things,* there must be hundreds who know only Lévi-Strauss's essay on the Oedipus myth, or Althusser's study of the Piccolo Teatro, or Lacan's seminar on "The Purloined Letter," or Foucault's discussion of *Las Meninas.* One can argue that Barthes's study of "Sarrasine" borrows much from *Tel quel* theory, but the ruminations of Julia Kristeva and Philippe Sollers were never presented in such a beguiling piece of "practical criticism" as *S/Z.*[68] In these and kindred works, "theory" becomes explicit as seldom before in the study of the arts. Now the film critic was expected to show that the interpretation reinforces or revises or replaces a theory about how movies work. After structuralism, the catchphrase "a——ian reading of X" came into film study. At the same time, theory became streamlined; its complexities and nuances were often ignored, and it served to fuel ordinary interpretive activity.

To these developments *Cahiers du cinéma,* still the vanguard Parisian journal, was of course not immune. The early 1960s saw the *Cahiers* incorporate some structuralist advances.[69] Yet not until the crisis around Henri Langlois and the Cinémathèque in 1967–1968 and the events of May 1968 did the *Cahiers,* under the editorship of Jean-Louis Comolli and Jean Narboni, enter the era of politicized structuralism.

Like their peers in literary and art theory, the *Cahiers* editors began to write texts pitched at a new level of elliptical abstraction. (*Positif*'s most virulent polemicist, Robert Benayoun, dubbed the converted *Cahiers* crew "les enfants du paradigme."[70]) Some of this work, such as Jean-Pierre Oudart's essays, has enjoyed continuing influence, and one theoretical manifesto, Comolli and Narboni's "Cinema/Ideology/Criticism" of 1969, has become a canonized work. Here the editors lay out a taxonomy of the possible relations between a film and the dominant ideology. Their most influential formulation (borrowed primarily from Macherey) pertained to those films which, they claimed, belonged to dominant ideology only superficially. In certain Hollywood films "an internal criticism is taking place which cracks the film apart at the seams. If one reads the film obliquely, looking for symptoms; if one looks beyond its apparent formal coherence, one can see that it is riddled with cracks; it is splitting under an internal tension which is simply not there in an ideologically innocuous film."[71] This passage, cited dozens of times over the next two decades, became a search warrant in the investigation of repressed meanings.

The *Cahiers* case centered upon the analysis of auteur films. There was, for example, Jean-Pierre Oudart's claim that Buñuel's *Milky Way* created a cinema which was the site of many incomplete and incompatible readings, all revolving around structural contradictions.[72] There was also Raymond Bellour's painstaking dissection of the Bodega Bay sequence of Hitchcock's film *The Birds.* Bellour's analysis was heavily indebted to the structuralist stylistics of Jakobson, but it was praised by Narboni for opening the path to an Althusserian-Lacanian account: Bellour had revealed the process by which a film could bear the traces of what it must exclude.[73] *Cahiers* furnished still more applications of the symptomatic approach during the years 1970–1971 in a series of "collective texts": detailed studies, composed by members of the editorial board, of repressed meanings in Renoir's *La Vie est à nous,* Ford's *Young Mr. Lincoln,* Sternberg's *Morocco,* and Kozintsev and Trauberg's *New Babylon.*[74] Although the variety of this critical work is greater than is often assumed, I can pause only to consider the Ford essay, which has in English-language criticism become the prototype of modern symptomatic interpretation, and is probably the central exemplar of academic film criticism as such.

The essay, written by the *Cahiers* board around an unusually opaque submission by Jean-Pierre Oudart (section 25 of the essay as published), stands as a summation of many trends in late 1960s French theory. Its scene-by-scene segmentation and its insistence on the work's "intertextual spaces" recall Barthes's recently published *S/Z*. It draws on Althusserian and Lacanian concepts to identify "discourses of overdetermination" that should explain the film's repression of politics and sexuality. More centrally, the essay relies on Macherey's model of how a text embarks on an ideological project and then subverts it by creating "constituent lacks." *Young Mr. Lincoln*'s ideological project—to portray Lincoln as a mythically perfect Republican—seeks to rewrite history by linking him to Law, family, and politics. To transpose this project into narrative form, the film avails itself of two structural models. The "biography of a great man" functions in the future-perfect tense, setting the stage for the great deeds which the hero will perform in later life. At the same time, the detective story furnishes a plot organized around a murder, clues, a witness who won't talk, red herrings, and a courtroom denouement. Up to a point, then, both ideological project and narrative structure hold the film together.

But the ideological project is thrown off course by several factors. First, it secretes certain incompatibilities. Lincoln both incarnates the Law and rises above it; he acts as a mother's son but also must stand in for a missing father. As the film works itself out in action and imagery, Lincoln becomes constituted by absences. There are significant omissions: his mother, his fabled origins, his stand on slavery, the outcome of his choices (between plaintiffs, pies, and brothers), and especially his relation to women. The *Cahiers* editors argue that the political sphere "represses" Lincoln's erotic identity. It is through women (Mrs. Clay, Ann Rutledge) that he accedes to the Law; but to be true to it, he must renounce sexual pleasure. The film also presents notable distortions of the ideological project. The Law is depicted solely as prohibiting violence ("castrating"), yet it is also paranoid, trying to ground itself in nature. And the editors point to certain "excessive" moments: Lincoln exhibits a "castrating stare," a paranoid self-confidence, an excessive violence, and a final "monstrous-

ness" reminiscent of Nosferatu. In sum, an ideological project beginning from a myth of Lincoln as the great unifier and upholder of
natural Law succumbs to ambivalence: the great father figure derives
his authority from the mother, and the Law is revealed as repressing
desire, castrating the Oedipal son while also nominating him as the
restorer of an ideal, maternally based law. Hence the essay's most
notorious Lacanian apothegm: "Lincoln does not have the phallus, he
is the phallus."[75]

However novel it may have seemed, this symptomatic reading had
one ingredient that assured its continuity with earlier *Cahiers* work.
Macherey had already suggested that Jules Verne could create a "faulty
narrative" out of the theme of capitalist exploration. Now the *Cahiers*
editors attributed the absences, distortions, and excesses undergone
by the film's ideological project to Ford's "scriptural work," his filmmaking practice. Recurrent motifs of Ford's oeuvre—the community
celebration, the centrality of the family and the mother—serve to
short-circuit aspects of the originating myth. Lincoln "can only be
inscribed as a Fordian character at the expense of a number of distortions and reciprocal assaults (by him on the course of the fiction and
by fiction on his historical truth)."[76] In the "Cinema/Ideology/Criti-
cism" manifesto, Narboni and Comolli had mentioned Ford as a
director who could reveal and denounce the overt ideology within a
film. Now Oudart's portion of the *Young Mr. Lincoln* text asserts that
the ideologically overdetermined presentation of Lincoln as Law has
been "declared by [Ford's] writing and emphasized by his comedy"
and has yielded an indictment of the Law's castrating discourse.[77] The
text is contradictory chiefly thanks to the auteur—a subversive textual
force rather than a visionary individual, but no less fundamental for
that. The film is truly "John Ford's *Young Mr. Lincoln*."

The *Cahiers* collective texts had many effects, one of which was to
encourage critics to scrutinize films with unprecedented exactitude.
Bellour's 1969 article on *The Birds* had already initiated what is now
called "textual analysis,"[78] a genre of criticism whose attention to the
minutiae of technique and narrative construction far surpassed anything attempted by *Movie*'s close readings: Thierry Kuntzel's study of
the opening of *M* (1972), Bellour's breakdown of a scene in *The Big
Sleep* (1973), an exhaustive collaborative analysis of *Muriel* (1974),
and *Communications* 23 (1975), which included such now classic essays
as Kuntzel's study of the opening of *The Most Dangerous Game*, and
Bellour's staggering 115-page dissection of *North by Northwest*, com-

plete with stills, charts, and a bird's-eye diagram of the crop-dusting scene.

Significantly, the most influential of these studies ascribed symptomatic meanings to the patterns and processes yielded by analysis. In *North by Northwest* Bellour discovers a dialectic of desire: the hero achieves identity by forcing the woman to participate in a fantasy that eventually installs him as the good father and projects his aggression onto the villain. Kuntzel treats a film as analogous to Freud's "dream work" in that the opening offers a matrix of images like that of the primary process, a passage of condensed motifs that the later portions of the film will "linearize" into displaced fantasy forms. For Bellour the classical film creates rhymes and parallels whose differences stage a sliding Lacanian game of lack posited, filled, and recreated that echoes the movement of the hero in the intrigue. For Kuntzel, the classical film fuses, and thus confuses, what culture normally keeps apart, and the film's progress is a series of displacements and inversions that are eventually halted by the reassertion of difference. For both, textual analysis reveals the film's "unconscious," its repressed material that may surface in the slightest details of form and style.

The Contradictory Text

In English-speaking countries, awareness of the Parisian symptomatic approach coincided with a rise in Marxist film theory and criticism. Translations of Althusser, Lacan, and Foucault spurred interest in the political ramifications of post-structuralist thought, while Barthes's 1957 *Mythologies* took on a new life from being translated into English at this period. In the spring of 1971 *Screen,* under a new editorial board and editor Sam Rohdie, launched an ongoing inquiry into film and ideology—spearheaded by a translation of the *Cahiers* "Cinema/ Ideology/Criticism" essay. Soon *Screen* translated the *Young Mr. Lincoln* article and devoted an entire issue to semiology, conceived as a "science" along Althusserian lines.[79]

Some of the *Screen* writers sought to show the illusory basis of the unity which explicatory critics had imputed to the auteur film. In a critique of Perkins' *Film as Film,* Rohdie charges that an insistence on coherence and wholeness links *Movie* to Romantic and realist aesthetics and cannot comprehend "modernist" filmmaking or locate the contradictory forces within a film practice.[80] For some critics, accepting *Cahiers*'s gaps-and-fissures argument required an explicit break with the compromise of auteur structuralism. In his 1972 afterword to the new edition of *Signs and Meaning in the Cinema,* Wollen asserts that the auteur film, and Hollywood itself, is contradictory, although "like a dream, the film the spectator sees is, so to speak, the 'film-facade,' the end-product of 'secondary revision,' which hides and masks the process which remains latent in the film 'unconscious.'"[81] The unconscious work that Wollen once assigned to the filmmaker's mind is now located within the film. The modern conception of the "text" presents "fissures and gaps which exist in reality but which are repressed by an ideology, characteristic of bourgeois society, which insists on the 'wholeness' and integrity of each individual consciousness."[82] Nowell-Smith, who confessed in 1973 to having been "a star-struck structuralist," suggests that auteur structuralism makes sense only as a step toward a scientific, materialist film theory.[83]

To a great extent, such theoretical pronouncements answered a need that was already being articulated in practical interpretation. Marxist criticism has long been preoccupied with the need to explain how progressive or otherwise valuable art can arise within oppressive economic and political circumstances. By the early 1970s, the New Left's emphasis on consciousness and culture had given a strong impetus to ideological analysis of popular cinema. Some concepts already introduced help us identify three broad critical options.

One approach, often called "demystification," aims to show up artworks as covert propaganda, sugar-coated pills. Whatever explicit meanings can be ascribed to the work, the demystifying critic constructs reactionary implicit ones that undercut them. A second, contrary approach posits progressive implicit meanings lying behind whatever reactionary referential or explicit meanings the film may present. Engels seems to have set the pattern for this approach when he praised Balzac's fiction for satirizing the very class with which the author sympathized most deeply.[84] In film journals of the late 1960s and early 1970s, critics employed both the demystifying and the progressivist methods of interpretation. *Cinemantics, Cineaste, The Velvet Light Trap,* and *Jump Cut* ran articles that either damned Hollywood for embodying the values of American capitalism or praised Hollywood films which suggested radical meanings.

The concept of the contradictory text, predicated on repressed meanings that disrupt explicit or implicit ones, permits the critic to take a more synthetic and dialectical stance. The critic may unmask ideology by pointing out all the patent distortions in the film, but go on to "save" the film by showing how it either contains progressive elements or embodies in its very incompatibilities some instructive indications of how fiercely ideology must struggle in order to maintain its authority. Just as the conception of symptomatic reading supported *Tel quel*'s analysis of masterworks of the literary avant-garde, a parallel notion allowed film critics to continue to study, with a new sense of political purpose, that Hollywood cinema already revealed by auteur and genre studies.

By 1974 the political possibilities of symptomatic reading were emerging clearly, informed by ideas from anthropology, Marxism, and psychoanalysis. An early and influential effort was Charles Eckert's article on Warners' 1937 *Marked Woman*. Like the *Cahiers* editors, he seeks to situate the film within a concrete historical context, that of New York gangsters' control of prostitution. In the film, Eckert finds a "dialectical" relationship between melodrama and factors that treat the women's plight "realistically." Eckert interprets the latter elements as symptomatic of the film's latent content, class conflict. The film struggles to displace this economic conflict into a series of Lévi-Straussian antinomies in the sphere of regional differences (city/small town) and personal morality ("smartness"/"dumbness," wrong conduct/right conduct). These masking oppositions are very near the text's surface, set out in the songs sung in the nightclub and governing the melodramatic action. The film also condenses class-based conflicts of rich/poor and exploiter/exploited onto the figure of the gangster himself. He is at once capitalist and immigrant, a thug who can be criticized on moral grounds rather than economic ones. The film's aim throughout is "to attenuate conflicts at the level of real conditions and to amplify and resolve them at the surrogate levels of the melodrama."[85] Nevertheless, *Marked Woman* cannot wholly defuse its tensions, and thus it intermittently exposes normal ideological maneuvers. At the end of the film, for instance, the effort to sentimentalize the women's plight pales before their implacable expressions as they walk toward the camera. Progressive aspects of the text are thus "saved": the critic's therapy cannot cure this film, but it can reveal how baring key contradictions of capitalism somewhat redeems a tawdry gangster movie.

Nowhere in this period are the cultural politics of the contradictory text more evident than in the critical writing that emerged out of the Women's Movement. Kate Millett's *Sexual Politics* (1968) had already produced demystifying readings of contemporary literature, and the early 1970s saw the consolidation of what soon came to be identified as the "images-of-women" approach to cultural texts.[86] This tended toward either a demystifying or progressive interpretation of character types and situations: unmasking films which yielded demeaning role models, praising those which presented women more "realistically." The critic might show how 1930s Warner Bros. films promulgated stereotyped conceptions of women (golddigger, girl reporter, prostitute), or how a film like *Klute* captured "a very common female conflict."[87] The "images" approach quickly became a target for feminist critics who sought to treat texts as internally contradictory. A recent formulation concisely summarizes the issues:

> In the relative absence of works by women (except for the explicitly feminist works created by the women's movement itself), feminist critics have become increasingly adept at "reading against the grain" of the classical cinematic text. In this kind of reading, the critic is less concerned with the truth or falsity of the image of woman than with gaining an understanding of the textual contradictions that are symptomatic of the repression of women in patriarchal culture. This tendency in feminist film criticism has been enormously fruitful—expanding our understanding not only of the strategies of filmic texts which work to support and sustain patriarchal constructions but also of the weak spots, the failings of those constructions. [88]

Yet in practice "images" criticism did not necessarily rule out either symptomatic interpretations or textual incompatibilities. In *From Reverence to Rape: The Treatment of Women in the Movies* (1974), often taken as a landmark "images" study, Molly Haskell follows 1940s critics like Deming in insisting that Hollywood's "American Dream machine" does not function flawlessly. "Like the latent content of any good dream, unconscious elements, often elaborately disguised, came to trouble our sleep."[89] She can, for example, treat the sex goddess as a "schizophrenic" phenomenon, both acceding to gender stereotyping and, perhaps unwittingly, struggling against it.[90] One can argue that a basic assumption of all feminist criticism is some conception of a split "cultural consciousness"; the feminist critic will tend to consider ideological products as, in some broad sense, symptomatic of repressed cultural forces. If so, then Marxist and psychoanalytic versions of symptomatic meaning—versions deriving from *Cahiers*'s *Young Mr. Lincoln* exemplar—drew upon existing tendencies within the feminist tradition.

Not surprisingly, the new developments centered around the BFI/ *Screen* group. The result was a mixture of ideas drawn from Lévi-Strauss on kinship (the importance of which had been signaled by Simone de Beauvoir and Juliet Mitchell), Brecht's critique of representation (as refracted through Althusser, Barthes, and Walter Benjamin), auteur structuralism, and the sort of Machereyan and Lacanian concepts at work in the *Cahiers* essay on Ford. All of these sources offered an explanatory grounding for the incompatibilities that feminist critics had recognized in mainstream films. Now one need not merely add up the film's ideological pluses and minuses; one could show how the logic of a narrative, a characterization, or a thematic progression could create disparities in the representation of gender. In addition, the Women's Movement offered something that most symptomatic readings lacked: a concrete political base, from which a feminist critique could not only reveal the weak points in patriarchal ideology but also launch an oppositional filmmaking and film viewing.

By 1973, Claire Johnston was attacking the images-of-women position for its "crude determinism" and calling for film critics to use "the sciences founded by Marx and Freud," informed by semiology and auteur theory.[91] Johnston recasts the idea of stereotypes in terms of Barthesian myth and Freudian fetishism, thus scotching the question of realism.[92] She translates the antinomies of Wollen's *Signs and Meaning* into feminist terms: Hawks treats the woman as nonmale in order to negate her "traumatic presence," while Ford makes her a cipher around which the garden/desert tension revolves.[93] Further implications for practical criticism were developed in a 1974 essay by Johnston and Pam Cook. Here they draw on Lacanian and Lévi-Straussian concepts in order to interpret Raoul Walsh's work as constructing woman as an empty sign to be circulated within a patriarchal order. On her devolve the male protagonist's castration fears. As an object of exchange, she becomes analogous to money. In *The Revolt of Mamie Stover*, however, this pattern changes: at certain moments Mamie seeks "to transgress the forms of representation governing the cinema itself."[94] Like young Abraham Lincoln, she possesses a threatening look (here sometimes trained on the camera): as the phallic woman, she is at once seductress and castrator. Yet she remains confined by the symbolic dimension of the text. Both its narrative and its imagery seek to make her into a commodity, an object and not a subject of desire. The essay's ending, citing the Comolli and Narboni passage quoted earlier, exhorts us to treat the text as fissured and to situate authorship within ideology. "The tasks for feminist criticism must therefore consist of a process of de-naturalisation: a questioning of the unity of the text; of seeing it as a contradictory interplay of different codes; of tracing its 'structuring absences' and its relationship to the universal problem of symbolic castration. It is only in this sense that a feminist strategy for the cinema must be understood."[95] In its presentation of a basic narrative trajectory (the threat posed by woman contained by larger textual operations) and its suggestion of the power of characters' glances to channel the ideological undercurrents of the text, the *Mamie Stover* essay came to constitute an exemplar for feminist film analysis.[96]

Even more influential was Laura Mulvey's article "Visual Pleasure and Narrative Cinema."[97] Resolutely "theoretical" but written in lucid language, never so abstract as to ignore examples, it remains a key text for guiding symptomatic interpretation. Mulvey argues that classical patriarchal film must represent woman as a lack, but this entails an inherent contradiction: the phallus is valorized, but woman's lack of a penis is a constant reminder of the threat of castration. The film must therefore offer a fantasy that denies woman's threat while maintaining the law of the Father. The results are two versions of visual pleasure, scopophiliac voyeurism and narcissism.

So much would probably not have offered much purchase for practical criticism, but Mulvey goes on to translate these theoretical concepts into concrete terms. She asserts that film technique inherently favors scopophilia, particularly through the camera's relaying of characters' acts of looking. At this level, sexual difference consists of making the woman the looked-at object, the man the looking subject.[98] At the level of narrative structure, though, narcissism comes into play. The male becomes the active protagonist, controlling the forward-moving action in a three-dimensional space, while the female is the passive "one-dimensional" object. Mulvey specifies still more helpfully: Sternberg's films are prototypes of fetishistic scopophilia and Hitchcock's typify as well the structure of voyeurism. The woman may, in the course of the narrative, evolve from an "icon" into a mate, as in Hawks, or she may be investigated and punished, as in *Vertigo*.

Apart from the article's purely theoretical arguments, Mulvey's recurrent emphasis on the necessary contradictions in any attempt to represent woman provided strong support for an interpreter seeking gaps and fissures in the text. Just as important, the essay itemized a host of interpretive cues—the look as bearing power and sexual difference, the equating of the camera with the viewer, the notion of woman as fetishized spectacle, plot patterns such as surveillance and punishment. And, like the Johnston and Cook work, "Visual Pleasure and Narrative Cinema" proved compatible with such continuing concerns of practical criticism as studying Hollywood cinema, maintaining canons of interpretability, and pursuing auteur analysis.[99]

Mulvey's essay was published in 1975, which constituted a crucial year for consolidating the new symptomatic model. That was the year of *Communications* number 23; of Johnston's essay on masquerade in Tourneur's *Anne of the Indies;* of *Ça*'s special number on Christian Metz; of the BFI booklet on Dorothy Arzner that included Cook's Brechtian analysis of two Arzner films; and of Stephen Heath's two-part *Screen* article "Film and System, Terms of Analysis." While Heath's essay is innovative in many ways, it also synthesizes ideas drawn from the most influential traditions of the moment: hard-core structuralism (Lévi-Strauss, Todorov, Greimas, early Barthes), post-1968 *Tel quel* (Kristeva, later Barthes), Althusserian Marxism, Lacanian psychoanalysis, feminist interpretation, and textual analysis à la Bellour and Kuntzel. As Heath's title indicates, he undertakes a meta-critical task, the theorizing and redirecting of current film analysis. Once more, however, the theory would have had less impact had it not been framed as a dense, filigreed analysis of a single auteur film, *Touch of Evil.* The result is a virtuoso exercise in symptomatic interpretation.

According to Heath, a classical film's textual dynamic consists of a stabilizing narrative "economy" and an excessive "logic of production," the "other scene" of repressed meaning. In a model structuralist analysis, Heath establishes the coherence of *Touch of Evil:* its strands of action, its construction of character, its spatio-temporal organization, its oppositions and alternations, its delays, its exchange of characters and roles, its parallel sexual relationships, its attempt to achieve thematic unity around the struggle between Vargas and Quinlan over justice. But Heath situates such systems within a larger dialectic of contradiction, that process fundamental to such ideological systems as narrative, gender, and subjectivity. Narrative is held to be inherently contradictory because it transforms one stable state (the beginning) into another (the ending) by means of a disruption: "Aimed at containment, it restates heterogeneity as the constant term of its action— if there is symmetry, there is dissymmetry, if there is resolution, there is violence."[100] Thus *Touch of Evil*'s initial explosion interrupts Vargas and Susan's kiss, opening the need for closure and a final embrace; it also creates a chain of events around sexuality and violence. This problem is figured forth in those "dead spots" during which Quinlan visits Tanya's brothel. Heath thus treats narrative as a dynamic attempt to control repressed meaning.

Once the violence establishes woman as a threat, a psychoanalytic scenario emerges. The problem of woman is everywhere: a father is murdered (so the resolution must restore Vargas and Law); the women (Zita, Marcia) must be done away with; and above all Susan must be made guilty so as to keep the male secure in his identity and to ward off the anxiety of homosexuality. Susan becomes a point of contradiction, her body generating "panic images of its sexuality."[101] The stripper Zita, the Night Man, and the sexually equivocal Grandi family all emerge as so many symptoms, as does the scene of Quinlan's murder of Grandi, during which the narrative lets slip excessive images of its own repression, "Susan obliterated at the very point of desire."[102]

Finally, Heath considers how contradiction informs the social identity of both character and viewer. As a textual construct, a character is only a moment in the film's systematic sliding between economy and logic. The character, as agent, hero, or star "image," helps bind the text; but as a "figure," the character may be a site of dispersion. The spectator is similarly divided. The coherence of the film requires a conversion of public symbolic systems—family, gender relations, language, film conventions—into an imaginary unity in which the viewing subject misrecognizes himself as a counterpart to the Other. But that unity is purchased at the cost of repression; and narrative triggers a set of displacements and condensations which offer, if only momentarily, the possibilities of Barthesian *jouissance,* a "radical heterogeneity."[103] In such ways, Heath suggests, overtly ideological products like Hollywood films harbor not just messages or myths but processes that threaten to overturn the very stability that ideology seeks to maintain.

Symptoms and Explications

A man with only one theory is a lost man.

—Bertolt Brecht

In Western Europe and the English-speaking countries, 1970s-style symptomatic interpretation is currently the most influential form of academic film criticism. The historical scenario I proposed in Chapter 2 suggests why. A new event attracted young workers to a sparsely populated field. A rhetoric of absolutes pulled the new approach sharply away from its predecessors. Broad exploratory work generated some powerful exemplars. As the field expanded, "application" set in. Studies became more detailed and discriminating, and concepts began to be used in more diffuse and eclectic ways.

Symptomatic reading became identified as the most sophisticated form of "ordinary criticism." Pick up a recent issue of the Slovenian journal *Ekran* and you will find an article claiming that Hitchcock's traveling shots illustrate the look of the Other.[104] *Movie*, once the enclave of auteurist exegesis, now publishes lengthy Marxist-psycho-analytic essays. For most writers, the symptomatic approach provides a frame of reference to be filled out in detail, transferred to fresh domains (a new director, film, or genre), or recast with more finesse (for example, the essays that revise and correct the *Cahiers* account of *Young Mr. Lincoln*).[105] The normalization of this trend can also be seen in the expanding publication of introductory texts such as Annette Kuhn's *Women's Pictures: Feminism and Cinema* (1982), Kaja Silverman's *Subject of Semiotics* (1983), E. Ann Kaplan's *Women and Film: Both Sides of the Camera* (1983), *Esthétique du film* (1983) by Jacques Aumont and others, and Pam Cook's *Cinema Book* (1986), all of which aim to train students in the rudiments of symptomatic reading. More recent developments in the symptomatic mode—such as positing a time when Hollywood films contained and resolved their contradictions, as opposed to a later period when the films collapse and expose their contradictions[106]—continue to rely on the concept of repressed meaning. Even what are perceived as new developments, such as the borrowing of concepts from Foucault or Bakhtin, or the various appeals to audiences as "conjunctural appropriators" of texts, operate from gaps-and-fissures premises. The fundamental compatibility of such novelties with the commitments of symptomatic reading has been neatly summed up by Paul Willemen as "the familiar conclusion that the 'text' under analysis is full of contradictory tensions, requires active readers and produces a variety of pleasures."[107]

Today, symptomatic criticism often presents itself as a radical challenge to traditional criticism; yet in many respects it is not. Most fundamentally, the Freudian conception of the unconscious is of a piece with "folk" psychology in crucial ways, such as the assumption that a causal chain runs from hypothesized motive to real or imagined satisfaction.[108] Part of the Freudian story is scandalously uncommonsensical, of course, but its underlying explanatory structure and many of its premises (for example, self-deception) tally closely enough with the canons of everyday inferences about behavior to render it appealing. (See the Wittgenstein passage at the head of this chapter.) In a more historical context, the comparatively swift success of symptomatic interpretation suggests that it fulfilled a particular role within the American educational institution. Roughly speaking, in its first phase academic film study was conceived as a domain parallel to the disciplines organized by objects of study—such as French literature or the visual arts. But with the rise of Grand Theory in the humanities during the 1970s and 1980s, cinema studies became a vanguard discipline, a place where people keen on theory could work more freely than in other fields. At the same time, however, film studies was legitimating itself by specialization. Like literary or art criticism, film studies could be seen as housing "humanist," Marxist, feminist, and psychoanalytic "schools." Institutionally, this paralleled that division of labor by "approaches" installed in literary criticism after the Second World War. "Theory" could be a part of film studies as long as it interlocked with a conception of specialization, a development that confirms Mary Douglas' observation that if a new set of ideas is to gain institutional acceptance, it must square with the procedures guaranteeing existing theories.[109]

The Parisian sources of these new ideas, themselves shaped by forces within French academic and media institutions,[110] attracted intellectuals interested in forging a political criticism in the post-1968 period. Yet to succeed, this had to accord at least partly with overarching institutional demands. Here the critics in the United States stole a march on their colleagues in other countries, academicizing the new discourse to a degree still unmatched elsewhere. Once auteurism had shepherded film studies into universities, a self-consciously theoretical criticism could convincingly present itself as more truly academic than its predecessor. Not that Marxist, psychoanalytic, and feminist readings were welcomed with open arms; it is just that, in American institutions of higher education, intellectual disputes among competing premises and methods tend to be avoided simply by adding the "new approach" onto existing structures.[111] All that was necessary was that symptomatic readers demonstrate that they deserved a place, however controversial, within the university.

This proved fairly easy to do. In the 1960s, trade publishers, hoping that anything about movies would sell, had disseminated auteur studies; now academic presses sought out manuscripts that used "new theory," a growth market in the 1970s and 1980s.[112] Refereed journals appeared. The trappings of scholarship—footnotes, complex methods, Continental pedigrees, recondite allusions, specialized nomenclature— could differentiate this hypernew criticism from more informal expli- cation while also marking it as appropriate for institutions granting advanced research degrees. If explication was very teachable to under- graduates, symptomatic reading was ideally equipped for graduate training. (It would eventually trickle down to freshmen, who now perhaps tell their younger brothers and sisters about it.) Indeed, as the object of study became more controversial—first cinema, then Hollywood auteur films, then genre films, and finally current movies and television—the approach became more explicitly cultural and po- litical, the methods more diverse, abstract, and intricate. Hence the present situation, whereby in many American universities film criticism is legitimated by virtue of the theory that underwrites it, not by reference to claims about the intrinsic value of cinema or even the strengths of particular interpretations. "Theory" justifies the object of study, while concentration on the object can be attacked as naive empiricism.

Just as explicatory criticism arose with the decline of the Hollywood studio system and the rise of European art cinema and American experimental film, so the success of symptomatic criticism paralleled the waning of the art cinema and the avant-garde. In the 1970s, few filmmakers served as touchstones for symptomatic criticism, and so theory became almost by default the central reference point. As I shall argue in Chapter 9, *theory* became an invocatory term, functionally parallel to the appeal to values or art or human nature in explicatory criticism, and it could be used as a "black box" to sustain both film interpretation and filmmaking.

Despite the many changes which it created in the social role of film study, symptomatic criticism as an approach was less innovative than is generally recognized. Standard versions of its history stress the break with New Criticism, here conceived as an asocial and ahistorical "in- trinsic" criticism. Yet in a broader sense—that which takes the critical task to be interpretation of one or more texts—symptomatic criticism is the newest avatar of the New Critical practice of close reading. Moreover, the break with purely "intrinsic" criticism had been made long before by myth and cultural criticism. Academic critics had al- ready pioneered symptomatic readings of literature in such works as

Henry Nash Smith's *Virgin Land* (1950), Richard Chase's study *The American Novel and Its Tradition* (1957), Leslie Fiedler's scandalous *Love and Death in the American Novel* (1960), and Leo Marx's *Machine in the Garden* (1965). This trend influenced the "culturalist" slant of symptomatic film interpretation and made it more acceptable within academic circles.

Going still further back, it is evident that many of the concepts underpinning this criticism were already present in the culture-based critiques of the 1940s and 1950s. Far from being simple "content analysis," these studies assume films to be contradictory texts harboring repressed meanings. The 1940s critics are sensitive to "structuring absences," as when Warshow finds that *The Best Years of Our Lives* revolves around "a denial of the reality of politics"—specifically class differences—that is disguised by an appeal to personal morality.[113] Long before Kuntzel popularized the term, Deming describes *The Impostor*'s "dream-work."[114] Tyler calls a film's gaps in logic or naturalism its "crevices."[115] Certain feminist motifs are anticipated in Warshow's account of *Best Years* as a male fantasy of passive wish fulfillment,[116] or in Wolfenstein and Leites' analysis of the "good-bad" girl.[117] The contemporary assumption that a film's overall narrative structure will seek to tame its disruptive elements is stock in trade for these early critics. Kracauer and Deming are especially sensitive to the ways in which endings present false resolutions, while Tyler shows his awareness of the arbitrary closure of narrative structure by comparing Hollywood's happy ending to Christian theology and assuming that "all endings are purely conventional, formal, and often, like the charade, of an infantile logic."[118] The notion of subversion, so central to 1970s symptomatic study, is present here too. Riesman might be a contemporary advocate of emancipatory readings.[119] In the gangster film Warshow finds both conformity and resistance: "Even within the area of mass culture there always exists a current of opposition, seeking to express by whatever means are available to it that sense of desperation and inevitable failure which optimism itself helps to create."[120] As usual, Tyler is most poetic. He closes *The Hollywood Hallucination* with the suggestion that Hollywood can be pernicious or liberating, and he ends with two sentences that few contemporary critics would be ashamed to have written: "After all, everything proceeds by contradictions. That is our intrinsic social hope."[121]

In indicating such similarities, I do not deny that there are important differences between contemporary symptomatic criticism and its earlier avatars. Yet it is noteworthy that virtually nowhere in the post-1968 tradition can one find an acknowledgement of these predecessors. There is scarcely any attempt to read them, let alone dispute them. Perhaps one proof of the institutional authority of contemporary symptomatic criticism is exactly this partial and suppressive—or repressive—awareness of its own history.

As a practice, contemporary symptomatic criticism also displays strong affiliations with the explicatory trend. Barthes's revision of Saussurean semiotics encouraged the equation of "the signified" with "content" or "meaning," thus licensing critics to search for themes under the rubric of unveiling the "production of meaning." What was "ambiguity" in New Criticism could become "polysemy"; condensation and displacement accorded well with traditional motif analysis; symbols could become signifiers, and variety-in-unity could be translated into textual contradictions. Art-cinema explicatory commonplaces could continue in force, as when a trio of symptomatic analyses of Godard's *Sauve qui peut (la vie)* suggest that the film is ambivalent, that the hero is a surrogate for the filmmaker, and that the film treats the difficulties of human communication.[122]

The call to analyze style put forth by Bazin, Sarris, and *Movie* was paralleled by 1970s critics' emphasis on cinematic specificity. Here one can find an important difference from 1940s symptomatic work. The wartime and postwar critics had treated the film as a dream or a daydream, and they were thus inclined to disclose transmedia symbols, either on the text's surface or in its depths. The 1970s critics, treating the film on the analogy of the patient's symptom-ridden discourse, were far more attuned to issues of "film language." From the start, these critics looked more closely at formal procedures. Yet one is hard pressed to isolate any film technique discovered by the symptomatic tradition. The interpretion of film as "discourse" has derived virtually all its categories from the work of the classical film aestheticians. Typically, current symptomatic criticism ascribes symbolic meanings to recognized sorts of stylistic or narrative devices and then claims that those meanings "contradict" the film's explicit or implicit meanings.

The explicatory and symptomatic trends share another assumption: authorship. We have already seen how central Ford is to the *Cahiers* interpretation of *Young Mr. Lincoln;* later *Cahiers*'s symptomatic studies would concentrate on auteur works such as *Morocco, Hangmen Also Die,* and *To Be or Not to Be.*[123] Auteur structuralism and early feminist studies likewise insist that the auteur remains pertinent. Wollen makes the director the source of the text's contradictions,[124] while Claire Johnston remarks: "Our interest in Walsh is not that he is a victim of patriarchal ideology, but in how the ideology of the patriarchal order is mediated through all the other interests that he developed in his films, partly consciously and partly unconsciously. Almost all directors are patriarchal in different ways, and the ways that they differ are extraordinarily interesting."[125] Symptomatic criticism has often left open the possibility that the director, especially the subversive director, might act at least somewhat deliberately in creating the film's contradictions. A Hollywood director like Douglas Sirk could be considered an intentional agent.[126] Or oppositional filmmakers like Godard and Jean-Marie Straub might be valorized for consciously forcing ruptures in the classical system of representation. In either event, the contradictory-text approach offered a way to save auteurism: the director could, as Comolli and Narboni put it, "throw up obstacles in the way of the ideology."[127]

Individual critics' personal trajectories also testify to how compatible the explicatory and symptomatic trends could be in practice. In 1984 Colin McArthur could castigate classic auteurism as sheer romanticism and still maintain that the "besetting sin" of auteurism "is not the identifying of themes but the construing of them as *personal* rather than *social*."[128] The most remarkable transformation in this respect has been that of Robin Wood, who, after becoming the most influential explicatory critic in English, gradually moved to embrace a conception of repressed meaning. The writer who found in *Rio Bravo* a justification of the beauty and moral force of American cinema now writes that Hollywood classicism has been "always to a great degree artificially imposed and repressive, the forcing of often extremely recalcitrant drives into the mold of a dominant ideology."[129] Yet Wood's critical practice continues to identify themes, chiefly by constructing parallels of character or situations, highlighting certain passages as directorial commentary, and ascribing emotional qualities to significant details. Although Wood grants that every text is incoherent, he finds films like *Taxi Driver* and *Cruising* to be extreme cases, "works in which the drive toward the ordering of expression has been defeated."[130] *The Deer Hunter,* however, is valuable because its confusions are thematically "rich."[131] Invoking *S/Z,* Wood praises *Heaven's Gate* for emphasizing the code of symbolic oppositions and "the code of implied meanings out of which the work's thematic structure is developed."[132]

Wood's recent writing illustrates how, even if the critic disavows notions of organic unity, an auteur thematics and the appreciation of ambiguity can continue to flourish.

If Wood has shifted between implicit and symptomatic conceptions of meaning, other critics have played them off against each other. One of the most neglected of these writers has been Raymond Durgnat, whose work illustrates Kenneth Burke's maxim that the critic should use all that there is to use. During the 1960s, Durgnat's monographs on Buñuel and Franju proved him an ingenious, iconoclastic explicator possessed of a dark sense of humor. At the same time, he had a persistent interest in cultural criticism, and his books on American comedy, British cinema, Hitchcock, and Renoir treated films as often duplicitous portrayals of social tensions.[133]

More recently, most interpretive schools have tacitly agreed to treat mainstream films symptomatically while assuming that some form of alternative cinema harbors only implicit meanings. For example, Dudley Andrew acknowledges that the ordinary Hollywood product exhibits "flaws and tensions," which leads him to disclose "productive discords" in *Meet John Doe:* "Hollywood is most interesting when its authoritative voice is in question."[134] Yet Andrew also celebrates the art film that proceeds from an auteur. Vigo's vision, for instance, transcends his text's disparities and manages "to express a dimension of life closed to most fiction films."[135] Similarly, E. Ann Kaplan suggests that although Hollywood cinema systematically represses the woman's voice, a countercinema can "examine the mechanisms through which women are relegated to absence, silence, and marginality."[136] Thus she interprets films like *Camille* and *Blonde Venus* symptomatically, but claims that Sally Potter's *Thriller* "is important in implying a progression from looking at structures as they affect the individual internally (ie psychoanalytically) to looking at them as they affect the individual in society."[137]

The tendency of the symptomatic critic to switch into the explicatory mode is especially evident in the interpretation of avant-garde cinema since the mid-1970s. As the contradictory-text model gained supporters, critics could look to oppositional films as exemplifying that "other scene" repressed in classical cinema. (Here *Tel quel* was perhaps the most proximate influence, although a long-standing canard holds that avant-garde cinema, in its violation of taboos, represents Hollywood's underside.[138]) This development suggested that the oppositional film, in laying bare the contradictions of dominant cinema, would not itself be conceived as harboring repressed meanings. If *Touch of Evil* contains its contradictions in order to address a unified subject position, the structural/materialist film, according to Heath, aims to break down unity and address a spectator "at the limit of any fixed subjectivity, materially inconstant, dispersed in process, beyond the accommodation of reality and pleasure principles."[139]

Thus return several communicative or expressive assumptions of the explicatory trend. Critics lauding alternative cinema have tended to impute to the filmmaker or the film a considerable awareness of textual operations. In Martha Haslanger's *Syntax,* writes one critic, "there is a deliberate attempt to confront the spectator with the processes of identification."[140] No less than in the explicatory tradition, experimental films or filmmakers are said to propose, investigate, attempt, or challenge—not despite themselves, but calculatedly. For the post-1968 *Cahiers* critics, the works of the Dziga Vertov Group hold the spectator at a distance in order to produce knowledge: "These films also, ideologically, struggle against the passivity of the spectator, as Brecht struggled in his day."[141] Similarly, Paul Willemen commends certain Steve Dwoskin films because they "encourage the viewer to become aware of the kind of structure of subjectivity in which he/she is implicated."[142] Two feminist critics praise Carola Klein's *Mirror Phase* in wholly voluntaristic and communicative terms: it is "a personal statement in images and sound," noteworthy for "the emotional messages it examines and transmits."[143]

Accordingly, when symptomatic writers judge an oppositional film to have failed, they characteristically do not invoke the concepts of repression, symptom, or contradiction. Rather, they appeal surprisingly often to the communication model's criterion of failed intentions. For example, one critic suggests that in *Dora,* the connotations of certain techniques interfere with the film's "carefully prepared themes."[144] Auteur-structuralism had suggested that in the creation of a film, the Hollywood director's unconscious serves as a catalyst for processes that then undergo secondary revision; Peter Gidal is not far from this view when he recommends that the radical filmmaker become immersed in the material process of filmmaking and then, before finishing the film, bring "a (more) conscious theory and criticism to bear."[145] In short, if their theory dictates that the author is dead, a great many symptomatic critics continue to hold séances.

All this is perhaps to take the critics too much at their word. If there is a general disinclination to interpret the works of the avant-garde (or at least the avant-garde that the critic prefers) in symptomatic terms, that may be because the critic can treat these films as aspiring to the status of written theory or criticism. Like the critic's hermeneutics of suspicion, political modernist cinema is held to lay bare the repressed material hidden by dominant ideology. Humanist critics could reveal implicit humanist themes in their canon; modernist critics could reveal modernist themes in theirs; now theoreticist critics could disclose theoretical themes, consisting of the doctrines, problems, questions, issues, and challenges to be found in the critical literature (ideological naturalization, sexual difference, the power of the look, the split subject, and so on). Consequently, the filmmaker could be assigned a degree of self-consciousness and textual authority quite beyond the capacities of Ford, Brakhage, or Truffaut, who as mere points of overdetermination in a structural field could only raise questions unawares. The interpreter could also criticize an oppositional film on the same grounds that one criticized an article, for its misinterpretation of a point of doctrine, its strategic miscalculations, or its ignoring of pertinent issues. To perform a truly symptomatic interpretation of *Fortini/Cani, Crystal Gazing,* or *Journeys from Berlin* would open the door to a symptomatic interpretation of post-structuralist theory itself and, mutatis mutandis, of the critic's own discourse. By definition one cannot directly inspect the repressed contradictions in one's own thought or speech. It is far more pragmatic simply to treat the avant-garde film as symptomatic interpretation carried on by other means.

Symptomatic criticism's therapy, then, is usually trained upon those sick but popular films which constitute "dominant" cinema, while the filmmaking practice favored by the critic is judged robust. Hence an intertextual one-upmanship is in progress, even if the players seldom acknowledge one another. Andrew and Kaplan can perform symptomatic interpretations of Hollywood but explications of their chosen modes—art cinema, feminist countercinema. There are symptomatic studies of art cinema, of historical-materialist cinema (Soviet directors, Godard, Jancsó), and of the American underground.[146] Advocates of one avant-garde trend can disclose repressed meaning in another trend.[147] Still, a symptomatic critic will characteristically rescue some films by discussing them only at the level of implicit meaning. Even the critic who interprets *October* symptomatically can treat *Othon* sympathetically.

My most skeptical readers will still insist that the *theoretical* innovations from which symptomatic reading claims to derive render this mode of criticism fundamentally different from its predecessors. Even if this were the case, it would not address the basic issue I am raising: the very *relation* of "theory" to practical interpretation. The current assumption is that one's theory, of whatever sort, *determines* one's criticism. Old (that is, less aged) Criticism is said to have been blind to the ways its tacit theory governed its practice, whereas New (that is, really new) Criticism consciously derives its interpretations from a comprehensive and coherent theory. Now one can challenge this story on purely theoretical grounds, as I tried to do, sketchily, in Chapter 1.[148] More simply, though, one can ask whether a particular theory of meaning determines the concrete details of interpretive practice.[149] Given the institutional framework within which every critic operates; the problem-solving nature of interpretive thinking; the need to produce novel and plausible interpretations; the cutting and stretching of theoretical constructs to fit the film at hand; the general indifference of practicing critics to explaining or defending theoretical concepts beyond the interpretive needs of the moment; the rhetorical appeal to "theory" as legitimating one interpretation over another; the critic's shift to explication when confronting films that oppose classical cinema and mimic the theory of textual contradiction; and the persistence of the strategies and tactics I shall be examining in the next several chapters—given all this, there is strong evidence that film critics' conception of symptomatic meaning, like the notion of implicit meaning, operates chiefly as an enabling set of assumptions. The critic is expected to accomplish concrete tasks, and he wants some conceptual scheme that might help out. If symptomatic critics were to surrender the enabling theory without embracing another, equally efficacious one, they would lack something to do.

Since the practices of interpretation antedated contemporary symptomatic trends, those trends may have become successful at least partly because they provided a theory that ratified inferential moves that were already acceptable.[150] The conceptual differences between implicit and repressed meaning have had important local effects, but they have not significantly changed the pervasive, perduring routines that constitute the craft of interpretation.

5

Semantic Fields

There are moments, and I would not begrudge it this, when the play, if we can call it that, and I think on balance we can, aligns itself uncompromisingly on the side of life. *Je suis,* it seems to be saying, *ergo sum.* But is that enough? I think we are entitled to ask. For what in fact is this play concerned with? It is my belief that here we are concerned with what I have referred to elsewhere as the nature of identity. I think we are entitled to ask—and here one is irresistibly reminded of Voltaire's cry, *"Voilà"*—I think we are entitled to ask—*Where is God?*

—Tom Stoppard, *The Real Inspector Hound*

Our critic has embraced beliefs about implicit or symptomatic meaning. They will probably never have to be defended at a philosophical level. What counts is that they help produce an interpretation. The skilled interpreter knows that those notions, inconsistent or approximate as they may be, work.

But how do they work? What enables the critic to produce interpretations? At the end of Chapter 2 I asserted that, broadly speaking, three activities are involved. The interpreter must construct semantic fields that can be ascribed to the film. The interpreter must also find cues and patterns onto which the semantic fields can be "mapped." And the critic must, in the act of writing up her interpretation, utilize rhetorical tactics appropriate to the institutional audience sought. Later chapters will consider the mapping process and the nature of interpretive rhetoric. Here I want to show how critics use semantic fields in building up meanings.

As Chapter 1 suggested, I use the metaphor of construction in order to suggest that interpretive activity is an inferential process. Texts, as occasions for perception, cognition, and emotion, possess properties which can function as *cues*—"prompts" for meaning-making. In order to assign explicit, implicit, or symptomatic meanings to the cues, the critic must bring to the film some hypotheses about appropriate semantic fields.

A semantic field is a set of relations of meaning between conceptual or linguistic units.[1] Thus *city/country* can be said to constitute a semantic field, unified by a relation of opposite meaning. *City/town/ village/hamlet* also constitutes a semantic field, organized by diminution in size. *City/state/region/country* constitutes a semantic field defined by inclusion. When one asks the meaning of *city* or *country,* one is partly asking into what semantic fields it can be inserted.

It should be evident from these examples that interpretation of a film (or any other work) cannot get off the ground unless the interpreter, like Moon in my Stoppard epigraph, posits some relatively abstract semantic fields.[2] If we are to construct implicit or symptomatic meanings, we must use semantic fields in producing the final interpretation. Even a structuring absence must be part of a semantic field: the symptomatic critic opposes the "not-said" to the "said" and thus makes evident a set of meanings that are related to the manifest ones.

A semantic field is not identical to what is usually considered a "theme." In literary criticism, the theme is usually assumed to be a "governing idea," even a universal concept.[3] A semantic field is, in contrast, a conceptual *structure;* it organizes potential meanings in relation to one another.[4] Such fields may be organized in different ways. As I shall suggest, we can think of a "theme" as a node in a cluster of associated semantic features.

There is thus no such thing as a strictly intrinsic interpretation. The critic must ascribe to the film meanings which are, as Gerald Prince has suggested, extratextual, intertextual, and extra-artistic.[5] The "extrinsic" quality of semantic fields can be seen in at least two stages of the critical process. In seeking to construct an interpretation, the critic must, often only on a hunch, start to project cultural frames of reference onto the text. These frames of reference include already existing semantic fields. In the course of building the interpretation, the critic selects, shapes, and sharpens fields to match them to the text. The resulting interpretation, as proposed by the critic, will display particular semantic fields as the meanings finally ascribed to the text. These fields could, and usually do, exist outside this film. As far as interpretation is concerned, there are no "cinematic" meanings as distinct from "noncinematic" ones; even a reflexive theme, such as the idea that film is an illusion, could be ascribed to a novel or painting. Semantic fields, then, are at once a precondition for interpretive activity and an output of it. Because I am not studying the critical process step by step, I shall be concentrating upon semantic fields as the final meanings ascribed to the film.

As I indicated in Chapter 2, I argue that the critic's interpretive operations follow a logic of problem-solving. The long-range aim is to produce an acceptable and novel interpretation. In the short term, when ascribing semantic fields to films, the critic must balance a concern for generality with a need to discriminate among textual data. At any particular moment in the history of critical interpretation, the critic's institutional context will consider certain semantic fields schematic or unsophisticated. (Today, the good/evil dichotomy is a pariah.) Yet every interpretive semantic field, as a conceptual abstraction, is apt to seem reductive. The critic must check this tendency by keeping aware of contemporary standards of delicacy, sensing exactly what aspects and how much detail of the film should furnish evidence for a semantic field. Today, for example, an academic critic who utterly ignored film style would probably be considered jejune, no matter how intriguing the semantic fields he employed.

There are in principle many ways of solving the problem, but the critic uses two main rules of thumb. The first takes into account the film's *specificity* (though not its uniqueness): the semantic fields should have a plausible fit with the cues found in this film. Second, they should cover the *entire* film. The modern academic interpretive institution assumes that critics should seek to account for the text as a whole (even if it is conceived as a contradictory whole). Using these two guidelines, the critic can select and combine semantic fields so as to produce meanings pitched at acceptable levels of delicacy. The norm of specificity and totality thus often trade away logical validity for the sake of particularity. Once more, for even the "theory"-grounded critic, the niceties of theoretical consistency take a backseat to heuristic devices that yield institutionally approved results.

Meanings in Structures

In surveying the practice of film interpretation, one might initially be struck by the great variety of semantic fields deployed by different critical schools and trends. Contrast the 1940s Columbia social scientists with contemporary feminists, or Andrew Sarris with Stephen Heath. What can there be in common between a 1959 interpretation of *Ivan the Terrible* as the modern tragedy of art in society and a 1970 interpretation of it as a covert Oedipal drama?[6]

We cannot ignore such differences. Broadly speaking, explicatory criticism has gravitated toward what we might call "humanist" meanings—semantic fields revolving around moral categories. Here the heritage of New Criticism is evident. The theme of a poem, write Cleanth Brooks and Robert Penn Warren in a textbook, is "a comment on human values, an interpretation of human life."[7] The explicatory critic typically conceives of the film's meaning in terms of the significance of individual experience. Thus the meaning of a film will often revolve around individual problems (suffering, identity, alienation, the ambiguity of perception, the mystery of behavior) or values (freedom, religious doctrines, enlightenment, creativity, the imagination). In 1953, R. S. Crane listed a set of pairings that remain characteristic of the humanistic frame of semantic significance:

> . . . such familiar and all-embracing dichotomies as life and death (or positive values and negative values), good and evil, love and hate, harmony and strife, order and disorder, eternity and time, reality and appearance, truth and falsity, certainty and doubt, true insight and false opinion, imagination and intellect (as either sources of knowledge or guides in action), emotion and reason, complexity and simplicity, nature and art, the natural and the supernatural, nature as benign and nature as malignant, man as spirit and man as beast, the needs of society and individual desires, internal states and outward acts, engagement and withdrawal.[8]

Cahiers in the 1950s exemplifies how critics could exploit such dualities. Here is Eric Rohmer on the central oppositions of American cinema: "the relations between power and the law, will and destiny, individual freedom and the common good."[9] *Cahiers* found the theme of fate in such diverse works as the films of Lang, in *Strangers on a Train,* in *Rebel without a Cause,* and in *The Man Who Knew Too Much.*[10] Fereydoun Hoveyda confessed in retrospect: "All our favorite *auteurs* were, ultimately, talking about the same things. The 'constants' of their particular universes belonged to everyone: solitude, violence, the absurdity of existence, sin, redemption, love, etc."[11]

As the art cinema became more influential, other humanistic fields emerged and have remained in force. Works by Bergman, Fellini, Kurosawa, and others encouraged critics trained in modern literature to propose interpretations that highlighted themes of reality and illusion, the artist's vocation, the alienation of modern life, the difficulties of loving.[12] One persistent semantic node is the problem of personal communication. In 1962, V. F. Perkins found it in *King of Kings.*[13] In 1967, David Thomson disclosed it in Hitchcock.[14] In 1985, Seymour Chatman found it in Antonioni.[15] In 1986, Jim Jarmusch found it in his own films: "In the films, the stuff I write, the dialogue is so minimal and often there's—well, *always*—there's some kind of communication problem between people."[16]

Post-1968 symptomatic criticism, as befits a hermeneutics of suspicion, traffics in somewhat different semantic fields. The individualist perspective is replaced by an analytical, almost anthropological detachment that sees sexuality, politics, and signification as constituting the salient domains of meaning. The theme of fate is replaced by the duality power/subjection. Love is replaced by desire, or law/desire. Instead of the individual there is subject/object or phallus/lack. Instead of art there is signifying practice. Instead of society there is nature/culture or class struggle. In the previous chapter I have traced out enough of the history of this mode to suggest how particular films have been interpreted, but perhaps another instance can suggest the pool of meanings from which the symptomatic critic can draw.

In 1983 the British journal *Framework* published three brief essays on Godard's *Passion*,[17] all of which frankly admitted to be no more than first thoughts after a single viewing. In these remarks one can find at least the following semantic fields, which represent a fair sampling of those dominating interpretation today: work and love, power, exhibitionism, critique of bourgeois codes of representation, pleasure, linearity, class conflict, illusion, fiction, labor/desire, image/language, fetishism, narcissism, hysteria, woman's body, speaking/muteness, repression, male violence/female victimization, presence/absence, binarism, dialectics, knowledge, art/nature, aesthetics/politics, spectacle/narrative, voyeurism, excess, distortion, politics of representation/representation of politics, individual/society, alienated labor/non-alienated labor, interior/exterior, fantasy/reality. As this list suggests, critics working in the symptomatic tradition have drawn upon some semantic fields typical of the humanistic trend, and not only as examples of textual disguise.

Probably the most basic of these shared fields is the order/disorder couplet. As a staple of auteur and genre criticism, order has often been treated as a positive term, identified with tradition or stability.[18] But the humanistic critic can also delight in disorder, as do writers discussing how comedy overturns hierarchies.[19] Here the symptomatic trend runs parallel, for it is a commonplace of "contradictory text" criticism that order is linked with social and sexual oppression while disorder arises from impulses that have been subjugated. Sandy Flitterman writes of *Guest in the House:* "With gripping determinacy it represents the domestication of the uncontained excesses of female passion in favor of a family rigidly constituted and intractably defined ... It is precisely [Evelyn Crane's] sexuality and its representation, exceeding as it does the more acceptable definition of femininity in bourgeois culture—the position of wife and mother—which brings chaos into the home."[20] A similar semantic field, unity/disunity, can figure as a source of symptomatic interpretation; here again, the disunity is valorized.

By a reciprocal movement, certain semantic fields that developed under the aegis of symptomatic criticism have become attractive to exponents of the explicatory approach. Most popular have been those fields associated with "reading" a linguistic text. In 1967, a *Cahiers* critic suggested of *Torn Curtain:* "Spectator and hero are both involved ... in a systematic discovery of the powers of cinematic language, a veritable lesson in *reading,* with its exercises, its codes to decipher."[21] During the 1980s, this field came into general currency. An explicatory critic can now describe Hitchcock's "wrong" men as "misread" men who seek to establish the "legibility" of their innocence and to "reread" the world.[22] Another critic of humanistic inclination declares that Mizoguchi treats his subjects as "texts" which he "reads," the result having in turn to be "read" by the spectator.[23] So widespread has this semantic domain become—film as "text," form as "writing," critic or filmmaker or character as "reader"—that now critics of all sorts unabashedly call their interpretations "readings."

In addition to outright borrowing across traditions, there are looser affinities. A critic trained by the humanistic tradition to build a field around "the individual's search for identity" could recast this as "the reconstitution of the human subject"—especially if the imagistic cast of the Lacanian account offered better coverage of the film's details (glances, mirrors, use of language, and so on). A critic already inclined to see films as centering on problems of communication or the nature of art does not have to take a giant step in order to treat the same films as being about the opacity of representation or the nature of signification. And why not take the step? Whatever semantic fields best yield novel interpretations that are judged faithful to the film's totality and its specificity (at some institutionally accepted level of delicacy) are prime candidates for critical adoption, even if making the choice compels the critic to switch allegiance to a symptomatic conception of meaning.

The most currently powerful semantic field shared by all schools of criticism centers on the notion of "reflexivity." The history of this notion as a resource for critics in all media remains to be written. As early as the mid-1940s, Parker Tyler was putting forth symptomatic interpretations that were ingeniously reflexive: Sam Spade's job as duplicating the role of studio actors; Kane's story as a "super-condensation" of the agonies of directing and acting in movies; and *Arsenic and Old Lace* as taking revenge upon Broadway by entangling the drama critic in a purely Hollywoodian romance and melodrama.[24]

The real boom in such interpretations took place in the 1960s. It was then that critics of avant-garde films, relying on various tenets of modernism, accepted more or less explicitly Leo Steinberg's contention that "whatever else it may be about, all art is about art."[25] Thus one critic can argue that Warhol's films make us aware of cinema and its intrinsic limitations.[26] A comparable reflexivity surfaces in explicatory criticism of auteur or genre films. *Cahiers du cinéma* and *Movie* frequently cited auteurs' works as "testaments," ruminations on the essential conditions of the medium. Paul Mayersberg praised Renoir's *Testament of Dr. Cordelier* as a film in which "the spectator thinks constantly of the film's technique: the illusion is never complete."[27]

In the same period, a reawakened interest in Brecht encouraged film and literary critics to treat avant-garde art as laying bare its own operations. With the rise of structuralism, reflexive interpretations were licensed by the assumption that all art could reflect upon signification; *Madame Bovary* could be taken as "ultimately 'about' signs and meaning."[28] Now every film could, if interrogated from a certain angle, reveal reflexive aspects.

In any discussion of reflexivity as a theoretical concept, a great many distinctions have to be made. Few of them are my concern here.[29] I am concerned with critics' use of reflexivity as a "black box," a tool to get the interpretive job done. The critic need not defend this semantic field on general grounds, since the institution of criticism has long deemed reflexive semantic fields to be eminently applicable. And lest this be thought wholly a matter of high art or esoteric doctrine, it is worth noting that reflexivity is a widely available strategy. A 1968 manual for high school teachers of literature states that the critic can employ an "aesthetic mimetic interpretation" ("the work of art is imitating or talking about the way the artist works"), an "aesthetic typological interpretation" ("Kubla Khan is the poet and his pleasure dome is the poem"), or an "aesthetic hortatory interpretation" ("Joyce, through Stephen, tells us of his ideal artist").[30] Once again, the evidence suggests that various schools of criticism often ratify an interpretive move that is already a pervasive institutional routine.

Sometimes the reflexivity field is used "intratextually"; the critic claims: "This film is about some attribute of this film." One writer says that "Sirk's films are about their own style," another that the burning image at the start of *Persona* metaphorically foreshadows the conflicts to come.[31] The more common interpretive claim, and the one that I will concentrate on here, is, "This film is about some attribute of cinema as a whole."

Some films can be said to take reflexivity as part of their referential and explicit meanings. That *A Star Is Born* (1954) is "about" filmmaking registers at the level of comprehension: its diegetic world portrays the Hollywood film industry, and one explicit meaning might be said to be a critical judgment on that milieu. But one can go further to suggest that, say, the film is *implicitly* or *symptomatically* reflexive. For instance, certain shots in *A Star Is Born* comparing cinema and television may be taken as subtle valorizations of the former, or symptoms of Hollywood's unease when faced with its new rival. From such a relatively clear-cut case one can move to films in which a film is shown or mentioned. Beyond that are films centering on other media, such as *Lola Montès* or *The Golden Coach;* the circus or the stage becomes analogous to cinema. One step further, and a film's reference to any form of spectacle may warrant the appeal to reflexivity. For example, *North by Northwest* has been interpreted as being about the illusion of cinema because it alludes to theatrical artifice.[32] The mirrors in *Rules of the Game,* according to another critic, suggest "a private stage" with entrances, wings, and footlights—all of which increase the film's reflexive dimension.[33] The critic can go on to propose that even in a film not evoking spectacle of any sort, stylistic devices and narrative patterns indirectly designate aspects of cinema. At this extreme, any aspect of cinema may form the basis of a reflexive interpretation. One critic claims that *The Bitter Tears of Petra von Kant* becomes reflexive because, "like the audience, [Marlene] wears the same clothing throughout the film while other characters change theirs."[34] Stanley Cavell's essay on *North by Northwest* summons up a host of reflexive parallels: characters' comments about the protagonist Roger Thornhill's looks establish the film's concern with acting; Van Damm and the Professor are like movie directors; the echoes of *Hamlet* pose the problem of a film's sources; the faces on Mount Rushmore evoke a film projection; the tourist-stop telescope parallels the movie camera, as does the crop-dusting plane, which "shoots" at its victims and coats them with "film."[35]

In all cases that go beyond referential and explicit meanings, the tacit inferential moves would seem to run this way:

> This film has property X (a convention or aspect of representation).
> This film is about property X.
> Property X is a property of cinema.
> This film is about cinema.

Here, in skeletal form, is a reflexive discussion of *Lola Montès:*

> *Lola Montès* shows audiences watching performers.
> *Lola Montès* is about audiences watching performers.
> Cinema involves audiences watching performers.
> *Lola Montès* is about cinema.[36]

As a sampling, consider how various attributes of cinema can form the basis of a reflexive semantic field.

Attributes of the film industry. One of the earliest reflexive interpretations I have run across takes Gance's film *La Roue* as a symbol of cinema, a business spinning in place and constantly repeating the same errors.[37] More recently, another critic construes *In a Lonely Place* as demonstrating how "the disturbing effects of discourse" can "possess" workers in Hollywood.[38]

Attributes of film technology. "Warhol's movies state unequivocally that what is being seen is the product of a recording mechanism."[39] According to one critic, the guns in *Rules of the Game* are like Renoir's camera in their aggressiveness.[40]

Attributes of film history. One critic claims that the tension between reality and imagination in *Citizen Kane* parallels the split between Lumière and Méliès.[41] Jane Feuer asserts that late musicals interrogate their predecessors' assumptions about spontaneity and the role of the audience.[42] Jean Douchet suggests that the film projection in *Fury* constitutes Lang's condemnation of his German films, especially *Metropolis*.[43] And Annette Michelson reinterprets *Wavelength* as laying bare cinema's historical sources in the conventions of painting.[44]

Attributes of the role of the filmmaker. Since Cocteau's *Blood of a Poet*, an allegory of the artist's creative odyssey, critics have often interpreted films as harboring general comments on the nature of film direction.

Gerald Mast suggests that for Hawks, every vocation is actually a surrogate for filmmaking, so that in *Twentieth Century* Oscar Jaffe as storyteller and star-maker represents the film director.[45] In *Rules of the Game,* according to another writer, Octave's becoming entangled in events acknowledges "that the director, supposedly the authoritative and manipulating figure, is as much victim as originator of circumstances."[46]

Attributes of the film screening situation. Rear Window is the paradigm case: Douchet claims that Jefferies is the spectator, watching on the "screens" across the courtyard a spectacle which is only the "projection" of his own fears and desires.[47] Another critic declares that during the home movie scene in *Adam's Rib,* Kip's cynical commentary makes him a surrogate film critic.[48] Stephen Heath takes the flickering pages of Sergeant Brody's book in *Jaws* as resembling a film in projection.[49]

Attributes of the film spectator. By making a character a surrogate for the spectator, the critic can turn the film into a reflexive exercise. The most common semantic linkage is through vision. In *Hangmen Also Die,* a character looks into a mirror; a secondary character watching the action and reflected in the mirror thus becomes "a spectator-function . . . watching us watching."[50] In Mizoguchi's films, the prevalence of detached onlookers enables us "to draw an analogy between these people and the audience in relation to the screen."[51]

Attributes of doctrines or theories concerning cinema. This sort of interpretation is particularly common in discussions of Godard, who, in such films as *Les Carabiniers,* seems to be challenging conceptions of cinema as a record of reality. But the field can be applied to less explicit critiques. Tyler sees *Persona* as metaphorically refuting both Kracauer's conception of film's objectivity and Langer's notion of it as a "dream-mode."[52] Another critic has proposed that when in *Rules of the Game* Christine looks through the field glass, she is taken in by the reality of the view, "its ontological lie," whereas Renoir's film will demonstrate the deceptiveness of this conception of cinema.[53]

In sum, critics of all stripes have used virtually any means available to secure reflexive interpretations. Such semantic fields are believed to give the critic greater access to the totality or specificity of the film—

regardless of any theoretical questions attending such an unconstrained extension of the concept.

Structures of Meaning

It is not enough to catalogue the most popular semantic fields, even if the exercise does enable us to see that explicatory and symptomatic critics often draw on the same ones. We also need to recognize that semantic fields are organized by various principles. Charting them will help us survey other widely used strategies of critical practice. Such a survey also raises tacit knowledge to the level of awareness, helping us see the choices that are available to the critic.

In the study of literature, there have been some attempts to classify ways in which semantic fields can be organized.[54] My own taxonomy is adapted from D. A. Cruse's systematic overview of lexical semantics.[55] Cruse outlines four fundamental types of semantic fields: clusters, doublets, proportional series, and hierarchies. There is considerable evidence that these structures reflect the ways in which speakers of a language store items in the mental lexicon.[56] In this first section of the chapter, I shall show the ways in which film interpretation, in both its explicatory and symptomatic modes, makes use of all these structuring relations.

Clusters

A cluster is a semantic field in which items have a semantic overlap and a low degree of implicit contrastiveness.[57] Lexical examples would be synonyms *(violin/fiddle)* and plesionyms *(foggy/misty)*. Mentally, such fields might be organized as identity relations, as "family resemblance" relations, or as core/periphery relations. In film interpretation, clusters best answer the question posed by Brooks and Warren back in Chapter 2: "What is the theme?" The interplay of themes in the film is often presumed to be a cluster of more or less strongly associated semantic units that are not set in rigorously inclusive or disjunctive relation to one another.

Some examples will establish how semantic clusters underlie an interpretation. P. Adams Sitney proposes that the "true theme" of recent avant-garde film autobiographies is "the very quest for a cinematic strategy which relates the moments of shooting and editing to the diachronic continuity of the filmmaker's life."[58] Sitney goes on to claim that this is associated with other themes, such as absence, the comparative representational adequacy of film and language, cinema's inability to recover time, and the fantasy of origins.[59] None of these concepts relates by inclusion or disjunction to the main theme. Instead, some features of each can be associated with it by semantic overlap: the moment of shooting cannot capture what is absent; a film or photograph inspires reflection on its source; and so on.

More explicit is Seymour Chatman's claim to find in Antonioni "not themes taken singly but something like a coherent network of themes."[60] Thus the director's central theme is "the perilous stance of our emotional life," and it overlaps the themes of diseased love, the problem of communication, escape, and distraction.[61] Similarly, there is nothing that inherently links "isolation" with "a challenge to advanced capitalism," but a critic argues that these semantic units are clustered around the individualistic subjectivity characteristic of Peter Handke's films.[62]

Auteur criticism of the 1950s and early 1960s had a propensity for thematic clusters. If Hitchcock's work is centrally concerned with confession, the critic is encouraged to associate legal forms of the process with psychoanalytic and Catholic forms.[63] Sarris can claim that the central theme of *The Seventh Seal* is that illusions are necessary if modern man is to endure life; then, through semantic overlap, he introduces themes concerning the continuity of life and art's transcendence of everyday existence.[64] In such interpretations, we see how semantic clusters tend to have a rudimentary core/periphery organization: the central theme or themes of the film are linked to less central ones. By adding more associated themes, the critic can account for more of the text's aspects.

Cluster-fields remain important in contemporary symptomatic criticism. Interpreting *Letter from an Unknown Woman,* one critic gathers around the concept of female hysteria several semantic units—loss, silence, a repetitive sense of history, the possibility of male hysteria, the destabilization of identity.[65] The term *discourses* often seems to bring in a thematic cluster, such as in the proposal that the James Bond films display "the ways in which the discourses of nation and nationhood are articulated with discourses of class."[66] "Postmodernism" as employed in recent interpretations seems also to constitute a cluster.[67] One critic, for example, finds playfulness, pleasure, the shallow space of display, the alliance of electronics and corporate power, and other postmodern themes to characterize 1970s and 1980s science-fiction films.[68]

Doublets

To think of current interpretive practice is automatically to think of semantic fields organized as polarities. Active/passive, subject/object, absence/presence—these and other semantic doublets pervade contemporary criticism. The lexical category of doublets includes not only logically exclusive and exhaustive pairings (for example, *living/nonliving*) but also simple antonyms (for example, *dominating/dominated,* which does not exclude a relation of equality). In practice, most doublets or "binary oppositions" deployed in film interpretation are antonyms.

Cognitively, doubling calls on the fundamental tendency of human meaning-making to categorize by contrast. E. H. Gombrich has suggested the power of this strategy by recalling how many phenomena can be classified by means of a simple doublet like *ping/pong*.[69] (Day is ping, night is pong; Toyotas are ping, Cadillacs are pong; Clair is ping, Dreyer is pong.) Typically the critic has a doublet ready to apply, inherited from prior critics. If not, the critic can posit a theme and label it with a lexical item. Since any word can form the basis of an inference about a complementary or an antonym, the critic can go on to test various opposites for their applicability to the film.[70] As Dan Sperber indicates with regard to Lévi-Strauss's binary method, the principle does not constitute a theory. It is instead a powerful heuristic, enlarging the range of textual data that the critic's interpretation can cover.[71]

British cine-structuralism, with its Lévi-Straussian affinities, refined auteurism by replacing thematic clusters with thematic dualities. Sarris claimed that Budd Boetticher's films dealt with machismo, but Jim Kitses found them to rely on a clash of romanticism and cynicism.[72] Since the 1970s, the semantic doublet has become an almost indispensable interpretive tool. Laura Mulvey's "visual pleasure" argument depends upon the psychoanalytic doublet voyeurism/fetishism. One critic uses the active/passive pairing to contrast characters' behavior during two attacks in *The Birds*.[73] Another declares *Dog Day Afternoon* to be organized around the "contradiction" between transnational late capitalism and older national cultures.[74]

Contemporary criticism has learned to use doublets in a thoroughgoing way, but we should recall that this semantic pattern is not new. Kracauer's *From Caligari to Hitler* treated German cinema as torn between tyranny and chaos.[75] For Jacques Rivette, Hitchcock's films revealed a duality of external appearances and hidden secrets.[76] A *Movie* critic found Arthur Penn's films to be about the difference between the physical world of gestures and the symbolic world of language.[77] Contemporary criticism, even of the symptomatic sort, systematized existing tendencies toward using semantic doublets.

Proportional Series

After the critic constructs one doublet, the impulse is to create more. Cruse calls such a semantic structure a *proportional series,* whereby *a* is to *b* as *c* is to *d.*

Interpretation's most constrained form of proportional series is A. J. Greimas' semiotic square, according to which the A/non-A opposition generates a positive assertion, a contradictory, a complementary, and a contrary.[78] For example, in a discussion of *Alien,* James Kavanaugh uses the square to plot out the film's semantics of *humanness* (see Figure 2).[79] On the whole, however, film critics have not embraced Greimas' system, principally because it misses much of the text. (Where, for instance, do *Alien*'s other characters fit into the square?) Most interpreters prefer a looser heuristic that is more comprehensive.

Such a broadening of scope can be achieved by simply stacking doublets atop one another in a double-column list. Jonathan Culler describes the relevant reasoning strategies well: "If the text presents two items—characters, situations, objects, actions—in a way which suggests opposition, then 'a whole space of substitution and variation is opened to the reader' (Barthes, *S/Z,* p. 24) . . . The reader can pass from one opposition to another, trying them out, even inverting them, and determining which are pertinent to larger thematic structures which encompass other antitheses presented in the text."[80] We have already seen this sort of semantic field at work in the auteur-structur-

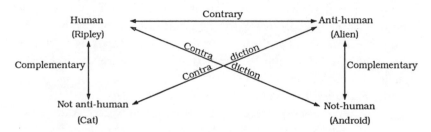

Figure 2. The semiotic square and *Alien*

alists' discussion of "antinomies" at work in directors' oeuvres and Hollywood genres. In mainstream film criticism, proportional series become chiefly *oppositional* series.

As Culler indicates, the critic often moves from referential oppositions to implicit or symptomatic ones. In discussing *Day of Wrath,* Jean Sémolué tallies the diegetic doublet nature/exteriors with life/ death and freedom/confinement.[81] For *The Naked Kiss,* Peter Wollen starts with the referential oppositions brothel/children's hospital and prostitute/child and then goes on to line up hate/love, sterility/possibility, and outward beauty/inward purity.[82] Gerald Mast interprets the first scenes of *Bringing Up Baby* by positing an opposition of indoors and outdoors, Miss Swallow and Susan Vance, a binding black dress and a flowing white one; to these he assigns the more abstract doublets confinement/freedom and death/life.[83] On the basis of characters, Pam Cook arrives at a lengthy proportional series of oppositions in *Mildred Pierce* (see Figure 3).[84] One can also embed one oppositional series within another, as Teresa de Lauretis does in her analysis of Roeg's *Bad Timing* (see Figure 4).[85]

Whereas strictly logical entailments purportedly govern the Greimasian series, much looser relations hold between the items in the opposing columns. The chief such relation is analogy. The critic of *Mildred Pierce* is committed only to saying that passive/active parallels womb/phallus, not that *womb* is the logical complementary of *passive.* And if the critic finds an aspect of the text that the oppositions don't already capture, he can simply add another doublet that does the trick. The practical critic can scarcely resist a rule-of-thumb strategy that

Female	Male
Tellurian	Uranian
Material/Corporeal	Spiritual/Intellectual
Night	Day
Dark	Light
Passive	Active
Left	Right
Mass solidarity	Individualism
Womb	Phallus

Figure 3. Oppositions in *Mildred Pierce*

Male		Female
Film noir, thriller		Woman's film
Subject		Object
Family		Refusal of family
Order		Disorder
Crimes against property		Crimes against propriety
Voyeurism, fetishism		Sexual excess
Dialectical oppositions:		Radical difference
Inspector Netusil	Dr. Linden	Maria
Law	Psychoanalysis	
Power	Knowledge	
Detection	Confession	
Vaginal examination	Rape	
Metonymy	Metaphor	
Oppression	Recuperable resistance	Unrecuperable resistance
Linear time	Obsessive repetition	Time as now

Figure 4. Embedded oppositions in *Bad Timing*

retains abstract conceptual differences but which adds oppositions, of varying degrees of specificity, *ad libitum*. When the critic wishes, a relation of association may be added to link items in the same column. For de Lauretis, it is not just that in *Bad Timing* the fetishization of woman is roughly comparable to rape, obsessive repetition, and loss; these semantic values are conceived as overlapping.[86] In this way, stacked doublets can gain the stronger bond that characterizes the semantic cluster; in effect, each column forms a semantic cluster with each term's opposite spelled out in the facing column. With both analogy and association available to the user of opposites, it is no wonder that 1970s film interpretation was inclined to see the text as endlessly productive.

Hierarchies

Semantic fields can also be structured hierarchically, either in branching or nonbranching forms.[87] Without entering into all the technicalities of Cruse's exposition, we can seize several structuring principles employed in critical practice.

A hierarchical field orders semantic units by relations of inclusion or exclusion. The taxonomic series *pekinese/dog/animal/living thing* would be an instance. Such hierarchies are occasionally used in interpretations. For example, Bill Simon takes the basic theme of Frampton's *Zorns Lemma* to be "the nature of representation, especially filmic representation in relation to other art forms and media."[88] In the course of the argument, Simon surveys the ways in which the film presents and interrogates different media. The semantic field underlying his argument can be diagrammed as a branching hierarchy (see Figure 5). Such a conceptual configuration enables Simon to assert that the film examines representation in a fairly exhaustive way.

Explicatory critics sometimes attributed hierarchical semantic fields to those films of the 1950s and 1960s that sought to survey the landscape of modern moral life (*Voyage to Italy, Nights of Cabiria, La Dolce Vita*). For example, a *Cahiers* critic could treat *Europa 51* as a journey through a variety of false doctrines.[89] (This ascribes a *meronymy*, or part/whole hierarchy, to the film's semantic level.) Nevertheless, it was structuralist and post-structuralist theory that brought branching hierarchies to prominence in film interpretation. Psychoanalytic theory supplied a large set of such fields: Family divided into Father/ Mother/Child, the psychic field as Ego/Id/Superego or as Imaginary/ Symbolic/Real. To take only one case, Raymond Bellour's interpretation of *North by Northwest* rests upon the hierarchy shown in Figure 6.[90] A comparable, though less elaborate, scheme underlies Wolfenstein and Leites' discussion of the "concealed triangle" of certain movies, in which the hero (son) is pitted against a strange man (father) and a mysterious woman (mother).[91]

You will have noticed that these hierarchies are logically incomplete or inconsistent. (Where does *Zorns Lemma* account for music, sculpture, or other modes of representation? Where is the daughter in the

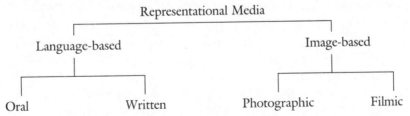

Figure 5. A semantic hierarchy in *Zorns Lemma*

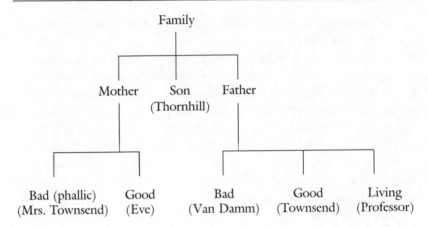

Figure 6. A semantic hierarchy in *North by Northwest*

North by Northwest family, and how does the "living" father square with the good/bad distinction?) Such flaws are characteristic of the way critical interpretation constructs hierarchical semantic fields. To demand logical stringency would miss the point of using them. The fields aim to cover the data of the film, not to meet purely deductive criteria.

It may be, as one cognitive researcher has suggested, that taxonomies are not even psychologically realistic: they may make excessively "logical" what are in fact far looser routines of thought.[92] Evidence of this is provided not only by the logical deficiencies of interpretive taxonomies but also by critics' tendency to reduce taxonomies to doublets. The Lacanian Imaginary/Symbolic/Real trio is, in practice, frequently handled as an opposition between the first two terms.[93] Wood interprets *Alphaville* as centering on the battle of Superego and Id, but he does not assign a place to the Ego.[94] A skeptic could argue that by ignoring some semantic values demarcated by the theory, the criticism is weakened as a theoretical enterprise; but again the norms of practical criticism outweigh scruples about theoretical coherence. Rough opposites are usually easier to work with than a strict taxonomy, which may, in the name of rigor, generate extra categories that do not "fit the film."

This fit can also be achieved with what Cruse calls nonbranching hierarchies. Although he discusses several sorts of these, for my purposes two are salient: the *graded series* and the *chain*.

The graded series consists of continuous variation along an axis (for example, *cold/cool/warm/hot*). Within film interpretation, one finds this in the phenomenon of the "thematic continuum." In the 1940s, critics were fond of turning the good/bad couplet into a spectrum. Deming speaks of "villain-heroes" and "non-heroic heroes," Tyler of the "good villain" and the "bad hero." Wolfenstein and Leites range their female types along an axis (see Figure 7).[95] More explicitly, Wood argues that if the formula for the horror film is "Normality threatened by the Monster," then *Psycho* presents a graded semantic field. "In *Psycho* normality and the monster no longer function even superficially as separable opposites but exist on a continuum which the progress of the film traces."[96] Janet Bergstrom creates a graded series by starting with two Freudian doublets: sexual object as male or female, sexual aim as either active or passive. She then asserts that each category in fact constitutes "a spectrum of real or imaginary choices."[97] She can therefore conclude that Murnau's films yield a passive contemplation that encourages the spectator "to relax rigid demarcations of gender identification and sexual orientation."[98]

For the practical critic, the most useful nonbranching hierarchies have proven to be what Cruse calls *chains,* those in which units are strung out "in linear sequence on either a spatial or temporal axis."[99] Lexical examples would be *wrist/forearm/elbow* or *summer/fall/winter/spring*. What comes to mind in interpretive practice are those semantic successions that the critic ascribes to narrative patterns in a film. For example, one may describe Bergman's work as displaying the recurrent progression from sadness to wise joy.[100] Cyclical patterns, which Cruse calls "helices," also constitute instances. One critic finds in Warren Sonbert's *Divided Loyalties* a thematic cycle of creation/destruction/regeneration.[101]

Evidently the critic can convert any sort of semantic field into chains by stringing the terms out temporally. The critic may claim that in the course of a film one "side" of an opposition cancels, defeats, or

Good girl———Good-bad girl———Bad-good girl———Bad girl

          (appears bad)   (prostitute redeemed)

Figure 7. Wolfenstein and Leites' semantic continuum

absorbs the other. Summarizing the tendency of classical Hollywood films to "recuperate" woman, Annette Kuhn writes: "A woman character may be restored to the family by falling in love, by 'getting her man,' by getting married, or otherwise accepting a 'normative' female role. If not, she may be directly punished for her narrative and social transgression by exclusion, outlawing, or even death."[102] Or the critic may construct a term that synthesizes semantic oppositions. Rick Altman proposes that a semantic doublet—work/entertainment—structures the Hollywood musical, and he suggests that marriage functions to mediate the terms.[103] One can go still further and claim that even if there is an absorption or synthesis, the contradictory text will retain *traces* of the repressed oppositional term. This is the strategy Charles Eckert pursues in discussing the ending of *Marked Woman,* in which the nominal defeat of the villain is followed by a symptomatic recollection of the women's suffering. (See my discussion in Chapter 4.) Other sorts of semantic fields can be strung out temporally, as in Kavanaugh's Greimasian analysis of *Alien,* which traces the plot as moving toward an alignment with the "human" terms in the matrix.[104]

The most common semantic chain, though, is that provided by a preexisting story that the film can be seen as replaying. When a critic finds that *Double Indemnity* centers on "the Oedipal trajectory of the hero—the problem of the knowledge of sexual diffrence in a patriarchal culture,"[105] she posits a string of developmental phases (attraction to mother/fear of castration/accession to paternal authority) as a semantic chain governing the interpretation. Any twice-told tale may serve the critic's turn, but myth, religion, and psychoanalysis furnish the standard instances. The American avant-garde film has long been considered to offer parables of sacrifice and rebirth; Hollywood has been interpreted as presenting veiled Christian parables; and all sorts of films have been translated into Freudian, Jungian, and Lacanian narratives. Since such detailed narrative patterns are not only chains but homologies, they present *allegories* of the entire film. As such, they will be analyzed in Chapter 8. For now, it suffices only to observe that contemporary theory has supplied semantic chains which can serve as either initial hypotheses or final outputs for practical criticism.

For the purposes of illustrating the four major types of semantic fields—clusters, doublets, proportional series, and hierarchies—I have had to schematize critics' arguments a fair amount. In practice, most interpretations mobilize various sorts of fields within a single interpretive project. Let me take up two examples for quick scrutiny.

In an analysis of Blake Edwards' *Darling Lili,* Peter Lehman and William Luhr posit that the film "deals centrally with different ways of looking and performing."[106] The phrasing of the claim suggests that the underlying semantic field is organized hierarchically, and so it is, but within a master doublet: looking/being looked at. The result is traced out in Figure 8. Laid over this schema is a graded series ranging from control to lack of control. Lili starts in control of her performance space and of the audience's space. As the film progresses, her control recedes and that of Major Larrabee increases. (This semantic chaining relies on taking the female/male opposition as a referential cue.) In the film's last scene, Lili's audience invades her performance space, and Major Larrabee's complete control is established.[107] The interpretation deploys both different semantic fields and different *sorts* of fields. The value of this is apparent: for any part of the film, the critics can invoke a field that lets them construct implicit meanings.

In discussing *The Most Dangerous Game,* Thierry Kuntzel combines semantic fields in another way. He seeks to interpret a carved door-knocker that appears under the film's opening credits. The knocker depicts a centaur, wounded by an arrow and carrying a prostrate woman. According to Kuntzel, this image generates semantic units ("signifieds") combined in what he calls "constellations." He starts by clustering: the arrow suggests Cupid's dart and a wounded heart; the woman calls to mind mythological virgins. Then the centaur leads him to posit a set of doublets—man/beast, hunter/hunted, civilization/savagery—of which the centaur is less the mediating term than the

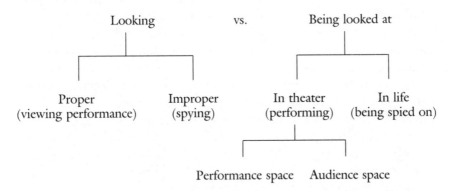

Figure 8. Semantic fields in *Darling Lili*

transgressive mixture. This particular oppositional series suggests that one can also place the woman's figure within a doublet: male as hunter/ female as prey.[108] Like Barthes in *S/Z,* Kuntzel claims that the blurring of oppositions represented in the centaur poses a problem for the film's plot to work out. The narrative will work to eliminate this transgression, drawing a clear line between the poles and letting one emerge the victor. Kuntzel's constellations consist of clusters, proportional oppositions, and a tacit semantic chain that enables the film to repress mediating terms. Like most critics, he is an unabashed *bricoleur,* adding together semantic fields to maximize coverage and particularity.

These interpretations are instructive on two more counts. First, the critics are not simply combining various sorts of semantic fields but are blending them into a whole. Fields are not simply adduced seriatim but are, to one degree or another, synthesized into a coherent significance. *Darling Lili* is "centrally" about looking and performing; *The Most Dangerous Game* is primarily about the danger of blurring socially distinct terms. Schools of criticism differ as to the degree to which the text can be reduced to a coherent structure of significance, but typically the critic moves from particular meanings to overall meaning.

Second, both these interpretations exemplify a general strategy to which I shall often return: interpretation claims to shadow comprehension. Semantic fields become plausible by virtue of being connected to meanings that the critic has already identified as referential or explicit. The most obvious example is the way that, in nearly all criticism, the male/female pairing operates. As a contingently universal opposition, it serves as an "output" of comprehension: this character is a man, that one is a woman. A plot based on heterosexual romance and ending in a marriage is unintelligible to a spectator who does not have the concept of gender difference. But because this opposition is in all cultures freighted with many abstract values, it also becomes a salient cue for interpretation. Upon it the critic can stack semantic oppositions such as active/passive, subject of desire/object of desire, and so on. Even if one wishes to posit a reversal, such as feminized men or masculine women, one must base the switch on an appeal to referential meanings (for example, behaviors in the diegetic world) or to explicit meanings.[109] Although semantic fields are a major source of innovation within the critical institution, they are usually constrained by a pressure to "respect" the text.

The Role of Semantic Fields

In 1953 R. S. Crane hurled a devastating broadside against the semantic fields dominating literary interpretation. He argued that abstract significance could be found in any literary work:

> It requires no great insight to find an inner dialectic of order and disorder or a struggle of good and evil forces in any serious plot; or a profound dialectic of appearance and reality in any plot in which the action turns on ignorance or deception and discovery; or an intention to inculcate poetically "the wholeness and complexity of things, in contrast with a partial and simple view" (to quote a recent formula for *Romeo and Juliet*) in any plot in which the characters become progressively aware that their enemies are not as bad or their friends not as good as they had thought.[110]

More recently, Richard Levin has revived Crane's cause, mocking the reflexive turn as "the new leading candidate for all-purpose thematism."[111] The challenge might lead one to ask: If we agree that these fields, at work in criticism of all the arts, are so general as to be uninformative, should we simply discard them?

We cannot do without semantic fields, for several reasons. First, interpretation needs *some* abstractions. If we seek to build implicit or symptomatic meanings, we must go beyond the concreteness of referential meanings. Moreover, we cannot ban broad semantic fields from interpretation as long as the same fields may be used in comprehending a film's overt "point" or "message." "Be a man" or "Resist patriarchy" or whatever a film might be taken to say explicitly will mobilize the same abstract semantic fields (active/passive, strength/weakness, oppression/resistance) that the critic could ascribe to other films implicitly or symptomatically.

Second, the broad fields to which Crane and Levin object pervade our culture. There are no strictly "artistic" semantic fields. All are learned and used across a wide range of social activities. This is what makes an interpretation "relevant": it connects a novel, painting, or film to semantic fields which interest people generally. To refuse to employ such fields would, in the eyes of most critics and consumers of criticism, render interpretation irrelevant to broader social life.

Finally, certain semantic fields are probably so ingrained that we, and perhaps other cultures, cannot do without them. Individual/ group, culture/nature, order/disorder, appearance/reality, and others have been used throughout history to ascribe significance to human life.[112] The interpreter can hardly give them up. Perhaps here we confront an anthropological Kantianism: certain meanings may simply constitute the grounds, or the limits, of interpretive reason.

Of course, Crane and Levin have a reply. However necessary semantic fields are to interpretation, they remain undiscriminating and banal. Perhaps, then, we should stop doing interpretation. To this I offer no answer now; I shall explore the problem further in the final chapter.

6

Schemata and Heuristics

The critic's mind is a department store: you can find everything in it: orthopaedics, sciences, bedding, arts, travelling rugs, a large selection of furniture, writing paper, smokers' requisites, gloves, umbrellas, hats, sports, walking sticks, spectacles, perfume, etc. The critic knows everything, sees everything, hears everything, eats everything, confuses everything and still manages to think.

—Erik Satie

Semantic fields are central to interpretation. They form the basis of any implicit or repressed meanings which the critic assigns to the text. This chapter and the two following seek to show that the ascription of meaning consists in *mapping* semantic fields onto textual items and patterns. The mapping metaphor, implying selective projection according to prior coordinates, follows from this book's basic assumption—that in interpretation, meaning is arrived at through an interplay of conceptual schemes and perceived cues.

Mapping as Making

In the previous chapter, for the sake of expository clarity, I assumed that the interpretive critic straightforwardly maps semantic fields onto aspects of the film. A simple version of the process is illustrated in Figure 9. As the diagram indicates, a field is typically mapped "one-to-many" onto the film. For each semantic field the critic employs in the interpretation, there will be at least one textual feature (even an "invisible" feature, as in the "structuring absence" approach) that can be correlated with each unit in the field. Often, however, several aspects of the film will bear the same semantic unit. For example, the nature/culture doublet may be manifested in the film's characters, settings, props, dialogue, and so on. The advantage of one-to-many mapping is that it produces a comprehensive interpretation while gaining in economy.

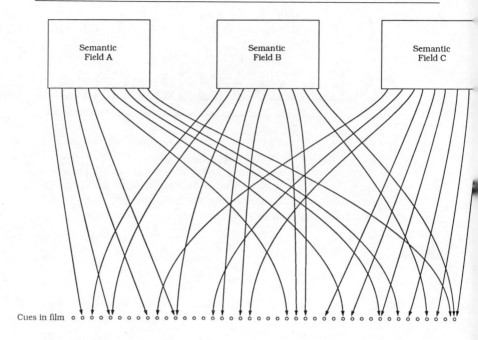

Figure 9. Mapping semantic fields: a first approximation

It is just as evident that a critic may map a field "many-to-one" onto the film. Here a single textual unit bears different semantic values drawn from distinct semantic fields. A single character may represent nature, masculinity, power, and voyeurism. (Recall, for an example, the *Movie* explication of the first shot of *Marnie*.) Many-to-one mapping yields obvious advantages: by multiplying semantic fields, the critic may attribute polysemy to a textual item. In practice, critics mix both one-to-many and many-to-one mapping, seeking a balance between explanatory breadth and economy on the one hand and local density on the other. In this mixture criticism attains its particular thickness of conceptual texture. Even gross or banal semantic units become linked or opposed, discriminated, incarnated in various guises, qualified by expressive attributes of image or sound, and come out looking comparatively nuanced.

Finally, the diagram presumes that all mapping is selective, that complete coverage of every discriminable cue offered by the film is impossible. Various theoretical justifications can be offered for this— the unique subjectivity of each critic, the infinite polysemy of cinema as a signifying system, the inevitable disjunction between meaning and material. The institutional fact remains that no critic acts as if he has completely absorbed the text into the set of semantic fields deployed. At best, the critic can declare that he has accounted for the most important or puzzling or unusual features of the film (and *this* is claimed fairly often). But no critic could claim to have wrung the film dry. This pluralism is productive; it helps interpretation keep going.

Because no critic's interpretation can encompass the film, a certain "perspectivism" is built into the contemporary interpretive institution. It is a truism that different interpreters, employing different semantic fields, will activate different aspects of the text, or will activate the same ones differently. If two interpreters set out to build implicit or symptomatic meanings from the same film, we can revise our diagram (see Figure 10). Already things are getting pretty tangled, but let us

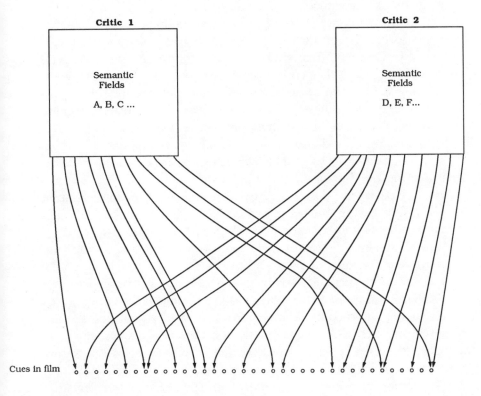

Figure 10. Competing semantic mappings

stop at two interpreters, and assume that there will still be cues which they ignore or play down.

Of course in other respects this new diagram does not go far enough. For it is misleading to present semantic fields as being projected straight onto the text. The critic has to know what aspects of the film may legitimately—that is, according to institutional protocol—prompt the interpretive act. In my terms here, the critic must learn to recognize appropriate textual *cues* for constructing interpretations. E. H. Gombrich's constructivist slogan "Making precedes matching"[1] must be supplemented by another, "Marking precedes mapping." The semantic fields, of themselves, provide no indications of what may properly bear them. Nothing about the nature/culture doublet stipulates that I must map it onto people rather than abstract patterns on the hero's wallpaper or vowels in street signs or those punches in the frame corners that indicate reel changes. Something else must mediate, helping the critic assign semantic fields to a proper range of textual features.

What mediates are reasoning processes—assumptions, hypotheses, organized bodies of knowledge, and well-practiced routines. I suggested in Chapter 2 that critics produce interpretations by using inductive inferences. The critic faces several problems—appropriateness (picking a film that is an acceptable candidate for interpretation), recalcitrant data (adjusting elements of the film to match reigning notions of what ought to be interpreted), novelty (making the interpretation fresh), and plausibility (making the interpretation persuasive). In learning to solve these problems, the critic has acquired skill in seeking out significance, interpretability, salient patterns, and exemplary passages. I also suggested that proficiency in interpretation consists in having a repertory of schemata and routines. Although these call upon more basic skills, such as analogy-making, they are not general laws but are "localized" to some degree, aimed at dealing with concrete and frequently occurring situations.[2]

These more particular schemata and routines will be my concern shortly. At this point it is simply worth recalling that the critic's search for cues is governed by normalized traditions. The critical institution steers the interpreter away from trivia toward those zones which are taken to be (a) presumably effective in spectators' responses (either potential or actual), and (b) traditionally capable of bearing meanings. With point (a), we again encounter the dependence of interpretation upon comprehension. The critic takes as given, at least initially, a posited "ordinary" viewing that makes referential sense of the film (identifies agents and settings, follows a story or argument). If explicit meaning (the film's point, moral, or message) is assumed to be un-contentious, this too can be taken for granted. The "output" of these processes of comprehension creates, more or less tacitly, points of entry for interpretation. As for criterion (b), that of traditional ac-ceptability, the interpreter relies upon her or his training, study of exemplars, disputes with other critics, and other prior experiences to determine what cues should be selected.

It is risky to be innovative in picking out cues. If we want to prove that reel-change marks are worthy vehicles for semantic fields, then we will need at least to show that they are comparable to already acceptable cues or that they have an effect on spectators' comprehen-sion of the film. The most striking recent success of this sort—Thierry Kuntzel's argument for the interpretability of credit sequences—makes a strong case for the significance of such cues on both these grounds.

The question of criteria for cues illustrates how institutionally grounded assumptions necessarily shape the process of mapping se-mantic fields. In a similar fashion, the inductive process is guided by particular, socially implanted hypotheses about how texts mean. While there are probably several such hypotheses worth spelling out, I want to concentrate briefly on the two I consider most pertinent to film interpretation: the hypothesis that textual units cohere, and the hy-pothesis that the text bears some relation to an external world.

Some presumption of unity is essential for the construction of referential and explicit meanings. Northrop Frye remarks: "'Every poem must necessarily be a perfect unity,' says Blake; this, as the wording implies, is not a statement of fact about all existing poems, but a statement of the hypothesis which every reader adopts in first trying to comprehend even the most chaotic poem ever written."[3] Again, interpretation shadows comprehension in starting from the premise that the text, as a singular and materially bounded entity, has some degree of internal coherence. Of course, the elevation of unity to a major feature or even a criterion of value is a historically variable process. Some traditions, such as midrash and Freudian dream anal-ysis, do not set much store by overall coherence. Aristotelian poetics and New Criticism, by contrast, have bequeathed to today's interpre-tive institution a predisposition to make texts cohere to a very consid-erable degree. But this is not to say that critics will always and everywhere *find* such coherence. "Organic" critics have their notion

of tension-in-harmony and variety-in-unity. Contradictory-text pro-
ponents argue that effects of unity merely camouflage deeper rifts.
The point is that for the working critic, the hypothesis of unity is in
force until it is knocked down; the text is presumed coherent until
proven otherwise.[4] Even the critic who discloses gaps and contradictions must initially posit a unity that is undermined by textual processes.

One could, moreover, argue that all critics adhere throughout their
inquiry to a hypothesis of *minimal coherence*—say, the presumption
that everything in any text is significantly related (if only by negation)
to everything else and to the pertinent semantic fields. In other words,
even the contradictory-text approach hypothesizes a degree of affinity
among textual elements. And certainly in practice most contradictory-
text readings do not posit a thoroughgoing fragmentation. Usually it
is a matter of finding one or two sore spots, or of tracing the disin-
tegration of particular semantic differences, or of pointing to a slight
falling-off of coherence. For example, Pam Cook's interpretation of
Dorothy Arzner's work as a set of contradictory texts relies on such
factors as irony, episodic construction, interruption, narrative reversals,
and an explicit play with stereotypes—none of which, even in a Hollywood film, constitutes a radically disunifying device.[5]

The other primary hypothesis I want to examine is that the text,
until shown otherwise, is held to be related in some way to an external
world—one of general human affairs and concerns—or a historical
context. In making referential meaning, the ordinary perceiver brings
into play real-world assumptions about space, time, causality, identity,
and so forth. She also makes use of vast bodies of "encyclopedic"
knowledge (English cars put the steering wheel on the right end of
the dashboard; when *Casablanca* was released, America was fighting
on the side of the Allies). The film's diegesis cannot be *wholly* other
than the world we know. It should thus come as no surprise that the
critic must posit some text-world relations in the course of building
an interpretation.[6] More specifically, these relations are taken—under
a *regulative* hypothesis—to be verisimilar.[7] In the course of problem-
solving, the critic often faces a "mimetic moment": the need to posit
some correspondence between a textual entity and some other construct derived from prior traffic with realms of experience attributed
to an intersubjective external world.

To some readers, this claim will be as scandalous as my arguing for
a coherence hypothesis, but much of its shock value drains away when

I explain that my formulation is indifferent as to theories of what the "external world" is like. I happen to believe that its physical, social, and psychic properties and patterns are not usefully characterized as just more texts to be "read" (as in the formulation "All reality is discourse"). But even if you believe that your bedroom or your friend is just another text, or is best treated as one, my point will hold. You will comprehend and interpret the settings of *The Little Foxes* according to spatial schemata derived in large part from your experience of rooms like your bedroom, and you will make sense of the film's characters largely on the basis of presuppositions about how people, such as your friend, act. Or rather, you will until you find conventionally acceptable grounds for doing otherwise. Like the coherence hypothesis, the mimesis hypothesis is a regulative one, resting on "default" or *ceteris paribus* ("all things being equal") conditions.[8] Contemporary film theory has spent a great deal of time damning mimesis as illusory (characters are not "real people," art does not copy life), but, as with the coherence hypothesis, the demystifying or contradictory-text critic must presuppose that some verisimilitude is at least sought; otherwise the critic could not reveal the text's antimimetic machinations.[9]

I must be very clear here. I do not argue on ontological or epistemological grounds that films directly copy life. I assert only that critical practice requires the interpreter to draw upon schemata and procedures built up in the context of situations outside this film and, indeed, outside any film. Chapter 7's discussion of personification and Chapter 8's account of text schemata will, I think, show that in making meaning, all critics, whatever their philosophical or ideological commitments, hypothesize particular text-world correspondences. Once again, theory proposes (doctrines) but criticism disposes (of films).

Knowledge Structures and Routines

In considering the sort of reasoning that governs mapping, I have discussed some basic assumptions, such as the need to discover cues on the basis of some actual or potential viewer's experience, and two principal regulative hypotheses, that of minimal coherence and that of mimesis. All, I stress once more, function within a particular institution at a particular time. While some are probably used in all interpretive traditions, others would not necessarily be as salient in other institutions or periods. I want now to look, in general terms, at the process of interpretive inference, for that puts the assumptions and hypotheses to work in the mapping process.

Despite differences in terminology and assumptive frameworks, cognitive theories from various disciplines have in recent years converged on a central fact about our ways of thinking. Human induction achieves its goals by using organized, selective, and simplified bodies of knowledge. For example, to understand an event as a *purchase* or a *sale* summons up a conceptual structure consisting of two agents, buyer and seller; a piece of property; and money.[10] These are taken to be the necessary components of the situation. The transaction is mentally represented as an exchange of the property for the money. In understanding that I sell a bike to Ben, you pick out the pertinent features of the empirical situation according to this structure and you assign them to the buyer/seller/property/money/exchange slots. You map, one to one, the conceptual structure onto the concrete case.

The "buy-sell" conceptual construct is internally organized: it consists of a set of relationships among types of agents, objects, actions, and states of affairs. It is also made up of data, so that you can, in a concrete case, fill in slots that are left blank. For instance, if I say, "Vance came home from the showroom with a jeep," you will probably apply the buy-sell construct and will fill in the other agent slot (the salesperson) and Vance's payment of money. Yet the construct remains a regulative one, functioning not as an absolute guarantee but only as the best current candidate for understanding the situation. If I say, "Vance came home from the showroom with a jeep. The police arrested him ten minutes later," you will probably discard the buy-sell construct and opt for a less charitable one.

Although it contains data, the construct is quite *schematic*, or diagrammatically simplified. A great many cases of buying and selling do not exactly fit the schema: a third party may act as an intermediary, or corporations may transfer stock by computer. As a simplifying construct, the schema also relegates a lot of data, such as the weather or the cut of the seller's clothes, to a low point in the hierarchy of importance. Nevertheless, the schematic structure is "basic" in that one starts with it under default assumptions and then adapts it to the concrete situation (for example, the seller slot could be filled by a company, or the money slot could be filled by a credit card). However incomplete or in need of revision the structure may be, it remains a point of departure. Whatever we call such structures—frames, scripts, models, or, as I shall here, schemata—they centrally mediate our cognitive activity.[11]

Of course, particular schemata are culturally variable. A society may lack the buy-sell schema; it may have only a "barter" schema or a "gift-giving" one or indeed nothing remotely similar. But in every society, human reasoning utilizes *some* schemata, and the principles undergirding their formation and use must be cross-cultural. This presupposes, in turn, that practical inductive reasoning is a fundamental feature of human thought, achieved by native endowment, cultural evolution, or a combination of both.

The concept of a "schema" runs back at least to Kant, who seems to have applied the term to both the knowledge structure itself (conceived, it would appear, primarily as a mental image) and the rule or procedure by which the mind produces and uses such structures.[12] Both usages can be found in the cognitive theory literature as well. For my purposes here I shall refer to the data structures used in interpretation as *schemata* and to interpretive activities (however "schematic") as *procedures* or *routines*.

The next two chapters will consider several schemata that guide the process of mapping semantic fields. For now, I need only suggest that they all constitute bodies of knowledge organized according to a basic logic and a simple structure. The buy-sell schema exemplifies what Mark Johnson and George Lakoff call a "link" schema. The underlying structure consists of two entities (buyer and seller) with something connecting them (the act of exchanging property for money). The underlying logic is that of symmetry and reciprocal dependence.[13] I shall sometimes call on Johnson and Lakoff's taxonomy to reveal the patterns underlying certain interpretive schemata.

Schemata typically generate "prototype" effects—the selection of one sort of instance as the clearest representative of the schema's essential features. The prototype of the buy/sell schema is that of a face-to-face transaction involving two individuals exchanging cash for a tangible piece of property. A televised auction in which buyers pledge to pay next year is comprehensible in terms of the schema, but it is not the "best" instance. As Lakoff indicates, prototype effects can arise from stereotypes, typical examples, ideals, and other sorts of samples.[14] All the interpretive schemata I shall be discussing produce prototype effects.

Schemata are retrieved, applied, adjusted, and rejected in the course of all perception and cognition. Within interpretive problem-solving, schemata are typically employed in what psychologists call a "top-down" manner: guided by more or less explicit goals, the critic tests abstract schemata against the empirical case. (By contrast, some aspects of comprehension, such as perception of shape or movement or color, are "bottom-up," or data-driven. Still other aspects of comprehension, such as story construction, involve both top-down and bottom-up processing.) Thus it becomes necessary to consider how schemata are *used* in a cycle of interpretive action. The routines or procedures in question consist mostly of *heuristics,* rules of thumb that have proven useful in meeting the interpretive institution's demands for novelty and plausibility.

Such heuristics are commonplace in the history of interpretation. Academics trained in New Criticism who could not reproduce, say, Richards' theoretical arguments about the psychology of language were nonetheless able to produce proper interpretations by following the hunch that metaphors and paradoxes were productive spots to look for meaning. A heuristic can be spelled out, as in St. Augustine's advice: "We must meditate on what we read till an interpretation be found that tends to establish the reign of charity."[15] This is no theory, merely a recommended step toward solving a problem. It is like the suggestion "In the classical narrative cinema, to see is to desire."[16] Unlike an algorithm, a heuristic does not guarantee a solution, but it is the best strategy for solving the ill-defined problems characteristic of interpretation in the arts.[17]

There are certain general heuristics that most problem-solvers apply in all domains. There are, for instance, what researchers have called the *representativeness* heuristic, whereby problem-solvers tend to reduce all inferential tasks to judgments of similarity, and the *availability* heuristic, whereby solutions are sought among what is most readily accessed in memory. Both are affected by a tacit criterion of *vividness,* whereby the most sensorily concrete data are given saliency. If you are considering buying a car, you are likely to take a friend's experience with the same make and model as more important than abstract information about its technical specifications, performance, and frequency-of-repair record. Deciding whether to buy the car is made easier if you let your friend's situation represent your own; the instance is also more vivid and more easily called to mind than a tangle of specifications.[18] Similarly, the critic is likely to solve the interpretive problem by likening the film to others, by seeking out the most easily recalled aspects of it, and by making the most concrete aspects of the film the most prominent cues. A corollary of these heuristics is that people tend to underutilize null or negative instances; the problem-solver is attuned to information that *confirms* the hypothesis rather than challenges it. By this logic, the critic who associates a certain object with a certain character's trait will be likely to ignore scenes in which the character displays the trait in the absence of that object.[19]

Consider, as an extended example, a common and simple interpretive routine. The critic can create a cue by making a pun. Donald Spoto writes of *Stage Fright* that the motif of cars "points to the characters' need to be authentically 'moved.' Hitchcock uses the car similarly elsewhere . . . to connote the possibility of flight and equally of motivating the will, of 'moving on' in ways more meaningful than merely geographic."[20] Another writer suggests: "Hallways and alleyways are obvious symbols of passage, and most of Ozu's late films center around passages from one stage of life to another."[21] Of *Notorious,* Andrew Sarris claims that Alicia is never more appealing to Devlin than "when she is most poisoned (figuratively as well as literally), degraded, humiliated, and disordered."[22] A symptomatic critic proposes that Dreyer's films often contain a motif of bars, a signifier of repression which appears in *Ordet* as a checkered pattern in Inger's dress and on her tablecloth; this signifies "a potentially productive female body precisely 'in check.'"[23] Quotation marks and the use of the word *literally* are clear marks of the punning maneuver.

This particular heuristic belongs to an ancient tradition. Punning often guided Stoic allegorizing of Homer and rabbinic and patristic exegeses of Scripture.[24] Freud too had constant recourse to what Josef Breuer called "a ridiculous play on words."[25] When Dora drags her leg, Freud tells her that she fears that her fantasized pregnancy is a "false step."[26] The procedure could be quickly learned: one of Freud's patients dreamed he was kissing his uncle in a car, and he supplied what Freud considered the correct interpretation: auto-eroticism.[27]

In literary criticism, Jonathan Culler suggests, puns are permitted "in cases where they contribute to coherence and do not displace a satisfactory literal reading"[28]—that is, when they satisfy what I have discussed as assumptions of unity and of pertinence to comprehension. The film critic, however, must take an extra step to arrive at puns. The interpreter of a literary text confronts a determinate lexical item which can then be punned upon.[29] The film interpreter, by contrast, must first retrieve such an item from her vocabulary and affix it to an item in the text—cars, alleyways, a poisoned woman. The lexical item must denote the cue in referential terms (it *is* a car, a passageway, and so on) and possess at least one other meaning that, although metaphorical in this context, can be synonymous with a term in an abstract semantic field. We can lay out the inferential logic of some of the above examples:

Pun: *check*
   referentially, in the diegetic world: "checkered pattern"
   figuratively: "to restrain"
      semantic unit: repression of woman's desire

Or, to take the more complicated *Stage Fright* case:

Pun: *movement*
   referentially, in the diegetic world: "to travel"
   figuratively (a): "to undergo emotional change"
      semantic unit: susceptibility to emotion
   figuratively (b): "to alter one's life" ("move on")
      semantic unit: will to change

The extra step of describing a visual or sonic cue grants the film critic more interpretive leeway than the literary critic enjoys. In a film, any image or sound permits an indefinite number of verbal descriptions, many of them rich in metaphorical implications; these can be linked by synonymity to a great number of semantic fields. It is also significant that the critic typically feels no need to justify the pun etymologically, as scriptural exegesis did. Critics can draw on metaphors that belong to sociolects that the filmmaker presumably did not share (for example, "moving on" and "passages" as 1970s Me Generation catchphrases). Indeed, in my examples, films in Japanese and Danish are redescribed using lexical items from English. Here, as in our study of semantic fields, we find that the plurality of meaning which theorists commonly assign to the text, to verbal language, or to the cinematic medium turns out to be a product of comparatively unconstrained interpretive procedures.

The conventionality of the routine is shown not only by its underlying logic but by recurrent puns appealed to by all schools of criticism. A mirror in the shot invites the critic to talk of characters "mirroring" one another or the film "mirroring" reality.[30] Characters descending from a height call forth a pun, as when the critic treats Hitchcock's characters as morally "fallen."[31] Another favorite pun involves the frame. *Beyond a Reasonable Doubt* includes a shot of a police car, framed in a rearview mirror, it in turn framed by a car windshield, with the windshield in turn enclosed by the film frame. The critic comments: "All in all a fitting climax to Spencer's attempt to 'frame' Garrett for the Patti Grey killing."[32] This is a very handy heuristic, since the critic will never see a shot that is *not* framed at least once. More generally, the pervasiveness of such puns suggests that their figurative component draws upon some of the basic metaphorical schemata involving bodily states (up/down, inside/outside) analyzed by George Lakoff and Mark Johnson.[33]

The punning maneuver illustrates how critics rely on the general problem-solving heuristics I mentioned earlier. Puns such as the ones just cited constitute judgments of *representativeness* in that they rely upon a two-step similarity inference. (The alleys *are* like passages, and spatial pathways *are* acceptable metaphors for temporal changes in life.) Puns are also attractive because they are highly *available*. They call on no specialized knowledge, only the native speaker's vocabulary. In addition, they involve easily recalled material. Psycholinguists have found that words are often stored in the mental lexicon by their sound and their rhythmic contour.[34] Puns also rank high on the *vividness* criterion, in being at once concrete and calling on sensory metaphors. Finally, the punning heuristic is remarkably easy to acquire in our culture. Any teacher of film criticism knows that college students, like Freud's uncle-osculating patient, are already predisposed to it.

This prior inclination makes punning a pointed illustration of one role of abstract theory in ordinary criticism. As part of a general appeal to theory which arose in 1970s symptomatic interpretation, critics justified the punning heuristic by reference to conceptions of language or the psyche. *Screen*'s discussion of Vygotsky's doctrine of "inner speech" endorsed criticism's use of the "literalism"—the image or line of dialogue that homonymically reduces to a metaphor.[35] Thus Willemen invokes Ophuls' own explanation of why the camera never enters the Tellier establishment in *Le Plaisir:* it is a *maison close* ("closed house," or brothel).[36] More recently, an interest in Bakhtin's theories of "polyglossia" has had as one effect the ratifying of the same routine. "Camera angles," write a pair of critics, "can literalise specific locutions such as 'look up to' or 'oversee' or 'look down on.'"[37] According to the same critics, in *The Wrong Man,* the line "Manny plays the bass" refers literally to his instrument but figuratively to something else: "He also plays the role of the *base* when he is falsely accused and forced to mimic the actions of the real thief."[38] Significantly, the interpretive maneuver long preceded the theoretical rationale. In 1927 a *Variety* critic mocked *The Street* because a character constantly carried an umbrella. "Perhaps it's there to show that into each life some rain must fall."³⁹ Theorists would claim that inner speech or polyglossia helps explain comprehension; I am arguing that long-standing habits of interpretation explain why theorists are drawn to these concepts. This heuristic is not a rule derived from deductive reasoning but another cognitive procedure developed by the institution for craft-centered ends.

As the punning heuristic suggests, most routines aim at helping the critic find applicable semantic fields.⁴⁰ To take another example: Interpreters employ a "stepping-stone" procedure to move across clusters or oppositional series. In interpreting *The General,* one critic argues that woman is associated with passivity, and thus stasis, and thus photography. Each shift requires the critic to posit a semantic unit that overlaps with, but is not identical to, the next.⁴¹ The tactic is often mandatory for critics working with theoretically defined semantic fields, as when the psychoanalytic critic must pass from a given premise (for example, voyeuristic fetishism is associated with the representation of woman) to a particular clinical category (for example, hysteria, paranoia, psychosis).⁴² As a problem-solving procedure, this calls on the same skills tapped by the associative word game called "stepping stones," which sets such tasks as "Move from *drinks* to *cricket,* by way of *transport* and *Christmas.*"⁴³ In the puzzle and in critical interpretation, the necessary steps depend on the semantic similarity revealed by the representativeness heuristic and, during some steps, on availability and vividness.

Mapping as Modeling

These schemata and routines, pervading human problem-solving practices, feed into a particular routine that is central to film interpretation. In mapping semantic fields onto the film, guided by schemata and heuristics, the critic produces approximations of the film at hand—mental *models* of it.⁴⁴ Unlike schemata, which are stable, persistent, and of general application, mental models are "transient, dynamic representations of particular unique situations."⁴⁵

Suppose that I am trying to produce an interpretation of *Raw Deal* (1948). I might hypothesize that the driven male protagonist and the film's overall style put it into the class of film noir. This move will recast the film along certain lines, throwing particular cues into relief and downplaying others. I might then follow interpretive traditions within the institution and start to project some semantic fields—say, male castration anxieties. This will lead me to refine my model by picking out particular cues to carry those fields. But since the institution also suggests that I incorporate beginnings and endings into my model film, I might notice that the film is organized around a woman's flashback. The model film gets revised again, with the temporal rearrangement and the woman as "center of consciousness" becoming more prominent. These features in turn might recall *Mildred Pierce,* but with this difference: *Raw Deal* does not make the woman the protagonist; she is only a passive witness. My model now starts to shape up as a sketch for a contradictory text. In a male-dominated genre like film noir, turning the narration over to the woman can be taken as a symptomatic expression of the threat that the genre normally seeks to repress. And so the process goes. Using various schemata (such as those of genre and textual structure) and skills of analogical inference, the critic may build up several versions of the film before finding an acceptable fit.

The one that fits—that, in the critic's judgment, solves the interpretive problem, yielding sufficient particularity and "coverage"—becomes *the* model, the final "output" of the mapping process. That output is not just semantic fields plus certain aspects of the film. The critic produces a totality—the film unified under a description which organizes those aspects of the film she has picked out and weighted with semantic values. In constructing an interpretation, the critic has in a sense reconstructed the text. The critic can come to conclusions about many things—the nature of art, the wellsprings of virtue or oppression—but insofar as she claims to be interpreting a film, she produces a model film. And as semantic fields and the aspects of the film activated will vary among critics, so will the model films produced. If you think that *Rules of the Game* implies the decadence and decline of the bourgeoisie of prewar France, your model film is organized around that meaning, highlighting certain cues, playing down or omitting others, and bringing in certain schemata. If you take *Rules of the Game* to be symptomatically betraying the male's fear of castration, you will construct a different model film—perhaps sharing some features with the other one, but still differing in its patterning, weightings, and assigned meanings.

Because of the selectivity and "perspectivism" involved in the process, the model film is inevitably an approximation. It offers a thinned-out revision of the film as comprehended (itself a reconstruction of that posited entity, the "film itself"). At the same time, however, by being more cleanly organized and freighted with definite conceptual significance, the model film becomes a sharper, neater version. It is like the fashion "model" who, spurning the vivacious disorder of wearing clothes for everyday purposes, offers instead an immediately available contour, an assured stance, and a conventional elegance.

By now it should be clear that mapping semantic fields onto the film is far from a straightforward affair. The fields are mapped selectively, many-to-one and one-to-many. The critic frames hypotheses about what may count as acceptable vehicles for such fields. The critic makes hypotheses about unity and the relation of the text to the world. More specifically, the interpreter possesses a great many schemata, some geared to comprehension and others, more the province of experts, involving interpretation. And the interpreter makes use of both general and particular problem-solving heuristics, such as drawing analogies, deriving puns and overlapping associations, and building mental models. The final product of interpretation—the film-as-interpreted, the "model film"—is the result of a complex, highly mediated process. Not until the end of Chapter 8 will it be possible to represent this process fully in a diagram, but for now, let Figure 11 stand as a revision of my earlier ones.

Note that no mastery of theory need play a part in this process. A critic trained in the proper assumptions, hypotheses, schemata, and routines should be able to produce an acceptable interpretation without benefit of theoretical knowledge. This is not to say that these activities do not have theoretical implications; they do in any realm of reasoning. Nor is this to say that film theory, like other bodies of knowledge, cannot help in particular cases. Nor is it to underestimate the importance of theory as a rhetorical appeal; later on, I shall argue that the invocation of theory may encourage a particular audience to find one's interpretation novel or plausible. I claim only that skill in creating, understanding, or defending theoretical arguments is neither a necessary nor a sufficient condition for the solving of interpretive problems. As usual, we must look beneath what critics say and examine what they—concretely, practically—do.

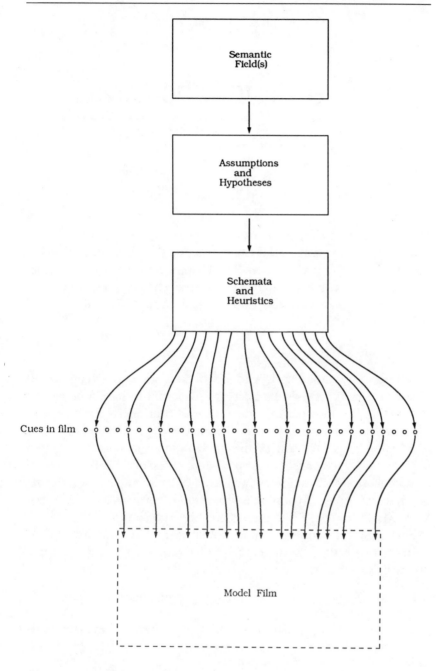

Figure 11. Mediations in the mapping process

7

Two Basic Schemata

What do *those* balloons mean?

—Dr. Cheryl Kinsey

If schemata are as important as I have claimed, we ought to be able to identify the most significant ones. I argue that four principal schemata govern film interpretation. This chapter considers category schemata and person-based schemata; the next chapter concentrates on two schemata that represent textual organization.

Is There a Class for This Text?

Perception and thought depend upon categories. To recognize an object or event is to possess a schema for it and to have a procedure for judging it a member of some class.[1] Critical interpretation splendidly exemplifies the importance of categories in problem-solving. The critic cannot treat the text as absolutely unique; it must belong to a larger class.[2] Here again, interpretation relies on the processes of comprehension. Making referential sense of a film requires several acts of "framing" it: as a fiction, as a Hollywood movie, as a comedy, as a Steve Martin movie, as a "summer movie," and so on.

The most common grouping mobilized in film interpretation is associated with the idea of genre. The concept actually involves three problems of categorization:

1. The definition of genre as a *principle*, distinguishing it from other types of concepts.
2. The framework that defines a *system* of genres, discriminating one from another.
3. The definition of a *single* genre.

One could try to spell out necessary and sufficient conditions for any of these definitions, but film critics have been notably uninterested in doing so. Indeed, all the results so far indicate that no such conditions can be found. Theorists have been unsuccessful in producing a coherent map of the system of genres, and no strict definition of a single genre has won widespread acceptance. A Western seems identified primarily by its setting, a science-fiction film by its technology, a musical by its manner of presentation (song and dance). Thus one could have a science-fiction musical Western, in which Martians visit Billy the Kid and everyone puts on a show. (Of course, this could also turn out to be a comedy, but how is *that* genre defined?) One cannot safely appeal to historical norms, since many currently accepted genres, such as melodrama or film noir, did not exist as categories for audiences or filmmakers of the 1930s or 1940s. One could instead try, as several scholars recently have, to define a genre by certain thematic materials. Yet while the musical or the Western may display recurrent themes, any theme may appear in any genre, for the simple reason that no semantic field is barred from appearing in any sort of film. Efforts to date suggest that Boris Tomashevsky was right sixty years ago in claiming that because genre markers vary and overlap, no strictly deductive set of principles can explain genre groupings: "No firm logical classification of genres is possible. Their demarcation is always historical, that is to say, it is correct only for a specific moment of history; apart from this they are demarcated by many features at once, and the markers of one genre may be quite different in kind from the markers of another genre and logically they may not exclude one another, only being cultivated in different genres because of the natural connection of compositional devices."[3]

The difficulty of defining *a* genre is nothing compared to the task of defining *genre* as opposed to *mode, cycle, formula,* or whatever. Is film noir a genre, a style, or a cycle? Is experimental film a style, a genre, or a mode? Are animation and documentary film genres or modes? Is the filmed play or comedy performance a genre? If tragedy and comedy are genres, perhaps then domestic tragedy or slapstick is a formula. One could, following Tomashevsky's hint, argue that the concept of genre is so historically mutable that no set of necessary and sufficient conditions can mark off genres from other sorts of groupings in ways that all experts or ordinary film-goers would find acceptable.[4]

Yet critics have not let theoretical difficulties stop the march of interpretation. Interpreters no more have strict definitions of genre than speakers of English have definitions of *game* (to take the most famous example in the philosophical literature).[5] Genre would seem to be an "open-textured" concept, and genres are treated as "fuzzy" categories, definable neither by necessary and sufficient conditions nor by fixed boundaries. The processes by which people construct a fuzzy category do not define it but rather provide a loose set of more or less central, more or less strongly linked expectations—default hierarchies—that are taken to hold good unless contradicted by other information. Musicals are typically comic, but *A Star Is Born* (1954) causes us to revise our expectations, not redefine the musical. Such categories are organized, in Johnson's and Lakoff's terms, as a core/periphery schema, with the more "central" members of the category creating a prototype effect. Just as chess serves as a prototype of games, so *Singin' in the Rain* is a prototypical musical. Any acceptable notion of the musical must include it, and it is taken as a better, more vivid example of the genre than, say, *Ivan the Terrible,* which has plenty of song and dance numbers. Horrific as *Close and Rocking Encounters with Billy the Kid* promises to be, it will not demolish our notions of musicals, Westerns, and science-fiction films; we will probably just shove it to the periphery of all these categories, never using it as a prototype for any of them. Far from being concerned with definition or reasoning from genus to species, critics often identify the genre only to aid in interpreting the particular work.[6] The identification is transitory and heuristic, like that of nearly all the categories we draw upon in everyday life.[7] Genres, and genre, function as open-ended and corrigible schemata.

The handling of genre serves as a prototype of the critic's acts of classification. Fiction/documentary, narrative/nonnarrative, mainstream/oppositional—such alternatives function in critical arguments, as they function in comprehension, as enabling schemata, not closed, deductively guaranteed categories. The separating stroke can always be blurred, the categories are always permeable. (Indeed, often the critic's aim is to show that the film at hand has broken out of its category.) The variety of categories at work in film criticism—grouping by period or country (American films of the 1930s), by director or star or producer or writer or studio, by technical process (CinemaScope films), by cycle (the "fallen woman" films), by series (007 movies), by style (German Expressionism), by structure (narrative), by ideology (Reaganite cinema), by venue ("drive-in movies"), by purpose (home movies), by audience ("teenpix"), by subject or theme (family films, paranoid-politics movies)—all this should bewilder only the system-builder. This diversity is rather the mark of an institution that offers the interpreter many tools for making meaning.

Such categories, for instance, allow the critic to establish referential or explicit meaning (guaranteed by genre conventions) as a point of departure. Thus Constance Penley can use the conventions of the science-fiction subgenre of "critical dystopias" to identify explicit meanings in *The Terminator*.[8] Accepted categories also permit the critic to appeal to the semantic fields that critical tradition has already assigned to that category. Ozu's films can be taken as centering on the dissolution of the family, melodramas as questioning the basis of romantic love and kinship ties. The default hierarchy for the Western encourages the critic to start with the wilderness/civilization, nature/culture doublets. Reciprocally, any semantic field can found a category schema if the critic can find some prototypical cases and some guidelines for mapping the field onto recurrent cues. Watch a group of critics construct a new category, complete with prototypes: "One can associate *The Reckless Moment* with a (trans-generic) cycle of films which emerge in Hollywood during the 'forties, alongside the themes and iconography of the 'film noir' and which express that increasingly disturbed preoccupation with the tensions and ambiguities of 'settlement' and the family which reaches full, conscious, elaborated expression in the work of, say, Ray and Sirk in the 'fifties."[9] Reflexivity is likewise not only a semantic field; it also serves as the basis of a category of films, possessing a default hierarchy based on the presence of explicit or tacit references to cinema and a set of core cases *(Man with a Movie Camera, 8½)* that can provide analogies for building a model of the film at hand.

Perhaps now we can see one reason why critics committed to a symptomatic theory of meaning do not apply it to films which oppose mainstream practice. The category schema of "oppositional cinema" highlights a self-consciousness about representation that also underlies the critic's own interpretive act. The film simply belongs to a category which does not (at least at its core) harbor repressed meanings. The oppositional film's revelation of repressed contradictions functions as its central "genre convention."

Like any schemata, received categories can be revised. They offer fruitful points of difference and dispute. *Touch of Evil* can be discussed as a thriller, a film noir, a Welles film, a 1950s film, an expressionist film, or, from Stephen Heath's perspective, a prototype of "obvious" cinema.[10] At a certain point in history, the critic may recast a commonplace about the category. If previous writers have said that film noir is concerned primarily with the loss of secure identity, a critic may argue that this theme is in fact a by-product of the assignment of certain roles and values to the female characters.[11] By and large, the contradictory-text movement accepted categories estabished by studies in genre and authorship, arguing that each one harbored gaps and disparities. Eventually, the "contradictory text" itself became a category schema with its own prototypes (*Young Mr. Lincoln, The Birds, Touch of Evil*).

Perhaps the most powerful category schema of recent years has been that of a "classical" American filmmaking, and it has undergone repeated revision. Bazin saw classical cinema as a tradition that assured aesthetic stability, technical proficiency, and generic variety. Yet for the auteurists, classicism often provided a backdrop of bland efficiency against which the idiosyncratic director stood out. During the rise of structuralism, the classical cinema was conceived chiefly as a myth machine. With the coming of symptomatic criticism, the poise that Bazin had ascribed to the classical film was shown to be precarious, produced at the cost of massive repression of ideological tensions. Within contemporary critical schools the category continues to be reworked. For the 1970s *Cahiers* critics, *Young Mr. Lincoln* typifies the gaps and fissures produced by authorial intervention; for Robin Wood in his symptomatic phase, the film exemplifies such a high degree of control and moral certitude that it can form the background for a truly incoherent work like Penn's *The Chase*.[12] Classical Hollywood cinema can be seen as a form, a style, a set of themes, or a mesh of ideological and psychic processes, and each version of the schema will produce different prototypes, privilege diverse semantic fields, and make various cues salient within a film.

Sometimes new category schemata are derived from other arts or media. Auteurism and genre studies are obviously modeled on groupings at work in literary and art history. "Avant-garde cinema" as we understand it today is grounded in the category of American avant-garde painting, whose major movements (abstract expressionism, Pop, minimalism), strategies (reflexivity, flatness), and techniques were "matched" to particular tendencies in filmmaking.[13] During the late 1960s, "Brechtian film," made analogous to Brechtian theater, became a category schema that could help map new semantic fields onto new cues.[14] The critic can acquire some individuality by creating his or her own genre, as Stanley Cavell has in interpreting the "comedy of remarriage," while Comolli and Narboni were able to persuade many practical critics of the usefulness of the "Cinema/Ideology/Criticism" taxonomy delineating various ways in which a film could relate to

ideology.[15] Most recently, "postmodernist" films have come to constitute a category possessing salient cues, prototypes, and characteristic
semantic fields.[16]

To ensure wide coverage of the film's details, the skillful critic
mobilizes several category schemata within any one enterprise. Robert
Stam consigns *Sauve qui peut (la vie)* to three classes: Godard's oeuvre,
reflexive films, and erotic films.[17] For Roswitha Mueller, *The Image of
Dorian Gray in the Yellow Press* can be interpreted in the light of Lang's
Mabuse films, Ottinger's other films, Oedipal dramas, and literary
adaptations.[18] The academic institution encourages critics to mix their
tools; textual cues that do not fit into one category schema invite the
critic to bring in another category that will invoke pertinent semantic
fields.[19]

No thought starts from scratch, and no interpretation can do without category schemata. Although they form what Wittgenstein calls
"a complicated network of similarities overlapping and crisscross-
ing,"[20] they are indispensable tools for the practical critic. The apprentice critic must learn these categories' range, their specific powers,
the etiquette of their use, and the proper times to recast or reject
them.

Making Films Personal

"Teeth remember," says my dentist, thereby endowing them with
properties that help me understand why he can't put in a new filling.
"It thinks it should get its queen out early," complains a software
designer about a rival chess-playing program.[21] The program thinks
no such thing, but the characterization enables me to schematize the
contraption as a rational human opponent, and perhaps even win
against it. We project humanlike properties onto so many domains of
activity that we ought not to be surprised that they also feature in
that esoteric realm known as film criticism.[22] The mimetic hypothesis
reappears: the notion of the person is basic to our making sense of
the external world.[23] The person schema also exemplifies the vividness
heuristic. It is easier for a patient to imagine teeth remembering than
to recall a string of X rays and charts.

In similar ways, the critic scans the text for cues that answer to
criteria for "personhood." In what follows, I shall treat the notion of
the person not as a logical or metaphysical category but as a social
and psychological schema, for it is chiefly in this respect that it func-

tions in interpretation.[24] It generates several heuristics that move the critic toward institutionally acceptable interpretations. Furthermore, I shall assume that the schema of the "person," at least in contemporary Western cultures, includes at least the following folk-psychological features:

1. A human body, presumed to be singular and unified.
2. Perceptual activity, including self-awareness.
3. Thoughts, including beliefs.
4. Feelings or emotions.
5. Traits, or persisting dispositional qualities.
6. The capacity for self-impelled actions, such as communication, goal-formation and -achievement, and so on.

The person schema, in ordinary thought as in interpretation, functions as a context-bound cluster of these features. The common-sense prototype of the person is the putatively sane, mentally active and un-coerced human adult. In any given instance, some of these features may be absent or present in lesser degree; to this extent, the case will be problematic. An infant, we might say, is on the way to becoming a person. A prenatal child or a permanently comatose adult is not as clear a candidate for personhood.[25]

It is part of the critic's mapping process to ascribe such folk-psychological traits to aspects of the film, and this can be done by following particular routines. The critic uses the schema to build up more or less "personified" agents in, around, underneath, or behind the text. Such agents, once endowed with thoughts, feelings, actions, traits, and bodies, become capable of carrying semantic fields.[26] I shall call this set of heuristics *personification*. Although my usage deviates significantly from classical precedent, I defend it on two grounds: I can't think of a better term ("personalization" reminds me too much of monogrammed bracelets and cryptic license plates); and it is at least faithful to one way of construing the term's etymology—*persona* ("person") plus *facere* ("to make").[27] To ascribe memory to teeth, chess strategy to swarms of electrons, hauteur to cats, voyeurism to movie cameras, and duplicity to narrators is to make meaning by "making persons."

Characters as Persons

Let us take characters to be any agents, fictional or not, assumed to inhabit the film's world. From this perspective, Roger Thornhill, Bob

Dylan, and Donald Duck are characters in certain films. It is evident that constructing characters on the model of the person is fundamental to comprehension. The simplest "referential" construal gets nowhere if it does not identify persons or personlike agents in the film. In fact, this process would seem to be a culturally universal feature of humans' ways of making sense of texts.[28]

Of course, interpreters would not *have* to follow such commonsense heuristics. We could decide to ignore personification and assign semantic fields to any other perceptible variables. We could, say, plot the shifts of color in the frame's lower left corner, and assert that when the color black is present, that means "culture," and that when the color white is present, that means "nature," and that when gray is present, there is a mediation. We could do all this; but no one would listen. We could devise any number of interpretive heuristics, as complicated as we like. The institutional fact remains that such systems would seem fancifully arbitrary. Critics rank cues hierarchically, and at the top of the list are human agents performing actions. Moreover, it seems likely that such a ranking is justified as a case of interpretation's shadowing of comprehension. Humans are predisposed, biologically and culturally, to attend to humanlike agents in representations. The character-as-person schema seems obvious because it is ours; it is us.

The person schema allows the critic to ascribe several features to represented human agents in a film. Characters are embodied; they can be assumed to perceive, think, and feel; they seem to display traits and to execute actions. Any description of their personal qualities can be reworked so as to bear semantic fields. For example, in *Cahiers's Young Mr. Lincoln* exemplar, Lincoln's awkwardness at Mary Todd's party becomes a symptom. The scene "involves him (socially and sexually) in a seduction relationship which simultaneously *integrates and excludes him;* this causes a confusion which is not resolved dramatically." The critics produce a repressed meaning: Lincoln cannot be integrated because the Law (which he represents) is symbolically "Other."[29] In order to pinpoint an ideological disparity in the text, the critics draw an ordinary inference from Lincoln's behavior and use that as a basis for mapping a semantic field. In such ways, interpretation plows more deeply the ground first broken by comprehension.

My survey of semantic fields in Chapter 5 revealed something relevant in this connection. The clusters, doublets, proportional series, and hierarchies discussed there typically took characters as their vehicles. The opposition confinement/freedom which Mast located in the opening of *Bringing Up Baby* tallies with the opposition Miss Swallow/

Susan Vance; de Lauretis' discussion of *Bad Timing* groups the characters into males versus female, and then separates the two male characters along another duality; Kavanaugh's Greimasian analysis of *Alien* assigns different slots to the characters. We can now see that what makes this possible is personification. Starting from concrete descriptions of characters along the lines of bodily features, traits, actions, and so on, the critic can align them with semantic fields.

Indeed, any aspect of the person schema can serve as a cue for applying a semantic field. We can concentrate on gesture or comportment, as Jacques Rivette does when he attributes significance to the "lassitude of demeanor" in *Voyage to Italy*.[30] Or, like most critics, we can pay special attention to dialogue. Teresa de Lauretis is able to treat *Bad Timing*'s Milena as signifying a purely feminine temporal register because at one point she shouts, "What about my time?"[31] More circuitously, J.-P. Oudart makes Efrosinia in *Ivan the Terrible* a mother-figure by treating Ivan's praise of her as an inversion of the calumnies which the boyars flung at his mother.[32] It may not be too much to say that verbal language, supplemented by facial expression and narrative role, forms the most important cue for critical interpretation of narrative cinema. As in life, we make inferences about individuals largely on the basis of what they say.

In mapping semantic fields onto the film, the simplest strategy is to assign different units of meaning to different characters. Pick out a range of behaviors, a set of traits, a line of dialogue, a costume, or some other cues. Then make them, by virtue of the representativeness heuristic, stand for an abstract semantic value. Typically, what a character *is* or *has* can be translated into what the character *means*.[33] Movie critics popularized the gambit of making a character stand for "a way of life," which in turn implied values of semantic consequence. For V. F. Perkins, *River of No Return* presents the opposition between Kay's emotionalism and Matt's reliance on law and reason.[34] According to Robin Wood, in *Persona* Alma represents the "hollow conventionality" of unfulfilled normality while Elisabeth represents a deeper awareness of life's horror.[35]

As such examples suggest, there is a strong tendency to align semantic fields with relations among characters. Two characters in conflict not only represent oppositional doublets but also enact a more abstract struggle between the terms. In Murnau's films, a critic writes, one character represents the threat of sexuality (for example, Nosferatu), while another will represent feminized masculinity (for example,

Jonathan Harker).[36] The same strategy yields results when the semantic fields are structured in other ways. In *I Vitelloni,* Eugene Archer finds, each character illustrates the theme of entrapment: Fausto pursues sexual conquests, Leopoldo is the failed intellectual, Alberto is the introverted clown, and Moraldo is tied to childhood.[37] James Collins sees Joe Dante's *Explorers* as contrasting two kinds of "postmodernist subjects" (a semantic field which in itself eases the move to a character-centered account). Here the alien creatures, incapable of recognizing difference, represent postmodern subjectivity as theorized by Jean Baudrillard. In contrast, the children represent a subjectivity that seizes on one "discourse" and makes it the privileged mode for representing experience. Collins then proposes a branching hierarchy whereby the three children correspond to three such modes: "semi-hard science," nineteenth-century fantastic adventure, and contemporary rock culture.[38]

As persons, characters talk, think, feel, and act. They also perceive—which is to say that they mostly look and listen. Characters probably listen almost as much as they look, but for a long time critics have taken visual activity to offer the more valuable interpretive cue. Since 1930 or so, the "Kuleshov effect" has alerted film aestheticians to characters' gazes and glances. In a chapter of *The Movies* called "Performers and Onlookers," Wolfenstein and Leites claim that Hollywood films treat the act of seeing as a displacement of Oedipal conflicts, echoing the situation of the excluded child spying on parents.[39] Later, throughout the 1950s and 1960s, discussions of Hitchcock's technique induced critics to note and interpret shifts in point of view.

After Lacan and Foucault mapped new semantic fields onto the act of looking, film critics fastened on the look in earnest. The *Cahiers* editors wrote of young Mr. Lincoln's "castrating" stare; Pam Cook and Claire Johnston treated Mamie Stover's look to the camera as asserting herself to be a subject of desire; Laura Mulvey distinguished between the voyeuristic look in Hitchcock and the fetishistic look in von Sternberg. Looking for the look is currently one of the critic's most productive heuristics, and whatever semantic quality gets assigned to it—power over the object of the look, the constitution of subjectivity through the look of the Other, sadism or masochism, external directorial authority or a character's narcissism—it remains inextricably part of the character's embodiment, traits, goals, and relations with other characters. It is pure, if sometimes abstruse, personification.

The critic can make persons out of characters in still other ways. There is the possibility, for instance, of elevating a character to the status of *raisonneur*. Marie, in Truffaut's *Domicile conjugal,* remarks, "If you don't follow politics, politics will get you in the end." The critic can thus take her as Truffaut's mouthpiece.[40] The critic can also treat characters as different aspects of a single personality, as when Laurence Wylie suggests that in *Rules of the Game,* Robert's two women represent two aspects of his character, civilized manners and naive virtue.[41] Conversely, the critic can make two persons out of the same body. Since the 1960s, the influence of Brecht has alerted critics to the possibility of ascribing divergent traits, goals, thoughts, and so on to the performer and to the character. "The real conflict," writes a critic of Warhol's narrative films, "is of the actors with their roles."[42] Or the critic can simply opt for the broadest ascriptions possible, taking a character as a new incarnation of a mythical figure or symbolic force. The anonymous woman on the bed in Bruce Conner's *A Movie* can seem, by the film's end, "Eve or Circe or Prime Mover."[43] Here the specific character's actions or qualities are mapped onto those traditionally aligned with particular semantic fields.

Some readers may object that my account of character personification holds good only for the explicatory tradition. The symptomatic critic, according to this account, does not subscribe to such a naive view of character because he does not fall into the illusion that the film, even the documentary film, presents "real people." Every film is a fiction film in that the profilmic event is thoroughly "textualized" by the discursive processes at work. "Character" is considered as much a structural process and effect as is spatio-temporal continuity or unified meaning.

Once more I need to clarify my claim. The critic does not believe that the film presents "real people." The critic constructs the characters by means of a schema she also applies to real people (and animals, teeth, computers, and whatnot). This schema shapes our conception of agents within the film, and whatever character constructs result may be more *or* less consistent, variable, or fleshed out than any conceptions we have of the people we know around the house or the gym. Moreover, the examples cited in this chapter and earlier ones overwhelmingly show that critics of all stripes, whatever their articulated "theory" of character, rely at the outset on folk-psychological intuitions about persons. Criticism as we know it would not be possible if the critic did not assume that, for instance, a person's overt speech and action are *ceteris paribus* caused by traits, goals, or other internal states. (Here ordinary criticism calls on another traditional meaning of *personification,* which implies that only through externals—the *persona,* or mask— can the perceiver identify the character's inner qualities.) In a loose sense, character is "an effect of the text," but it is more accurate to say that the spectator reworks cues provided by the text to produce inferences about referential, explicit, implicit, and/or symptomatic meanings. Treating character construction as "active making" might lead to a more precise explanation of the pertinent processes than structuralist conceptions of character (and before them Aristotelian and Slavic Formalist accounts) have yielded.[44]

But all this is theory. In contemporary practice, "person perception" provides a point of departure for even those critics who insist that the textual structuration creates characters, and character. Consider one case. Interpreting Carlos Saura's *Carmen,* Marvin D'Lugo asserts that the male protagonist, Antonio, "is less an individual character than the figuration of a kind of social mentality." Likewise, Carmen comes to operate "not so much as a psychologically-defined character, but as the embodiment of an instinct and naturalness which are the antithesis of the rehearsed and performed."[45] Yet in order to make the protagonists bear abstract semantic values, D'Lugo must treat them as full-blown conscious agents. Antonio has "a culturally-determined mentality"; he "listens intently" to a tape; he displays a "profound submission to art as an intuitive response to personal experience."[46] On one occasion his words betray a "painful knowledge."[47] True, Antonio has a *false* consciousness; the spectator comes to see his life as an imposture. Nevertheless, such a realization requires the viewer to construct the character as a person. Carmen is less exactly delineated, but she can still learn dance steps, engage in rivalry with other women, "transpose her real-life animosity against Cristina into the theatrical role she is playing,"[48] and, most important, decide to tell Antonio that everything is over between them. However the critic may wish to make the characters represent abstract semantic fields—spectacle, artistic bad faith, spontaneity, or repressed aspects of Spanish history— they are, if only as an initial step, constructed according to the person schema.

The Filmmaker as a Person

The critic can use the person-based schema to construct another agent capable of bearing semantic weight: the filmmaker. One or more people can be taken to be the source of the film. The filmmaker can be cast as director, writer, producer, star, "film artist," collaborator, or whatever. (For consistency of exposition and in deference to the strongest critical tradition, I shall treat the filmmaker as the director.) Consequently, the film can be considered a product of individual or group activity: a statement, message, symptom, or artifact.

The personification of the filmmaker follows the same path as the interpretation of character. A personlike agent is posited, and external cues—here, aspects of the film—are taken to reveal perceptions, thoughts, feelings, decisions, communicative goals, and so on. Now, however, these are ascribed to an absent body, the filmmaker, who exists but who is not usually incarnated in the film.

Despite their debts to the objectivist, text-centered side of New Criticism, most explicatory critics use the schema of the personified filmmaker. And although symptomatic critics often declare the irrelevance of the creator's intention, the emptiness of crude auteurism, and the death of the author, we find this heuristic in the symptomatic camp as well.

Personification of the filmmaker clearly underlies auteur criticism. Bazin admired the *politique des auteurs* for its attempt to discern "the man behind the style."[49] But this formulation covers a lot of ground. The critic can utilize a "rational-agent" personification. On the assumption that the folk-psychological schema endows persons with the capacity to adjust means to ends, the interpreter assumes the filmmaker to aim at particular effects. Because Douglas Sirk, the man, is familiar with modern theater, Paul Willemen argues that he consciously creates symbolic, nonillusionist works.[50] Once Godard's voice enters the soundtrack of *Two or Three Things I Know about Her,* says another critic, we understand that he is the agency choosing and ordering the shots.[51]

The rational-agent personification also appears frequently in those writings of symptomatic critics in an explicatory mood. Here the oppositional filmmaker is granted considerable voluntary control over meanings and effects. For one critic, Peter Greenaway's *Draughtsman's Contract* achieves the critique of representation that the director attempted.[52] In D'Lugo's essay on *Carmen,* he quotes Saura on the relation of the dance spectator to rehearsal mirrors; the director's words are used to establish the interpretive significance of "the eyes of the other."[53]

The critic's very description of the avant-garde filmmaker's activity can point to an agent energetically posing questions and making points. The task is easiest when the filmmaker is explicitly present, in the frame or as a voice-over. Then the critic can, for instance, refer to Laura Mulvey and Peter Wollen's *Amy!* as offering "a psychoanalytic reading of what is happening to Amy through the device of Mulvey's words, spoken in her authorial persona role."[54] Usually, however, the critic infers the filmmaker-as-agent from the film text. One essay on Leslie Thornton's *Adynata* asserts that the filmmaker *investigates* the representation of the Orient, *aligns* it with femininity, *shows interest* in the traces of sexual difference on the soundtrack, *displays an obsession* with found footage, *mimics* scientific genres, *cuts* language apart, *chooses* sounds and images, and seeks to *explore* overly familiar language. The critic also quotes the filmmaker to exhibit the latter's awareness of controlling meaning.[55] Assumptions about origin-of-the-text author-ship are hard to avoid, even for critics who are—in theory—aware that since medieval exegesis, the string of terms *auctor, auctoritas, authenticus* inevitably linked author, authority, and authenticity.[56]

Someone might retort that much of this directorial personification is mere phrasing, that one could rewrite such claims as statements about what the *film* does. I shall argue in more detail in Chapter 9 that wording actually matters quite a lot. But even when the film, not the filmmaker, is the subject of the sentence, the rational-calculator personification can be implied. The film can be made analogous to a deliberate act—an "essay" (*High Noon* as "a very beautiful essay on solitude"[57]), a "commentary," an analysis, an experiment, a reflection.[58] Avant-garde criticism that calls on phenomenological reflexivity often characterizes the film as "demonstrating" the flatness of the screen or the illusionistic aspects of perspective—the verb being in keeping with the didactic purposes which other traditions impute to the filmmaker.

To the filmmaker as rational calculator we can counterpose the idea of the filmmaker *expressing* himself or herself. Now the film becomes analogous to a confession, a lyric, a journal, a diary, an intimate revelation, even a dream. As I indicated in Chapter 3, the rise of the art cinema, with its emphasis on personal expression and marketable directorial differences, encouraged critics to rake films for implicit meanings of this sort. Godard's later films, according to a critic, are "profoundly personal endeavors" arising from "real existential pain."[59] For Colin MacCabe, the "dissatisfaction" at the center of *Sauve qui peut (la vie)* expresses the director's attitude to filmmaking, a mood that became evident "on the occasions that I visited Godard last year."[60] The salient schematic features here are the person's emotions and memories, the latter because autobiography tends to accompany this personification. *A King in New York* can be said to be about Chaplin's travails in America.[61] The projection scene of *Muriel* can reflexively represent the director's nostalgia and despair over the political film that could not be made.[62]

Classic auteur criticism, while not at all averse to autobiography, made use of a milder version of the "self-expression" heuristic. Just as the critic builds a character's personality out of bits of comportment and repeated actions, so he can infer the director's personality on the basis of aspects of the single film and repeated elements from film to film. From Bazin's monograph on Welles to the end of the 1960s, the thrust of the *Cahiers*-Sarris-*Movie* tradition was to show how the director's work embodied what Jean Domarchi in 1954 called "a personal conception of the world."[63] In particular, the artist's personality is assumed to be revealed in film style. "The way a film looks and moves should have some relationship to the way a director thinks and feels."[64] *Cahiers* applauds Sirk for not subordinating his personality to Faulkner's in filming *Tarnished Angels;* Sirk's pointless camera movements reveal only his enjoyment of technique; his excessive artificiality is more sincere because more authentic.[65]

The self-expressive conception of the filmmaker is particularly prominent in interpretation of the American avant-garde. After linking Stan Brakhage to abstract expressionism, Sitney treats the lyrical films as finding a form "in which the filmmaker could compress his thoughts and feelings while recording his direct confrontation with intense experiences of birth, death, sexuality, and the terror of nature."[66] The symptomatic critic can also stray into this region, as when the filmmaker is personified as a gendered body. Patricia Erens finds that one amateur moviemaker unwittingly expresses cultural differences by framing shots of women against foliage and sunlight, while shots of males are set against tree trunks and other verticals.[67] Dorothy Arzner's films are often taken as marked by feminine, even feminist, qualities, while, say, Ophuls and Lang involuntarily present contradictory texts partly because of their gender identity. "For any 'man-subject behind the camera' the steady gaze at the female figure effectively constitutes an absence of narrative."[68]

Whether conceived as a rational calculator of effects or a self-expressive individual, the filmmaker-as-person can occasionally borrow a body. As early as 1953, Rivette was suggesting that the detective in *I Confess* incarnates Hitchcock, who also tracks down unfortunate creatures and makes them admit their guilt.[69] Twenty-five years later a critic finds the same director represented in *The Man Who Knew Too Much* by an "alter ego"—Bernard Herrmann, the orchestra conductor.[70] The reflexive analogies can become very elaborate, as in William Rothman's account of *Rules of the Game*. Octave is taken to be the filmmaker's surrogate. He creates a "production" by orchestrating situations ("stage setting") and instructing others in their "roles." This leads to the conclusion that Octave, as *character,* eventually realizes that he is in a film and that he shares his identity with the film's author.[71] In such interpretations, the critic's person-making economically fuses the filmmaker with the character.

Personifying Style and Narration

As we move gradually away from instances of fairly definite persons—on-screen characters and flesh-and-blood filmmakers—we find that the critic builds up personlike entities on the basis of analogy.[72] Some cue in the film can be taken as displaying perceptual, emotional, or cognitive qualities like those of a sentient being. This is another traditional sense of "personification," as seen in a medieval definition: "the fashioning of a character and speech for inanimate things."[73] Most commonly, critics who personify disembodied elements concentrate on aspects of film style (mise-en-scène, cinematography, editing, and sound) or on narration (the process of producing and channeling narrative information).

It is generally thought that the rise of auteur theory in France pioneered the study of film style. "Through technique," wrote Fereydoun Hoveyda, "we are looking for the meaning of the work."[74] With few exceptions, however, the *Cahiers* critics did not achieve the precision Bazin displayed in his analyses of Welles or Wyler at the end of the 1940s. Not until *Movie* did critics offer blow-by-blow interpretations of cutting, composition, color, or camera movement. But how to personify such aspects of the film? It seems to me that the stylisticians of auteurism constructed two complementary personlike agents: the *narrator* and the *camera*. These were taken up by later critics, both explicatory and symptomatic.

The auteurist notion of "directorial personality" usually mixed qualities which one might observe in the filmmaker and qualities which one could ascribe to the filmmaker on the basis of the film. Thus Hitchcock might be a phlegmatic, witty, and cynical man, and such qualities could be found as easily in the films as in his chats with François Truffaut. But often the auteur critic ascribed to the film qualities which need not, and perhaps could not, be ascribed to the filmmaker in the flesh. Bazin writes of the *Cahiers* auteur that from film to film, "he has the same attitude and passes the same moral judgments on the action and on the characters."[75] The auteur becomes, implicitly, a narrating agency in the text. Since Bazin's day critics have been far more explicit. Rohmer and Chabrol speak of the narrator's point of view in *Suspicion*,[76] and this has become a common personification in interpretation. An explicatory critic can speak of Ford's "narrating presence,"[77] while a symptomatic one talks of "'Hitchcock,' the narrator of the tale."[78] For Nick Browne, the narrator of *Stagecoach* is "the originating authority who stands invisible, behind the action," and who delegates the justification of the imagery "to his masks within the depicted scene"—a description that echoes the etymological link of *persona, personification,* and *personage*.[79]

Other critics have personified this authority as a "speaker." André Labarthe discusses Welles's films as "spoken" through an "unheard voice."[80] Raymond Bellour locates in *Marnie* traces of Hitchcock ("i.e., the director, the man with the movie camera") as "author-enunciator."[81] Beverle Houston finds that the female director Arzner is also an enunciator, but one who reveals contradiction, excess, and an active absence.[82]

Even if the narrating agency goes unnamed, the critic can invoke it, as Philip Rosen does with regard to the shaft of light that concludes *Seventh Heaven:* "The filmmaker, as God, absorbs the multitude of gaps which the fictional world cannot contain."[83] Another critic suggests that the carbon arc rods in the movie projector shown at the start of *Persona* function as a "persona" of the narration.[84] Critics can multiply such entities at will, as when one proposes that every film actually has both a *narrator* (a "teller") and a "mega-*monstrator*" (mega-"displayer"), which in turn consists of two "sub-*monstrators*" (one for the profilmic event, one for framing).[85]

Attitudinizer or judge, narrator or enunciator or deity, the agency personified in style and narration has usually been granted vision. "In the cinema," writes Perkins, "style reflects a way of seeing; it embodies the filmmaker's relationship to objects and actions."[86] The relationship requires the creation of another personified agent, the *camera*. This is not a physical object (the critic never mentions its weight or cost) but another heuristic construct that can make meaning out of spatial cues.[87] The shot, as a spatial display, need not be discussed as the "view" of a "camera," but this is a more available and vivid construct than an abstract conception of visual configurations. The camera construct allows the critic to posit the image as a perceptual activity (that is, as a framed vision), as a trace of mental or emotional processes (something is shown because it is significant, or shocking), and as a bearer of decisions or traits (the camera deliberately shows us this, is obsessed with that). Once such properties are ascribed to the camera, the critic is free to map them onto the filmmaker, the narrator, or other personified agents. Thus even though Bellour speaks of Hitchcock as the "enunciator," he claims that this speaker's chief goal is to control "the relationship between the camera and its object."[88]

In documentary cinema, the camera is relatively easy to associate with the empirical filmmaker. Michael Renov suggests, for instance, that in Joel DeMott and Jeff Kreines's *Seventeen,* the filmmaker behind the camera becomes a "receptor of complaint and imprecation for whom the pretense of invisibility is never an issue."[89] But such a linkage of camera and filmmaker is not confined to the documentary mode. Annette Kuhn uses the connection to support a male/female semantic division in *Jeanne Dielman, 23, quai du Commerce, 1080 Bruxelles:* "Chantal Akerman, the film's director, has said that the relatively low mounting of the camera corresponds with her own height and thus constructs a 'woman's-eye-view' on the action."[90]

More commonly, the critic personifies the camera in order to link it to the narrator. The phrase "Hitchcock's camera" may suffice to suggest both the narrating presence and what it sees. Tyler portrays the camera as the eye that creates a narrational omniscience.[91] A discussion of Godard's *Passion* emphasizes the camera as a moving "look" that can also physically "enter" the tableau, as if it were a penetrating intruder.[92] By now, the identification of camera and narrator has become a commonplace of the theory of cinematic narration.[93] It is likely that here, as so often, theory followed practice. Criticism's ad hoc heuristics put the camera-as-narrator notion on the agenda, and theorists justified it by means of an abstract system that has in turn ratified critical practice.

The most prevalent personification of the camera involves an opposition of close and distanced framing. This pair of cues can bear the semantic field involved/detached, which is then transferable to the narrator. The roots of this heuristic go back to those early film theorists who categorized the medium's aesthetic options. It remained for practical critics to "thematize" the opposition by assigning it meaning according to the vivid, available metaphor of "getting involved in" something or "backing out of" it. Sarris was explicit in equating emotional and aesthetic distance with physical distance. At the end of *La Notte,* "Antonioni drifts away from his coupled protagonists with the evasive camera movement and overhead angle of the biologist." In Rossellini's *Viva l'Italia!,* however, a zoom back from a girl on a beach allows the camera to attain the "cosmic distance" of "historical perspective."[94] In a hypothetical example, Sarris outlines the pertinent heuristic with admirable clarity:

> If the story of Little Red Riding Hood is told with the Wolf in close-up and Little Red Riding Hood in long-shot, the director is concerned primarily with the emotional problems of a wolf with a compulsion to eat little girls. If Little Red Riding Hood is in close-up and the Wolf is in long-shot, the emphasis is shifted to the emotional problems of vestigial virginity in a wicked world . . . One director identifies more with the Wolf—the male, the compulsive, the corrupted, even evil itself. The second director identifies with the little girl—the innocence, the illusion, the ideal and hope of the race.[95]

Other critics picked up the personification, making, say, Warhol's distant camera passive or voyeuristic.[96] With the rise of Brecht-influenced criticism, the appeal to certain shots as more uninvolved and "objective" became a commonplace. A critic quotes Sirk ("Art should establish distances") in order to show that the filmmaker criticizes his characters through detached and isolated views.[97]

Just as we can take Sarris' fairy tale not as a piece of film theory but as a heuristic for mapping semantic fields onto personifications of the camera and the narrator, so we should consider the more recent personification of cinema's "three looks" as a guide for practical interpretation. The schema was first, and most simply, set out in Mulvey's 1975 article on visual pleasure. "There are three different looks associated with the cinema: that of the camera as it records the profilmic event, that of the audience as it watches the final product, and that of the characters at each other within the screen illusion."[98] The critic can now link a privileged aspect of one personification (a character's looking) to a metaphorical personification of narration and style (the camera as looking) and thus project meaning onto both. Mulvey starts from the male/female and looker/looked-at cues, then maps the dominance/subjugation doublet onto them. Since the camera is also a "looker," Mulvey can use the same semantic field to make the camera's "look" into an act of repression and to interpret the object filmed as "subordinated to the neurotic needs of the male ego."[99] Subsequent interpreters in this tradition have accepted the premises that the frame is the "camera" and that it has an ability, even an urge, to "look." They have gone on to ascribe to this look certain semantic fields (voyeurism, fetishism, scopophilia). However novel the symptomatic critic's semantic fields may have once been, treating the camera as enacting them remains within the terms of personification pioneered by the explicatory tradition.

The most extreme sort of personification of technique has moved away from perceptual metaphors. Instead, critics have made style "somatic" by drawing an analogy between the person's body and what is called the "body" of the film. Freud and his contemporaries found that certain psychic disturbances left paralysis or spasms as traces; now symptomatic critics can compare such traces to textual gaps, contradictions, and excesses. Discussing melodrama, Geoffrey Nowell-Smith claims that "material that cannot be expressed in discourse or in the actions of the characters furthering the designs of the plot" appear, as in Freud's conversion hysteria, "in the body of the text."[100] This creates a "hysterical moment" when realist representation breaks down. Mark Nash likewise interprets the "Dreyer-text" as a hysterical discourse which displaces the characters' desire onto a chaste mise-en-scène that is analogous to the stasis of hypnosis or hysterical paralysis.[101]

The Spectator as Person

I have already argued that the critical institution seeks to make interpretation at least notionally relevant to comprehension. Claims about spectatorial effect, as registered consciously or unconsciously, are a practical means to this end. More specifically, the critic can make personlike agents in the text analogous to the spectator. Historically, the operational concept here has been *identification*. This is one of the most pervasive and useful heuristics at work in interpretation, and like most, it has its sources farther back than current practitioners often acknowledge.

For the critics around *Movie* in 1962, a concern for style led to questions of *effect*, and this was principally conceived in relation to identification. Two directors were believed to pose the question in sharply opposed forms. Hitchcock became the master of intense emotional absorption. According to Ian Cameron, *The Man Who Knew Too Much* undermines our security to the point where we participate in Jo's breakdown.[102] For Perkins, *Rope* "destroys the detachment of the long take by a technique which, without resorting to subjective camera-work, makes us share in the characters' feelings."[103] At the other extreme stands the impersonal Preminger. "He presupposes an intelligence active enough to allow the spectator to make connections, comparisons, and judgments. Preminger presents the evidence but he leaves the spectator free to draw his own conclusions."[104] A considerably elaborated version of the Hitchcock/Preminger model of identification was eventually presented in Perkins' *Film as Film*.[105]

Movie's treatment of these issues coincided with broader trends. In the mid-1960s, Brecht's duality of "Aristotelian" versus "epic" theater was becoming widely popular among critics in various arts. Godard's *Vivre sa vie* (1962) and *Masculin/Feminine* (1965) had a share in making cinephiles aware of Brechtian ideas, and in 1964, the publication of John Willett's *Brecht on Theatre* and Barthes's collected pieces on the Berliner Ensemble made those ideas widely available. Identification could now be correlated with emotional saturation and "illusionism." Detachment could be equated with ratiocination, "alienation-effects," and "distantiation." This trend reinforced the influence of painting's "modernist" schemata, which were circulating at the same period (see Chapter 4). By the early 1970s, critics were primed to claim that classical films created absorption, passivity, and political quiescence; that avant-garde or political films sought detachment and critical reflection; and that identification was a fundamental process which film theorists had to explain, preferably psychoanalytically. *Movie's* identification/detachment polarity formed a rough draft of ideas which later accounts of the spectator would revise, expand, and ground in theory. Here again, a concrete interpretive practice tacitly set the course for theoretical navigation.

Identification is an instance of Johnson's and Lakoff's "link" schema: a process connects one agent, the spectator, with another. That agent can be personified, most obviously as one or more characters. Again, perceptual, emotional, and cognitive qualities yield the salient features. In discussing *The Man Who Knew Too Much*, Cameron claims that the viewer identifies emotionally with the MacKennas. Mulvey suggests that the female spectator may identify with a male hero, through a nostalgic fantasy of "tomboy" activity.[106]

This routine can take a more reflexive turn when the characters are personified as not only sharing but *representing* our attitude to the situation. Thus for David Thomson, the protagonists of *Rear Window* and *Woman in the Window* are stand-ins for the spectator, enabling the filmmaker to comment on viewers' narrative expectations.[107] For Sitney, the end of Conner's *A Movie* includes a mediating figure that represents the audience.[108] One can also present the character as taking an option which the viewer does not take, as when Mary Ann Doane points to a scene in *Caught* in which the heroine laughs during her husband's screening of a film. "Both her laugh and the fact that she faces *away* from the screen indicate her refusal of this position as spectator, the marked absence of that diegetic spectatorial gaze which would double and repeat that of *Caught*'s own spectator."[109]

The narrator and the camera are also available as personlike agents with which the spectator can be said to identify. The personification may be abstract, picking out only fundamental perceptual or cognitive features, as when Michelson claims that Snow's *Région Centrale* uses the camera to personify the spectator as the transcendental, centering subject of post-Cartesian philosophy.[110] Alternatively, the critic can offer a very specific role to the spectator. Tadao Sato holds that since Ozu's narrating persona is analogous to a host, the characters become, in effect, our guests.[111] Michelle Citron's *Daughter Rite,* according to E. Ann Kaplan, lets the female spectator "position" herself either as daughter or as therapist.[112]

The heuristic of constructing spectatorial identification through personified narration has become the basis of a great many theoretical claims, most notably Christian Metz's distinction between the spectator's "secondary identification" with the characters and a "primary identification" with the camera.[113] The idea has also become a commonplace of journalistic writing. Scriptwriter and ex-film student Neil Jimenez comments that the director of *River's Edge* was right to use close-ups of the dead girl's body, in a line that could have come out of a 1962 critical essay on *Rear Window:* "It implicates the audience voyeuristically."[114]

Given such a productive heuristic, it is no surprise that spectatorial detachment is as useful as identification. For the *Movie* writers, Antonioni and Ozu keep the spectator at a distance, reflecting on the characters and their behavior.[115] Contradictory-text critics could shape the concept to their purposes, as when Rohdie claims that in *House of Bamboo,* the "contradictions" in the protagonist's personality preclude identifying with him. "An audience must think about what goes on, decide upon identity, hence its own loyalties, but is disallowed from any kind of unthinking acceptance, of losing itself in the movie fantasy."[116] This in turn permits the critic to invoke the illusion/reality semantic doublet and apply it not only to the characters but to the spectator. Similarly, we have seen that various versions of avant-garde "modernism" pushed the critic toward emphasizing the spectator's knowledgeable detachment from "transparency" and "illusion."

For the sake of expository clarity, I have teased apart different objects to which the personification schema may be applied: characters, filmmakers, style or narration, spectators. My last few examples, however, should show that the practical critic often uses several of these constructs as bearers of semantic traits. Just as the interpreter can insert the film into several categories in order to account for various aspects of it, so can she move freely from the filmmaker to the narrator to the camera to the spectator in search of appropriate cues.

Category schemata and person-based schemata are common coin of all schools of interpretation; they help make the critical institution cohere. As tacit knowledge, they help the critic pick out cues that are proper candidates for semantic mapping. As worked out in heuristics, these schemata guide the critic's problem-solving. Like the carpenter's rules of thumb, they enable the interpreter to do a professional job. The next chapter surveys more tricks of the interpretive trade.

8

Text Schemata

Of students' papers: "I am generally very benevolent [said Shade]. But there are certain trifles I do not forgive." Kinbote: "For instance?" "Not having read the required book. Having read it like an idiot. Looking in it for symbols; example: 'The author uses the striking image *green leaves* because green is the symbol of happiness and frustration.'"

—Vladimir Nabokov, *Pale Fire*

To be interpreted, the film cannot be amorphous. The critic must start from some partially structured version of it, a kind of all-purpose rough cast from which he can shape the model film. A schema for textual form will enable the critic to begin picking out cues and building patterns. I shall argue that, on the basis of institutional assumptions and critics' actual interpretations, we can infer two broad, tacit, and powerful schemata. One represents the text at a particular moment, "frozen" synchronically; the other represents the film as a diachronic totality, as a linear unrolling. Each one involves particular heuristics and, occasionally, some more particular schemata.

These text-based schemata are products of the history of the interpretive institution. Depending as they do upon the hypothesis of coherence among parts, they reflect the belief of modern interpreters that the text hangs together more or less meaningfully. At the limit, the critic may try to produce an interpretation that projects the privileged semantic fields onto as many parts of the work as possible. The demand that the interpreter be sensitive to a passage's place in the overall text has emerged at various points across the history of interpretation: in Jesus' interpretations of prophecy, in the Judaic *peshat,* in Spinoza's insistence on overall textual coherence, in Schleiermacher's demand for unity and integration, in Lanson's "centrifugal" movement from the passage to the text and historical context.[1] Romantic poetics' celebration of organic form and symbolic richness is perhaps the most powerful source of modern literary studies' notion of the textual whole; the most proximate source of the conception in film criticism is doubtless Anglo-American New Criticism.[2] Like the person-bound schema and the category schema, the interpretive schemata I shall examine are not logically necessary, but they are so deeply ingrained within the institution that they seem natural.

A Bull's-Eye Schema

One way to ascribe coherence to the film is to imagine that, at any given moment, discriminable elements serve as vehicles for the same semantic field. When Susan Sontag explains the tank in Bergman's *The Silence* as "an immediate sensory equivalent for the mysterious abrupt armored happenings going on inside the hotel," her pun-plus-metaphor rests upon an assumption that a unit of setting should carry the meaning that applies to characters' actions.[3] Such an interpretive move proceeds from a "synchronic" schema that combines what Lakoff calls "container" and "core/periphery" schemata.[4] It can be conceived as a set of three concentric circles, as in Figure 12. By putting characters at the center, this schema makes their traits, actions, and relationships the most important interpretive cues. Less salient but still potentially significant are the characters' surroundings—setting, lighting, objects, in short the "diegetic world" they inhabit. These surroundings are in turn enclosed by the film's representational techniques. The schema presents, as usual, a default hierarchy: if the film contains no characters, then only levels 2 and 3 come into play.

Like the person schema and the category schema discussed in Chapter 7, this concentric-circle schema seems obvious because it is so widely used. It promotes those personified agents we call characters (fictional or not) over less prominent cues. The schema also suggests fruitful correlations: between character and setting, between setting and camerawork. It thus offers a way for the critic to map semantic fields onto stylistic or narrational qualities. In addition, the bull's-eye schema faithfully reflects the comprehension process, since the viewer has already produced a referential meaning in which characters are prominent. "So important is character to fiction," write Brooks and Warren in their college textbook, "that one way in which to approach the basic pattern of a story is to ask: 'Whose story is this?' In other words, it usually is of first importance to see whose futures are at stake—whose situation is settled by the events that are described."[5] Of course this is very commonsensical, but so is practical criticism.

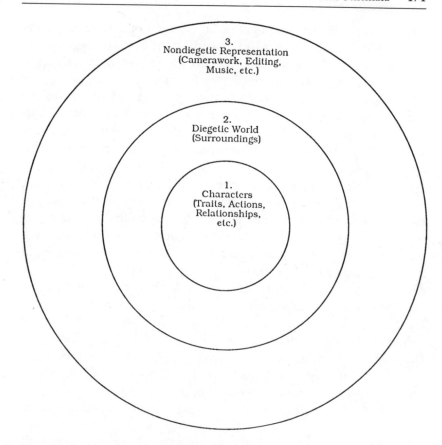

Figure 12. A core-periphery schema for textual structure

No theory other than the folk psychology we use every day is needed to justify the weight which critics assign to character action and dialogue. The mimetic hypothesis steers us unswervingly toward such cues.

Assume that our interpreter has used personification routines to construct characters and has begun to map semantic fields onto them. At any particular moment, these characters will stand out against the diegetic world, which consists essentially of a set of illuminated locales. Lighting and setting are subsidiary to character in two respects. First, they command less of the critic's attention. They can be treated sketchily and sporadically. Second, lighting and setting gain their semantic pertinence *in relation to* characters' actions and attitudes. For example,

Bill Nichols interprets the lighting in *Blonde Venus* in terms of the heroine's progress. A shot which is dark at the bottom suggests "her rise, floating up from obscurity toward the radiant allure promoted by the high-key, soft-focus lighting of her face . . . Later, during her fall (and flight), blackness extends across the top and bottom of the frame emphasizing her entrapment in a world not of her own choosing."[6] Most critics use the central realm of character as the basis for judging how cues in the diegetic world can become correlated with semantic fields.

Critics seldom discuss lighting unless it is outré (as in film noir); this is probably because, again, criticism follows our everyday perceptual routines, which favor inferences about substantial objects rather than inferences about illumination. Like other critical routines, the search for significant objects is partly initiated by high school training in reading literature. One textbook suggests: "This story should be read on more than one level. Many of the small particulars have larger implications. For example, what might the ocean liner represent? The small boat? Is there any point to the two directions the vessels are going? Is there any significance in the name of the boat [*The Flying Dutchman*]?"[7] Such explicit instruction, in high school education and after, is accompanied by ostensive example. It does not take too many critical essays or film courses to lead apprentices to assume that, for instance, unhappy characters will often languish in confining surroundings.

If character becomes the base-term in the extension of meaning to setting, we can identify several concrete ways in which the critic can control the process. Discussing *Strike*, Pascal Bonitzer assigns semantic values to the characters and then maps the differences onto various settings: subhuman qualities embodied in the spies and the lumpenproletariat living *below* earth; simple human qualities embodied in the workers living *on* earth; "excessive" human qualities embodied in the bosses living *above* earth.[8] Or one can start by positing semantic differences in setting, and then look for character traits or actions to confirm the pertinence of the cues discovered. One can, for instance, look for inside/outside cues. Lucy Fischer notes that *Meshes of the Afternoon* presents a split between the house interior and the outdoors, and she suggests that this reflects a common theme in the American avant-garde, the dialectical tension between the self and the external world.[9] More elaborate is Annette Kuhn's interpretation of Geiger's house in *The Big Sleep*. Assuming a symptomatic conception of meaning, she treats the house as the repository of sexual material not otherwise representable. "It is shadowy, closed-in, cluttered and messy—the *mise-en-scène* of the Unconscious, of Freud's uncanny, at once both familiar and alien, reassuring and threatening."[10] These qualities are, of course, bound up with the action of the film, in particular Marlowe's investigation of the Rutledge family.

The critic can map semantic fields onto settings by identifying symbolic objects. *Movie* critics proved ingenious at projecting several semantic fields onto a single prop. In Bresson's *Trial of Joan of Arc,* Paul Mayersberg finds a close-up of the cross to be full of implicit meaning. Trembling, it reminds us that a person holds it (and thus the church is human); the cross's design resembles a window (making Jeanne's death parallel to the burning of a building); the iron of the cross suggests Jeanne's determination; when the cross is lowered, it conveys the priests' sorrow at her death.[11] All these meanings, of course, depend on the traits and interactions of the characters.

Props are important to symptomatic critics as well. Kuhn finds in the Geiger household a statuette of a woman, which signifies "the menacing riddle of female sexuality."[12] Jacques Aumont's interpretation of *The General Line* takes the dairy walls to stand for the "old" life and the cream separator to stand for the "new" one.[13] A deconstructionist critic seeks to open up the text by showing how each instant offers an opportunity for "continual dissemination" and urges us to consider the death's-head in one scene of *The Seventh Seal:* "We take this, quite naturally, as significant. But why not the white canvas of the coach as a sign of hope? Why not the wheel as the wheel of fortune (which would make us think of the knight in a different way)?"[14] Here the critic seeks a plurality of meanings while adhering to the standard procedures by which the meanings are made: his interpretations derive from the same inferential routines that Mayersberg applies to Joan of Arc's cross, and the meanings are still validated by appeal to character action.

Across all schools, film interpreters have raked settings for symbols of sexual difference. To take only one instance: Andrew Britton interprets *October* as creating, in the attack of the bourgeois woman upon the demonstrating worker, a symbolic opposition of parasols and rigid banner-staffs: "The parasol eliminates space and dwarfs the man, overwhelming him spatially in anticipation of the subsequent onslaught, and suggesting an engulfing vagina. At the same time, the women become phallic monsters, jabbing at the man's naked torso with *furled* parasols and castrating him (one of them stamps on the shaft of the banner, breaking it)."[15] In recent symptomatic criticism, the act of looking offers a more convenient cue for mobilizing the desired semantic fields. To build from the text by way of the phallus/vagina pairing, one must (1) find cues in the settings that resemble the two organs; (2) correlate the referential opposition male/female with it; and (3) associate other doublets, such as power/subjugation, with the result. Assume instead that men look at women, who function chiefly to be looked at, and the correlations follow swiftly. A cane or a cave is only an analogy, but a look is there, so to speak, for all to see. In addition, since in most films characters spend a lot of time looking, the critic is seldom at a loss for an occasion to disclose an ongoing power struggle. And symbolic objects can still supplement the looking cue.

The dependence of interpretable items of decor upon character becomes fully apparent in criticism's most meaningful object: the mirror. We have already seen in Chapter 7 that the appeal of this prop lies partly in the personifying possibilities lurking within the word itself. Even when there is no pun involved, though, the critic will itch to make a mirror mean. The character before the mirror may be narcissistic or self-aware (or, if turned away, lacking in self-knowledge), or may have a split or layered identity. As producer of images, the mirror can also be taken as reflexively designating cinema.[16] Multiply the mirrors and critics respond ardently. In *Two or Three Things I Know about Her,* Godard uses a pair of mirrors "to propose that the image of [Juliette] must be multifaceted."[17] Mirrors in *Rules of the Game* are "a privileged locus for understanding the way characters choose to think of themselves," so the panel mirror becomes a "private stage" for the film's theatrical reflexivity.[18]

In the core-periphery schema, the characters (circle 1) and the diegetic circumstances they inhabit (circle 2) are enclosed within a third circle, that of what I shall call nondiegetic means of representation. These include a wide range of devices, but usually critics confine their discussion to processes of framing, change of shot, and nondiegetic sound. This domain is not identical with what is usually called "style," since lighting, setting, and performance are no less important stylistic features. Nonetheless, critics have tended to assume that framing, editing, and certain sounds come from "outside" the world of the fiction, while in most cases the techniques of mise-en-scène and diegetic sound are construed as operating "within" that world. In terms of the tacit schema, the third circle always includes the second: framing or editing encompasses character-in-setting. In practice, however, non-diegetic means of representation typically receive less commentary than does character behavior. And, like the second circle, the nondiegetic realm gains its pertinence in relation to the core domain of characters' actions and interactions.

Explicatory critics were the first to call attention to framing and editing as cues for mapping meaning. The American symptomatic critics of the 1940s concentrated primarily on the first circle in the diagram, but Bazin and his auteur followers were far more sensitive to "direction" (what was called *mise-en-scène*). Perhaps the most concise statement of the position that all three realms must be taken into account comes in Astruc's 1948 essay on *la caméra-stylo:*

> We have come to realize that the meaning which the silent cinema tried to give birth to through symbolic association exists within the image itself, in the development of the narrative, in every gesture of the characters, in every line of dialogue, in those camera movements which relate objects to objects and characters to objects. All thought, like all feeling, is a relationship between one human being and another human being or certain objects which form part of his universe. It is by clarifying these relationships, by making a tangible allusion, that the cinema can really make itself the vehicle of thought.[19]

Astruc's statement licenses the extension of interpretation to decor and framing. Not surprisingly, character remains the reference point.

One legacy of auteur criticism is thus the assumption that framing—usually personified as "the camera"—is meaningful in relation to the action and the setting. One particular tactic is to equate long shots with context (for example, society) and closer views with a part (for example, the individual's isolation). So Perkins can argue that Losey's tight close-ups in *The Criminal* are appropriate to the claustrophobia of characters in prison,[20] while Fred Camper suggests that Mizoguchi's long shots present metaphors for the undetermined role of the individual in society.[21] Another tactic is to take the framing as a cue to characters' freedom or lack of it. The most common phrase here is "frame within a frame." Hawks's compositions in *Dawn Patrol* can be said to "enclose" and "imprison" characters who, as part of the shot design, "subordinate their personal feelings to a larger sense of duty."[22]

Such treatments of framing are firmly established in post-auteur criticism as well. In discussing *Two or Three Things,* Brian Henderson brings into play not only familiar humanistic semantic doublets but also the equation of camera movement with freedom and dynamism:

> Toward the end of the sequence, the voice-over speaks of a rising of consciousness. Godard achieves this cinematically, not philosophically, by cutting to four fluid, somewhat repetitive shots of Juliette walking outside. Aided by Beethoven's String Quartet #16, the passage suggests a rising up out of the coffee cup and the isolation/immobility of the café into motion, space, joy. Even if that too is solitary, the sense of emergence into the world from the prison of the self, and into clarity from ambiguity, is achieved strikingly.[23]

Similarly, Nick Browne points to a shot in *The 39 Steps* that represents the characters behind a barred window while a police searchlight shuttles across it; he interprets it as a "trope" for imprisonment that connects to the general theme of guilt and innocence.[24]

The aesthetics of cinema, especially as developed by pioneer poeticians like the Soviet filmmakers and Rudolf Arnheim, provided practical critics with parameters of framing that could be correlated with semantic units. If a framing can be either balanced or unbalanced, each property can be taken as *representing* something else, as when Pam Cook suggests that balanced compositions in *Mildred Pierce* stand for maternal plenitude.[25] Similarly, a divided composition can become a vehicle of meaning. For one explicatory critic, the center bar of a jeep's windshield in *Carmen Jones* separates two characters' "worlds"; for one symptomatic critic, a similar windshield in *Out of the Past* not only suggests the male/female opposition but also points up the splitting of the protagonist's psyche.[26] If a shot shows a character from a low angle, that framing can be mapped by "power" as a semantic value (especially if another character is shown from a high angle). Camera movement, dynamically relating characters to settings, can come to mean temporal movement of various sorts. Sarris finds that Ophuls' camera movements imprison characters in time,[27] while Dana Polan sees Oshima's camera movements in *Night and Fog in Japan* as representing "the movement and changeability of historical reality."[28] Whereas classical film aestheticians sought to classify framing devices and point out their perceptual and emotional effects, film critics—both explicatory and symptomatic—have assigned the devices abstract meanings.

The capacity of a framing device to bear character-centered meaning becomes clear if we compare two interpretations of a single scene in

Hitchcock's *Rebecca*. Both critics treat the film as a contradictory text. For Tania Modleski, it is about female Oedipal relations, which emerge symptomatically before being suppressed by patriarchy. For Mary Ann Doane, *Rebecca* displays contradictions *within* patriarchy: it translates the woman's desire to be looked at into a fear of being looked at. The critics also concentrate on different characters and relations. Modleski's model of the film centers on the matriarchal figure of Rebecca, the mother whom both male and female desire, and Mrs. Danvers, the masculine woman. Doane's version emphasizes the nameless protagonist played by Joan Fontaine; she must bear the aggressive look of the male.

Both critics discuss the scene in which Maxim reveals that he hated Rebecca. While he describes her behavior on the night of her death, Hitchcock's camera moves over empty space. For Modleski, this camera movement enacts Rebecca's action on the fateful night; it thereby celebrates her mocking playfulness. "Rebecca flaunts her 'lack,' making her absence vividly present when the hero and the spectator least expect it . . . Not only is Rebecca's absence stressed, but we are made to experience it as an active force."[29] The camera movement enacts the return of the repressed. Doane, by contrast, treats the shot as itself repressive. She takes it as Fontaine's optical point-of-view shot, transferred from Maxim and synchronized with his voice-off explanation. Fontaine comes to identify with his gaze, and the shot concludes on him as the anchoring-point of meaning: "The story of the woman culminates as the image of the man."[30] For Doane, the shot negates the threat of femininity by rendering the woman absent and by identifying activity and the control over looking and movement with the male.[31] Whether the camera movement is taken as male or female, active or passive, a sign of activity or of domination, it is made to mean by being connected with traits, desires, beliefs, and actions of characters, both alive and dead.

Like framing, editing has furnished cues for semantic mapping. Take two characters. If a shot of one is followed by a shot of the other, any semantic values that have been mapped onto them as persons and onto the setting can now be assigned to the shots in which they appear. And since any shot-change is both a break and a join, one can argue that the semantic values are either opposed or connected. For Vlada Petrić, the argument between Geneviève and Robert in *Rules of the Game* is correctly rendered in a shot/countershot construction, and the shots of the characters alone in the frame "epitomize the dissonance of the liaison between Renoir's protagonists."[32] Another critic finds both possibilities in *Pursued:* "Walsh cuts between close-ups of Adam and Jeb staring at one another, conveying at once an opposition, on which the subsequent narrative will enlarge, and a symbolic likeness—Jeb's face left of frame, Adam's right of frame, suddenly become, across the cut, reflections of each other."[33] Alternatively, post-1970s psychoanalytic criticism has ascribed to editing the possibility of representing the fantasy of the "body in pieces." In *You Only Live Once,* when Eddie cuts his wrists, one critic describes the shot as one that "emphatically dismembers his body."[34] Another critic finds the editing in *La Passion de Jeanne d'Arc* to parallel the "decoupage" to which Jeanne's body is subjected and to support an interpretation of the film as a "hysterical" text.[35]

For the symptomatic critic, editing, like any other technique, can be construed as an act of textual repression. Philip Rosen traces how Frank Borzage's *Seventh Heaven* must overcome its thematic duality of the physical and the spiritual. Institutional religion fails to do so, since the priest tells Diane that Chico has died in battle. Yet Chico miraculously lives and returns to Diane. At the level of nondiegetic representation, the disparity is authoritatively overcome by the cut from the sorrowful Diane to the living Chico in the streets outside. By linking the physical and the spiritual, the cut absorbs the differentiated terms into a transcendent unity.[36] Alternatively, editing can be taken as a symptom. Lea Jacobs asserts that in *Now Voyager* the protagonist, Charlotte, speaks from the position which Jerry assigns to her, thus creating a contradiction between enunciative structure and sexual difference. Examining editing dissymmetries in one scene, Jacobs finds "a disruption of the typical shot/reverse-shot formation, a violation of syntax which points to a violation of the categories of sexual difference."[37] In both cases, the interpretive significance of the technique derives directly from *données* of character action.

The interpretation of framing and editing also has recourse to one of film criticism's most routine tactics—what we might call the "same-frame" heuristic. Explicatory critics have straightforwardly explained it:

Sarris (1968): "If two figures are shown in the same frame, a bond is established between them. Cross-cutting would establish separate-ness and opposition as the point of view changed back and forth."[38]

Donald Spoto (1979), on *The Man Who Knew Too Much:* "Apart

from this single gesture [Ben's giving Jo the sedative], they are never in the same frame, which stresses their distance."[39]

Richard Thompson (1980), on Daffy Duck's habit of entering the action from a separate shot: "Even the mise-en-scène designates him as an outsider, less privileged, disenfranchised."[40]

William Paul (1983): "Where the cutting is used to isolate the individual and his particular responses, the camera movement, as it reintegrates space, reunites the individual with his group to establish a sense of wholeness."[41]

Symptomatic criticism has frequent recourse to the same heuristic. *Cahiers* critics of the 1970s stressed the "impossibility" of putting proletariat and bourgeoisie in the same shot of *The New Babylon,* since such mixing would contaminate ideological oppositions.[42] Deborah Linderman notes that in Dreyer's *Passion de Jeanne d'Arc,* the heroine is isolated from her interrogators by cutting which "atomizes" her space, whereas the monks are linked by a camera movement.[43] In a discussion of *Lady from Shanghai,* E. Ann Kaplan asserts that in one scene on the boat, while men talk among themselves, the shots of Elsa sunbathing on the roof create "a kind of alternate space for Hayworth, since for much of the time she is not seen in the same frame with anyone else . . . She is isolated in her cold beauty."[44]

Practical critics seldom discuss the use of nondiegetic sound, but those who do so follow the rules of thumb elaborated for framing and editing. Michel Chion remarks that by employing diegetic speech and avoiding off-screen dialogue, *Ordet* refers to "the symbolic force of incarnated language, and not . . . to the black magic of the bodiless voice."[45] Similarly, Graham Bruce treats parts of Bernard Herrmann's score for *Vertigo* as clarifying associations between vertigo and fascination with the woman, while Royal S. Brown finds the same film's prelude to employ motifs and harmonization that suggest two sides of the protagonist's obsession.[46] Music becomes another vehicle for the semantic fields already projected onto the central core of the schema.

In all this, my bull's-eye picture of the film may seem to apply only to narrative cinema. What of the avant-garde? Needless to say, many avant-garde films include personified agents, and as we have seen, that schema helps the critic pick out cues in the represented world and in nondiegetic representation that can carry abstract meaning. In Brakhage's *Loving,* for example, when a couple makes love in the grass, a series of quick shots of pine needles can suggest "the tickling pain of the foot in contact with them."[47] If the experimental film does not include characters, the critic simply drops that circle out of the schema and maps semantic fields onto the film's use of settings and objects and its uses of nondiegetic techniques. Thus shots of windows in Brakhage's *Scenes from under Childhood* can be reflexive: they form a metaphor for cinema, "its framing process and illusory depth and movement."[48] The most abstract cinema can be interpreted: even Duchamp's rotating spirals in *Anemic Cinema* can be taken as representing the sexual act.[49] Criticism of avant-garde cinema has no difficulty in mapping semantic fields onto any stylistic feature of a film, with or without characters.

In considering the synchronic text-schema, we have veered close to the notion that critics of all stripes essentially seek out "symbols." The term has an enormously complex history, part of which is purely rhetorical. (Critical school A can accuse school B of harboring mechanistic symbol-mongers; school A can thus promote its own rich, dynamic, context-sensitive, and comprehensive interpretations.) Theoretically, there are important and subtly different conceptions of the symbol.[50] For my purposes here, however, there is no reason to quarrel about labels. The practical critic possesses an underlying schema that proposes which textual features can carry abstract meaning. Most members of the critical institution share that schema, and those features thereby become common property, like semantic fields. The centrality of character traits, dialogue, and action goes without saying, like most of the more specialized heuristics of checking mirrors, looking for looks, picking out shots that enclose characters or endow them with power, and so on. In practice it does not much matter whether critics call such cues signifiers, figures, tropes, emblems, metaphors, or just representations. They all function as symbols.

Hence, perhaps, their appeal for certain contemporary filmmakers. So great is the influence of the text-schema promoted by the interpretive institution that we find Brian DePalma directing *Obsession* according to the protocols of Hitchcock criticism. We find an avant-garde filmmaker explaining why one scene shows the camera reflected in a mirror: "The sequence was about reflection, which is very close to the whole subject of the film: the relationship and reflection between mother and child. Bringing the camera in at that point was to bring up the concept that the camera, in taking the film, was making another reflection."[51] And we find filmmaking students encouraged to convey a character's energy through a camera movement. The instructor suggests: "Give the camera a life and energy as well."[52] As filmmaking has grown more closely intertwined with academic criticism (the rise of the school-trained "movie brats," the reliance of the avant-garde on college exhibition, the tendency of film theorists to make films), filmmakers have used interpretive practices as artistic rationales.

Meaning, Inside Out and Outside In

> I thought a fire-chief was a nice metaphor for a man who's on fire inside himself.
>
> —Steve Martin, explaining how he decided on the protagonist for *Roxanne*

The simplest textual heuristic, then, seeks synchronic correspondences between the cues in different rings of the circle. A more dynamic heuristic treats meaning as having its primary source in either the innermost circle or the most enveloping one, and as passing "through" the others. In other words, meaning "moves" outward or inward.

Discussing the disjunctive style of *A bout de souffle,* a critic writes: "The conspicuous arbitrariness of these cinematic choices reflected the fitful decisiveness of Godard's characters, all of whom recognized the urgent need for selecting a defined lifestyle."[53] Here the critic makes the film's nondiegetic representation embody aspects of characterization. Many of the examples cited in the previous section take the same tack. I shall call this the *expressivist* heuristic. Meaning is taken to flow from the core to the periphery, from the characters to manifestations in the diegetic world or the nondiegetic representation. I call it "expressivism" because the term echoes "expressionism" in art, as well as the root meaning of "ex-press"—to "press out."

The auteur tradition emphasized expressivist mappings of meaning. This was strategically appropriate, since the vaunted "invisibility" and economy of the classical Hollywood cinema entailed that stylistic choices were usually subordinated to diegetic factors. Bazin may have set the tone in his discussions of Welles and Wyler as directors who emphasize performance. His analyses of the kitchen scene in *The Magnificent Ambersons* and of the father's death in *The Little Foxes* seek to show that "cinema begins when the frame of the screen or the proximity of the camera and the mike serve to present the action and the actor to the best possible advantage."[54] During the 1950s and

1960s, many Hollywood directors were praised for not obtruding on the character, for depending more on *what* is shown (that is, characters and diegetic world) than on *how* it is shown.[55] Hawks very quickly became the prototype of this elegant sobriety, but the extreme position on such "transparency" was taken by Michel Mourlet, who argued that on this score, Cecil B. DeMille would have to be the greatest director of all.[56]

More stylistically self-conscious directors could also be discussed as transmitting meaning arising from within the action. The *Movie* group often held to this line, with V. F. Perkins developing the most articulated defense. In Nicholas Ray's *The Lusty Men,* Susan Hayward stands by a curtain while a party goes on behind it. "The shot," writes Perkins, "describes her dissatisfaction with the new way of life and her longing for a secure home: the curtain has a symbolic value of its own—the fabric is very 'domestic' in its design—but it also divides the image vertically, to separate her from the environment which she wishes to renounce."[57] Perkins' 1972 book *Film as Film* argues that great subtleties can be achieved by a director who does not impose meaning on the diegetic world but who builds up implications from it.[58]

In employing an expressivist heuristic, auteurism bears the marks of interpretive strategies elicited by the art cinema of the 1950s and 1960s. Critics often sought to make such films mean by rendering passages, or the entire work, *subjective.* For Fellini, claims John Russell Taylor, a landscape becomes "an objective correlative to the mental and spiritual states of his characters."[59] The punning heuristic could assist here, as when Tyler writes of *Persona* that the shifting focus of the face in the prologue suggests that Elisabeth cannot "focus" on the world.[60] The subjectivist heuristic has continued to provide a major resource for interpreting films circulating under art-film auspices. A study of *Lucia* starts from the premise that in innovative Cuban cinema, "conflicting visual styles are used to represent the perception of individuals from different historical periods or belonging to different classes."[61] The critic goes on to discuss particular shots as expressing social cohesion, resistance to colonial culture, or psychological imbalance.

Symptomatic critics have utilized the same heuristic. Hollywood melodramas of the 1940s and 1950s are commonly treated as enacting in their setting, lighting, and framing the psychic tensions of the characters. Recall the expressivist interpretations of *Rebecca*'s camera movement as reflecting the dead woman's traits (Modleski) or as embodying other characters' points of view (Doane). The symptomatic critic working in an explicatory register can apply the same routine to oppositional works. One example is Henderson's discussion of the freedom-evoking tracking shots in *Two or Three Things;* another is this account of a shot from Sally Potter's *Thriller:* "The ideological positioning becomes manifested as physical positioning within the frame, the woman as circled by the male presence."[62] Treating meaning as a flow from character through environment to nondiegetic presentation can either help identify contradictions in the text or make a point about textual coherence.

Alternatively, the source of meaning may be located in the most encompassing circle of the scheme. Here meaning is projected from the nondiegetic realm onto the diegetic world and its inhabitants. Consider as a prototype the claim that Sirk creates "a melodramatic machine around the characters that seems to deny their powers of free will."[63] The writer discusses the reframings in the beach scene of *Magnificent Obsession:* "It is a relatively stationary tableau and yet Sirk's camera consistently asserts its presence by readjusting to—or sometimes leading—every small movement the relatively active Judy makes. She turns over, she sits up, she leans forward—and each time the camera moves with her. The effect of these movements is to deprive the characters of any sense of force or will."[64] I shall call this the "commentative" heuristic. It suggests that something—narration, presentation, narrator, camera, author, filmmaker, or whatever—stands "outside" the diegetic realm and produces meaning in relation to it. As in any application of the concentric-circle schema, the commentative heuristic takes character traits and actions as its reference point, but here they are "placed" within a qualifying or negating frame of reference. If the expressivist heuristic stresses the semantic compatibility among character personification, diegetic world, and overarching representation, this heuristic emphasizes the *disparity* that can arise between the characters and the other realms.

The disparity becomes operative when the critic invokes the non-character personifications I outlined in the previous chapter. The claim that Lubitsch's shots reflect his hierarchical sense of society points to a commenting filmmaker behind the camera.[65] Or commentary may flow from a narrator, as when Bill Nichols suggests that in *The Battle of San Pietro,* Huston undercuts the film's official message.[66] And of course the personified camera can be used in this connection. Peter

Wollen writes of Godard's *Passion* that the moving camera's "look" at the Orientalist tableaux represents a metaphorical penetration, a fantasy replacement of the Father.[67]

The difference between the core and the two enclosing circles is most evident when the critic attributes to the commentary a knowledge of upcoming events—something the character cannot have. Wood takes an early sequence in *The Scarlet Empress* as "an extraordinarily vivid prophetic metaphor for what becomes of Sophia Frederica in the course of the film."[68] According to Richard Abel, in the torture sequence of *La Passion de Jeanne d'Arc*, Jeanne remains central to spatial continuity, and this "suggests that her spirit remains unbroken and that she will ultimately triumph."[69] The greatest power of the commentative representation is its ability to hint at the future.

Constructing a commentative source of meaning takes relatively few forms in contemporary interpretive practice. Perhaps the mildest is *irony*.[70] In *The Birds*, a low-angle framing of the characters is said to present "the heavily ironic, and final, 'bar' of visual imagery at the end of the attack . . . The 'heroic' low angle seems unearned by characters who can at best withstand but not control the adversity they face; Melanie's position lacks weight in the aftermath of her isolation during the attack. A retrospective reading would suggest she is being supported by Mitch and Lydia rather than wedging herself between them."[71] At the level of narrative, Claire Johnston finds Arzner's films ironic in refusing a happy ending[72]—a refusal that most critics of Sirk's films also take as a sign of authorial commentary.

More radically, the commentary imputed to the film can be treated as *distanciation*. Greenbergian modernism and popularized Brechtian theory encouraged critics to seek out cues whereby the film breaks our putative absorption in its illusion. Here is a discussion of the automobile-driving sequences in Jean-Marie Straub and Danièle Huillet's *History Lessons*:

> These driving passages may be described as a meditation upon the process of representation, its compositional implications. First we note the series of frames that are on the screen: at the most obvious level, there is the frame delimited by the edge of the screen, that contains the interior of the car. Then there is the windscreen of the car, which is our "window upon the world," through which we gaze upon "reality." There is also a less conventional "window on the world"—in the roof of the car, a sliding roof which opens another frame, through which pass more oblique perspectives on the "real-

world." The fourth frame is that contained in the driver's rear-view mirror, and in it we see his eyes and nose—through this mirror we find our link to the narrator (otherwise faceless, as befits his minimal visual presence in the film). Through this mirror we are, however, implicitly thrown back to ourselves, it enforces awareness of our position as specular subjects—the nature of our relationship to the images on the screen is raised once more. And the appositeness of Godard's Brechtian maxim that cinema is "not the reflection of reality, but the reality of the reflection" is also stressed, through the double reflections that occur within this series of frames: the windscreen bears the reflection of the driver's hands—thus becoming screen rather than window, and the glass of the speedometer dial reflects the sky passing overhead, via the hole in the roof. These series of frames within frames are important not only in so far as they underline the flatness of the screen (in direct opposition to the Bazinian elevation of the "long take" and "depth of focus" as the devices essential to a transparent capturing of an ineffable reality), but also relate to the notion of a distanciated history which is central to both Brecht and Straub/Huillet.[73]

In what is virtually an anthology of interpretive tactics, the claim about commentative distance is coordinated with the frame-within-a-frame heuristic, the personification of the narrator and spectator, the granting of saliency to the diegetic world, the characterization of the film as posing questions, the punning on "reflection," and the commonplace of flatness/illusion.

Although symptomatic critics have found the commentative heuristic useful for spotting "subversive" qualities in mainstream works or for praising oppositional or avant-garde works, the procedure goes back to the days of auteur stylistics. During that period, critics urged that some personified "external" agent—filmmaker, narrator, or narration—could strike an attitude toward the diegetic world and thus contextualize it properly for us. After noting that during one scene in *Ride the High Country* Peckinpah isolates Heck in a single shot (the same-frame heuristic again), a *Cahiers* critic remarks that in such films, direction presents attitudes to events, and that this yields interpretive results: "The opposition between the 'objective' action and the director's judgment extends to thematics."[74] In any such case, ironic commentary was a likely possibility. *Movie*'s construction of authorial personas for Preminger or Hitchcock also depends crucially on the possibility of such external authorial commentary. Thus Preminger's camera movements in *Carmen Jones* suggest that the characters have a certain freedom, while Hitchcock's cutting in *The Man Who Knew Too Much* makes Jo resemble Louis Bernard.[75]

The critic may use the expressivist and commentative heuristics simultaneously. The *Movie* analysis of *Marnie*'s first shot (discussed in Chapter 4) suggests that the setting magnifies aspects of the character (the shot connotes holding to a course despite the "schizophrenia" of the composition) but also that some meaning is imposed "from without" (the character's movement is determined by the shot).[76] Similarly, Tag Gallagher asserts that *How Green Was My Valley* echoes Huw's mood through lighting, cutting, and setting; yet this becomes "an expressivist fantasy of ritual whose subjectivity Ford faults" by means of framing and cutting.[77] Using both heuristics can help the critic align the semantic fields with a broader range of cues across the film.

Finally, we should note that both the bull's-eye schema and the alternative flow-of-meaning heuristics function as default values, to be overridden if the critic wishes. Consider Kaja Silverman's discussion of voice in classical Hollywood cinema. She posits that Hollywood anchors the voice-off in the diegesis and the voice-over outside it. She goes on to propose that in order to conceal the contradiction arising from male anxiety concerning female lack, the film displaces the inside/ outside distinction onto the diegesis itself. In this argument, woman is assigned to the "inside" and man to the "outside," as in those scenes in which the female voice becomes the source of the spectacle or, within the psychoanalytic session, the transmitter of repressed trauma.[78] Thus male discourse "frames" female discourse, functioning as an "external" source of meaning controlling woman's "recessed space" within the story. (In effect, Silverman asserts that circle 1 includes two domains congruent with circle 2 and circle 3.) Silverman emphasizes the artificiality of this construct and implies that non-Hollywood films might obey other principles. Still, even if the schema and the heuristics are to be revised, criticized, or superseded by the critic, they remain necessary points of departure.

Textual Trajectories

The diegetic-nondiegetic schema functions as a tacit guide for unifying aspects of any particular moment in the film. But the critical institution demands that such moments be connected, linked into an overall pattern that carries the semantic fields across the text. There must be a *holistic enactment* of semantic fields. This is a clear extension of the pattern hypothesis I discussed back in Chapter 6. Theorists of criticism have, in fact, generally identified interpretation with the ascription of pattern to a text.[79] Any aspect of ongoing structure—imagery, sound, or action—can become the basis of an acceptable interpretation.[80] Only by ascribing successivity to the text can the critic solve the interpretive problem in terms that the institution encourages—an encompassing view of the text's variety, adherence to a notion of the unity of form and content, respect for the viewer's ongoing experience of the film.

It would be possible to trace how this notion of global form became explicitly acknowledged in film criticism of the 1950s and early 1960s: Rohmer's declaration that modern directors create autonomous works,[81] *Movie*'s embracing of organicist New Critical aesthetics, the structuralists' insistence upon the film as system, and the subsequent idea of the text as a contradictory unity. But the critic's basic allegiance to diachronic coherence is best seen in the more mundane practice of motif analysis.

When rabbinic commentators treated one passage as part of a "progressive revelation" of meaning, when Gnostics posited a series of "new" testaments that fulfilled previous ones, and when the church fathers used "typological" interpretation to show that events in the Old Testament prefigure events in the New, all were utilizing a heuristic that reveals "horizontal" affinities among textual motifs. Much later, it became a tenet of symbolist aesthetics that the artwork creates its enclosed "intrareferential" meanings through the patterning of recurrent elements. Folklorists and art historians use the concept of motif to indicate a conventional unit used as material in several texts, but, significantly, this definition never became as central to literary criticism as did the concept of the motif as a unique component of the particular work's unifying strategies. The musical motif was a far more congenial analogy for postsymbolist literary aesthetics.

By the 1950s, the victory of New Critical method guaranteed that motif-tracing was to be a basic skill for every critic. Not only does the recurrent motif ensure organic unity, but the modifications attendant upon each recontextualization also allow one to trace changes within and among semantic fields. Because of film interpretation's close ties to literary interpretation, all schools of criticism have assumed the motif to carry meaning. Repeated objects, colors, lines of dialogue, elements of lighting or setting or costume, recurrent framings or musical passages—all translate semantic structure into architectonic unfolding.

In order to become genuine cues, motifs must be situated within some temporal schema of textual form. The most general one in film interpretation constructs the film as a *trajectory*. This is Johnson and Lakoff's "source-path-goal" pattern, which presumes a starting point, a destination, a series of intermediate points, and a direction.[82] The critic postulates that the text will reveal a *progression,* one that not only organizes time and space but also mobilizes semantic fields in a sequential interplay. As Jonathan Culler puts it, "The reader must organize the plot as a passage from one state to another and this passage or movement must be such that it serves as a representation of theme."[83]

The most obvious examples come from narrative forms. The schema's prototype is the *journey,* a spatio-temporal progression that is easily grasped. It can be represented as a quest, an investigation, a maturation, and so on. Semantic fields can be projected onto any component of the schema. Thus Eugene Archer says that Bergman's essential theme is "man's search for knowledge in a hostile universe," while Robert Burgoyne finds Fassbinder's *In a Year of Thirteen Moons* to constitute "the quest for a metalanguage which will deliver the characters from the muteness of their surroundings."[84] The *direction* of the trajectory can also be invested with meaning, as when Burgoyne makes the search for a metalanguage trace a descent.[85]

Within such an itinerary, motif analysis gains its force. For instance, Mary Ann Doane employs the cue of the look, some puns on framing, the commentative heuristic, and a trajectory schema to show how *Humoresque* depicts the objectification of the woman. Early on, eyeglasses enclose Helen's gaze (a "quite literal framing"); later, she stands before a framed mirror; "within the general frame of the film, Helen is framed even more precisely by the male gaze," by editing, and by being surrounded by watching men. At the film's end, before Helen commits suicide, she is framed in the baroque grillwork of a door. "The insistent, obsessive framing indicates the inevitability of a continual transformation of the female subject of the gaze into the object of the gaze. And here, in this scene which precedes her suicide, the syntax of the film insures that the transformation of femininity into object—framed and fetishized—is synonymous with death."[86] Since the trajectory forms what cognitive theorists call a "template" schema, motif analysis becomes a matter of slotting concrete items—here, the framing cue—into the overall pattern.

As these instances suggest, the trajectory schema is very powerful.

It allows the critic to correlate stages along the pathway with changes in the imputed spectator's response. The *Movie* critics, for instance, argued that Hitchcock and Preminger, in the course of their films, subtly compel the viewer to revise judgments about the characters.[87] The schema can also be applied to nonnarrative cinema. One might think that Frampton's *Zorns Lemma* invites application of atemporal classificatory patterns, but critics typically envision it as a progression—from symbolic modes to spatio-temporal reality; from human knowledge as factual information to knowledge as contextual understanding; from oral literature to the sound film and "from reality to seeing"; or from spoken language through film montage to cinematic realism.[88] Because of the critic's desire to account for the entirety of the film, even a conceptual catalogue can be schematized as having a source, path, and goal.

The trajectory is internally differentiated. Lakoff's schema has primary parts (source, path, goal) and secondary ones, the steps along the path. Part of the critic's skill lies in the ability to treat the film's pattern as a series of discrete segments which can, at several levels of generality, be compared or connected. The critic must choose what segments best support semantic projection. The best candidates are those "nodal" or "summarizing" segments which gather together several semantic values.[89]

In locating these passages, the interpreter can employ two complementary heuristics. The critic may assume that the portions most salient in comprehension—beginnings, endings, key causal turning points, and so on—are most pivotal to the interpretation. Or the critic may provisionally assume, as Frank Kermode puts it, that "no part is less privileged than the other parts. All may receive the same quality and manner of attention."[90] (This heuristic is especially effective when the critic wishes to dislodge existing interpretations.) Soon certain passages, perhaps ones overlooked by previous critics, come to seem opaque or anomalous, and these call for special cognitive work; they become subproblems to be solved. Later, as semantic fields are tested out and recast, the interpreter discovers that although all parts are potentially equal, some are only weakly connected to the semantic fields. Either heuristic helps the critic arrive at some highlighted passages that will become central to the critic's model film.

To pass institutional muster, every interpretation must show that its semantic fields are pertinent to a film's opening. Here again, interpretation tracks comprehension, since a text's beginning creates a "primacy" effect and intrinsic norms against which later developments are measured.[91] Which item does not belong in this series?

skyscraper   cathedral   temple   prayer

Most people will answer "prayer." Now consider this series:

cathedral   temple   prayer   skyscraper

Most people will exclude "skyscraper."[92] The sequencing gives one item greater saliency and changes the category the perceiver constructs.

Because of its agenda-setting function, a film's beginning typically becomes a summarizing segment for interpretation. Here the critic often finds the film's major semantic fields locked into place. Of *History Lessons,* a critic notes that the first three shots (maps of the Roman empire) present territorial history, the fourth shot (a statue of Caesar) presents the mythical history of the heroic individual, and the fifth shot (a view from a car driving through Rome) yields several semantic values: history as flux, the demythologizing of monumental history, cars as the new monuments, the traces of the past in the present, and questions about cinematic representation.[93] Even if the opening is retracted or canceled by what follows in the film, as in Ken Jacobs' *Blonde Cobra,* it needs accounting for—as, in this case, the first challenge to the viewer's concentration.[94] The most elaborate account of films' beginnings, Thierry Kuntzel's discussion of them as motivic and thematic matrices to be "linearized" by succeeding textual units, tacitly acknowledges the tendency of all interpretive schools to treat the opening as the "source" of the trajectory.

Once the film is launched, the path must be schematized as points or stages. Tacitly or explicitly, the interpreter marks out segments that delineate phases of the pattern. There seem to be two subschemata available. The critic can consider the stages as parallel *replacements,* as when the journey carries the traveler through comparable locations or situations, or the investigation takes the inquirer to different suspects. Thus Archer will suggest that the quest in Bergman's films traces its path through a set of parallel possibilities; the *Zorns Lemma* critics treat the various representational systems as paradigmatic equivalents. The notion of replacements allows portions of semantic fields to be aligned with the distinct alternatives ascribed to the text. This can coordinate with style-centered routines like the same-frame heuristic. In discussing the Chinese film *The In-Laws,* Chris Berry points out an early scene in which the family is united within a 360-degree pan; but the pan is soon replaced by shot/reverse-shot cutting, suggesting a breakdown. At the film's close, a smooth panning shot shows the family at the table, and then a bird's-eye view shows them sitting in a circle. "Finally, they are reunited in the same frame."[95] A pan shot is replaced by cutting, then by a new pan, then by an encompassing view—all parallel cues that bear the unity/disunity doublet.

By contrast, the trajectory may also be made interpretable by positing each phase of it to be a *struggle*. Conflicts between or within characters, or disparities among settings or techniques, may become cues for applying semantic fields. BFI structuralism of the late 1960s, and much genre criticism since, has found each term of the film's thematic doublets to be incarnated in one or more agents, and the ongoing exchange of blows, the actions and reactions that involve the characters, are easily interpretable as a confrontation of abstract values. In a study of Dreyer's films, I interpret *La Passion de Jeanne d'Arc* as organized around "a dialogical clash of texts," in which Jeanne's expressive, ahistorical speech contends with the impersonal, historicizing writing of the church.[96] For the symptomatic critic, the concept of struggle can be applied to both manifest and latent forces. Frank Tomasulo takes the scene in the workers' rehearsal hall in *The Bicycle Thief* as articulating an antinomy between art and politics; the song's lyrics treat oppression, but "the debate over pitch displaces the political content onto aesthetic form."[97] As this example indicates, locating a struggle may lead the critic to a semantically informed contradiction within a summarizing segment.

The currency of "struggle" and "replacement" subschemata may be readily seen in a pair of contrasting studies of *Mildred Pierce*. Pam Cook treats the film as a conflict between "mother-right" and "father-right," played out in terms of genre (melodrama versus film noir), style (uses of lighting), and characterization (Mildred versus her men). In both the flashbacks and the present-tense investigation, the maternal principle resists patriarchy but is eventually overthrown. The "past" sequences show that Mildred's matriarchy eventually deteriorates through its inability to create social order. Thus patriarchal order must reassert itself. When Mildred falls under suspicion of murder, her original husband, Bert, takes control of her life. In the present-day scenes, Mildred seeks to assert her power by taking the blame for Monty's death, but Inspector Peterson breaks down her lie, reasserts the power of patriarchal authority, and returns her to Bert.[98] Cook depicts the struggle in apocalyptic terms: "The consequences of the retreat from patriarchy are represented as the complete upheaval of social order leading to betrayal and death, in the face of which the reconstitution of the patriarchal order is seen to be a necessary defence."[99]

By contrast, Marc Vernet presents the diachronic patterning of *Mildred Pierce* as a series of replacements. He personifies Mildred as passing among the other characters, progressively substituting one trait or action for another until she finds a just mean that avoids others' excesses or shortcomings. Mildred is mother, entrepreneur, and sexual woman; but by being too much the woman and not enough the mother, she loses her daughter Kay, while in being too much the mother, she loses Veda. The film becomes a *Bildungsroman*, Mildred's journey through unacceptable options toward a proper balance of qualities: "After undergoing economic, romantic, and social adventures, after having explored the different paths of fulfillment which are revealed as impasses (Lottie and Ida, Wally and Monty, the Bert of the beginning and the Veda of the ending), after having climbed so high that she cannot fall too low, Mildred-Candide can at the end of her trip return, light of heart, to cultivate her American garden."[100] Both Cook and Vernet adopt the trajectory schema but map semantic fields onto the phases in accord with its two principal subschemata. It should now be evident that the critic can also combine the two— treating a pattern of replacements as containing more localized struggles, or treating struggles as including exchanges and substitutions of equivalent units, or treating the film as alternating replacement segments and struggle segments.

Needless to say, any portion of the film's trajectory may be interpreted as a "summarizing" one, depending on how the critic has mobilized semantic fields, selected person-based and category schemata, disclosed cues on the basis of the concentric-circle schema, and so on. Whatever such promontories are disclosed along the way, though, the interpreter in good standing must show how the selected semantic fields pertain to the trajectory's goal.

Like the beginning, the film's ending plays a summarizing role in ordinary comprehension. The interpreter therefore has good reason to highlight it. And the ending offers great freedom of interpretation because critics have available several heuristics for making it mean. We can itemize four possibilities.

1. The simplest routine is to assume that the film resolves its referential meanings and its more abstract ones. For instance, a *Movie* critic

finds the ending of *The Courtship of Eddie's Father* to unite the worlds of reality and make-believe in a synthesis that coincides with the plot's establishment of the family.[101]

2. If the plot or argument seems "deliberately" to leave some events or effects unresolved, the interpreter can find correspondingly "open" meanings. This heuristic became prominent with critical discussions of the early "waves" of the European art cinema. Here is a prototype, from a 1961 book on Antonioni (himself the prototypical artificer of unresolved endings): "Will the external condition of existence be capable of exerting an influence on man's happiness, on his equilibrium? These new conditions will create new problems, will involve man in a new web of dependencies. Where will they lead him? No one can answer this question."[102] The same strategy continues to be used. Richard Abel ascribes a thematic ambiguity to Epstein's *Glace à trois faces*, in which the final image of the hero in the mirror leads to a thematic irresolution: "In a crisis of recognition, the enigma of the hero's identity and desire shifts onto us."[103]

3. Conversely, even if confronted with an "open" dramaturgy, the critic can assert thematic closure. Bazin, for example, recognizes the "accidental" plotting in *The Bicycle Thief* but still argues that it forms a coherent semantic structure, chiefly because it ends by marking a new phase in the father-son relationship. "The son returns to a father who has fallen from grace. He will love him henceforth as a human being, shame and all."[104] Decades later a critic could claim that although *Blow-Up* is narratively open, it presents a finished statement about art as a willed imaginative act.[105] Edward Branigan uses Greimas' semantic square to claim that *8½* contains four endings, each based on one term, and that despite plot ambiguities, the system of implicit meanings achieves closure.[106]

4. In a reversal of the third strategy, the interpreter may find a diegetically "closed" film semantically "open." Richard Levin calls this "refuting the ending," a procedure which often produces ironic interpretations on the assumption that "all's not well that ends well."[107] This too runs back to art-cinema interpretive tactics, when even "closed" comedies like *Smiles of a Summer's Night* could be seen to harbor lingering tensions: "One may suppose that each triumph is transitory: the mistress will soon grow bored again, the count vows eternal fidelity 'in his fashion,' the theologian will soon be overcome with remorse, the coachman's promise is retractable after the dawn.

The game reaches its preordained conclusion, but life, constant and incalculable, goes on, and in the end they all go in to breakfast."[108] In the heyday of auteur-structuralism, the routine proved useful in showing such directors as Sirk to be subversively ironic. One could look past the apparently settled denouements and raise questions about the characters' values and futures. A contemporary genre critic summarizes the relevant inferential move: "Sirk always resolved the immediate love story, but left unresolved the contradictory social conditions in which the story was 'embedded' and that had prevented the lovers' embrace until some arbitrary event near the film's end. His resolution is ultimately unsatisfactory, challenging the viewer's expectations on virtually every level of engagement. Thus Sirk's 'unhappy happy end,' to encourage the audience to 'think further, even after the curtain goes down.'"[109]

Because these four heuristic options are available, the ending has a particular significance in contemporary symptomatic criticism. The critic analyzing an oppositional text can adopt a sympathetic stance, valorizing the film for asking the right questions and leaving matters for the audience to resolve. Ruth McCormick praises Oshima's *The Ceremony* because "he presents us with seemingly insoluble problems and invites us to solve them. If his films are difficult, making a revolution is more so."[110] Less often, the critic can charge the oppositional film with not asking the right questions, or giving wrong or excessively definite answers.[111]

But the most striking variations in interpreting endings emerge when symptomatic critics turn their attention to contradictory texts from Hollywood. Since most "classical" films are assumed to strive for plot resolution and closure, the critic faces a choice. Using a variant of option 1, the critic can posit that the ending works to contain symptoms revealed earlier in the film's trajectory. Such is the tack taken by the *Cahiers* editors on *Young Mr. Lincoln* and by Heath on *Touch of Evil*. Thanks to this heuristic, dramaturgical and semantic closure becomes a proof of the power of the text to tame its disruptions.

If the arbitrary-closure heuristic presents an "adjusted" text—that is, one better at disguising its neuroses—another heuristic enables the symptomatic critic to show that all's not well that ends well. The ending, while superficially well wrapped up, betrays symptoms of persisting problems. Some earlier examples offer instances. In ascribing matriarchal meanings to *Rebecca,* Modleski finds that, because the males' pursuit of the law does not arrive at the truth, patriarchy does not unequivocally vanquish feminine desire and so "the threat of matriarchy is not entirely dispelled at the film's end."[112] In discussing *Mildred Pierce,* Cook claims that the film's last shot, which shows two women on their knees, closes the film on a reminder of woman's sacrifice.[113] For contemporary symptomatic critics, refuting the ending of a classical film involves finding motifs or personifications that can be taken as symptoms of repressed meaning.

Doctrines into Diachronies

The interpretive institution, then, furnishes the critic with a large repertoire of tools for ascribing meaning to the film's unfolding pattern. The trajectory schema provides a basic template into which actions and diegetic or nondiegetic motifs can be slotted. Along it the critic can also plot ongoing personifications—of character, narrator, spectator, or whomever. The less general schemata of replacement and struggle allow the critic to conceive of the trajectory as having an origin, phases, and a goal. In addition, critics can exploit particular heuristics in order to find cues that inflect a beginning one way, an ending another. There remain, however, still more specific diachronic schemata upon which the critic will draw. I cannot inventory them all, but it is worth indicating how the most prominent ones utilize one of the institution's most revered practices: allegory.

Broadly speaking, all criticism is "allegorical" in looking for another meaning than the one overtly presented.[114] In a narrower sense, allegory is a type of holistic enactment in which the trajectory of this text is interpreted as being congruent with that of some other text, or with the categories or precepts of a preexisting doctrine. John Fletcher's *Essay on Allegorical Poetry* (1715) puts it fairly well: "An Allegory is a Fable or Story, in which, under imaginary Persons or Things, is shadowed some real Action or instructive Moral."[115] If we add to this that texts not intended allegorically can be interpreted in this fashion, we can examine one last set of diachronic strategies for ascribing implicit or symptomatic meanings to films.

As an interpretive convention, allegory has known fluctuating fortunes. Central to classical and medieval interpretation, attacked in the romantic era as merely illustrative, it was rehabilitated in this century by Freud and his followers, who linked it to myth and psychic universals.[116] Jung, Panofsky, and Benjamin all brought the concept to a central place in literary and art-historical studies, while Maude Bodkin, Richard Chase, and Francis Fergusson domesticated the concept for ordinary criticism.[117] For the latter critics, myth and ritual provided the "under-text" in terms of which works could be interpreted. After Northrop Frye's *Anatomy of Criticism* (1957), various mixtures of allegorizing myth criticism and psychoanalytic interpretation of literature, such as Simon Lesser's *Fiction and the Unconscious* (1957), Leslie Fiedler's *Love and Death in the American Novel* (1960), and Harold Bloom's *Visionary Company* (1961), were offering an "extrinsic" complement to the "intrinsic" analyses of official New Criticism.[118] In France, Gilbert Durand's *mythocritique* came into prominence during the same period.[119]

These developments paved the way for the rehabilitation of purer forms of allegory. Frye treated allegory sympathetically, and subsequent works, such as Edwin Honig's *Dark Conceit* (1959) and Angus Fletcher's *Allegory: The Theory of a Symbolic Mode* (1964), made a case for its range and power. (In a synthesizing gesture characteristic of the period, Fletcher linked it to myth, ritual, and psychoanalytic processes.) In the post-structuralist age, allegory has come to be prized for its semiotic self-consciousness. In stressing the gap between levels of meaning, it not only incarnates the differential nature of symbol systems but offers a scale model of interpretation itself.[120] It was perhaps inevitable that a mode of writing which explicitly demands decipherment should, when taken up into an institution that puts interpretation at the center of its concerns, become the very paradigm of textuality.

If allegory bids fair to become the scriptural exegesis of postmodernism, psychoanalysis may furnish the appropriate semantic fields. A major exemplar for contemporary film studies is Jacques Lacan's 1956 reading of "The Purloined Letter." For Lacan, Poe's story allegorically enacts the displacement of desire and, concomitantly, the subject's constitution in and through the symbolic process of language. In interpreting Poe's tale, Lacan makes use of many schemata and heuristics I have already considered. He maps such semantic fields as power/powerlessness, Symbolic/Real, and so on onto characters and actions. By building structural parallels between two scenes, he is able to display a series of positions with respect to knowledge and desire through which different characters pass. Lacan produces his allegory by means of punning (the letter is the "literal," or the signifier), localized symbols (the letter is like a female body which Dupin's eyes "undress"; it is placed in the "vagina" of the fireplace), and personification and motif analysis (when the Minister occupies the Queen's structural role, he becomes "feminized"). Furthermore, Lacan takes as his foremost cue the act of looking, which puts each character in a specific relation to the letter (in both senses). The act of narration is allegorized as well, since the fact that it is filtered through various sources makes it represent language as necessarily mediated by the Other, an important premise of Lacanian doctrine. Overall, Lacan's model of the tale centers on the repetition compulsion, itself based on the materiality of the signifier; along the way, he finds traces of male narcissism and the fetishization of the woman.[121] Lacan's interpretation of "The Purloined Letter" becomes, in the words of one commentator, both an allegory of psychoanalysis and an allegory of reading.[122]

In film studies, the most salient allegorizing tendency is squarely in this tradition. Very often the schema is some version of the "Oedipal trajectory." Heath, for instance, reverts to Freudian myth analysis in discussing *Touch of Evil:*

> The swollen foot (Quinlan hobbles along as a result of his gammy leg), the stick of the riddle (the key to the crime), the man who uncovers the truth of himself as the criminal (Quinlan ends up a murderer), the theme of blindness (wanting to phone Susan, Vargas enters a shop kept by a blind woman), the baby left to die (Susan lets herself be photographed because a baby is suddenly held up in front of her and which she turns to admire: it is the symbolic that reasserts its dominance in this abandonment of the narrative, the baby that is given no life in its development: before he enters the blind woman's shop, Vargas finds another baby in his path—he puts on dark glasses, refuses to see clearly).[123]

In another version the critic may apply Lacan's language-based trajectory. For example, Kaja Silverman claims that Werner Herzog's *Kaspar Hauser* "deftly literalizes all of the key terms in Lacan's abstract grammar" and goes on to trace the film's "endless circulation of the name-of-the-father between fathers and sons."[124] She construes the film as a comprehensive allegory of the human subject's development: Kaspar starts out as a Lacanian *hommelette,* meets an old man who initiates him into the Symbolic, gets constituted as a subject via the paternal gaze, and so on.

The Lacanian template does not always appear in a pure form. Like any schema, it can be recast to suit critics' various purposes. One revision has combined it with a form of myth analysis derived from Vladimir Propp. Propp, a Russian folklorist, proposed to define a certain form of fairy tale, the "heroic wondertale," by breaking it down into thirty-one functions, various auxiliaries, seven roles, and a limited set of "moves," or lines of action.[125] Propp's work proved of importance to French structuralism, although Lévi-Strauss, Greimas, and Bremond all found it necessary to revise and correct his theoretical conclusions. Soon after Barthes's 1971 application of Propp's method to a passage in Genesis, film critics began to remold Propp's scheme into a suitably allegorical subtext.[126] Peter Wollen's 1976 "morphological analysis" finds that *North by Northwest* conforms to Propp's set of functions. In the process, Wollen turns Propp into a proto-Lacanian. The hero's task now involves liquidating a "lack" by finding "an object of desire."[127] By such revisions, Wollen seeks to relate his analysis "to such psychoanalytic concepts as fantasy-scenario or family romance."[128] This reformulation provides the symptomatic critic with a sort of "linking" template: the film's "surface" patterning can be transposed into the fairy-tale format (in the process obeying virtually none of the constraints which Propp set upon his method); this schema, thanks to pivot-concepts such as desire and lack, may be further allegorized by reference to the "deeper" structure of the Lacanian scenario.[129]

Both Lacan and Propp tell stories centered on male protagonists. Consequently, a second, more influential revision of the Lacanian scenario has emerged. By combining the psychoanalytic story with Laura Mulvey's discussion of the woman as source of visual pleasure and castration anxiety, symptomatic critics have produced a comprehensive and flexible allegorical pattern. The heuristic goes roughly like this: Take male characters to be functioning as father figures or undergoing the Oedipal trajectory. Take female characters to be playing the role of mother or as posing a castration threat. Then trace the ways in which (1) the male either (a) succeeds his father or (b) loses his identity; and (2) the woman is either (a) transformed into a fetish for male desire, (b) eliminated from the text, or (c) transported into a realm beyond patriarchal definition.

Two examples display the heuristic at work. Steven Jenkins' study of *Metropolis* presents young Freder as initially fascinated with Maria as idealized mother. By evoking pleasure and anxiety, she threatens the Law of the Father. Eventually, Freder's trajectory leads to his acceptance of his role in patriarchy. But only after the woman's threat is displaced onto the robot Maria can the human Maria, after suitable punishment, assume the limited maternal role.[130] Alternatively, the woman can be valorized as beyond patriarchy's power. In Elizabeth Cowie's interpretation of *Now Voyager*, the father is eventually excluded from the text. He is replaced by an idealized mother-child relation that springs from the original Oedipal fantasy.[131]

Within such interpretations, all the Lacanian cues of language, looking, and so on can be utilized. At the same time, the critic can draw on other material that lets the interpretation include more aspects of action and surroundings than can the narrowly Lacanian script. Moreover, the schema is also open to revision at various points, as when Modleski treats *Rebecca* as enacting the female Oedipal trajectory in relation to matriarchy. Construals of the ending may also draw upon any of the options enumerated in the last section. For instance, the critic may seek out cues that show that even if woman is cast out from the text, symptoms of her disturbing presence linger on.

Although the feminist revision of the Lacanian story assumes that such patterns are constructed by culture, the pragmatic reasoning strategies reflect a schema that *functions* in critical interpretation in the same way that the archetype of the Wanderer or the Earth Mother functions within interpretations that depend on purportedly universal myths. Both tendencies derive allegories from processes assumed to be at work when humans discover their personal and social identities. This should not surprise us, as it points up yet another continuity between recent symptomatic criticism and its predecessors. Interpreting a literary text as a journey toward self-definition is a commonplace of postromantic criticism.[132] New Criticism, myth interpretation, and postwar psychoanalytic criticism have all made use of the trajectory of the individual who, lacking a stable identity, undergoes painful encounters with the world before acquiring some, perhaps illusory, sense of self.[133] It is this humanist myth that Lacan revises and retells; and it is his tale that psychoanalytic film criticism revises and retells. Whether Lacan's account has universal application or is culture-specific, whether it "explains" only patriarchy or all social formations, in the hands of film interpreters it becomes an allegorical template that assists in building a model of the text.

It might be objected that my analysis does not take notice of the originality of the feminist-Lacanian schema. Unlike the psychomythography of Freud, Rank, and the American critics of the 1950s and 1960s, this approach deals not only with the actions of the characters but also with the narration that represents them—the outer circle of my bull's-eye text schema. Lacan, for instance, discusses the "triple subjective filter" in "The Purloined Letter"; and Mulvey offers the "three-looks" version of personification as a means for designating power relations at the level of visual representation. This account of narration, however, conforms to the traditional assumption of an "outward flow" of meaning from the central core. Lacan's relay clearly runs in an expressivist direction: the story of the purloined letter passes from the Queen to the Prefect to Dupin to the narrator to the reader. Likewise, in most Mulvey-influenced criticism, characters' gazes and glances establish the power relations that the camera's "look" will reinforce, qualify, or contradict.

Consequently, interpretations of narration can offer no less thoroughgoing allegories of theoretical doctrine. A vivid example is E. Ann Kaplan's discussion of Sally Potter's *Thriller*. Kaplan treats the diegetic realm as a feminist-Lacanian allegory of woman's relation to the Symbolic. In order to investigate the place of Mimi in *La Bohème,* the heroine, Mimi I, must return to the Mirror Phase. Potter conveys this in a shot that shows Mimi I with her back to a mirror, which nevertheless, à la Magritte, reflects her face. This suggests, Kaplan says, that Mimi I has recognized the fundamentally split nature of all subjectivity. Further, when her shadow is cast across a wall, Kaplan invokes the search-for-self pattern: "The shadow across the screen signals that Mimi I has asserted her own identity rather than letting herself be named, given a character/identity, like Mimi II in the opera. The sound of a heartbeat accompanying these shots signifies the rebirth that is taking place."[134] Thus both its diegetic action and its nondiegetic representation make the film an allegory of contemporary theory itself. In having the protagonist pass from the level of the unconscious to historical awareness, *Thriller* is said to present a progression from psychic and individual determinations to social ones. According to Kaplan, the film challenges Lacanian theory by representing change. "We *see* the women, formerly split both internally and externally, turn to each other and embrace, recognizing their oneness while the men slink away."[135] This is a perfect example of allegorical commentary.

In using such emblematic imagery, *Thriller* can also be considered an allegory in the traditional sense summed up by Frye: "when a poet explicitly indicates the relationship of his images to examples and precepts, and so tries to indicate how a commentary on him should proceed."[136] Here is another reason why symptomatic critics turn explicatory when confronted with certain oppositional films: those films are more or less deliberate allegories of contemporary symptomatic theory. Works like *Sigmund Freud's Dora* and *Riddles of the Sphinx* enact issues, categories, and processes. In doing so they strive to foreclose certain interpretations and point the critic to the correct meaning, even if the meanings include the possibility that the issues are difficult, the categories problematic, and the processes polysemous. (Recall the semantically "open" trajectory of art cinema, discussed earlier.) Of course, as in any allegory, the meanings require expert decoding, but the critic who is stumped has the recourse of asking the filmmaker to explain the text. Typically, the filmmaker will oblige with a contemporary equivalent of that "instructive Moral" which John Fletcher located at the heart of allegory. Here is Mulvey in an interview, explicating aspects of *Riddles:*

> I think of the Sphinx as standing for the danger, the threat posed by femininity in patriarchal society, which is closely linked to motherhood . . . for two reasons: (1) It's the power that the child invests in its mother, bonded by the strength of emotional ties, that has to be overcome for "him" to be able to achieve independence and social maturity. (2) The unconscious of patriarchy sees the mother as a source of anxiety and castration threat if it's not kept strictly ideologically in check, and even then anxiety remains . . . I see the Sphinx as also standing for that which is in or of femininity which cannot be described/understood by a society that assigns the feminine inferior value.[137]

Whereas classical allegories channel the reader toward the desired sense by attaching a running commentary or a summarizing moral, the allegorical theory-film aspires to the evocative richness of implicit meaning. It rarely wears its doctrine on its sleeve. But the institution of film interpretation, by publishing filmmakers' interviews and writings, still helps the critic determine what this or that stands for.

My survey of synchronic and diachronic schemata and their attendant heuristics aims to convey both the variety and the conventionality of text-based schemata. Along with the semantic fields and the category- and person-based schemata, the text schemata offer the critic many ways of building an interpretation that will meet the demands of novelty and plausibility.

In practice, all the schemata work together to guide the critic to proper cues. The category "Hitchcock films" enables the critic to be sensitive to a certain narrating persona, while the category "melodramas" alerts the critic to certain character types, behaviors, and "excesses" of mise-en-scène or music. Similarly, the diachronic schemata help define the range of personifications that are appropriate, focusing on character actions that constitute phases of a struggle or choices between alternatives. These schemata and routines vary enough to cover diverse aspects of any film but remain sufficiently redundant to reinforce some cues, such as human action or the framing of a shot, which are central to the interpretive enterprise.

Once more, I should stress that I am not offering a "real-time" model of critical inquiry (though that would be a worthwhile goal for empirical research[138]). I am not claiming that every critic conceives semantic fields, then runs them through assumptions and hypotheses, then invokes various schemata and heuristics. What I have proposed is an anatomy of the logic of mapping and modeling that underlies interpretive problem-solving. One critic may start with concrete textual cues and then cast about for schemata, heuristics, and semantic fields that seem appropriate; another critic may start by presupposing certain semantic fields and then, finding some cues that fit, call upon schemata and heuristics that will extend the interpretation. In any event, conceptual structures of the sort I have laid out would seem to be central to the process. At this point, I can offer a diagrammatic representation of how schemata and heuristics mediate the projection of semantic fields onto the text and contribute to the production of the critic's "model film" (see Figure 13).

All this, we might say, is very largely what separates the academic critic from the reviewer and from the ordinary spectator. A critic is not necessarily a master of theory or an expert on cinema, or art, or life. A critic is a person who can perform particular tasks: conceive the possibility of ascribing implicit or repressed meanings to films, invoke acceptable semantic fields, map them onto texts by using conventional schemata and procedures, and produce a "model film" that embodies the interpretation. Though acquired by each individual, these skills and knowledge structures are institutionally defined and transmitted. And though it is possible to abstract a critical "theory" or "method" from individual "readings," and thus to reify that theory

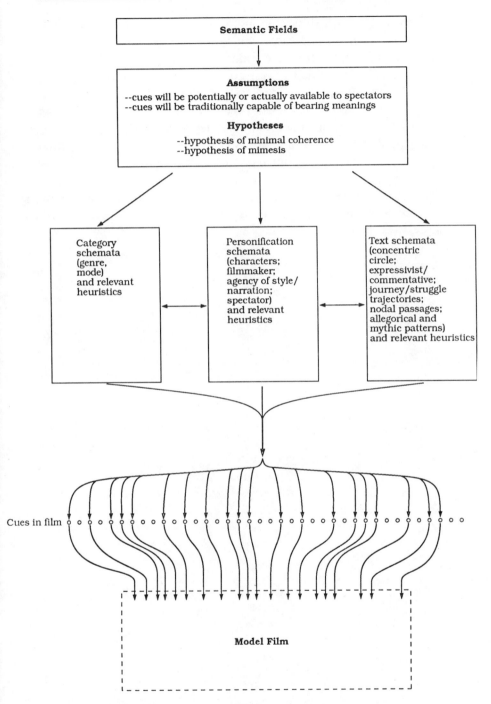

Figure 13. A cognitive model of critical interpretation

or method as a self-sufficient procedure of discovery or validation, employing such an apparatus will not carry any critic all the way through an interpretation. Decisions about cues, patterns, and mapping must still be made by "just going on," as Wittgenstein puts it, and following the tacit logic of craft tradition. Further, I have tried to show that in the operations of interpretation, such skills are more functionally significant than many of the theoretical positions enunciated by distinct methodological schools. Indeed, the schools often take the practices as unexamined premises for their more programmatic statements.

A critic is, however, something more. She is a person who sets out interpretations in language. The critic, as the next two chapters will show, uses rhetoric.

9

Interpretation as Rhetoric

It is very much more difficult to talk about a thing than to do it. In the sphere of actual life that is of course obvious. Anybody can make history. Only a great man can write it.

—Oscar Wilde

In contemporary theoretical inquiry, the study of rhetorical processes often reduces to tropology, with special attention to those "master figures" of metaphor and metonymy.[1] As Chapter 2 indicated, this book takes a broader and more old-fashioned view. I treat rhetoric as a matter of *inventio* (the devising of arguments), *dispositio* (their arrangement), and *elocutio* (their stylistic articulation).[2] This scheme allows me to discuss how a wide range of factors, including the critic's persona and the constructed reader, will shape the finished interpretation. The classical outline also lets us trace how the schemata and heuristics that operate in the problem-solving process emerge as premises and evidence for arguments. Throughout, I shall be insisting that rhetoric is a dynamic factor in exploring issues, sharpening differences, and achieving consensus within a community.

High-minded as this sounds, there is a potential danger. Few critics like having their arguments treated as instances of rhetorical conventions, and so this chapter risks seeming cynical or destructive. Such is not my intent. I am hoping that contemporary critics' commitment to the analysis of how positions are "discursively constructed" will make my inquiry seem not only timely but revelatory. Critics who believe that discourse can never be a neutral agency ought to welcome analysis of the intersubjective presuppositions and implications of their own writing.[3] Further, and more plainly, for me rhetoric does not amount to a disinterested manipulation of language. One can be sincere and rhetorical at the same time; indeed, rhetoric can help one be sincere. (Forster: "How can I know what I think till I see what I say?") Rhetoric is the shaping of language to achieve one's ends, and in the act of shaping the language, the ends get sorted and sharpened. The rhetor's purposes may be cynical or selfish ones, but they may also be—*should* be—ones which are grounded in socially desirable goals. Such is, at least, the way I take not only my analysis of critical rhetoric but also the rhetoric I deploy myself. If nothing else, this chapter offers tools for analyzing my own persuasive strategies throughout the book.

Sample Strategies

"The speaker," writes Aristotle, "must frame his proofs and arguments with the help of common knowledge and accepted opinions."[4] Rhetorical argument is adjusted to the audience's preconceptions, even if the rhetor aims to change some of them. If the critic's audience will not assume that a home movie or an educational documentary or a "slasher" film is an appropriate object of interpretation, the critic must generate arguments for discussing such despised genres.

From the rhetorical standpoint, the interpreter's basic task—building a novel and plausible interpretation of one or more appropriate films—becomes a matter of negotiating with the audience's institutionally grounded assumptions. There is a trade-off. Risk a more novel interpretation, and you may produce an exemplar; fail, and you will seem merely odd. Stick closely to the limits of plausibility, and you will pass muster, but you may seem routine. In general, the best preparation is to study exemplars. This teaches the critic what will go down with an audience and what degrees of originality are encouraged by particular institutional circumstances.

In creating a novel and plausible interpretation, the critic draws upon strategies associated with rhetorical *inventio*. For instance, the critic must establish her expertise—by reviewing the literature or the state of a question, by making fine distinctions, by displaying a range or depth of knowledge about the film, the director, the genre, and so on. These ethos-centered appeals create the critic's persona—a *role* (Partisan, Judge, Analyst) and a set of *attributes* (rigor, fairness, erudition).[5] A rare recognition of ethos emerges from a moment in a 1959 *Cahiers* roundtable on *Hiroshima mon amour*, in which Rivette follows mentions of Stravinsky, Picasso, and Braque with the observation: "Well now, we've mentioned quite a few 'names,' so you can see just how cultured we are. *Cahiers du cinéma* is true to form, as always."[6] So pervasive is the power of rhetoric that the remark endows the speaker with a self-conscious honesty.

Another aspect of invention is *pathos,* the appeal to the reader's emotions. This is evident in belletristic film interpretation, and is no less present, though more circumspectly, in academic writing. A critic writes that one scene of *L'Atalante* "humanizes the thief, modeling his frail body wasted by cold and hunger."[7] The description triggers feelings which drive home the interpretive claim. The critic who probes for symptomatic readings also uses pathos, at least insofar as he seeks to gratify an urge for knowledge, mastery, or refined discrimination. The defiant call for analytical sobriety, such as Mulvey's claim in "Visual Pleasure and Narrative Cinema" that she aims to destroy the pleasure of the image, can excite feelings of liberation, a "passionate detachment."[8]

Whatever the critic's approach, she will also create identificatory roles around which the reader's emotions can crystallize. One such role is that of the constructed reader, a kind of parallel to the rhetor's own persona. The other role is that of the "mock viewer," the hypothetical spectator who responds in the fashion best suited to the critic's interpretation. The interpreter must give each role some emotion-laden attributes and relate the two—making them congruent, or demystifying the activities of the mock viewer in order to heighten the constructed reader's awareness. For instance, the *L'Atalante* critic cited above ends his essay with an invitation:

> If the film charms rather than preaches, it is because for Vigo, as for Père Jules, there is nothing transcendent about art or morality. These are not achievements so much as instincts, instincts, it is true, that civilization has lost, but instincts all the same. Catlike, Père Jules is the film's most artful and moral being, his sensuality a guarantee of his authenticity. The same rhythm of life, the same fever that drives the cats, drives Jules, Vigo, and each spectator not yet immunized against it.[9]

By this point the reader should have identified with the constructed reader of the essay, one who can appreciate the film's nonnarrative, richly physical qualities. Now the reader is asked to take the role of the sensitive viewer who welcomes the film's "fever." I shall suggest later how a critic's use of "we" often blends the rhetor's persona, the mock viewer, and the constructed reader into a single vague but rhetorically conventional entity.

Invention's case-centered proofs are no less significant than its ethical and pathetic ones. An argument often passes or fails by its use of *examples*. Michel Charles has proposed that in fact the key convention of literary interpretation is what he calls the *integral citation* of parts of the text under study. By absorbing stretches of the original text into his discourse, the critic presents that discourse as seeking to approximate the act of reading, while the fragmentation of the text gives him great freedom to arrange extracts in a compelling sequence.[10]

The film critic's examples are principally those nodal passages of the film that bear ascribed meanings. Through vivid writing and varied degrees of amplification, these passages must become what Frank Kermode, following Wilhelm Dilthey, calls "impression-points."[11] From one angle, the history of film interpretation looks to be one of steadily increasing finesse in the presentation of such examples: the incisive description practiced by Bazin, the richer detail work of *Movie,* and the shot lists, bird's-eye views, and frame enlargements that appeared in the late 1960s. The greater detail lets more cues activate more semantic fields—producing longer and more intricate interpretations. Although diagrams and stills offer the skeptical reader an opportunity to spot disparities in the interpretation, they convince the charitable reader through "presence."[12] Like Caesar's bloody tunic or the scientist's graph, these devices offer themselves as purified data, examples beyond words: the reader need only look and see.

Still, examples would not carry much force if tacit and widely accepted beliefs were not also giving the critic's case a logical cast. The *enthymeme* is an incomplete syllogism; the audience, from its stock of knowledge and opinions, supplies premises never set forth in the argument.[13] Some of these premises will be specific to different critical schools, as when the critic presupposes that the Oedipal trajectory or organic unity underwrites a certain interpretive move. Other premises subtend the institution as a whole. All the problem-solving processes I have brought out in previous chapters can operate enthymematically. When the critic personifies the camera or claims that a character's surroundings reveal a psychological condition, she is using an inferential procedure as a warrant for the conclusion. The rhetor typically makes certain interpretive moves seem logically inevitable by turning semantic fields into hidden meanings, schemata and heuristics into tacit premises, inferences into argumentative points and conclusions, and the model film into the film itself.

There are, however, widely used enthymemes that do not derive from cognitive discovery procedures. Chief among these is an appeal to authority.[14] The rhetor can count on his audience to trust knowledgeable individuals, and the appeal to respected names and writings is basic to an institution's coherence and continuity. Thus the critic can drop names (Leavis, Lévi-Strauss, Laplanche) or metonymically invoke the massive authority of vast realms of knowledge ("according to Marxism" or "semiotics"). In self-consciously theoretical criticism, the authorities cited often stand outside the institution, and the credibility arises from a belief that they possess knowledge about matters larger and more weighty than cinema. That is, claims about cinema now depend upon truth-claims about wider realms—social power, the nature of language, the dynamics of the unconscious. In this connection, the arrival of citational footnotes in *Cahiers, Screen,* and *Artforum* should be seen as a major event, signaling not simply "academicization" but a move toward arguments from external expertise.

The authority most frequently called upon is the filmmaker. In Chapter 4 I suggested that both explicatory and symptomatic critics habitually trace effects of the film back to such a source, and in Chapter 7 I showed that both trends personify the filmmaker as a calculating or expressive agent. Now we can see how the filmmaker's words can function as rhetorical backup for an interpretation. One critic can take a statement by John Ford as confirming the ideological problems of *Fort Apache,* while another can quote interviews with Sirk to show that his films are about happiness and knowledge.[15] Hitchcock's comments about fetishism can support a reading of *Marnie*.[16] A critic can describe *Riddles of the Sphinx* in terms established by the makers: the Sphinx presents 'a stream of questions, contradictions, and word associations' (Wollen), a 'voice asking for a riddle' (Mulvey). Implicit here is a conception of feminist strategy which is not solely in the realm of the conscious, for the Symbolic world into which women enter 'is not their own' (Mulvey)."[17] Interviews, manifestos, and essays furnish evidence for even the symptomatic critic who denounces the idea of origins or creative agency. If the author is dead, film critics are still holding seances.

More exactly, the appeal to the artist functions in relation to several alternative topoi, or commonplace enthymemes. The critic makes a claim about the film's meaning. If the filmmaker's statement confirms it, the statement becomes a piece of causal evidence. (The filmmaker "put" the meaning there, as either a rational or an involuntary agent.) What if the filmmaker's statement does not square with the reading? The critic can simply ignore it (a common tactic). Or she can cite D. H. Lawrence's dictum "Never trust the teller, trust the tale," and point out how unself-conscious the artist is. Alternatively, the symptomatic critic can use the filmmaker's counterstatement as just another trace of repressed meanings. In any case, the critic has great freedom. The *Movie* critics dismissed Hitchcock's answers at press conferences but used claims he made in more serious interviews as evidence for an interpretation.[18] More recently, another writer builds her interpretation of *Presents* out of statements by Michael Snow about the film's techniques and themes, but then she cites other Snow remarks to demonstrate that he is unaware that the film "leaves no room" for the female spectator's look.[19] In such exercises, film criticism plows long-broken ground; Kant, then Schleiermacher, took it as a goal of interpretation to understand an author better than he understood himself.[20]

Two can play this game. The flexibility of the ask-the-artist topos gives filmmakers a chance to manipulate the interpretive institution. In experimental production, the filmmaker's statement can lead the critic to preferred interpretations of an otherwise opaque work. If Peter Wollen claims that the Sphinx in *Riddles of the Sphinx* represents "a repressed instance of the female unconscious," critics can pick up the hint and expand the interpretive point.[21] (This tactic is not unknown in the history of avant-garde art; Joyce turned over his plan of *Ulysses* to Stuart Gilbert and helped a circle of friends write explications of what would become *Finnegans Wake*.[22]) Such skills can be wielded by more commercial creators as well. The director of *In a Lonely Place* tells critics that one of his constant themes is man's loneliness.[23] David Cronenberg acknowledges that in *Videodrome* he deliberately entices critics with a tension between medieval and Renaissance thought, as well as quotations from Yeats and Leonardo.[24] Chabrol supplies a more cynical reason for the literary citations in his films:

> I need a degree of critical support for my films to succeed: without that they can fall flat on their faces. So, what do you have to do? You have to help the critics over their notices, right? So, I give them a hand. "Try with Eliot and see if you find me there." Or "How do you fancy Racine?" I give them some little things to grasp at. In *Le Boucher* I stuck Balzac there in the middle, and they threw themselves on it like poverty upon the world. It's not good to leave them staring at a blank sheet of paper, not knowing how to begin . . . "This film

is definitely Balzacian," and there you are; after that they can go on to say whatever they want.[25]

If critics can use the artist's statements as evidence for their interpretation, artists versed in interpretive procedures can use the critics.[26]

A complete list of topoi at work in film interpretation would run very long, but let me pick out a few which have given pleasure over the years.

A critically significant film is ambiguous, or polysemous, or dialogical.

A critically significant film is strikingly novel in subject, theme, style, or form.

A critically significant film takes up an oppositional relation to tradition (old version: ironic; new version: subversive).

A film should make its audience work.

Putting characters in the same frame unites them; cutting stresses opposition.

Montage is opposed to mise-en-scène, or camera movement.

The first viewing is different from later viewings.

Lumière is opposed to Méliès.

The image always escapes verbal paraphrase (old version: through richness; new version: through excess or plenitude).

The filmmaker in question is not solely a master of technique; the film also harbors profound meanings.

In the artist's late period, technique is thrown aside and the work becomes simpler, more schematic, and more profound.

The film asks a question but doesn't answer it.

The film is a reflection or meditation on a sophisticated philosophical or political issue.

The film is Shakespearian (Anglo-American version) or Racinian (French) or Faulknerian (either).

The film's style is so exaggerated that it must be ironic or parodic (useful for Sirk, late Vidor, Visconti, Ken Russell, and so on).

Previous interpretations of the film are inadequate, if not downright wrong.

The critic may capsulize special topics in maxims such as: "If the woman looks, the spectacle provokes, castration is in the air," or "I daresay that ambiguity is an infallible sign of value in the cinema."[27] People are delighted, writes Aristotle, when the rhetor expresses as a general truth the opinions they hold about individual cases.[28]

We are now in a position to understand another function of self-consciously theoretical discourse within film criticism. Theoretical doctrines are often parceled out into enthymemes, topoi, and maxims that assist the rhetorical phase of interpretation. "Theory" has become a binding institutional force, creating tacit beliefs to which the rhetor may appeal. For instance, this book's analysis might be more persuasive to certain readers if whenever I mention critical "practice" or "discourse," I were to attach a quotation or two from Foucault. If debate within explicatory criticism rests on the premise "My theme can lick your theme,"[29] disputes within symptomatic criticism appeal to something like "My theory can lick your theory." In this respect, post-1960s film criticism turns from the Judeo-Christian tradition of putting philosophy at the service of the text and recalls the Stoic tradition of treating literature as a diversion to be mastered by the rigor of theoretical reflection.[30] The taken-for-granted power of the theory can appear to validate the interpretation; in turn, the interpretation can seem to illustrate the theory, confirm it, or extend its range of application. The critic may also grant an avant-garde or subversive film the power to investigate conceptual issues and reveal truths; a film becomes significant insofar as it aspires to the condition of theoretical writing (see Chapter 4).

So much, in overview, for the ethical, pathetic, and pseudological proofs that constitute "invention." *Dispositio,* the second major heading within classical rhetorical theory, concerns the organizational structure of the interpretation. Given the standard formats of criticism—the essay or the book chapter—we might want to make an initial distinction. The explicatory critic frequently structures the argument around an intuitively apprehended experience of the film, while the more "theoretical" critic characteristically mixes an exposition or elaboration of concepts drawn from the writings of an authority (Freud, Lacan, Althusser) with claims that the film illustrates or manifests those concepts. In recent years, however, the distinction between these approaches has become blurred, as academic protocol makes even explicatory critics lean on experts and received doctrines. A more basic argumentative structure is at work in both trends. The typical film interpretation follows the scheme laid down by Aristotle and revised by Cicero:

Introduction:
> Entrance: An introduction to the issue.
> Narration: The background circumstances; in film interpretation, either a brief account of an issue's history or a description or synopsis of the film to be examined.

Proposition: The statement of the thesis to be proven.
Body:
   Division: A breakdown of points that support the thesis.
   Confirmation: The arguments under each point.
   Confutation: The destruction of opposing arguments.
Conclusion: A review and emotional exhortation.[31]

Any piece of criticism may rearrange these components. Very often, the division of points is spread piecemeal throughout the essay, and the confutation (if present at all) is set close to the opening.

Beginnings are a problem. Whereas the journalistic reviewer strives for a novel, arresting opening, the academicization of film criticism has created a few predictable preliminaries. The critic will seldom start with a question, a provocative statement, or an abrupt, disorienting description of a stretch of the film at hand. The standard opening ritualistically positions this essay with respect to established or up-and-coming work, sometimes by a quick review of the current literature. At its most pallid, the essay's opening invokes "recent developments." This gambit conveys at least three things: (1) "I keep up with what's happening [ethos] and so do you [pathos]"; (2) "Film studies progresses; the more recent a work is, the more attention it demands"; (3) "I hereby put the top card on the pile; no work is more recent, hence more potentially significant, than what you're reading now." In the course of the essay, the rhetor can exploit the "recency" topos in two ways. Either: "I extend recent theory by showing how it applies to a fresh case," or: "I revise recent theory in a cooperative spirit by showing how, with some tinkering, the theory can account for an anomalous film." Very seldom will the critic challenge "recent developments" by using the film at hand to show that they have come to a dead end.

The body of the essay offers the critic an important organizational choice. Following the tradition of interlinear commentary and Lansonist *explication de texte,* she can move step by step through the film, letting "plot order" structure the argument. In effect, the "narration" component of the rhetorical framework swallows up the division and confirmation of points. The argument gains credence by apparently adhering to the contours of the viewing experience; but the essay risks conceptual diffuseness and makes any omission from the film's flow more glaring. Alternatively, the critic can organize the essay around the conceptual structure of the interpretation. Thus the "division" component becomes an outline of the film's principal semantic fields and a tracing of their interplay, while the "confirmation" portions will cite the nodal passages that instantiate those fields. The advantage of this strategy is conceptual clarity, elegance, and power. The critic subordinates the film to his overarching argument, ranging over the film and plucking out the datum that supports the point at hand. The disadvantage of this strategy is that it may seem partial and one-sided; the critic may appear to be concealing those parts of the film that don't fit. It is also significant that exponents of this pattern usually also resort to the step-by-step approach. Most often, the climax of the critic's argument coincides with a discussion of the climax of the film, and the critic achieves conceptual and rhetorical closure by ending with an interpretation of the film's final sequence.

The rhetor may vary the body of the argument by creating a comparative structure that sets two films off against each other: an ordinary genre film versus an auteur masterpiece, a "classical" film counterposed to a modernist or oppositional work.[32] In general, the more the critic seeks to make the film illustrate or demonstrate a theoretical argument, the more such comparative tactics can come into play. The risk is that the skeptical reader will argue that the theoretical framework distorts or impoverishes the films mentioned.

The ending of the interpretive essay is the most conventional aspect of critical *dispositio*. Whether the critic presents the interpretation as issuing deductively from a theoretical doctrine or arising inductively from the data of the film, the proposition announced at the outset must eventually stand affirmed. The thesis may be stated in a tentative fashion; the inquiry may present itself as exploratory; but the essay's ending will seek to establish the foregoing argument as a tenable interpretation. Richard Levin notes: "The critic will frequently claim or imply that the reading is to serve the function of testing his conception of the work's real meaning, which is presented initially as a kind of hypothesis. And his hypothesis always passes this test, because the reading . . . is a self-confirming demonstration . . . No reading on record has ever failed to prove the critic's thesis."[33]

The ending may also include, as Cicero recognized, a sharp emotional appeal. The critic can summon up particular feelings represented in or evoked by the film. (*Europa 51* shows that Rossellini is a "terrorist," presenting a cinema "of war, of guerilla action, of revolution."[34]) Or the critic can "place" the film's symptomatic qualities and remind the reader of social action. (*Klute* contains, despite itself, "fragments that refer forcefully to the images and problems of a struggling feminism."[35]) The appeal to pathos at the end of the essay (paralleling the ethos that must be established at the beginning) reveals the extent to which critical logic relies heavily upon rhetorical force.

The power of the film interpreter's *dispositio* lies largely in its familiarity. The essay has the structure of the standard literary or art-historical critical article. Like them, it derives from such forms of oral scriptural exegesis as the rabbinical *petihta* that introduces the Torah reading, and the Scholastic sermon that develops theme, protheme, and *dilatatio*.[36] The structure can be writ large across a book, so that the first chapter functions as the introduction, providing a review of the literature and a preview of the thesis, while the subsequent chapters produce interpretations of particular films, each chapter supporting points of the main argument. The conventions also acknowledge the interpretation to be part of a communal effort. Within such standard formats, social cohesion—of critic and reader, of critic and critic—can be reaffirmed.

Theory Talk

That critical *elocutio* is highly rhetorical probably needs no proving. Most film interpreters have considered themselves artificers of language. Some, such as Bazin and Parker Tyler, have been superb stylists. Academic critics have not shrunk from the stylistic flourishes of popular prose fiction.

On *Psycho:* "Does Marion imagine no one in the world with the power to make her feel this alive, no one to whom she might offer herself this freely and passionately?"[37]

On *Rebecca:* "If death by drowning did not extinguish the woman's desire, can we be certain that death by fire has reduced it utterly to ashes?"[38]

On *Empire of the Senses:* "Let us come back to the anecdote with which we began: Saito, the reception, the assassination, the abortive putsch. Yes, of course, *Naughty Marietta* has nothing to do with all that, is only, precisely, pure anecdote. And yet . . ."[39]

On *The Phantom of the Opera:* "The crowd freezes, the Phantom laughs and opens his hand to reveal that it contains . . . nothing at all."[40]

And no one can miss the blatantly persuasive effect of such passages as these:

On how the flatness of Antonioni's shots eliminates tactility: "To touch is to confirm, and people who are out of touch have a desperate need for tactile reassurance."[41] The punning heuristic discussed in Chapter 6 invites the critic to use homonymies metaphorically, as here with the "out of touch" phrase.

"If I were a gossip columnist, I would attribute this new tentative optimism [in *L'Avventura* and *La Notte*] to the arrival of Monica Vitti in Antonioni's life."[42] Here *praeteritio* ("I pass over this in silence") is used to get the biographical anecdote on the record while simultaneously attributing interest in such matters to scandalmongers.

"Think, for example, of Polanski's *Chinatown* and of Altman's *The Long Goodbye,* films which construct a whole set of discourses about voyeurism around the character of the private eye. Or think of individual scenes in any number of detective films and thrillers in which the central protagonist is engaged, simply, in secretive looking."[43] Rather than itemize the discourses or scenes, the critic invites the reader, who is presumed to share the rhetor's degree of knowledge, to recall a few. The phrases "a whole set" and "any number," like such phrases as "Had I sufficient time . . ." or "If space permitted . . . ," function to imply that the press of more important matters forces the writer to withhold information he could otherwise supply. (Figure: *periphrasis,* or circumlocution.)

On *Beyond a Reasonable Doubt* and Lang's earlier works: "What in fact do we see in each case? In the earlier films, innocence with all the appearances of guilt; here, guilt with all the appearances of innocence. Can anyone fail to see that they're about the same thing, or at least about the same question?"[44] The first sentence instantiates "reasoning by question and answer." The second, with its play on "guilt" and "innocence," is a fancy *isocolon,* like Herodotus' "In peace, sons bury their fathers; in war, fathers bury their sons." The third sentence asks a rhetorical question, then withdraws it in part by *epanorthosis* (correcting an initial claim); here it depicts the writer as seeking precision by qualifying his remark.

Less overt eloquence also serves the interpreter's ends. Consider the tactic I shall call "associational redescription,"[45] the movement from a comparatively neutral description to one keyed to the interpretive point. Here is a small-scale instance: "[In *Phantom of the Opera*] her unmasking of his face reveals the very wounds, the very lack, that the Phantom had hoped her blind love would heal."[46] The objectival phrase ("the very wounds") is uncontroversial, but the appositional phrase ("the very lack") functions as a redescription that carries an extra inference. Without the first phrase the interpretation would seem more forced; without the second phrase, there would be no interpretation at all. A more extended example comes from an explication of the ending of *Strangers on a Train*. In the scene, Guy and Ann are startled when a minister sits down across the aisle, and, as the critic puts it initially, they "look at each other, then smile and, without reply, quickly move away."[47] After the critic interprets this as symbolizing a rejection of stability, putting their future in "grave doubt," associational redescription occurs: the action is now a "fearful drawing back from marriage."[48]

Once film criticism moved into the academy, its diction took on the colors of its habitat. In scholarly writing, certain formulas signal rhetorical procedures. "As X has shown" (or pointed out, or argued) flags an appeal to authority. If I assert that "it is no accident" that something happens, I make the weakest causal claim in a decisive way. If I say that Y "forgets" a crucial point, I credit Y with once having known it—that is, agreeing with me but straying from the path. There are still more minute conventions, such as the colon in the title ("Told by an Idiot: Enunciation and Voice in the Films of Jerry Lewis") or the casually dropped "of course," "needless to say," and "it goes without saying" that soothe the reader while bringing crucial presuppositions into view.

Within the discourse of Academese (which really deserves a book to itself[49]), the rise of theory has generated particular formulas. The opacity of theory has become the source of many jokes, such as the one about the deconstructionist Godfather who makes you an offer you can't understand. Despite the standard tirades against jargon, though, it serves important rhetorical functions. Jargon can yield the critic some ethos, especially if she invents a new term. C. J. van Rees points out that an academic critic's reputation can be made by coining a term, and subsequent users will tend to adopt the premises implicit in it.[50] Jargon also serves to close the ranks, shutting out the uninitiated and reinforcing communal solidarity. Here is an instance drawn from a discussion of Lang's *Man Hunt:*

Indeed, the scene of interrogation seems a condensation of Langian style, as Raymond Bellour and others have staked out its dimensions. First, there is a deconstruction of psychological and dramatic depth through a deliberate flatness—for example, the opening shot of the torture sequence which focuses on a mountain which is obviously a backdrop. Second, there is a deliberate emptying of the image until it becomes a virtual blankness against which a few objects emerge to gain a value that is emblematic, or to use Brecht's term, *gestic*. Third, despite (or because of) these obvious ways in which the "naturalistic" image is theatricalized, turned into a staging, there is a certain emphasis on the space of the frame as a potentially open space. Creating a kind of dialectic of onscreen and offscreen space, the visible image gives glimpses of another space beyond the frame: open doorways that we only get a glimpse into; windows that appear to indicate an elsewhere; entrances and exits that turn the framed area into an arbitrary cutout of space. But unlike, say Renoir, for whom openness can seem an attempt to create the reality effect of a real world in vibrant flux (as in Leo Braudy's reading of Renoir), Lang's openness seems one in which the notion of the frame as *analagon* of a real is displaced by a notion of the frame as mere element in a formal structure, a combinatory, whose value is the quasi-mathematical one of the articulation of forms, not the suggestion of human(ist) meanings of life's richness (33). In a film that has already begun to deprive its hero of agency and turn him instead into a mere figure of the enunciative apparatus, the very composition of space deprives the "hero" of a ground in which his actions could take on a full sense.[51]

Here quotation marks make terms function in oblique, deprecatory ways, and the diction is faintly French ("combinatory" and "real" as nouns). Many names are mentioned, but only Braudy's is footnoted. The constructed reader can catch references to Brecht's theory of representation, Burch's account of off-screen space, and the Bazinian tradition in Renoir criticism. To those in the know, "condensation" and "displaced" cite Freud and Lacan, "deconstruction" recalls Derrida and Burch, "reality effect" and *"analagon"* summon up Barthes, and "enunciative apparatus" echoes Benveniste, Baudry, Metz, and Bellour. The embedded parentheses, as in the morpheme "human(ist)," have, like the connection of words by slashes or spaces, become an emblem of theoretical discourse as such.[52] Strictly speaking, the passage relies on the device of the shibboleth: "a catchword or formula adopted by a party or sect, by which their adherents or followers may be discerned, or those not their followers may be excluded."[53]

"A certain emphasis," "a kind of dialectic"—such phrases in the passage quoted imply both specificity (this, not that) and generality (the writer is aware of larger implications). Theory's rhetoric can thus distinguish itself by diction which is not jargon in the usual sense. Critics use ordinary language in extraordinary ways. To say that a doctrine or thinker "teaches" something becomes formulaic, portraying the rhetor as pupil or disciple. Critics of the contradictory text are drawn to San-Andreas Fault metaphors: cracks, gaps, crevices, fissures, collapses, and explosions. Certain lexical items become fixed counters to be shuffled and recombined. (Some hypothetical examples: *Language/Politics/Desire: A Reading; Reading Language: Politics and Difference; Desiring Differently: Reading, Materialism, Language.*) Innocent italics, jutting up at the end of a sentence, take on an ominous urgency. Barthes: "Psychoanalysis teaches us to read *elsewhere*."[54] A film interpreter: "And now it is possible to *look elsewhere*."[55]

Self-conscious as contemporary film studies is, it has not acknowledged the role of such rhetorical tactics in the 1970s victory of theory. There persists the myth of an embattled Grand Theory triumphing over its predecessors by virtue of its sweeping conceptual innovations. Here is one retelling of the tale:

> Auteurism could have led cinema studies to adopt a conservative, Arnoldian role (can it be an accident that the American director most studied by the auteurists—John Ford—was one who celebrated the mythology of American society, especially the victory of culture over anarchy?). Historical developments, however, prevented auteurism from becoming the dominant approach in film studies; the most important of these was the radicalization of French film/literary criticism which followed in the wake of the upheavals of 1968, a radicalization most obvious, perhaps, in the *Cahiers* circle itself (which published a long, collectively-authored piece on the ideology of Ford's *Young Mr. Lincoln*). Structuralist and post-structuralist theory and approaches, imports from France though importantly mediated by those writing for the British journal *Screen,* greatly influenced the work of American cinema scholars in the formative years of the early seventies. These scholars were more open to new ideas in part because of their marginalized position within academe. During the middle seventies film scholarship in this country became a heavily theorized

enterprise, a complex intersection of Marxist (largely Althusserian), psychoanalytic (largely Lacanian), feminist, and traditional (mostly auteurist and genre) approaches.[56]

This book has sought to show that, on the contrary, these developments were hardly an abrupt change. Apart from the overarching interpretive practices that made new approaches "applicable," there were more gradual and piecemeal changes of the sort traced out in Chapters 2, 3, and 4: symptomatic criticism of the 1940s and cultural criticism of the 1950s; auteur premises governing *Cahiers*'s ideological critique, BFI structuralism, and *Screen* readings; the ratification of long-standing critical habits by theoretical fiat; and so on.

The standard story also neglects important material preconditions. For a critical school to win a share of power, it should dwell in an urban culture—Paris, London, New York, or some other "center of calculation" that attracts money, documents, public events, and talent.[57] The school should command a journal or a book series. It should have bright young people (important critics, like filmmakers, start before they are thirty) and tolerant elders (a Bazin, a Paddy Whannel). It also needs financing, which, since the 1970s, has tied successful schools of film criticism to the rising fortunes of higher education. Now nearly all important film periodicals in English are run by academics and attached to universities; on the whole, the same thing seems to be happening in Europe. In the United States, college film courses started in earnest in the 1960s, and the first wave of film students went on to graduate school in the late 1960s and early 1970s. By the end of the 1970s, the first generation of film scholars had been hired and tenured, moving into positions of leadership in the emerging discipline. This activity coincided with that academicization of writing and publishing mentioned at the outset of this book. The growth of film interpretation requires the sort of shared conventions I have described, but they have flourished chiefly because of the post-1960s consolidation of intellectual power within colleges and universities— a political development that is only now beginning to receive the analysis it warrants.[58] The emergence of "theory" is at once a symptom of this process and a powerful maneuver within it.

That maneuver's success also depended upon a rhetoric that kept skeptics and adversaries on the defensive. Choices hardened: one was either materialist, liberatory, conceptually sophisticated, rigorous, and interested in ultimate questions of mind and society; or one could be idealist, entrenched in the status quo, naive, impressionistic, and preoccupied with superficialities. In their "Cinema/Ideology/Criticism" of 1969, Comolli and Narboni attacked the empiricism of current film writing in the name of scientific dialectical materialism.[59] A rhetorical advantage always lay with the theorist, who could not only invoke powerful authorities to back up an argument but could also show *why* the opponent was bewitched by false ideas. The editor of *Screen* could denounce mainstream British criticism and *Movie:* "Both formalism . . . and semiology have revealed the essential realist and hence ideological impulse involved in this species of romantic aesthetics."[60] A feminist could show that Peter Gidal's attempt to create a "structuralist/materialist" cinema resembled "the *fort/da* game as described by Lacan in which the child plays out obsessively, repetitively the concept of separation, of loss."[61] Rhetorically, Marxism and psychoanalysis enjoy the ability both to propose arguments and to explain the etiology of opponents' errors.

The research program underlying the rhetoric of theory has yielded attractive strategies of proof and diction. Since theory is committed to asking questions, the writer can assume that all work is *in medias res.* The critic can point to difficulties, offer notes or reflections, and end the essay with an invitation to pursue the knotty problems disclosed. Consider this passage:

> This continuousness, the effect of framing as the disposition—the *Einstellung*—of the subject, is evident most immediately in the form of the "continuity" of the sequence-binding of the narrative functions. Festival of affects, a film is equally in the intermittence of its process of images a perpetual metonymy over which narrative lays as a model of closure, a kind of conversion of desire into affectivity as the *direction* of the subject through the image-flow (representation is much less a fact of the image in film than of the organisation of the images).[62]

Anyone who complains about the style here is rebuked by this reply:

> No one writes difficultly in *Screen* for the sake of difficulty; the difficulties come from the development of film theory within the perspectives mentioned above, from the fact that this development is a process. It is this that we recognise as a problem and it is this that we are determined to solve, not by simplifying but by an increased care in identifying and defining the points of difficulty, pres-

enting them as clearly as possible and carrying them through as points of debate in the magazine.[63]

Despite the exploratory qualities claimed for theory, however, the theorist remains pledged to some solid premises. There is not much allowance for questions, problems, and debate in one theorist's claim that the self-consciousness of semiology "puts the nail in the coffin of the unified self."[64] A rhetoric of musts and onlys, of always alreadys, of dangers and complicities portrays the writer as one guided by certainties.

> A feminist theory of film must examine the ideological effects of the cinematic apparatus on the spectator/subject, understanding the spectator as a social subject, a locus of ideological determination.[65]

> Nor can the Lacanian theory have any relation to those theories involving a concept of misrecognition as false consciousness, thereby assuming, even if it is always unknowable in any future sense, that reality can be described by theory, and that ideology operates a systematic distortion or falsification of that reality. This latter would have to rely on a privileged relation between knowledge and its object (to be in a position to know the real beyond the phenomenal forms); ultimately this can only rely on an idealist form of consciousness.[66]

> Although the introduction of the critical category of POV constitutes an attempt to locate the text in relations of subjectivity, it is still complicit with the ideology of centrality and identity, with the model of communication theory which the development of a theory of the subject seeks to displace.[67]

Over the last two decades, an aggressive rhetorical stance has helped win and maintain theory's institutional authority.

That authority might have been challenged by an equally attractive set of ideas deploying an equally vigorous discourse. None emerged. Instead, there appeared a rhetoric of conversion, confession, and abjuration. In "Cinema/Ideology/Criticism," Comolli and Narboni admitted that they had fallen into the two traps of structuralism ("phenomenological positivism and mechanistic materialism").[68] Looking back at his 1965 writing on *Vertigo*, Robin Wood finds it "shot through with a subtle and insidious sexism (at that time I had no awareness whatever of the oppression of women within our culture), and, closely related to this, it lacks any psychoanalytic account of the nature of 'romantic love,' accepting it as some eternal and unchanging given of 'the human condition.'"[69] Back in 1973, calling himself a "star-struck structuralist," Geoffrey Nowell-Smith offered a self-criticism of his *Visconti,* charging it with idealism, essentialism, and a "then fashionable historicist Marxism."[70] Soon thereafter, Charles Eckert repudiated his allegiance to Lévi-Strauss and announced that he had since been "educated" by the writings of Marvin Harris and Julia Kristeva.[71] He issued a ringing prophecy pledging support to the new vanguard: "There is a stiff, cold wind blowing against partial, outmoded, or theoretically unsound forms of film criticism—and it just might blow many of them away."[72] Two years later, I criticized my essay on *Citizen Kane* for idealist naiveté and announced my adherence to current work in theory (Russian Formalism, structuralism, and post-structuralism).[73] Again, I am not saying that such self-criticisms are insincere, or that the new positions which the authors take are not improvements on earlier ones. My aim is to show that the public articulations of such intellectual commitments have, inevitably, a persuasive component. In this respect, using "theory" as a topos and a stylistic appeal resembles other rhetorical procedures in social life as a whole.

10

Rhetoric in Action: Seven Models of *Psycho*

Resemblances are the shadows of differences. Different people see different similarities and similar differences.

—Vladimir Nabokov, *Pale Fire*

The last chapter's survey of rhetorical devices was merely indicative; one could go on much longer tracing out particular patterns of *inventio, dispositio,* and *elocutio.* But we do not need an atomistic taxonomy like those in ancient handbooks. For our purposes, some exemplars and prototypes will furnish more illuminating examples. This chapter seeks to display the dynamic role of rhetoric by analyzing, in historical sequence from 1960 to 1986, seven discussions of *Psycho.*

My emphasis on the conventions that run across different interpretive schools may sometimes seem oblivious to the disparities and disputes that riddle the institution. By tracing varying responses to the same film, I can show that such incompatibilities have a rhetorical dimension. Further, these differences can best be understood in terms of the categories which this book sets out. Interpretations vary according to semantic fields, textual cues, schemata, procedures, and, not least, rhetorical strategies. These studies of *Psycho* thus let me review in concrete terms many of the aspects of interpretation discussed in earlier chapters. We shall see that the critical institution offers a diversified but not unlimited range of interpretive options.

Jean Douchet, "Hitch and His Public" (1960)

From the start of *Psycho* criticism, the spectator is given a starring role. Douchet plots the film's trajectory as the viewer's journey through three "worlds": starting from everyday events, then through intellectual involvement in a mystery to a confrontation with subjective desire.[1] The viewer becomes a voyeur who at once desires Marion Crane and has contempt for her: thus emotions both "crazed and fascinating" attend the shower murder (p. 155). *Psycho* makes us accomplices in Marion's crime, and then in Norman's attempt to clean up. After this, the spectator's ties to reality and reason are completely cut. Every new scene becomes potentially terrifying, until scientific intellect, in the form of the psychiatrist's explanation, comes to release us. We can then contemplate Norman with pity.

The critic's task is to persuade us that his interpretation captures aspects of spectatorial activity. To this end, Douchet first organizes his presentation as a chronological account of the film. Most critics of *Psycho* take this option; in general, if the critic wants to prove a point about the viewer's experience, tracing the action's trajectory scene by scene often helps win the reader's assent. Moreover, Douchet opens the essay with a discussion of *Rear Window* as an allegory of Hitchcock's seduction of the spectator. James Stewart is the voyeuristic viewer who moves from the realm of reality through intellectual curiosity to the realm of projected desire. (This allows Douchet to use the "expressivist" heuristic to show how other couples in the courtyard personify the hero's attitudes.) In asking us to imagine that Stewart stepped down off the screen and sat in the audience, Douchet identifies *Psycho*'s spectator as a voyeur; this is a sturdy topos in film criticism generally. Third, Douchet goes on to treat this spectator as both abstract and empirical. On the one hand, his analysis would not be damaged if a reader protested that she or he did not feel terror around the corner in every scene. Douchet is describing a "mock" spectator. On the other hand, he strengthens his claim to validity by citing empirical evidence of spectators' response. He starts with the admonition not to read the essay unless you have seen *Psycho,* since he can attest that knowing the ending in advance spoiled some of his pleasure. Elsewhere, Douchet describes the opening scene in terms that address empirical spectators who have sexual desires: "If John Gavin's torso just satisfies at least half the audience, the fact that Janet Leigh is not naked is taken badly by the other half" (p. 153). Douchet's pathos-centered appeal profits from the elision between posited and actual spectators, as when he summons up the critic's characteristic plural pronoun: "We are with her all the way" (p. 153). In a movement that is hard to resist, the abstract and concrete spectators, the critic, and the reader merge into one entity.

Douchet's arguments are grounded in auteur premises, invoking the category schema "Hitchcock film" and personifying the auteur as a rational agent calculating effects. The critic believes that the director pursues two aims: inciting terror and conveying an occult meaning. Douchet's attention to the mechanics of spectatorial involvement becomes a way to explain how terror is evoked, since Hitchcock's work is based "on an exact science of audience reactions" (p. 150). The critic sustains this claim not only by drawing examples from the film but by citing authority: he and Jean Domarchi interviewed Hitchcock, who narrated and mimed the film in detail. This announcement, coming at the start of the essay, also bolsters the critic's ethos: he is an expert, he has talked to the auteur.

Because *Psycho* opens onto a world of desire, it has significance. The enthymeme could be put in a compressed form: *Psycho* makes the audience plunge to the end of their desires; such a movement must have some meaning (a tacit common opinion of readers); therefore the progress can be interpreted symbolically. Douchet sees the film—like all Hitchcock films—as enacting an occult duel between Light and Shadow, or Unity and Duality. He finds the theme capsulized at the opening, which starts in harsh, bright light and moves into the darkness of the hotel room. "In two shots Hitchcock states his proposition: *Psycho* will speak to us of the eternal and the finite, of being and nothingness, of life and death—but seen in their naked truth" (p. 157). These grandiose semantic fields are introduced in the last paragraph of the essay, where they have the effect of assigning profound significance to the emotional dynamics that Douchet has traced out. The most abstract interpretation may seem a logical conclusion to the concrete details of spectatorial engagement, while in terms of *dispositio* a satisfying closure is achieved by ending the essay with a recollection of the film's opening.

Robin Wood, *"Psycho," Hitchcock's Films* (1965)

Wood's book, the first interpretive study in English, sets out to demonstrate that Hitchcock is a serious artist—by no means an easy rhetorical task in 1965 British film culture.[2] His overall strategy is to link Hitchcock to indisputably great art. Hitchcock's work is like Shakespeare's in appealing to a popular audience while also exhibiting unity, diversity, richness of theme, and intricacy of method. In particular, Wood emphasizes the "therapeutic" theme that not only "cures" a character of a weakness or obsession but also makes the audience identify with the character's progress toward mental balance.

In this light, Wood undertakes to convince the reader that *Psycho* is a major work of art, indeed "one of the key works of our age" (p. 113). It can "contemplate the ultimate horrors without hysteria, with a poised, almost serene detachment" (p. 114). Thus he compares it to *Macbeth* and *Heart of Darkness*. But his concern is not wholly aesthetic: the essay presents the critic as one who is keenly concerned about the relation of art to life. Thus part of the *artistic* power of *Psycho* is its ability to recall the revelations of the Nazi concentration camps. Wood blunts criticism by admitting the extreme nature of the analogy ("I do not think I am being callous in citing the camps in relation to a work of popular entertainment," p. 113) and by turning *indignatio* on one critic who believes that Hitchcock's films are "light-hearted" entertainment. By the end of the essay, Wood's ethos—that of an aesthetic sensitivity inextricable from fine-grained moral awareness—comes through vividly. If one believes that art should confront us with our own worst impulses, one is strongly inclined to accept Wood's interpretation.

Like Douchet, Wood presents an extended plot synopsis with running commentary and a conclusion; and, as in Douchet's essay, the spectator is squarely at the center of things. But Wood's spectator is initially "healthier" than Douchet's. Whereas Douchet's viewer is split, both desiring and despising Marion, Wood's sympathizes with her almost completely. "We" identify with her. Wood secures this point by positing a unity of theme, plot, and narrational method. *Psycho* is about the continuum between normality and abnormality, neurosis and psychosis. The graded semantic series is holistically enacted in the film's action (the journey from Phoenix to Fairvale, from Marion to Norman to Norman-as-Mother) and in Hitchcock's use of audience-identification techniques. By making us identify with normal and likable Marion and by suppressing moments of critical decision, the film involves us in her theft. This is tantamount to involving us in her loss of rational control. Here Wood points out several episodes during her journey to Fairvale, showing how each one reinforces audience identification.

Wood places his heaviest emphasis on Marion's encounter with Norman in his parlor, since this scene most fully reveals the continuity between her behavior and his. The parallel is recognized by both the viewer and Marion, and her decision to return the money indicates her, and our, return to rationality. The shower murder, irrational and disturbing, disrupts the movement toward psychic health and breaks our identification. After a brief interlude of identifying with Norman, the spectator becomes the film's true protagonist, with the investigating characters (Arbogast, Sam, and Lila) becoming "merely projections of the spectators into the film, our instruments for the search, the easier to identify with as they have no detailed individual existence" (p. 110). This subargument also justifies devoting far less space to the second half of the film.

It is central to Wood's argument that the viewer, through identification, sees Norman as no less sympathetic than Marion. This drives home the key theme:

> That we all carry within us somewhere every human potentiality, for good or evil, so that we all share in a common guilt, may be, intellectually, a truism; the greatness of *Psycho* lies in its ability, not merely to *tell* us this, but to make us experience it. It is this that makes a satisfactory analysis of a Hitchcock film on paper so difficult; it also ensures that no analysis, however detailed, can ever become a substitute for the film itself, since the direct emotional experience survives any amount of explanatory justification.   (p. 112)

The invocation of the difficulties of analysis invites the reader to re-create the film along with the critic. Once more, the aesthetic sensitivity ascribed to the critic's persona implies a larger scrupulousness concerning the nuances of the emotional life. Yet Wood goes on immediately to display his ability to describe the viewing experience by a detailed discussion of camera movements, motifs of vision, and the sensation of vertigo evoked by a particular shot. Each aspect is invested with symbolic force within the semantic fields of the film.

Like Douchet, Wood sees the film's ending as releasing us from the spell of the abnormal, but he puts no faith in the psychiatrist's explanation. It is a glib and complacent reassurance, and it is undercut by the final scene. Wood's diction now turns hyperbolic. The last scene is "unbearably horrible," the sense of finality is "intolerable," Norman is denounced as a "savage butcher"; "we witness the irretrievable annihilation of a human being"; "we have been made to see the dark potentialities within all of us, to face the worst thing in the world"

(p. 113). The constructed reader is thus prepared for the concluding passage, which will invoke the death camps. More immediately, Wood's style reemphasizes the colossal artistic and moral stakes Hitchcock is playing for. Yet the commentary concludes on an optimistic note, claiming that the final shot sets the viewer free: "The last image, of the car *withdrawing* from the dark depths of the bog, returns us to Marion, to ourselves, and to the idea of psychological liberty" (p. 113). By opposing this backward movement to the forward tracking shots that dominate the film, Wood is able to imply a new psychological distance from the film's world, one which carries the thematic connotations of rationality and control. Norman is beyond therapy, but our cure is complete.

Wood's essay on *Psycho* is fairly brief, but its clarity and fecundity have made it, and indeed his entire book, an exemplar for the Anglo-American interpretive community.[3] The essay's careful explication of how the film enacts its semantic fields makes it a pedagogic model, and its rhetorical control remains instructive almost twenty-five years after its publication. There would be much else to study in it, such as its quiet introduction of religious discourse (salvation and damnation are mentioned almost in passing) and its use of Freudian symbols and themes (an opening epigraph quotes Freud: "We are all ill, i.e. neurotic").

Perhaps most interesting here is a rhetorical obstacle that Wood must overcome. As an auteur critic he is inclined to appeal to authority by citing the filmmaker's statements. Another of the opening epigraphs, Hitchcock's claim that he takes the audience through terror as if they were going through a haunted house, indirectly backs up Wood's claims about the film's identification processes. Yet in the same passage Hitchcock remarks that *Psycho* is a "*fun* picture . . . a film made with quite a sense of amusement on my part" (p. 106). Wood now has a difficulty: Hitchcock's remark seems to gainsay the film's artistic seriousness. At the very least, it makes the director seem as callous as the uninformed viewer. Wood solves the problem by arguing that Hitchcock "has not really faced up to what he was doing when he made the film" (p. 114). Hitchcock is a greater artist than he knows, so even if he thinks the film is a sick joke, we are not bound by that judgment. This also implies that we can trust Hitchcock when he explains the mechanics of suspense, but when it comes to implicit meanings, one should put one's faith in critical interpretation.

Raymond Durgnat, "Inside Norman Bates,"
Films and Feelings (1967)

Durgnat offers yet a third model film and model spectator.[4] For him *Psycho* moves in fits and starts, the plot abruptly "ending" with Marion's death, then Arbogast's. The result is not two large-scale parts pivoting around the shower murder but rather three "movements" (p. 219), each based on an investigation. There is also a bewilderingly premature "happy ending" when Marion decides to return the stolen money. These disjunctions point to a confusing tale, not the smooth trajectory outlined by Douchet and Wood. The film presents "emotional collisions" that are "quick, subtle and drastic" (p. 219). Like a musical piece, *Psycho* has "emotional chords and dissonances," with "haunting harmonies placed on a simple yet eerie melodic line" (p. 219).

By assigning the film a looser pattern, Durgnat can make his essay frankly digressive and exploratory. He can take the film as seriously as Wood does, but he can also treat it as a lavatory joke. He can find its semantic fields to be related not to the pervasive horrors of our age but to specific cultural values. The film is "a derisive misuse of the key images of 'the American way of life': Momism (but it blames son), cash (and rural virtue), necking (and respectability), plumbing and smart cars" (p. 218). The critic has time to jot down an odd line of dialogue or pursue a set of incomplete parallels (Lila as substitute mother, Arbogast as like the psychiatrist). He can also take the Freudian element further than Wood does, as when he contrasts the glossy bathroom with the "black sticky cesspool" of the swamp: "Norman has pulled the chain" (p. 213). As the last two quotations indicate, the more free-associational model of the film also permits the critic's style to become audacious and self-conscious. This is a critical performance, and if it risks losing the trust of the more staid reader, it attracts the reader who wants criticism to be a true "essay," a frank "attempt," a string of spontaneous insights.

Like his predecessors, Durgnat takes "identification" to be central to the film, but it is of a less homogeneous sort. *Psycho* displays not simply unity plus variety in Wood's sense, but sharply contrasting qualities created by our experiencing events along with different characters. The "sick jokes" and sudden surprises create a more dissonant relation of spectator to character. For Durgnat, Marion is no vessel of normality; his spectator regards her with both concern and curiosity. As the film goes on, this mock viewer, while identifying with Marion to some degree, is also simultaneously held in check.

Most saliently, the spectator is film-conscious. The viewer (and constructed reader) knows not only Hitchcock's other films but also *The Wild One, Orphée, The Old Dark House,* and the Hays Code. The viewer also knows that Marion cannot get away with theft ("Criminals never do, in American films," p. 210). This tactic lets Durgnat check potential objections to the film: of course the Bates home is stuffed with horror-movie clichés; of course the riddle is fairly easy to guess. These are all aspects of the film's entertainment ploys, pitched to our purely cinéphiliac pleasure. "We feel guilty about enjoying this film, but we have to admit we're having our money's worth of fun and fear" (p. 212). The knowing engagement of the viewer with the film profits the critic's argument by casting the reader as another connoisseur and injecting a tone of frivolous expertise into the interpretive act. Unlike Douchet and Wood, who prefer the spectator to be totally surprised by the denouement, Durgnat divides the audience into those who suspect the solution and those who haven't guessed it. This encourages his constructed reader to oscillate between alternatives, an act which entails a superior position of knowledge. It also allows Durgnat to play with phantom interpretations, to conjure up wisps of emotional commitment, and to write such sentences as this: "Norman grows more anxious and angry as Sam brutally presses him; he struggles to keep his temper, to quieten his tormentor's suspicions, while keeping Mom from breaking out in himself (if you know) or (if you don't) bravely protecting his Mom or (if you're not sure) both or neither or which?" (pp. 215–216).

By the time Durgnat gets to the psychiatrist's diagnosis, it becomes another, possibly valid explanation: this solution reveals that our surmise is only "the topmost level of nastiness" (p. 217). This film, in which our sympathies alternate so rapidly—"poured into so many moulds which are distended or smashed by contradictions, revelations, twists" (p. 218)—ends with an image of pure nihilism, which cancels our chaotic responses only by grotesquely simplifying them. "People leave the cinema, chuckling incredulously, groggy, exhilarated yet hysterical, half-ready to believe that everybody in the world is as mad as Norman" (pp. 217–218). Durgnat's spectator does not slide down the slippery slope from mundane rationality to horrific psychosis but is instead pleasantly outraged by the film's productive confusion, its "baffling maze of malevolent Nothings" (p. 217), its "brinkmanship of taste," its "powerful vagueness" (p. 219). And Durgnat finds no trace of Wood's therapeutic release, let alone the enlightened pity described by Douchet. The "sanity" to which we return is as hollow as a skull, and the human soul is revealed as a "diabolical nothing" (p. 218). Characteristically, Durgnat inverts the quest-for-identity schema: in defying society, "only Norman has found himself, and lost himself" (p. 218).

Once more the critic has outlined the film in chronological sequence; once more the critic speaks for the audience. By now we might suspect that what a critic traces is not the film but a second narrative, one based on the film but aiming to implicate the reader in an unrolling argument, a model film that selects and heightens certain cues, schemata, heuristics, and semantic fields; and that the spectator portrayed in this narrative merges with the rhetor's ideally convinced reader—here, one held enthralled by a display of critical ingenuity.

V. F. Perkins, "The World and Its Image," *Film as Film* (1972)

Perkins' theory of film, emphasizing organic unity and contextual significance, has been taken as an outgrowth of *Movie*'s New Critical version of auteurism. Since demonstrating his theory is the major purpose of *Film as Film,* Perkins' scrutiny of *Psycho*'s shower murder is only one step in a much larger argument.[5] Yet Perkins wants to show that his theory produces valuable interpretations, so he pauses in his survey of film techniques to perform an unprecedentedly detailed analysis of this "impression point." Whereas Douchet, Wood, and Durgnat appeal to synoptic effects of the film, passing over whole scenes in a line or a phrase, Perkins devotes eight pages to one brief sequence. This not only offers evidence for his theory but also lets the critic display skills different from those flaunted by Durgnat. Tidy and patient, this critic refers to no other films and to no works of literature. He does not invoke occultism, the Holocaust, or American culture. Avoiding appeal to outside authority, Perkins must establish that speaking the truth suffices.

To achieve this, the critic asks us to grant his in-depth knowledge of this film. The analysis itself is the final proof, but as an opening sally, he assures us that he could, given enough pages, go much further.

He apologizes for not considering the length of each shot and "the degree to which each image in its content, composition and movement reacts with its immediate neighbors" (p. 107). Only a critic of unusual modesty and very precise standards—remarkable in a 1972 context—could describe this study as "superficial" (p. 107). Here, and in Perkins' dexterity in projecting semantic fields onto the minutiae of the film, we find the beginnings of a persona that would eventually become a major option within "academic" film criticism generally.[6]

Confident in the force of his explication, the critic does not follow the trajectory of the film but uses *dispositio* to demonstrate a thesis: in a film in which the context creates a dense network of meanings, editing can bring out relationships that increase the work's complexity and subtlety. *Psycho* becomes an exemplum of such a film, achieving its complexity by means of the filming method and the choice of imagery. Perkins describes no fewer than seven consequences of Hitchcock's use of montage, including an aestheticization of the horror and a shifting of identification away from Marion.

Moving beyond such "technical" matters, Perkins shows how Hitchcock also achieves complexity by imparting significance to images that, in isolation, might seem unpromising. Perkins' motif analysis treats meaning as intrareferential, governed by local and long-range contexts. The knife evokes a bird's beak, and links with the bird motif; in its plunging trajectory, it also echoes the descending movement of the film as a whole, of Marion's body, and even the arc of the windshield wipers during Marion's rainswept drive. The shower evokes rebirth and recalls the driving scene. The eye motif anticipates the hollow sockets of the corpse, while the killer's dodgy exit foreshadows Lila's movements in exploring the Bates household. Even the knife's Freudian overtones must be contextually qualified: it gains its force in relation to vaginal symbols (the shower head, Marion's open mouth), and it is still, first and foremost, a particular object. The critic lays out all these echoes, parallels, and contrasts as a systematic inventory of an exhaustive pair of categories—objects presented, mode of presentation. No previous *Psycho* critic has so explicitly appealed to a categorical organization and so carefully controlled his "dissective attention."[7]

Perkins does not put his faith solely in the coherence among the motifs. They bear implicit semantic fields too, and he invokes a variety of heuristics to back up his case. The film's handling of the knife, for example, covertly indicates the underlying themes. As phallus, the knife yields not only a parody of intercourse but a suggestion that Norman's manhood is "catastrophically manipulated" by a false image of his mother (p. 110). As bird's beak, the knife makes Mother and birds into dead shells, reanimated by Norman's imagination and thus embodying the theme of an illusory past that erupts into the present. Moreover, the water imagery can provide the critic with puns. When Marion flushes her notes down the lavatory, she "washes her sins away"; as she dies, water "drains away" her life (p. 112). Constructing a parallel between the shower scene and the driving scene allows Perkins to link the former to the latter:

> This ingeniously constructed sequence of pre-echoes makes Marion's punishment not more justified but less completely arbitrary. It be-comes appropriate not to her actions but to her attitudes. She is destroyed by an explosion of forces existing within her own person-ality: the savage equation of sex and punishment, the self-comforting contempt for others' desires. "The dirty old man deserved to lose his money" is a short step from "The filthy slut deserves to lose her life." It belongs to the same order of psychotic reasoning. Implicated as we have been in Marion's thought, we can not entirely refuse the guilt of Mother's action. (p. 113)

While confirming Wood's general line of argument, this passage dem-onstrates how a single technique can create "exactness of imagery and concentration of meaning" (pp. 114-115). More than any other *Psycho* critic examined so far, Perkins makes explicit the expectation that, in accord with the bull's-eye schema, character-centered meaning is cor-related, in minute ways, with objects in the diegetic world and mo-ment-by-moment shifts in camera position and editing structure. He thus assembles an elaborate set of examples that call on the general enthymematic premise that in a great film, even the smallest details are contextually significant.

While Durgnat invites his reader to watch meanings ricochet off one another, Perkins exhibits the film's coherent patterns. The com-parison risks making Perkins look stodgy, but his stylistic tactics render his argument more fluid than his categories might demand. A less skilful writer would make the inventory of symbolic imagery a cut-and-dried list: a paragraph on what the knife means, another on what eyes mean, and so on. Perkins solves this problem by combining several motifs in a single paragraph, so that the imagery of water and eyes is discussed in relation to the downward movements in the film. At a still more local level, he practices a kind of enjambment, whereby a paragraph devoted primarily to one motif is introduced by a sentence that continues the discussion of a motif central to the *previous* paragraph. The intermingling of motifs enacts, in the critic's own discourse, the tightly knit connections he argues for in the films. Similarly, treating the driving scene as another "summarizing" segment allows him to analyze it as another nexus of imagery, but on a smaller scale: the paragraph devoted to it becomes a miniature version of his analysis of the shower scene itself.

Perkins' frame of reference remains explicatory and auteurist. Hitchcock is a rational calculator, achieving complex effects with little evident effort. Yet he is not treated as a virtuoso. Appealing to expressivist assumptions, Perkins claims that the meanings spring naturally from the diegetic context and never seem imposed upon it. Because of the subtlety of the implicit meanings here, the critic and his reader must learn to be as precise and attentive as the director.

Raymond Bellour, "Psychosis, Neurosis, Perversion" (1979)

By the mid-1970s, *Psycho* had entered the canon of indisputably great films. The rise of college film studies elevated Hitchcock to preeminence, and with the general unavailability of *Rear Window* and *Vertigo*, *Psycho* became the most-studied postwar Hitchcock film. Explicitly academic analysis of the film was initiated by James Naremore's *Filmguide to Psycho* (1973), a monograph offering background information on the director and the production, a lengthy scene-by-scene commentary, footnotes, filmography, and annotated bibliography. Until Naremore's book went out of print, it was widely used in American undergraduate courses. During the same period, directors of the "filmbrat" generation began to pay homage to *Psycho* with frank pastiches like Tobe Hooper's *Texas Chainsaw Massacre* (1974), John Carpenter's *Halloween* (1978), and Brian De Palma's *Dressed to Kill* (1980). These seemed to owe as much to college teaching and academic criticism as to the original film.[8] From now on, *Psycho* criticism would be unremittingly academic. It would display a familiarity with prior writing. It would often fill out areas left sketchy by earlier work; so, for instance, one could write entire essays on Herrmann's score.[9] And it would revise the model film, subsuming it to a theory of cinema, of culture, or of criticism.

Bellour's essay, which first appeared in the academic feminist journal

Camera Obscura, is evidence of how much the critic could demand of the reader by the end of the 1970s.[10] Armed with thirty footnotes and starting with an epigraph from Philippe Sollers about Roland Barthes, the article constructs a reader who follows *Screen, Camera Obscura, Ça,* and the vagaries of French semiotics and psychoanalysis. Yet the essay also keeps one foot in tradition. It treats the film as part of Hitchcock's oeuvre, and it appeals to Hitchcock's comments on the film. Bellour also amplifies what had become commonplaces of *Psycho* criticism, such as the two-part structure (Marion's story/Norman's story), the three-part movement indicated by Durgnat, the centrality of the supper scene in Norman's parlor, and the overall shift from neurosis to psychosis. More generally, Bellour ascribes hidden motives to characters in a fashion congruent with interpretive tradition. He suggests that Marion's theft is partly a response to Sam's aggression; later, he says that Norman, alone in the mansion, will "imagine what will happen next" (p. 321). He also, as we will see, uses the bull's-eye schema and conceptions of motivic unity. The essay's persuasiveness proceeds in part from its command of the auteurist paradigm; in part from its commitments to ordinary schemata and heuristics; and in part from an orientation that aims to anchor its interpretation within a larger scheme.

Central to that scheme is a set of general principles associated with "theory." Bellour assumes that his audience accepts French research on his principal category schema, the "classical text." "The principle of classical film is well known: the end must reply to the beginning" (p. 311); the idea of the opening as a motivic matrix is "one of the laws of classical film" (p. 326). Like Perkins, Bellour must assign meanings to the patterning of repetitions and variations, but he harnesses motif-analysis to psychoanalytic theory. Some traditional critical topoi, like the knife as phallus, thereby become absorbed into a larger field of reference. Bellour also draws on a Freudian syntax to demonstrate that the film's plot patterns involve substitution, condensation, and displacement of motifs. For example, when Marion visits Norman's parlor, shots of Marion alternate with shots of the menacing stuffed birds. Afterward, similar cutting alternates between Marion and Norman. Therefore Norman, in replacing the birds, becomes equated with them. Likewise, the opening shots' explicit voyeurism and male/female split are condensed into the penultimate image of Norman's staring "body-look" (p. 327). Bellour also uses Freudian "both/and" logic to multiply interpretive possibilities, as when he argues (homonymically) that the motorcycle cop's dark glasses signify at once the law's "super-vision" and a breaking of the law through fetishistic psychosis (p. 327). In such ways, psychoanalytic doctrine supplies the interpretation's semantic dimension.

It also allows Bellour to treat *Psycho* as no problem for the theory. The film does not seem "classical" in that the ending (which he identifies with the psychiatrist's speech) does not seem to echo the opening. His answer—that the film is at once a subversion of classicism and an overt demonstration of its basic principles—requires careful rhetorical maneuvering. If he succeeds, he will not only have said something new about *Psycho;* he will have subsumed the film to a theory that aims to explain much larger psychic and cultural mechanisms.

Bellour's interpretive conclusion is that *Psycho,* in aligning the neurosis/psychosis doublet with the female/male one, renders the woman a means for the male's achievement of narcissistic identification; yet the film also reveals this as grounded in psychotic fetishization. Bellour's theoretical warrants derive from Lacanian and post-Lacanian psychoanalytic writings. Here Bellour uses several rhetorical tactics. First, he presupposes the "classical dialectic" of castration anxiety, by 1979 sufficiently commonplace in academic film studies to function enthymematically. Mention of the woman-as-lack topos invokes the premise that since she functions as a castrating threat, woman will be fetishized and/or punished.

But this will not of itself secure the equation neurosis = woman, psychosis = man. So Bellour argues that in Hitchcock's other films this alignment is also present. Again, an enthymeme undergirds it (tacit premise: if Hitchcock does something in other films, he's likely to have done it in *Psycho*). Further, Bellour wants to link psychosis to fetishistic perversion, since that category—again, given contemporary academic film criticism's embrace of a version of psychoanalytic theory—will allow him to treat the woman as object of the male's aggressive, voyeuristic look. On one page, Bellour hedges a bit: perversion's denial of reality links it only "in some ways" to psychosis (p. 322). But after establishing that *Psycho*'s opening initiates a voyeuristic relation to the primal scene, and that the woman undergoes the camera's aggressive look, Bellour introduces perversion as a pertinent correlative to psychosis. He goes on, in two brief paragraphs, to appeal to authorities—Freud, Lacan, Guy Rosolato, and Luce Irigaray (all footnoted)—in order to conclude that in men "the scopic drive is dominant" (p. 324). He then takes the link as proven: "This explains the fact that Norman's psychosis, his inordinate object-desire that rushes headlong into murder, is entirely structured by a fetishistic aim carried to the point of madness" (p. 324). (Bellour need not justify his mimetic assumption that a theory of "real" human behavior necessarily explains fictional agents' actions; he assumes that the tradition of psychoanalytic criticism supplies the enthymematic grounds.) Once the castration-fetishization-perversion-psychosis cluster is in place, Bellour can utilize many topoi of the revised Lacanian story, such as the securing of male identity through staging the woman as spectacle (for example, Hitchcock's depiction of Marion's pleasure in the shower before the murder).

The psychoanalytic frame of reference also allows Bellour to argue that *Psycho* "designates" its own operations. He thus constructs a "commentative" flow of meaning. "Hitchcock" is throughout personified as an external agency that brazenly uses the diegetic world to stage his own fantasy, offering a "fascinated reflection on the logic of desire"—from, of course, a male standpoint (p. 317). This tactic permits Bellour to personify the camera as well, identifying it as the "subject of the enunciation" and giving it a range of traits: voyeurism, anxiety with respect to the primal scene, and finally psychosis itself (p. 322). Bellour goes on to make a reflexive move. Norman watching Marion through the peephole becomes a model of the "cinematic apparatus," sometimes likened to the projector and sometimes to the camera. Shot/reverse-shot alternation creates a mirror effect that evokes the cinema's structure. The policeman's dark glasses are a "metaphor" for the photographic lens. The bare bulb in the cellar recalls a spherical screen, with Mrs. Bates as the spectator and the swinging pulsations of the bulb evoking cinema. By means of a pun, Marion's last name is identified with the camera crane, that device that embodies an omniscient look and a "bird's-eye view" (p. 329). Reflexivity, long accepted in academic criticism, becomes a topos which allows Bellour to claim that *Psycho* does not simply retell the standard story of woman sacrificed to male identity, nor simply make it unusually evident (assisted by the critic's "reading"). The film shows how cinema engages the spectator's desire.

Bellour concentrates on the first half of the film, the psychiatrist's explanation, and the epilogue. These nodal passages help anchor the essay in tradition while making its unique features stand out. The piece's mingling of abstract theory and fine detail portrays the critic as an erudite *penseur*. There is more, though. The critic who has sought to portray the film as subverting the classical model and Hitchcock's own model reveals his own subversive aspirations. Listing men who possess the scopic drive, he adds himself, "the subject writing these lines in an attempt to fissure the system that holds him" (p. 324). The film critic as social critic, criticism as an assault on dominant ideology—these topoi too can be used by the academic film interpreter, who may depict himself or herself as using theory to reveal how a cultural system works, and who may excite the emotions of a reader who hopes to participate in the dismantling of oppressive political structures. Bellour's concluding apothegm, then, implies a social criticism as much as it ties together the psychoanalytic and reflexive components of his argument. Film and cinema, he says, are "the very institution of perversion" (p. 329).

Barbara Klinger, "*Psycho:* The Institutionalization of Female Sexuality" (1982)

Psycho criticism in the 1980s follows many lines similar to those set down by Bellour. William Rothman pursues a thoroughly reflexive reading of this and other Hitchcock films. His argument renders virtually every element of style and narrative a covert symbol of filmmaking or film viewing (the shower curtain as a film frame or screen, the shower head as both eye and lens, Marion's inner monologue as a "private film," and so on).[11] Kaja Silverman uses reflexive semantic fields to discuss *Psycho*'s editing: the stabs of the knife, timed to the "cuts" in the shower scene, mean that "the cinematic machine is lethal; it too murders and dissects."[12] In a more recent essay, R. Barton Palmer treats the film as a "metafiction" that refuses to contain its melodramatic excesses.[13] Larry Crawford extends Bellour's segmentation techniques to other scenes.[14]

Barbara Klinger revises Bellour's conclusions while remaining within his overall theoretical orientation.[15] Like him, she takes a symptomatic and feminist-psychoanalytical approach. She starts her article with a summary of his, tacitly invoking the "recency" topos and granting that sexual difference and the problem of the film's beginning and ending are crucial to understanding the film. Even her title derives obliquely from his last line about the "institution of perversion." Unlike him, however, she betrays no interest in authorship. (Hitchcock's name appears once in the essay, when she discusses the opening credits, and no other films are mentioned.) *Psycho* becomes an instance of the classical text, as allegorized under the feminist revision of Lacan: it yields a trajectory of woman's threat/repression of threat. Klinger contends that the film achieves closure by a massive containment of textual symptoms.

She organizes her case around the beginning and ending of the film, thereby marking out certain semantic fields and narrative parallels. She takes the credits and the opening segments to establish central doublets:

subject	vs.	discourse
unlawfulness	vs.	law
female sexuality	vs.	family

In the opening, Marion embodies an unlawful sexuality that poses a problem for the narrative. Her erotic identity must be repressed (via the switch to the Norman plot) before reemerging (Norman as Mother) and finally being contained by law and family. Thus the film moves toward the semantic values in the right-hand column. More basically, the pertinent enthymematic premises would seem to be that female sexuality is a problem for any narrative and that (given the further premise of the contradictory text) a film will work to disguise and displace it. Klinger goes on to recast the standard conception of the film's "two stories." By arguing that the second is not Norman's but Mrs. Bates's, she is able to suggest a movement toward the family and a phallocentrically defined erasure of difference, as well as to contrast Marion's body (exposed, then concealed) with Mother's (concealed, then exposed). She also picks out key points on the trajectory, such as the shower murder, when Marion overtly falls victim to violent punishment at the hands of the family.

In tracing the film's progress toward closure, Klinger calls on several accepted procedures. Here is a sample:

> That there begins to be an indissoluble link between the family and the law in the second narrative is multiply represented. Lila's investigation to find Marion is motivated by familial concerns but serves the legal establishment which has labeled Marion a criminal; the figures of legal authority which she encounters are simultaneously defined familially—Arbogast, as a private detective, is a domestic version of a policeman, the sheriff is domesticized by the constant presence of his wife, and the psychiatrist is a doctor committed to unraveling the family mystery. Perhaps the bond between the family

and the law is most concisely presented in the dissolve from the just discovered mother's corpse to the courthouse, which begins the explanatory epilogue of the psychiatrist. (p. 337)

The critic personifies the characters through careful word choice. The brevity of the treatment and the use of "domestic" discourage the reader from asking whether Arbogast, hired by Marion's employer, is strongly associated with family values. Similarly, to treat a dissolve as a "bond" of two images presupposes that shot-changes, in connecting dramaturgical elements, also link thematic ones. In the essay's linear argumentation and diction, no less than in its flashes of academic humor (the film ends in a "res-erection" of family "members," p. 339), it adheres to the rhetorical norms within what has come to be considered "film studies."

The academic quality of the piece's rhetoric emerges in two other significant ways. First, although Klinger footnotes only Bellour, she uses many received concepts—the contradictory text, the centrality of woman as erotic spectacle, the "hermeneutic code." Why does she not cite *Cahiers* on *Young Mr. Lincoln*, Cook and Johnston on *Mamie Stover*, Barthes's *S/Z*, and other relevant predecessors? I surmise that her constructed reader dwells so wholly within the institution that mere mention of relevant concepts suffices to carry the point. By 1982 the premises of symptomatic criticism did not need to be explicitly presented, nor the authorities named; once artifacts, the ideas had become facts. Second, although Klinger acknowledges Bellour's precedence, and although her emphases and conclusions often confute his, she never disputes his arguments. She simply says that the links between the first and second narratives "remain largely unexplored" in his account (p. 333). This is a common strategy of academic film interpretation. Other critics are mentioned, but usually their work is characterized only enough to clear a space for this essay. The rhetor does not typically dramatize a clash of opposing views; he draws on various sources and weaves them into a new interpretation that, for the most part, sits peacefully alongside others.

Leland Poague, "Links in a Chain: *Psycho* and Film Classicism" (1986)

"The power of rhetoric," writes one sociologist of science, "lies in making the dissenter feel lonely."[16] Suppose that a discussion has been going on for twenty-five years, and you don't like the turn the conversation has taken. Rhetoric will be used to isolate you, so you will need to use rhetoric to switch the conversational flow.

This is, more or less, the task facing Poague.[17] Dissatisfied with the concept of "classicism" employed by Bellour, Klinger, and others, he seeks, in effect, to redefine the category schema. A classical film, he asserts, is not one which possesses certain features (continuity editing, the problem of sexual difference, or whatever); it is a film open to continuous reinterpretation within the critical community. Poague's is not simply, or even primarily, a theoretical sally. His definition presents the critic as willing to couch his case in theoretical terms—but ones which justify his attempt to say something new about a classic. Poague proposes a different set of semantic fields; in doing so, he links these to fields already accepted within the critical literature. More radically, he seeks to make this purportedly contradictory text into a unified work, and to turn its symptomatic meanings into implicit ones.

Poague wants to prove that *Psycho,* in going beyond the sexual dialectic traced by Bellour and Klinger, criticizes the value of money in American culture. (Compare Durgnat's interpretation.) "Institutions in the film's depicted world, preeminently the Ford Motor Company, threaten everything, even sight itself when characters let those institutions or paradigms delimit their field of vision" (p. 348). This leads to the most general theme of the film, the relation between social power (that is, capitalism) and individual freedom.

Poague's argument for this theme involves two steps. First, he activates new cues. He points to the prevalence of Ford autos in the film, suggests that Marion's second license-plate letters (NFB) stand for Norman Ford Bates, and infers an implied kinship between Norman and "the father of American assembly line capitalism" (p. 344). This allows Poague to push the film's money motif to a broader social level: the film is about capitalism. Here the critic has adopted the strategy of assuming that even "minor" elements of a text can become central to interpretation—a fruitful assumption if one wishes to say something new about an often-discussed film.

But if all the critic's cues were this minute, he would risk mounting an implausible interpretation. So Poague also reinterprets cues highlighted by earlier criticism, such as the stolen money, the twisting camera movements, and the motifs of eyes and doubles. His principal strategy is to concentrate on items of setting, often linked to character dialogue, as when the spinning motif is associated with money because Sam stands under a fan when he complains of his debts. Like the cues already mentioned, these tacitly appeal to the concentric-circle schema as an inferential warrant.

The dissenting critic must also carefully weave his line-by-line argument into a mesh of plausible inferences. Consider this passage:

> Let us say that money in the world of *Psycho* serves to twist or limit vision, to turn it back upon itself, and that the visual expression of this limitation is figured in the shot of the bathtub drain as water, life, even sight, is sucked into the swamplike darkness. The correlation between darkness, money, and obscured sight is seen initially in Marion's drive to Fairvale. The first water hits her car windshield immediately *after* the remark about her "fine soft flesh," a remark accompanied in the visuals by Marion's oddly self-satisfied, self-obsessed grin—which looks forward, as William Rothman points out, to the death's-head expression on Norman–the mother's face in the film's next to last shot. Indeed, the effect of the water on the windshield at certain moments is to fuse the headlights of the oncoming cars into a single circle of light (like the light bulb hanging over Mrs. Bates in the fruit cellar). Normal vision—seeing with two eyes, as it were—thus gives way to tunnel vision, seeing with a single eye, from a singular vantage point.
>
> The importance, the deadliness, of this species of tunnel vision is then reinforced by Norman's one-eyed glance through the peephole into Marion's motel room.   (p. 346)

The critic's "let us say" is ambiguous, recalling the traditional device of presenting what "we" experience during the film, but here the phrase hovers between the authorial "we" ("If you will grant me the chance to make my case . . .") and the collaborative "we" ("You and I may wish to say . . ."). And associational redescription is constant. Just before this passage the critic has discussed the spinning motif and the (literally) twisting camera. Now vision itself is (metaphorically) twisted; that is, distorted; that is, "limited." The reference to the film's penultimate image of Norman recalls the hollow eye sockets so often mentioned in the critical tradition, and thus evokes blindness, which is then linked to Marion's obsessional vision, and then to the fusing of headlights into one. Then this singularity of the *object* of light is redescribed as a quality of the sighting eye itself—"tunnel vision"—which then segues into Norman's monocular peeping at Marion. In subsequent paragraphs Poague goes on to equate, metaphorically, this partial *vision* with an incomplete *understanding* caused by money.

In effect, Poague's task is to make the film's flow of meaning commentative in a different way than Bellour has proposed. He aims to show that we do not have to identify with the characters, that we can detach ourselves and see "the degree to which they are victims of a culture which encourages possessiveness and limited perspective" (p. 347). To reinforce this implicit meaning, he constructs a Hitchcock—not a flesh-and-blood director but an omniscient "implicit character." This agency "knows what he is about, knows the ethical risks involved, knows it in every frame of *Psycho,* in every gesture and image" (p. 347). Didactically, this agency "shows us in *Psycho* how not to use money, how letting money use us condemns us to death; but he also shows us how to use it well, to forge a chain of images, let us say, which pulls from the heart of Norman's darkness a final image of a truth we would deny, the connection between capitalism, sexuality, and death" (pp. 347-348). The string of asyndetons is suitable for this climax of the argument, conveying as it does the excitement of a rhetor carried away by the force of the film's theme. This effect of spontaneity is balanced by the recollection of the film's final image of the chain pulling the car from the swamp and the half-buried allusion to the Conrad novella which Wood had cited twenty years earlier. Such techniques construct a reader who can entertain a view of the film and of the "classical" text which is as comprehensive as that of the wise narrator whom he portrays. Here filmmaker, critic, and reader transcend the limited perspective of *Psycho*'s characters and its previous interpreters.

Along the way, the argument seeks allegiances from other critics. Poague opens with a survey of recent developments, a hallowed way of portraying the interpretation as up-to-date. He cites authorities (Rothman, Culler) who can act as allies, and he even links his project to deconstruction (in his concentration on "marginal features," p. 348). Chiefly, however, he relies on already-accepted semantic fields, cues, schemata, and heuristics. These provide arguments and examples on which to build a case. No dissenter in this community can persuade his opponents without relying largely, if tacitly, upon basic concepts and routines. But the critical institution is so made that nobody can *be* a legitimate dissenter without having come to share them anyhow. The dissenter is not, finally, all that lonely, and his objection often triggers only a family quarrel.

These seven interpretations of *Psycho* can teach us much about the ways in which institutional problem-solving and rhetoric are related.

At first glance, we are likely to notice the interpreters' divergences. Some critics produce implicit meanings, others concentrate on symptomatic ones. One critic finds the film to display the normality/abnormality doublet, another concentrates on the sexuality-death-capitalism cluster. One writer focuses on license plates, another on Marion's body. Some interpreters categorize *Psycho* as a Hitchcock film, others as a classical film. One takes the film as an occasion for rhetorical ingenuity, while others present themselves as handmaidens to the text's true significance. Such differences, and others, produce different "model films."

This process is, I suggest, one source of the plurality that criticism traditionally ascribes to the text itself. What permits the endless variety of meanings to be generated from a film are in large part the critical practices themselves, particularly the indefinitely large variety of semantic fields and salient cues that can be "processed" by a set of schemata and heuristics in force. The ambiguity sought by the New Critic, the polysemy praised by the structuralist, and the indeterminacy posited by the post-structuralist are largely the product of the institution's interpretive habits. Our ability to recognize, however tacitly, these habits in action emerges in our praise for the text's "richness"; it *must* be polysemous if we can imagine using different, but equally permissible, procedures to make sense of it, and to make cases for its discrete meanings. (It is this notion of the text as the meeting-point of varying interpretive processes that beginning students often lack.) If we all agreed to limit our procedures, *Psycho* or *Rules of the Game* or *Last Year at Marienbad* might seem as univocal as a shopping list or a telephone book.

In the course of my survey, I have sometimes noted that a critic's persona significantly resembles the model film she constructs. Probably, within the contemporary interpretive institution, the critic characterizes her persona chiefly through the choice of semantic fields and the rhetoric employed. To declare that *Psycho* is about normality and abnormality, to suggest that it enacts our permanent capacity for evil, and to compare its force to the revelations of the death camps is to portray the critic as a compassionate but tough-minded humanist. For a male critic to claim that the film lays bare the psychosis implicit in male fetishism creates a more confessional quality, as if the critic's act of interpreting the film mimics a process of introspective analysis and thereby depicts him as struggling toward a knowledge of self within culture. Because such affinities between model film and critical text are likely to arise, the symptomatic critic who finds no emancipatory moment in the text will have to hold the film at a distance, as Klinger does by means of her mocking puns. And the various alternatives affect pathos no less than ethos. If Durgnat's model film gives us a shiver or nervous laugh that we can plausibly ascribe to *Psycho* itself, we are prone to accept his persona and his argument; while the half-fascinated, half-demystifying attitude of Bellour's persona can attract adherence if the reader can imagine attributing that complex of attitudes to her or his (reconstructed) experience of the film.

What is also clear from our survey of *Psycho* criticism is that knowing when to stop one's interpretation is not wholly a matter of cognitive problem-solving. Up to a point, one can try to exhaust the cues and semantic fields on purely intrinsic grounds,[18] but from the start one's efforts toward novelty and plausibility are governed by the hunch that one can make a good case for the reading. The trained critic scrutinizes the film while casting side glances toward his potential audience. Furthermore, one finds the "threshold of termination"[19] only by positing a meaning that is more subtle, pervasive, remote, or elusive than other meanings, particularly those already constructed by other critics. It is obviously in the critic's interest to postpone determinacy for as long as possible before locking in her candidate meanings. As Laura Riding and Robert Graves remark: "It is always the most difficult meaning that is the most final."[20]

But, as Riding and Graves also point out, no meaning will ever be difficult enough. In an institution that favors novelty, the stakes constantly rise. The critical exemplars get mastered, and for all their merits, they come to seem obvious. They must be surpassed. In the age of symptomatic readings, Wood can revise his 1965 model of *Psycho,* treating the film as "the transmutation of ideological conflict . . . into a significantly realized thematic."[21] Novelty demands topoi of improvement, revisions, breaks, and subversion; a display of *indignatio* aimed at previous critics; the savoring of that evanescent moment (perhaps only twenty minutes on a conference panel) when the critic's interpretation incarnates innovation, trumping its precedessors simply by being the most recent.

Again, however, the academic institution regulates novelty by criteria of plausibility. This process seems most obvious in the inhibitions of earlier eras—who in 1965 would have accepted an interpretation of *Psycho* based on license plates or puns on the camera "crane"?—but constraints are no less important, if more invisible, in criticism that sets itself in today's vanguard. When members of a school argue that a chasm separates them from the past, the critic not only gets a chance to make new interpretations but also receives clear signals for when to stop. (Quit when the interpretation starts to sound like those that we supplant.) And, since plausibility involves sanctioned problem-solving processes and rhetorical maneuvers, the most novel critical school is likely to be more old than new. As long as critics need to argue with one another, they will argue on the basis of shared schemata and procedures of the kind I have tried to adduce.

If one takes this survey of *Psycho* criticism as a record of changes in the interpretive institution, one historical trend stands out. The appeal to "theory" is at first nonexistent (Douchet), then tentative (Wood's quiet invocation of Freud), then explicit (Bellour), then tacit (Klinger), and again explicit (Poague, who wants to confute the reigning theory). Such fluctuations suggest a movement from working assumption to fact, from hypotheses to taken-for-granted premises divorced from their situation of discovery. In the course of this shift, the rhetor becomes vulnerable on different grounds: the "untheoretical" critic could be charged with ignorance; Bellour's array of terms, quotations, and names could be attacked (by specialists) as resting on misreadings of sources or as being too eclectic; Klinger's elliptical use of theory could be faulted for addressing itself solely to those in the know. The fact that no writer ever straightforwardly argues for the psychoanalytic frame of reference as superior to its rivals suggests that it functions as a strategically defined topos in the critic's interpretation. For Bellour and Klinger, the model film at once illustrates the theory and offers evidence for it. The theory gains credence from two directions at once.

Still, despite the divergences and struggles for novelty, the interpretations of *Psycho* display a high degree of consensus. All critics treat Marion and Norman as the primary characters, all accept the break in point of view and plot action, all take the parlor dialogue and the shower murder as pivotal segments, and most are obliged to interpret the psychiatrist's speech. All assume that, whatever semantic fields will be brought into play, they must be mapped onto the principal characters, especially along an opposition between Norman and Marion. Most critics also concentrate their interpretation on the first half of the film. One might reply that this is a result of *Psycho*'s obviousness. Yet the critical tradition around such cryptic works as *Last Year at Marienbad* or *Persona* or *Wavelength* also exhibits a remarkable consensus about what cues and passages are worth attention, and how they are best interpreted. Our skeptical students need not worry: academic critics will never really "read too much" into films.

This consensus would seem to spring from the interpretive institution's tacit dependence upon norms of comprehension. Genre conventions, beginnings and endings, character actions, decisive twists in the plot, key props—these factors are salient for viewers, and they are natural starting points for interpretation. (Perhaps only after the institution has taken them for granted do novelty-seeking critics attend to Ford automobiles or make puns on the "cutting" in the shower scene.) Such comprehension factors would appear to be the basis of category schemata, person-based schemata, text-based schemata, and their attendant heuristics. Comprehension, it seems, can often get along without interpretation, but interpretation must appeal to comprehension, especially when it most hopes to surpass it.

11

Why Not to Read a Film

I've put in so many enigmas and puzzles that it will keep the professors busy for centuries over what I meant, and that's the only way of ensuring one's immortality.

—James Joyce on *Ulysses*

This book has set forth an analysis of film studies' interpretive system. This chapter lays out some arguments about the overall validity of my project. I also contend, in the chapter's middle section, that the centrality of interpretive conventions in film studies has had unfortunate effects. In closing, I discuss some alternatives to an interpretation-dominated criticism of cinema.

The Ends of Interpretation

To interpret a film is to ascribe implicit or symptomatic meanings to it. The critic aims to present a novel and plausible interpretation. The task is accomplished by assigning one or more semantic fields to the film. Such fields are distinguished by substantive features ("reflexivity" or "active/passive") and by internal structure (clusters, oppositions, proportional series, graded series, or hierarchies). Operating with broad assumptions and hypotheses (for example, the unity hypothesis), the critic maps semantic fields which she judges pertinent onto cues identified in the film. The identification of cues, and the judgment of pertinence, depend upon conventional knowledge-structures, or schemata, and inductive inferential procedures, or heuristics. The critic deploys category schemata (genres or periods, for example), personification schemata (such as director, narrator, or camera), and schemata for overall textual structure (the concentric-circle schema for synchronic relations, the trajectory schema for diachronic progression). The heuristics that translate these schemata into action allow the critic to show the film *enacting* the pertinent semantic values. The critic must also present the interpretation by means of standard rhetorical forms—ethical, pathetic, and pseudological proofs, familiar patterns of organization, and stylistic maneuvers.

Throughout the interpretive process, the critic works primarily as an artisan, not a theorist. He uses what is to hand, including "theory," to build an acceptable and original interpretation. Since this is likely to be my most controversial conclusion, I should probably draw together my lines of argument about it.

Throughout this book I have assumed that interpretive writing differs from theoretical writing, which proposes, analyzes, and criticizes theoretical claims.[1] Prototypes would be Bazin's "Ontology of the Photographic Image," Christian Metz's "Imaginary Signifier," and Noël Carroll's *Philosophical Problems of Classical Film Theory*. I have also assumed that a theory consists of a systematic propositional explanation of the nature and functions of cinema. From this standpoint, we can see that "theory" plays many contingent roles in film interpretation. A theory can provide the critic with plausible semantic fields (for example, sexual relations as power relations); particular schemata or heuristics (for example, looking as a privileged cue); and rhetorical resources (for example, the appeal to a community holding the same theoretical doctrines in common). But the critic does not need to call on theory in order to produce interpretations. If theory as a body of doctrine consists of propositional knowledge, critical interpretation is principally a matter of *procedural* knowledge, or know-how. Producing an interpretation is a skill, like throwing a pot. The potter need not be a chemist, a minerologist, or a professor of pottery. In some cases, learning "theory" may help people acquire certain interpretive skills, but it cannot replace those skills.

I have also argued that when interpreters "apply" theory, they do so principally in a piecemeal, ad hoc, and expansionist manner. Theory functions as a black box; if it gets the job done, there is no need to look inside. While the constraints on "pure" theorizing are logical and broadly empirical, the constraints on using theory in interpretation arise from the needs of the immediate task. Reciprocally, pre-1970 film criticism furnishes contemporary film theory with many of its central concepts. (One can trace a great deal back simply to auteur discussions of identification, voyeurism, and authorial commentary in one director, Alfred Hitchcock.) For such reasons, the interpretive process has become quite uniform across theoretical schools. Both an auteurist and a Lacanian can employ the punning heuristic; a feminist and a deconstructionist can find that an enclosed setting expresses the character's entrapment, or that the camera is a viewing agent. "Theory" will be selectively assimilated by the normalized routines of interpretation.

Theory is not, of course, wholly a matter of propositional knowledge; it too is a practice, with its own procedures of reasoning and rhetoric. By and large, however, interpretation is not conducted in a theoretically perspicuous way. For instance, interrogation of one's presuppositions would seem to be the theoretical act par excellence, but critics seldom indulge in it. Why do oppositional works rarely seem susceptible to symptomatic analysis? On what theoretical grounds can one defend the claim that to look is to express power? What are the explicit criteria for identifying a film's false resolution? What is the basis for taking the image displayed on-screen to be the trace of "the camera," for assuming that camera to have a "look," for assigning that look to a filmmaker or narrator or enunciator or viewer? Why should spectatorial activity be made synonymous with "identification"? Why should one personify the text as a body, or indulge in puns for the sake of interpretation? Most basically, by what criteria can one identify a textual gap or contradiction?

Similarly, interpretive critics constantly ignore the theoretical precept that empirical claims should be open to counterexample. Take the same-frame heuristic. Two characters are discrete entities, in visual, auditory, and narrative terms. If they are in the same shot, I can say that they are united (by being in the same shot) or separated (by the space between them). If they are in different shots, I can say that the cut separates them (a cut is a break) or links them (a cut is a join). I can thus use stylistic features to back up any inferences about unity or separation already arrived at on the basis of my assumptions about genre, narrative, or other factors. A critic might reply that conveying a symbolic opposition between characters by putting them in separate shots is simply a historical convention. No one, however, has attempted to demonstrate that this is the case. More tellingly, there is no tradition of filmmaking to which the same-shot-equals-affinity heuristic could *not* be said to apply. The heuristic is impervious to counterexamples and thus carries no theoretical weight. But since it is useful for the production of interpretations, even "theoretical" critics do not question it.

Most interpretive concepts are as unconstrained as the same-frame heuristic. Every film is presumed to be equally interpretable, and in an equally relaxed way. Punning encourages an associative play of meaning, as do semantic clusters and doublets. The frames-within-the-frame heuristic allows the critic to invoke entrapment *ad libitum*. "Reflexivity" as a semantic field invites the critic to link virtually any object on-screen—windows, curtains, light bulbs—to some aspect of cinema. If we take the male to be conventionally designated as active and the female to be passive, we can interpret anything as "feminine" if it can be described as passive. The concept of textual contradiction now includes anomalies, disparities, tensions, loose ends, and quirks. The Proppian model of the magical wondertale in preliterate societies has been recast to fit *The Big Sleep* and *Sunset Boulevard*.[2] Terms like *bricolage, suture, deconstruction,* and *foregrounding* have been steadily expanded in sense, so that they now mean little more than (respectively) assemblage, homogeneity, critical dismantling, and emphasis. Contemporary criticism, in aiming to interpret everything it can find, has usually set itself against theoretical principle by refusing to stipulate when something will *not* count as a valid interpretive move or as an instance of meaning.

Let me be clear: *within the interpretive institution,* such conceptual moves do not count as errors. They help produce interpretations that are judged to be novel and persuasive. But this shows that the criteria governing *this* practice ill-accord with the conventions of another one, that called theorizing.

In Chapter 1, I argued that theory neither inductively nor deductively guarantees an interpretation; we are now in a better position to see why anyone ever thought it would. When critics began to divide labor by "approaches," the spotlight fell on the most explicit doctrines of critical theory, and these seemed to be the likely causes for the conflict among interpretations. Moreover, certain theories, such as semiotics and psychoanalysis, proved highly compatible with critics' intuitive conceptions of meaning. It was natural to assume that these theories determined the different interpretive practices.

Neither inductivist nor deductivist, the critic is better described as pragmatic—arguing to the particular case when wishing to attack a theoretical position, arguing to theoretical correctness when wishing to assail an alternative interpretation. In neither case need an exact relation of theory to practice be spelled out. Theoretical assumptions can simply function as a cluster of enthymematic premises, and the rhetor can appeal to any one as the occasion demands. Probably the operative assumption goes like this: "A good interpretation invokes a theory as warrant, or evidence, or authority, as well as drawing data from the film." This is, of course, a purely institutional criterion of value. Any writer, theoretically informed or not, can during apprenticeship acquire the knack of "applying" theory.

Although this book is not about film theory as such, my analysis of the norms governing practical criticism should be judged on theoretical criteria. First, the account distinguishes between what it will and will not explain. A refrigerator repair manual, a scientific report, and a plot synopsis in *Variety* do not count as interpretations here. Furthermore, my account possesses degrees of generality. It distinguishes broad concepts (for example, symptomatic meaning) from middle-range ones (for example, the bull's-eye schema) and fine-grained ones (for example, the tactic of associational redescription). One advantage of this feature is that even if the account proves wrongheaded on one level, it might still prove fruitful on another. The account also seems to me reasonably uncommonsensical, so it has a chance of being surprising. It is corrigible; one could try to find often-used schemata or heuristics that my account overlooks. It is falsifiable empirically, in that one could point to pieces of indisputably interpretive criticism and claim that my outline provides no explanation of what is going on there. The account seeks to be conceptually coherent; one could, for instance, argue that the schema/heuristic distinction is logically untenable. All these criteria—broad but not unlimited scope, internal coherence, empirical adequacy, the ability to be disconfirmed—are ones by which a theoretical argument ought to be judged, and my account of interpretation seeks to meet them.

If critics are as pragmatic as I claim, though, they will not be satisfied with an arid functional analysis. My argument also tries to put the practicalities of interpretation in fresh perspective. The problem-solving emphasis squares well with the sense that, at least in mainstream institutional circumstances, critics operate as rational agents. In addition, the categories I have laid out enable us to specify our everyday assumptions more precisely. For instance, using this book's frame of reference, one could distinguish interpretive "schools" or "methods" along several parameters (the semantic fields each one favors, the principal schemata and heuristics employed, and so on). Similarly, we might now be able to see that disputes about interpretations often turn on different presumptions about appropriate inferential moves or rhetorical devices.

Today, most academic humanists share a devotion to interpretation.

Critics in all disciplines utilize conceptions of implicit or repressed meaning and deploy accepted semantic fields, schemata, heuristics, and rhetorical strategies. The contradictory text, reflexivity, characters as bearers of meaning, the "trajectory" model, refuting the ending, and the punning heuristic have become as central to literary studies as to film criticism. More recently, postmodernist criticism in the visual arts and the emergence of "literary" inquiries into historiography and philosophy have expanded the interpretive horizon, but not, it seems to me, the strategies of inference and persuasion ingrained within the institution. This book may thus help characterize interpretive practices in other domains.

The End of Interpretation?

Interpretation can be considered one of the few thriving industries left in the Western countries. It is a diversified enterprise. Anthologies and special issues of journals rejoice in the ever-expanding diversity of critical methods on offer. For most academic critics, interpretation epitomizes that pluralism to which the university pledged itself after the Second World War. "The impressive variety of approaches to film that mushroomed in the seventies," announces one blurb, "is worthy of the celebration this anthology has staged. Intoxicating analyses of films dance alongside the most far-reaching theories of signification and history. What an era this was!"[3] Business is booming; books, journals, and graduate programs in interpretive theory proliferate. Like all industries, Interpretation Unlimited must advertise, as witness one critic's promise that the millennium will be that of "good readers": "I believe that what actually causes the materiality of history is bad reading."[4]

Given the massive investment in interpretation, one should be skeptical of claims, put forth by successive critical schools, to have transcended it. Structuralism's doctrine of the play of the signifier has not reduced interest in abstract, meaning-drenched signifieds. In 1966, after proposing "a science of the *conditions* of content, that is to say of forms," Roland Barthes admitted that criticism "deciphers and participates in an interpretation."[5] Five years later, he acknowledged that his method in *S/Z* unavoidably gave priority to the "symbolic" dimension of the text.[6] Just as Freud practiced a kind of literary criticism on his patients' narratives, Lacan treated Freud's case studies as literary texts. Indeed, it is perhaps the familiarity of Lacan's interpretive moves (as well as an appeal to the long-lived topos of the incomplete, divided, conflict-ridden subject) that has drawn many literary critics to his work. Derrida, in criticizing Lacan's reading of "The Purloined Letter," makes use of customary schemata and procedures, as when he takes the opening description of Dupin's library to initiate the problem of writing.[7] Likewise, one deconstructionist critic finds *Billy Budd* distinguishing between two characters on the basis of their contrasting "styles of reading."[8]

The critic may insist that he reveals not meanings but the production of meanings, not ambiguity but the text's need for it, not what the text means but how it means. Despite such waivers, the critic usually goes on to apply the strategies and tactics of ordinary interpretive practice. A recent proposal to pass beyond interpretation by treating texts as constituted by "reading formations" yields this utterly orthodox discussion of the gilded woman in *Goldfinger*'s title sequence: "At once sexually alluring and rewarding, as desirable as the gold of the title song, and finally laid on her back, in the ultimate demonstration of Bond's phallic power, she is at the same time deeply troubling and threatening to Bond in containing, within her body, the castrating threat represented by Goldfinger."[9] Likewise, we can change the object of study by looking at publicity photos or movie posters, television shows or theme parks, and calling our inquiry "cultural studies"; but this still leaves unquestioned the routine, rationalized business of interpretation.

Once critics have made interpretation the center of their concerns, it is natural to project the activity back onto "ordinary" or, as they are often called, "naive" viewers. Now they too are "readers" of films. They belong to "reading communities," or are constituted by "reading formations." By responding, spectators are overtly, tacitly, or unconsciously interpreting, and the professional critic simply lays bare this process. Now we can see one historical source for the broad usage of terms I criticized at the outset: by defining whatever viewers do as interpretation, the critic secures a rhetorical warrant for his more enlightened and enlightening enterprise.

Since the protocols of interpretation are so ingrained as to seem inescapable, the theoretically inclined critic might try to put the whole affair on a sensible footing. Some recent instances are the Beardsleyan aesthetics proposed by William Cadbury and Leland Poague and the Ricoeurian hermeneutics of Dudley Andrew.[10] Such foundational gestures, however, tend to ignore the social, cognitive, and rhetorical processes that make interpretation a distinctive activity in the first place. These writers, in both their theories and their practical criticism, take for granted the protocols discussed in this book. An aesthetics or hermeneutics will not necessarily reveal the concrete skills that constitute the practice of interpretation. I shall argue in the next section that this work is best tackled by a historical poetics.

Interpretation, then, is far from finished. It has come to dominate the critical enterprise. But what good is it? I want to argue that the value of interpretation-centered criticism lies in several diverse features. I want further to show that its drawbacks, at least at present, loom large enough to make us consider ways of posing fresh questions.

Most generally, interpretation-centered criticism organizes and regulates the institution's activities. The growth of interpretive conventions has created a tradition for film studies, perhaps the only substantial one we have. Knowing how to make movies mean is the principal source of such authority as film scholars possess, and there is little doubt that text-centered film study could not have entered the university without establishing its credentials as a hermeneutic discipline.

The virtues of the most innovative interpretive criticism should need no lengthy defense. Conceiving of the text as symptomatically revealing cultural tensions introduced a powerful frame of reference. To claim unity across an auteur's output, to posit that cinema contains "three looks," and to suggest that a genre may constitute an intersection of nature and culture organized a great deal of information within a new perspective. Many exemplars deserve praise because they have introduced conceptual schemes that reorient our understanding. They have activated neglected cues, offered new categories, suggested fresh semantic fields, and widened our rhetorical resources. Innovative frames of reference have heightened our awareness of what can be noticed and appreciated in artworks.

What of ordinary criticism, the application and extension of existing semantic fields, schemata, and heuristics? I think that it plays at least two roles. One is *domestication,* the taming of the new. The critic who finds a recent film to be a contradictory text is pulling that film into the field of the known. Domestication subsumes the unfamiliar to the familiar. Though avant-gardists may disparage this side of interpretation, it remains an institutionally necessary function. The unschematized film is the uninterpretable film.

A second role of ordinary criticism is *differentiation,* the reshaping of the known. By showing the applicability of existing conceptual schemes to a fresh case, the critic is often obliged to discriminate aspects of those schemes more exactly than heretofore. In addition, the critic can bring out new affiliations among familiar semantic fields, as when Bellour finds that in *Psycho,* femininity is linked to neurosis while masculinity is linked to psychosis. Both domestication and differentiation serve to reaffirm existing conventions, but they do so by demonstrating their range, power, and subtlety.

If science aims to explain the processes underlying external phenomena, interpretation does not on the whole produce scientific knowledge. Neither causal nor functional explanation is the aim of film interpretation. Indeed, in a certain sense, knowledge of the text is not the most salient effect of the interpretive enterprise. It may be that interpretation's greatest achievement is its ability to encourage, albeit somewhat indirectly, reflections upon our conceptual schemes. By taming the new and sharpening the known, the interpretive institution reactivates and revises common frameworks of understanding. Interpretation takes as its basic subject our perceptual, cognitive, and affective processes, but it does so in a roundabout way—by attributing their "output" to the text "out there." To understand a film interpretively is to subsume it to our conceptual schemes, and thus to master them more fully, if only tacitly.

We can be a little more specific about what conceptual schemes are mastered. Although critics are usually uninterested in their own schemata and reasoning routines, they are centrally committed to informally exploring and comparing semantic fields. The interpreter typically believes that purely philosophical abstraction and strictly "scientific" analysis cannot capture the subtle interplay of meanings which the mind can entertain. Films, like novels, plays, and paintings, become the occasion to display a dynamic of semantic implications. The critic who interprets *Psycho* does not *prove* that psychic normality and abnormality lie on a continuum, or that the male gaze is a symptom of psychotic repression; no more does the film. The critic and her reader agree to entertain such notions as imaginative possibilities, as intriguing juxtapositions of semantic fields suggested by the film at hand and the critical practices in force.

Such juxtapositions can command the reader's attention because, for a great variety of reasons, people often wish to explore the potential meanings which they encounter in their lives. As I remarked in Chapter 5, semantic fields are relevant to general human concerns. Interpretation answers to a widely felt interest in motives, intentions, and ethical responsibility by showing that artworks which do not offer explicit guides for behavior can raise significant issues of thought, feeling, and action. If critical interpretation yields not knowledge but "understanding" *(Verstehen)*, it may do so through a more or less disciplined speculation on the possibilities of meaning. Perhaps this is another reason why some critics believe that interpretation tests a theory; the film becomes an occasion for the critic to explore a theory's semantic implications and affinities.

Whatever virtues interpretation possesses might well be outweighed by its faults and excesses. Such, I believe, is currently the case. But let me hasten to add that I am not suggesting that interpretation grind to a halt. Calls for an end to literary interpretation extend back at least to Irving Howe's "This Age of Conformity" (1954) and run through Susan Sontag's "Against Interpretation" (1964), Geoffrey Hartman's "Beyond Formalism" (1966), and Jonathan Culler's "Beyond Interpretation" (1976). Such calls have gone almost completely unheeded; indeed, they are now part of the ritual of the interpretive institution itself. A thoroughgoing rejection of interpretation is likely to sway virtually no reader, and may well be dismissed as a rhetorical ploy for promoting one's own interpretation.

More important, for reasons I shall suggest, a criticism that ignored implicit or symptomatic meanings could not comprehensively account for artworks' construction or effects. This is not to deny that, as a practicing critic, I find many interpretive conventions forced and unproductive. The punning heuristic usually depends too much on atomistic, local effects, while the stress on doublets and oppositional series often forecloses the possible range of meaning in films. Personifying the camera and the narrator often strikes me as an unnecessary complication. Although such maneuvers are sanctioned by the current state of the critical institution, I would at opportune moments argue that they should be used more sparingly. Yet interpretation remains an important part of critical activity, and to outlaw all of its conventions would drastically impoverish film studies. Some schemata and heuristics—the personification of characters, the use of graded semantic fields, the appeal to category schemata—capture important aspects of films, partly because they accord with notions of comprehension that members of all critical schools share. Here I want only to suggest that we rely too much on this way of thinking and talking; making interpretation the basis of teaching and critical writing has created many problems.

Like many highly routinized practices, interpretation has tended to be deeply traditional in its assumptions. This has not been sufficiently acknowledged by the most experimental critics of our day. To watch contemporary exegetes embrace the form/content distinction or to explain that the work's symbolic field possesses "richness, density, and breadth"[11] is to recall that the presuppositions of explicatory and symptomatic criticism have a long history in Western culture. While not all societies believe that a symbol is inherently meaningful, Christianity has been a strongly hermeneutical religion, seeking the *kerygma*, that latent sense waiting to be called forth.[12] This tradition leads to what Susan Sontag calls "an overt contempt for appearances."[13] Forty years ago Erich Auerbach pointed out that figural exegesis tended to wrap the text's sensory qualities in a cocoon of abstractions:

> It is a visually dramatic occurrence that God made Eve, the first woman, from Adam's rib while Adam lay asleep; so too is it that a soldier pierced Jesus' side, as he hung dead on the cross, so that blood and water flowed out. But when these two occurrences are exegetically interrelated in the doctrine that Adam's sleep is a figure of Christ's death-sleep; that, as from the wound in Adam's side mankind's primordial mother after the flesh, Eve, was born, so from the wound in Christ's side was born the mother of all men after the spirit, the Church (blood and water are the sacramental symbols)— then the sensory occurrence pales before the power of the figural meaning.[14]

The same tendency has, by and large, characterized the history of film interpretation.

I am not making the commonplace complaint that interpretation impoverishes the work. The standard retort to this is that every ratiocinative act "reduces" the work, since we cannot know the work without the mediation of some conceptual schemes. This argument is correct, as far as it goes. But some conceptual schemes are more nuanced and comprehensive than others. It is one thing to say that the text's particularity can be known only through some conceptual frame of reference; it is another to insist that all such frames are equal in power and precision. Many current interpretive schemes, such as the semantic doublets of order and disorder or Symbolic and Imaginary, remain quite coarse-grained.

True, interpretation does not have to be so gross. If the critic's real aim is to use the text as a way to juxtapose and explore semantic fields in a speculative fashion, she might well be sensitive to differences in the cues that invite her to create nuances within and between semantic fields. Such a flexibility seems to me present in the very best interpretive criticism, such as Tyler's books, Bazin's writings on Welles and Renoir, and the early *Psycho* criticism I have surveyed. But as academic criticism has developed, it has assembled a battery of all-purpose heuristics that drill into a film at the standard junctures and mine out examples which can be sorted into the standard bins. Semantic fields are not so much explored as invoked to serve as fixed points of reference. The contradictory-text model once offered intriguing novelties, but its stark opposition between repressed and repressive elements, its intuitiveness and looseness, and its self-fulfilling scenario have become glaringly apparent.

This is not to say that for contemporary critics anything can mean anything. Actually, a handful of things will mean even fewer things. One lesson of this book is that while the particular results of any interpretive act are indefinitely numerous, the textual cues, the procedures that rank and organize those cues, and the semantic traits which are assigned to them have become quite limited. And the limits are, by and large, not logical but institutional. Does the interpretation "apply" a theory in a fresh way? Does it activate overlooked portions of films? Does it contribute to "recent developments"? These are constraints of habitual practice and reigning rhetoric. To use Todorov's term, film interpretation has become almost wholly "finalistic," based upon an a priori codification of what a film must ultimately mean. "It is foreknowledge of the meaning to be discovered that guides the interpretation."[15] Many of a film's nuances now go unremarked because the interpretive optic in force has virtually no way to register them.

A more concrete way to put the charge is to say that in recent film studies interpreters have paid scarcely any attention to form and style. (In this they follow the influential example of Freud, Lévi-Strauss, Lacan, and other "finalistic" theorists.) After a century's work in the study of narrative form, film interpreters continue to rely on very simple patterns: the allegorical journey of values, or the steps by which repressed forces emerge and are extinguished or linger on. The concentric-circle model, whereby aspects of setting or camerawork amplify or comment on characters' interaction, is a comparably crude way to understand film style. For both the old New Criticism and the new old criticism, style is chiefly a means to meaning: a window through which the critic watches characters embody semantic fields, or a mo-

mentary diversion—an intriguing camera movement, an abrupt cut—
that can be "read" in its turn. The "classical" system of continuity
staging, shooting, and editing can either be treated as a neutral ground
for the truly significant meanings arising from dialogue and deport-
ment, or it can be exploited for its symbolic potential (for example,
eyeline-matching as creating power-infused looks). Film style is like
the music in nineteenth-century melodrama: always subordinate,
vaguely there, of interest only when it underscores a point deemed
important on other grounds. Automatism or atomism: such are the
principal roles style can play in today's interpretation.

Significantly, most of the basic concepts for understanding the resources of the film medium have not issued from contemporary interpretive projects. Arnheim, Kuleshov, Eisenstein, Bazin, Burch, and
others defined the parameters of film style and structure with which
all critics still work. Perhaps most interpreters believe that form and
style are now well understood. This is a useful fiction to keep "readings" rolling along. Film interpretation charges its debts to the account
of classical aesthetics, but it pays very little back.

In sum, contemporary interpretation-centered criticism tends to be
conservative and coarse-grained. It tends to play down film form and
style. It leans to an unacknowledged degree upon received aesthetic
categories without producing new ones. It is largely uncontentious
and unreflective about its theories and practices. As if all this weren't
enough, it has become boring.

Barthes often confessed himself sickened by *doxa*, those banal signifieds he discerned in common opinion, popular literature, and film.[16]
We ought to be no less put off by the predictable moves that rule
belletristic and academic film interpretation. It seems to me likely that
the writings of Bazin, Tyler, and Deming, and of the *Cahiers, Positif,*
and *Movie* groups will endure for a long time. But the late 1960s,
fruitful for film theory in many ways, ushered in a mode of criticism
that has in the last decade or so become astonishingly barren. We need
no more diagnoses of the subversive moments in a slasher movie, or
celebrations of a "theoretical" film for its critique of mainstream cinema, or treatments of the most recent art film as a meditation on
cinema and subjectivity. In retrospect, the revamped symptomatic
readings of the mid-1970s look like originality's last gasp. We have
had no exemplars since then; we live in an era of ordinary criticism.
Theory too is waning.[17] Hence perhaps critics' desperate swerve to
television, to publicity materials, to cultural artifacts—as if the repet-

itiveness of Interpretation, Inc., could be disguised by a turn to new sorts of texts.

In a search for freshness, some critics have resorted to the academic equivalent of Las Vegas comedy: a grimacing playfulness depending on slashes, dashes, word-fracturing parentheses, obscure citations, and labored puns. But earnest glitz cannot disguise the blandness of the business. Academic legitimation has helped film interpretation turn into a new scholasticism, complete with a canon (Hollywood and some venerated oppositional works), received truths (Theory), highly regulated interpretive moves, and guaranteed points of arrival. Underlying all these features is an appeal to authority. Nothing could better describe most contemporary academic film criticism than Michel Charles's remark "Scholasticism would be a mode of thought and expression where all knowledge must be authorized by a text, however fluid or variable it becomes; an intellectual world in which the renewal of knowledge must come through the rereading of a text; a system in which, necessarily, nothing new can be produced outside the discovery of a new text (which can, of course, include the rereading of a canonical text)."[18] Film academics have perhaps been more prone to narrowness than their counterparts in literary study. The latter, at least until a few years ago, had to know something of empirical import about an author, a period, or a genre. New Criticism reacted against the positivist scholarship of the Academy, but film criticism had no tradition of historical scholarship to displace. Intrinsic interpretation and "close reading," taught in high school and college, swiftly became film studies' mainstream practice. Today the propositional knowledge underlying most critical essays consists of some theoretical beliefs and descriptions of certain internal features of the film at hand. This is what "application" means, which is not far from what it meant for the scriptural exegetes of the Middle Ages. Such scholasticism may become film studies' principal contribution to a *fin de siècle* in which *A rebours* is paralleled by a dozen texts of painfully ludic postmodernism and in which our *Decay of Lying* is David Lodge's *Small World*.

Structuralism and the concept of the contradictory text were promising initiatives, and they could have spurred lively, skeptical debate. Yet they have devolved into a practical criticism that claims theoretical terrain it has never logically staked out, squeezes film after film into the same half-dozen molds, and refuses to question its own procedures. The fact that critics may still enjoy this enterprise is not sufficient reason to keep it going. After all, in 1975 Laura Mulvey wrote that her theory sought to take the pleasure out of film viewing. Perhaps now is the time to do something more controversial: take the pleasure out of film interpretation.

Prospects for a Poetics

If my critique of interpretation-dominated criticism is well founded, some fairly obvious recommendations follow. Critics, the present writer included, could write with more precision, rigor, and vigor. They could build their inquiries around hypotheses and questions rather than "applications." They could be more theoretically ambitious and incisive, and strive to use specialized terms consistently. Above all, they could quarrel more. Dialogue and debate hone arguments, turn attention to fine points, and invite the reader to be skeptical.[19]

These reforms would create changes in the institution, but they would not push the ascription of implicit or symptomatic meanings out of its central place in critical practice. I have suggested that it is no longer useful to grant it this place. Yet interpretation has already accumulated an enormous inertia. It is not hard to do passably, especially for bright people who have imbibed thematics from high school onward. Anything else will take longer to master. My last task is to show that the time and trouble would be worth it. Assuming that one wants to study and write about cinema in an academic context,[20] what options are open?

Let us back up a step and ask: To what *questions* is ordinary critical interpretation offering answers? I have already suggested that one could consider ordinary interpretation to be tacitly asking: How does this film provide an occasion for us to entertain, as an imaginative possibility, the juxtaposition and development of certain semantic fields? But one might capture the critic's own sense of the activity by asking two more object-centered questions. First, how are particular films put together? Call this the problem of films' *composition*. Second, what *effects* and *functions* do particular films have? If criticism can be said to produce knowledge in anything like the sense applicable to the natural and the social sciences, these two questions might be the most reasonable points of departure.[21]

How does the interpretive critic answer these questions? He presumes, I think, that the film's composition and effects are the vehicles of its implicit and/or symptomatic meanings. Such meanings determine the films' use of subject matter, ideas, structure, and style; they also govern the film's effects on spectators within social contexts.

Yet this is only one way of conceiving matters of composition and effect. Other answers are possible, and perhaps better. For example, one could argue that ordinary interpretation conceives the problem of effect too narrowly. What may matter as much as implicit or repressed meanings is the surface of the work, which Auerbach claims has been ignored. For a long time literary and art criticism consisted of "impressionistic" descriptions of the faults and beauties of works. In this century, Shklovsky's "palpability of the object," phenomenology, and other trends argued for the perceptibility of the artwork. The most influential formulation in our time has been Susan Sontag's 1964 essay "Against Interpretation." In the face of interpreters' woolly abstraction, Sontag demands that we recover our senses and art's sensuousness. The critic can produce "a really accurate, sharp, loving description of the appearance of a work of art."[22] Tyler, Bazin, the *Cahiers* and *Movie* critics, and Sarris were often adept at this, but the real masters are a few reviewers like Manny Farber. Here he is on *His Girl Friday:*

> Besides the dynamic, highly assertive pace, this *Front Page* remake with Rosalind Russell playing Pat O'Brien's role is a tour de force of choreographed action: bravado posturings with body, lucid Cubistic composing with natty lapels and hat brims, as well as a very stylized discourse of short replies based on the idea of topping, outmaneuvering the other person with wit, cynicism, and verbal bravado. A line is never allowed to reverberate but is quickly attached to another, funnier line in a very underrated comedy that champions the sardonic and quick-witted over the plodding, sober citizens.[23]

Such rhapsodic evocation is one way to sharpen the reader's awareness of phenomenal qualities that ordinary criticism plays down.[24] Yet the academic critic will point out that Farber is still "producing meaning" from *His Girl Friday.* This is one reason I have insisted upon different *sorts* of meaning, at different levels of concreteness. In my terms here, the critic ascribes expressive qualities to certain referential and explicit meanings. A sensuous criticism needs rich models of perception, and the best ones currently available emphasize that perceiving is structural and categorical. Perception is not a mere grasp of abstract shape or a flicker of vivid sensations; it is an "effort after meaning"—though not necessarily implicit or symptomatic meaning.

A criticism attentive to "perceptibility" does not discard meaning altogether but ranges it among the film's effects.

Another approach to criticism's central questions would involve historical study of particular films. To analyze a film's composition and functions requires us to consider what processes brought it into being (for example, to what problems does its composition represent an attempted solution?) and what forces have mobilized it for various purposes. At the moment I write this, critics who a few years ago were immersed in "the text itself" or abstract theoretical inquiry are now "calling for" (a rhetorical study of this lexeme would be worthwhile) some form of historical study. Because cinema studies has lacked a strong tradition of historical scholarship, critics who know only how to read a film are discovering a terra incognita. The trend may be another symptom of the repetitiveness of ordinary criticism over the last fifteen years. It may also be a reaction to the prospect of completely "open" readings. (History can seem to pin them down.)

Plainly, the Historical Turn need not break with interpretation's business as usual. The critic can expand the object of study to include the film's genre, its audience, its period, its "discursive regime"—the aggregate to be pushed through the same sieve of contradictory meanings, personification schemata, puns, associational redescriptions, and whatnot. It is no great advance to treat a period as one vast text, or to dub "historicity" itself a new semantic field, or to study historical reception as a process of what critics or advertisements declare about a film, if we are never going beyond our familiar schemata and heuristics.

A better reason to study history is that the things people did and said in other times are less predictable than what our contemporaries do and say. We don't want a critical language to flatten out our predecessors' difference. Historical study touches off a Brechtian surprise: not "How like ourselves!" but "Who would have imagined that they could believe this?" There is no reason to assume that a historical perception of a work always has greater claim to some abstract truth or validity; but in an era of drab readings we can, if our conceptual schemes are flexible, turn to history to discover that films have functioned in ways that are not already known to us. For example, critics can expatiate freely upon the poetic implications of Dovzhenko's works, but Vance Kepley has shown that the films' mysterious mythographic elements had concrete extratextual references for the director's audiences, and that the films' explicit messages are the trace of various, sometimes conflicting, political purposes. Kepley can go on to describe "ideological projects" and propose informed symptomatic readings on the basis of the sort of specific historical evidence that Macherey and the *Cahiers* critics were never able to muster.[25]

Work like this points in two directions. One is toward the reconstruction of earlier acts of comprehension. Donald Crafton, André Gaudreault, Tom Gunning, Charles Musser, Janet Staiger, Kristin Thompson, Charles Wolfe, and other contributors to the new historiography have reconfirmed the precept that through time some potential referential and explicit meanings are lost.[26] These can be revivified through an analysis akin to the study of iconography in art history. Alternatively, the critic may seek to explain the historical mechanisms that produce the contradictions that critics impute to texts. For example, Lea Jacobs and Richard Maltby have traced out how concrete institutional negotiations among filmmakers, studio executives, and censors generated the disparities one may attribute to "fallen women" films of the early 1930s.[27]

It is thus not a question of repudiating interpretation but of situating its protocols within a broader historical inquiry. Current research into pre-1915 world cinema has not ruled out the interpretation of films, but it has subordinated it to a rigorous examination of subjects, stylistic norms, generic factors, and conditions of production and exhibition.[28] Instead of the reigning duality of "theory versus history," we would do better to recall the one with which New Criticism won its institutional victory: "scholarship versus criticism."

I am not claiming that historical research is inherently more reliable or certain than critical interpretation; it too depends on inferences. All knowledge involves the subsumption of a phenomenon to a conceptual frame of reference. But, again, some frameworks are more complex, precise, and nuanced than others; some reveal anomalies and counterexamples rather than mask them off. The inferences produced by broad and nuanced frames of reference are thus more likely to capture fresh and significant aspects of the phenomenon. A theoretically rigorous historical scholarship is at present a strong candidate for reinvigorating film study.

Most broadly and basically, I suggest that the questions of composition, function, and effect that interpretive criticism sets out to answer are most directly addressed and best answered by a self-conscious historical poetics of cinema. I conceive this as the study of how, in determinate circumstances, films are put together, serve specific functions, and achieve specific effects. This tradition has been developed by classical aestheticians of cinema—Arnheim, the Russian Formalists, the Soviet filmmakers, Bazin, Burch, and others. A paradigmatic instance of cinematic poetics is Bazin's model of the "evolution of the language of cinema," which proposes an account of changing norms of cinematic construction and style.[29] Another example is Noël Burch's extensive history of style in Japanese cinema.[30] Some interpretive critics have also shed light on these matters, as in the *Cahiers* and *Movie* critics' explorations of authorial style, in Durgnat's analyses of technique, or in such trailblazing analyses of classical norms as Thomas Elsaesser's writings for *Monogram* in the early 1970s.[31] Textual analysts like Bellour, Kuntzel, Marie-Claire Ropars, and others have revealed many aspects of narrative composition and stylistic functioning.[32] Occasionally semiotic and postsemiotic theory has addressed compositional issues, as in Metz's outline of the *Grande Syntagmatique* and Wollen's discussion of Godard's "counter-cinema."[33] In some of these cases, poetics remains secondary to hermeneutics; nonetheless these writings show that the construction of implicit and symptomatic meaning can coexist with the study of form and style in given historical circumstances.

A historical poetics can fruitfully start with the assumption that no a priori device or set of meanings can serve as the basis of an invariable critical method. (For this reason, Kristin Thompson has called "neoformalist" poetics an "approach" that can utilize different "methods.") To make all films mean the same things by applying the same critical procedures is to ignore the rich variety of film history. In a given film, any item may bear an abstract meaning; or it may bear none. It is all a matter of conceptual scheme, intrinsic context, and historical norms. Some films may make meaning their "dominant," as do allegories like *The Seventh Seal* and *Thriller.* In other films, narrative referentiality forms the basis of the film's composition and effects; abstract meanings remain secondary. This is the case with most popular commercial cinema. Or a film's composition and effects may depend upon a fluctuating relation of narrative structure to stylistic patterning, as in *Play Time* or *Pickpocket.* In yet other films, such as *Mothlight,* perceptual play may dominate the film to the extent that cues cannot be isolated and bear semantic fields. Taken singly, no interpretive schema or heuristic can be definitively abandoned, since an open-textured poetics of film might find anything appropriate to illuminate a given film in a particular historical context. By the same token, though, not every film will be interpretable to the same degree, and in many cases interpretive inferences will be the least pertinent ones.

Historical poetics takes on particular urgency within a critical milieu that appeals to conventions as a way of setting off the target film. By invoking norms the explicatory critic usually treats mundane tradition as a foil to the innovative filmmaker. The symptomatic critic typically uses norms to establish what is "natural" and "invisible" (as a camouflage for textual contradictions). Yet most such appeals to convention remain ungrounded in evidence. Without an awareness of historically existent options, critics often attribute historically implausible transgressions to a film. One critic claims that the ending of *Humoresque* creates a "disturbance of codification" when radio music wells up unrealistically as the heroine walks to her death; but such a move from diegetic to nondiegetic music is quite permissible in classical Hollywood cinema.[34] Likewise, many of the disruptive traits ascribed to oppositional or "subversive" films are simply conventions of postwar art cinema. One writer finds *Videodrome* to "radically challenge prevailing systems of signification" because it has an unresolved plot, does not set off flashbacks with dissolves, and breaks down the boundary between subjective and objective representation.[35] Another critic declares that *Bad Timing* "undercuts the spectators' pleasure by preventing both visual and narrative identification, by making it literally as difficult to see as to understand events and their succession, their timing; and our sense of time becomes uncertain in the film, as its vision for us is blurry."[36] On the contrary: such problems of identification and such temporal uncertainties constitute fundamental art-cinema conventions, and they have shaped viewing skills ever since *Hiroshima mon amour, Red Desert, Persona,* and similar films became models for ambitious directors.[37]

For the poetician, such conventions and skills become the center of attention. Since *poiesis* means "making," poetics could profit from a pun of its own: it focuses on the *work*—the film as an object, but also the regulated effort that produces and uses it. Filmmakers aim to make certain sorts of objects, which in turn produce more or less predictable effects when used in conventional ways.

On the compositional side, the film poetician concentrates on those processes that enable films to come into being. Interpretive practice has tended to play down the concrete activities involved in the filmmaking enterprise. For the explicatory critic, the film may express the creator's world view, or it may be an integral object whose implications escape its maker. For the symptomatic critic, the mainstream text's contradictions are involuntary. (The producers, as cultural agents, are on the whole blind to ideological forces.) Yet most textual effects are the result of deliberate and founding choices, and these affect form, style, and different sorts of meaning. Just as a poet's use of iambic pentameter or sonnet form is unlikely to be involuntary, so the film-maker's decisions about camera placement, performance, or editing constitute relatively stable creative acts whose situational logic can be investigated. This is not to ignore the fact that in most industrial circumstances filmmaking involves collective work, with choices made by various agents and defined in varying ways. In principle, the standardized compositional options should be specifiable.

As a historian of forms, genres, and styles, the poetician starts from the concrete assumptions embedded in the filmmaker's craft. Sometimes these are articulated by practitioners; sometimes they must be inferred from the product and the mode of production. The poetician aims to analyze the conceptual and empirical factors—norms, traditions, habits—that govern a practice and its products. Poetics thus offers explanations, of an intentionalist, functionalist, or causal sort. It has a propensity to the problem/solution model, to institutional frames of reference, and to rational-agent explanatory assumptions.[38] At present, research into early cinema, genre history, stylistics, and narratology manifests the gradual emergence of a self-conscious poetics of film.[39]

In some traditions, "poetics" has referred only to the "productive" side of the process; "aesthetics" was often assumed to account for the work's effects. But Aristotle was at pains to include in the *Poetics* a discussion of the audience's response to tragedy.[40] In this century, literary poeticians such as the Russian Formalists and the Chicago Neo-Aristotelians made the question a central one. Historically, interpreters have tended to reduce all effects to "meaning"; they have been attracted less to art's "pleasing" side than to its didactic side. In contemporary film theory, matters of effect have sometimes been treated under a Freudian notion of "pleasure." Certainly a poetics of cinema should recognize something like pleasure as an effect to be explained, but as it stands the concept is notably broad. In watching an image, we pay attention, make inferences, and perform both voluntary and involuntary perceptual activities that need analyzing and explaining. In following a narrative, we make assumptions and draw on schemata and routines in order to arrive at conclusions about the world of the story. Somehow all this may come out as pleasure, but we scarcely know how.

By situating matters of meaning within the framework of effects, a poetics need not adopt the communication model of sender-message-receiver, or what has been called the "conduit" metaphor.[41] Nor need it follow the signification model of sign, message, and code.[42] The poetics I would propose rests upon an inferential model, whereby the perceiver uses cues in the film to execute determinable operations, of which the construction of all sorts of meaning will be a part. To some extent, the filmmaker (being himself or herself also a perceiver) can construct the film in such a way that certain cues are likely to be salient and certain inferential pathways are marked out. But the filmmaker cannot control all the semantic fields, schemata, and heuristics which the perceiver may bring to bear on the film. The spectator can thus use the film for other purposes than the maker anticipated. There is nothing mysterious or surprising about this; any product of human labor can fulfill various functions. When operating within the institution of film criticism, perceivers are likely to use the film to produce implicit and symptomatic meanings, regardless of the filmmaker's intent. A historical poetics will thus study not only the practices of production but also those of reception. It will not let the former dictate the latter, but it will study the parallels and common grounds no less than the divergences.

From this perspective, interpretation's conceptions of implicit and symptomatic meaning take on new significance. In their most concrete form, they constitute protocols of reception, particularly within twentieth-century Western societies. More generally, they point to factors which must be part of any explanation which a poetics can offer. Any social phenomenon can be analyzed as intended action accompanied by unintended consequences. The explicatory conception of meaning, in attributing to the filmmaker(s) voluntary control over the implicit meanings of the film, acknowledges the undeniable power of social agents to make and execute plans. Yet the concept of culturally symptomatic meaning directs our explanation to those aspects of the film shaped by the "invisible hand" of larger social forces. Insofar as poetics aims at comprehensive explanation of causes and uses of films, these conceptions of meaning, revised in ways I have suggested earlier, can point the enterprise toward a modified rational-agent model of films' making and reception.[43]

At this moment, however, I believe that the most promising avenues for poetic analysis are those opening onto the compositional processes of form and style. After the 1970s flurry of "textual analyses" in the pages of *Screen, Camera Obscura,* and other journals, most English-language critics seem to have relegated such activities to pedagogy. Many writers on the classical Hollywood cinema assume that its narrative and stylistic dynamics are well understood; this enables the critic to pass smoothly on to the business of interpretation. In France, however, textual analysis of a rigorous and enlightening sort continues to be done.[44] Such work, which puts interpretation at the service of more global investigations of conventions of filmic structure and function, lies firmly within the purview of poetics.

If the critic analyzes films' form and style, she becomes open to noticing that some effects are not reducible to meaning in the sense that interpretive critics employ. In the classical tradition of film theory, Rudolf Arnheim and the Noël Burch of *Theory of Film Practice* pay particular attention to those effects of the medium that escape thematization. Some practical criticism also points in this direction. Stuart Liebman has exposed the perceptual basis of the patterns in Paul Sharits' *Shutter Interface,* showing how the film's synesthetic qualities rely upon manipulations of the phi phenomenon and lateral movement illusions.[45] Kristin Thompson has traced how perceptual "excess" takes on saliency in *Ivan the Terrible.*[46] Borrowing from E. H. Gombrich's account of decorative art, I have argued that "parametric" films organize film techniques in patterns that may create an ongoing spectatorial engagement independent of narrative action.[47] The films of Yasujiro Ozu, with their nonnarrative structures of locale and shot composition, offer good examples of what Gombrich calls order without meaning.[48] While the interpreter makes the film interpretable, the poetician may also display the film as intriguing or challenging, perhaps because its operations lie beneath or beyond interpretation.[49]

A poetics of effects will also be led to a study of comprehension. If historical scholarship can disclose referential and explicit meanings, a historical poetics can study the principles whereby viewers construct such meanings. What are the inferential strategies that allow spectators to identify a protagonist, grasp a camera movement as subjective, or understand that one cut denotes an ellipsis while another does not? In order to analyze the process whereby a spectator constructs the film's world and the story that takes place there, the poetician will probably have some recourse to the schemata I have outlined in Chapters 6, 7, and 8. But instead of treating schemata as devices for marking out cues that can support abstract semantic fields, the poetician can study them in their own right: to examine how the personification schema allows the spectator to construct character, how the grasping of setting relies upon spatial routines, how the trajectory schema yields inferences about causality, temporality, and parallel agents or actions. To take up an earlier example: the poetician could analyze those structural and substantive aspects of *Psycho* upon which critics have reached consensus and from which they launch their various interpretations.

Going further, the poetician will want *explanations* for the processes of comprehension. Such explanations will probably not be neat, and it is unlikely that they will draw much support from structuralist and semiotic conceptions of codes (that is, rule-governed sets of fixed units). It is now apparent that cinema has few, if any, such rules or units, and that the spectator usually employs cinematic norms as "default" values to be overriden if broader strategies of sense-making suggest more fruitful inferences. A flashback that is not signaled by a dissolve will not faze a spectator who has picked up other cues for temporal reordering and who, as the film progresses, comes to grasp the work's intrinsic norm. Adequate explanations of comprehension will invoke several quite diverse explanatory frames: biological capacities of the human organism (for example, the mandatory perception of apparent movement), acquired but very basic perceptual processes (for example, ballistic eye movements, object recognition), acquired but culturally widespread cognitive skills (for example, means/end analysis, personification), and acquired and culturally variable processes (for example, particular notions of personal identity, historical conventions of narrative construction). It seems likely that a tenable theory of this sort will have recourse to perceptual and cognitive research in anthropology, psychology, linguistics, and aesthetics.

If poetics is concerned to explain effects generated by films, it must include in its purview those effects I have been calling interpretive practices.[50] The inferential protocols of certain modes of viewing encourage the spectator to try out implicit and symptomatic meanings "spontaneously," as when art-cinema conventions invite the viewer to take an object symbolically. A historical poetics should show how such interpretive inferences constitute viewing conventions. In other cases, when interpretation becomes a primary end of film criticism, the poetician must examine how those inferences inform the work of another artisan—the interpreter. Critical writing, in highbrow reviews and academic journals, becomes rather like art itself: a body of historically distinct norms and customs, goals and shortcuts, exemplars and ordinary works. At this point, poetics becomes metacriticism.

Poetics is thus not another critical "approach," like myth criticism or deconstruction. Nor is it a "theory" like psychoanalysis or Marxism. In its broadest compass, it is a conceptual framework within which particular questions about films' composition and effects can be posed. In its accomplishments, poetics has proven too wide-ranging to constitute practical criticism and too concrete (too "practical") to be honored as theory. Yet it is crucial to both. Its empirical generalizations and conceptual distinctions supply assumptions, hypotheses, and enthymematic premises that neither criticism nor theory could do without. Analytical editing, the notion of the protagonist, character-centered causality, the long take, on-screen versus off-screen space, the concept of the scene, crosscutting, and diegetic sound are middle-level concepts which survive changes in theoretical fashion because they mesh tightly with the phenomena.[51] They are our primary analytical instruments, and their usefulness lies in the fact that they capture real and significant choices faced by filmmakers and viewers.

Along parallel lines, I have sought to lay out certain middle-level concepts which interpreters employ and show how they embody the institutional choices which critics make. I offer not a hermeneutics—a scheme for producing valid or valuable interpretations—but a poetics of interpretation. An indication of this, I think, is the extent to which criticizing this book's conclusions will entail using its own concepts. The interpreter can probe the preceding chapters for implicit meanings, expose what is repressed, project new semantic fields onto nodal passages, trace out a journey of values or an Oedipal allegory, pun on my terms, deflate my rhetorical pretensions, and so on. Like every poetics of writing, mine hands over to the reader the tools with which my own discourse can be taken to pieces.

Within the framework of a poetics, interpretation takes on its proper importance. We cannot keep critics from building up implicit and symptomatic meanings; nor should we. The dominance of interpretation is regrettable, but abstinence is not in order. Interpretation of individual films can be fruitfully renewed by a historical scholarship that seeks out the concrete and unfamiliar conditions under which all sorts of meaning are made. Further, interpretation should not overwhelm analysis of form and style; the critic should not strive to reduce every effect to the conventions of interpretive reason.

Film researchers can also go beyond practical criticism and launch broad and basic projects in historical poetics. Here everything remains to be done. We are far from understanding the formal and stylistic operations of the earliest cinema. We have no sophisticated analysis of most genres, no sufficiently complex history of acting, lighting, editing, music, camera techniques, or aesthetic uses of color. We lack a subtle and principled history of narrative forms. We do not know enough about such mundane matters as dialogue, scene construction, and optical effects. We are almost completely uninformed about the norms governing the ordinary output of most national cinemas, let alone the relations between those norms and conditions of production and consumption. Even the official classics—the works of German Expressionism or Soviet montage or Italian Neorealism—have not on the whole been considered from the standpoint of a historical poetics. Such tasks as these, and a hundred more, require us to forge fresh theories, to ask precise questions, to examine a wide range of films from various traditions, and to supplement study of "the text" with examination of a wide range of documents. Again, interpretive conventions would fall naturally into this line of inquiry, but they would not compose it wholly. The researcher could profitably concentrate on historical norms of comprehension, about which we know so little, and to which interpretation owes so much. Empirical without being empiricist, emphasizing explanations rather than explications, poetics can enrich criticism by putting cinema's social, psychological, and aesthetic conventions at the center of inquiry.

I cannot rely on much besides inference and rhetoric to persuade my reader that such research programs are worth pursuing. I have offered some arguments to show that a criticism dominated by interpretation has strong and intriguing rivals in accounting for films' composition and effects. But to convince the interpretive critic that changes are in order, I must appeal to other values we share—such as our old friends plausibility and novelty. Certainly the alternatives I have sketched out seem minimally plausible. As for the novelty . . .

In titling his 1923 study of conventionality in art *The Knight's Move*, Shklovsky created an image rich in implications. One of them is the necessarily oblique development of art. Like the chess knight, art does not progress in a straight line. It gets deflected because it aims to be unpredictable in relation to reigning norms. Criticism can progress in a similar fashion. The greatest novelty, at this moment, will come not from new semantic fields (postmodernism, or whatever will follow) but from a sidestepped dislocation of interpretation itself. It is time for critics to make the knight's move.

Notes
Index

Notes

1. Making Films Mean

1. Roland Barthes, "On Reading," in *The Rustle of Language,* trans. Richard Howard (New York: Hill and Wang, 1986), p. 33.
2. See, for example, John Reichert, *Making Sense of Literature* (Chicago: University of Chicago Press, 1977), pp. 114–115. Cf. Paul Kiparsky, "On Theory and Interpretation," in Nigel Fabb et al., eds., *The Linguistics of Writing: Arguments between Language and Literature* (Manchester: Manchester University Press, 1987), p. 195.
3. I will, though, continue to refer to the object of interpretation as a "text," whether it be a piece of writing, a painting, or a film. I would prefer to call it the "work," but this is often too ambiguous, evoking the idea of task or labor. The last chapter tries at one point to make something useful of the overlapping senses of "work."
4. See, for an explanation, E. D. Hirsch, Jr., *The Aims of Interpretation* (Chicago: University of Chicago Press, 1976), p. 19.
5. Paul Ricoeur, "Existence and Hermeneutics," in Josef Bleicher, ed., *Contemporary Hermeneutics: Hermeneutics as Method, Philosophy, and Critique* (London: Routledge and Kegan Paul, 1980), p. 245.
6. A contemporary instance of this dichotomy is Dudley Andrew's contrast between a film's structured and "grammatical" transmission of a "message" (literal meaning) and the transgressive "derailing" of clear meaning (figuration). See *Concepts in Film Theory* (New York: Oxford University Press, 1984), pp. 158, 167–169, 188.
7. Frank Kermode, *The Art of Telling: Essays on Fiction* (Cambridge: Harvard University Press, 1983), p. 24.
8. What follows is discussed at a little more length in my *Narration in the Fiction Film* (Madison: University of Wisconsin Press, 1985), pp. 30–40.
9. This version of constructivism assumes that it is possible to arrive at inferences which are at least approximately true; it is thus compatible with a critical realist epistemology. For a defense of "constructivist real-

ism," see Ronald N. Giere, *Explaining Science: A Cognitive Critique* (Chicago: University of Chicago Press, 1988).

10. Gerald Graff calls this "given and unrefusable" aspect of perceptual construction the "Godfather effect." See *Literature against Itself: Literary Ideas in Modern Society* (Chicago: University of Chicago Press, 1979), p. 202.

11. Marshall Edelson, *Hypothesis and Evidence in Psychoanalysis* (Chicago: University of Chicago Press, 1984), p. 46.

12. See Stanley Fish, *Is There a Text in This Class? The Authority of Interpretive Communities* (Cambridge: Harvard University Press, 1980), especially pp. 268–292, 338–371.

13. Jacques Lacan, "Seminar on 'The Purloined Letter,'" *Yale French Studies* 48 (1972): 40.

14. See, for example, Kaja Silverman, *The Subject of Semiotics* (New York: Oxford University Press, 1983), pp. 146–148.

15. Jonathan Culler, *Structuralist Poetics: Structuralism, Linguistics, and the Study of Literature* (Ithaca: Cornell University Press, 1975), especially pp. 117–118, 225; Peter J. Rabinowitz, *Before Reading: Narrative Conventions and the Politics of Interpretation* (Ithaca: Cornell University Press, 1987), chaps. 2–5.

16. For example, Culler models his notion of "literary competence" upon Chomsky's notion of linguistic competence; *Structuralist Poetics*, pp. 25–26, 122. But Chomsky's Transformational Generative Grammar conceives of rules as defining correct expressions and inference steps in a constitutive fashion, whereas the interpretive rules proposed by Culler are regulative, strategic ones. For a discussion of this distinction, see Renate Bartsch, *Norms of Language* (London: Longman, 1987), pp. 160–163. For Transformational Generative Grammar, syntactic rules define the very notion of what will count as a sentence in a natural language. Culler's rules, by contrast, express probabilistic expectations about textual structure. Most recently, Chomsky has suggested that knowledge of language consists not of rules but of "principles." See Noam Chomsky, *Knowledge of Language: Its Nature, Origin, and Use* (New York: Praeger, 1986), pp. 145–160.

17. This derives from David Lewis, *Convention: A Philosophical Study* (Cambridge: Harvard University Press, 1969), pp. 58, 78.

18. On the notion of overt versus covert conventions, see Robert M. Martin, *The Meaning of Language* (Cambridge: MIT Press, 1987), pp. 79–81.

19. See, for a relevant discussion, Barry Smith, "Knowing How vs. Knowing That," in J. C. Nyíri and Barry Smith, eds., *Practical Knowledge: Outlines of a Theory of Traditions and Skills* (London: Croom Helm, 1988), pp. 8–9.

20. For a discussion of these concepts, see Bordwell, *Narration in the Fiction Film*, pp. 48–62.

21. These types of form are discussed in David Bordwell and Kristin Thompson, *Film Art: An Introduction* (New York: Knopf, 1985), pp. 44–81.

22. My double-edged usage of the term—including both intratextual and extratextual referring—conforms to current thinking in linguistics and literary semantics. See Keith Allan, *Linguistic Meaning*, vol. 1 (London: Routledge and Kegan Paul, 1986), p. 68, and the essays in Anna White-

side and Michael Issacharoff, eds., *On Referring in Literature* (Blooming-ton: Indiana University Press, 1987).

23. For a discussion of how explicit meaning can be derived from referential meaning, see Gerald Prince, "Narrative Pragmatics, Message, and Point," *Poetics* 12 (1983): 530–532.

24. For detailed and wide-ranging discussions of implicit meaning (from different theoretical perspectives), see Catherine Kerbrat-Orecchioni, *L'Implicite* (Paris: Colin, 1986), and Dan Sperber and Deirdre Wilson, *Relevance: Communication and Cognition* (Cambridge: Harvard University Press, 1986).

25. It may be that only with explicit meanings as a model can we build up notions of implicit meaning. Thus in the life history of the individual, learning to see the moral of a fable or the point of a fairy tale may be a necessary step to learning how to find an implied theme in "high" art.

26. I sketch a model of comprehension for fictional cinema in *Narration in the Fiction Film,* pp. 29–47.

27. Other interpretive institutions do not fall within my purview, but it seems likely that they could be studied using the same categories of meaning. For instance, censorship as an interpretive activity would appear to aim at definitively determining a film's referential and explicit meanings while having a difficult time pinning down its implicit and symptomatic ones.

28. As in this claim about Godard's *Sauve qui peut (la vie)*: "The incidents of abuse are clearly presented as ritual humiliations, symptomatic instances of a general malaise." Robert Stam, "Jean-Luc Godard's *Sauve qui peut (la vie),*" *Millennium Film Journal* 10/11 (1981): 197.

29. Lindsay Anderson, "The Last Sequence of *On the Waterfront,*" *Sight and Sound* 24, 3 (January–March 1955): 128.

30. "*On the Waterfront:* Points from Letters," *Sight and Sound* 24, 4 (Spring 1955): 216.

31. Robert Hughes, "*On the Waterfront:* A Defense," *Sight and Sound* 24, 4 (Spring 1955): 215.

32. See Irene R. Fairley, "The Reader's Need for Conventions: When Is a Mushroom Not a Mushroom?" *Style* 20, 1 (Spring 1986): 12.

33. Dwight MacDonald, *On Movies* (New York: Berkley, 1971), pp. 47, 54, 56.

34. Pat Hilton, "Ask Pat," *TV Week, Wisconsin State Journal,* 16 November 1986, 35.

35. "*The Republic* (selections)," in Allan H. Gilbert, ed., *Literary Criticism: Plato to Dryden* (Detroit: Wayne State University Press, 1961), p. 25.

36. Aristotle, *Poetics,* trans. Gerald F. Else (Ann Arbor: University of Mich-igan Press, 1967), p. 33.

37. Longinus, "On Literary Excellence," in Gilbert, *Literary Criticism,* p. 153.

38. Quoted in Beryl Smalley, *The Study of the Bible in the Middle Ages* (Oxford: Blackwell, 1952), p. 3.

39. Frank Kermode, "The Plain Sense of Things," in Geoffrey H. Hartman and Sanford Budick, eds., *Midrash and Literature* (New Haven: Yale University Press, 1986), pp. 179–191; Barry W. Holtz, "Midrash," in

Holtz, ed., *Back to the Sources: Reading the Classic Jewish Texts* (New York: Summit Books, 1984), pp. 180–182, 201.

40. Robert M. Grant with David Tracy, *A Short History of the Interpretation of the Bible,* rev. ed. (London: SCM, 1984), pp. 19–20.

41. "Letter to Can Grande della Stella," in Gilbert, *Literary Criticism,* p. 202.

42. Excerpts from *The Book of Suger, Abbot of St.-Denis,* in Elizabeth G. Holt, ed., *A Documentary History of Art,* vol. 1, *The Middle Ages and the Renaissance* (Garden City, N.Y.: Doubleday Anchor, 1957), pp. 29, 30.

43. Jean Seznec, *The Survival of the Pagan Gods: The Mythological Tradition and Its Place in Renaissance Humanism and Art* (Princeton: Princeton University Press, 1953), pp. 11–121.

44. See Don Cameron Allen, *Mysteriously Meant: The Rediscovery of Pagan Symbolism and Allegorical Interpretation in the Renaissance* (Baltimore: Johns Hopkins University Press, 1970).

45. Susan Leigh Foster, *Reading Dancing: Bodies and Subjects in Contemporary American Dance* (Berkeley: University of California Press, 1986), p. 109.

46. Moshe Barasch, *Theories of Art: From Plato to Winckelmann* (New York: New York University Press, 1985), pp. 263–269.

47. Mark Roskill, *What Is Art History?* (New York: Harper and Row, 1976), pp. 139–144.

48. See Tzvetan Todorov, *Symbolism and Interpretation,* trans. Catherine Porter (Ithaca: Cornell University Press, 1982), pp. 131–143.

49. Richard E. Palmer, *Hermeneutics* (Evanston, Illinois: Northwestern University Press, 1969), pp. 81–83.

50. Ibid., pp. 78–79.

51. Ibid., pp. 84–97.

52. See Rudolf A. Makkreel, *Dilthey: Philosopher of the Human Sciences* (Princeton: Princeton University Press, 1975), pp. 267–272, and Edgar V. McKnight, *Meanings in Texts: The Historical Shaping of a Narrative Hermeneutics* (Philadelphia: Fortress Press, 1978), pp. 12–32.

53. Michel Charles, "La Lecture critique," *Poétique* 34 (April 1978): 144–146.

54. Ibid., p. 141

55. Gustav Lanson, "La Méthode de l'histoire littéraire," in Lanson, *Essais de méthode, de critique, et d'histoire littéraire,* ed. Henri Peyre (Paris: Hachette, 1965), p. 44.

56. See, for example, Emile Benveniste, "Remarques sur la fonction du langage dans la découverte freudienne," in *Problèmes de linguistique générale,* vol. 1 (Paris: Gallimard, 1976), p. 86; David Bakan, *Sigmund Freud and the Jewish Mystical Tradition* (New York: Van Nostrand, 1958), pp. 246–270; and Tzvetan Todorov, *Theories of the Symbol,* trans. Catherine Porter (Ithaca: Cornell University Press, 1982), pp. 248–249.

57. See Henri F. Ellenberger, *The Discovery of the Unconscious: The History and Evolution of Dynamic Psychiatry* (New York: Basic Books, 1970), p. 537.

58. Michel Foucault, *The Order of Things: An Archaeology of the Human Sciences* (New York: Random House, 1970), pp. 373, 374.

59. Useful summaries of this process are provided in Ellenberger, *Discovery,*

pp. 474–534; Richard Wollheim, *Sigmund Freud* (New York: Viking, 1971), pp. 59–111.

60. Erwin Panofsky, "Iconography and Iconology: An Introduction to the Study of Renaissance Art," in *Meaning in the Visual Arts: Papers in and on Art History* (Garden City, N.Y.: Doubleday Anchor, 1955), pp. 40–41.

61. Fredric Jameson, *The Political Unconscious: Narrative as a Socially Symbolic Act* (Ithaca: Cornell University Press, 1981), pp. 30–31.

62. See Gerald Graff, *Professing Literature: An Institutional History* (Chicago: University of Chicago Press, 1987), pp. 247–262.

2. Routines and Practices

1. See C. J. van Rees, "Advances in the Empirical Sociology of Literature and the Arts: The Institutional Approach," *Poetics* 12 (1983): 285–310. Other social groups which practice film criticism include censorship agencies and fandom. Neither lies within my purview, but a study of each one's interpretive norms would be worthwhile.

2. Janet Staiger discusses the rise of the academic canon in film study in her article "The Politics of Film Canons," *Cinema Journal* 24, 3 (Spring 1985): 4–23.

3. James Monaco, *How to Read a Film* (New York: Oxford University Press, 1977).

4. See Steven Mailloux, "Rhetorical Hermeneutics," *Critical Inquiry* 11, 4 (June 1985): 634–637, and Vincent B. Leitch, *American Literary Criticism from the 30s to the 80s* (New York: Columbia University Press, 1988), pp. 109–114, 150–151.

5. Mary Douglas, *How Institutions Think* (Syracuse: Syracuse University Press, 1986), p. 112.

6. See Jonathan Culler, "Beyond Interpretation," in *The Pursuit of Signs: Semiotics, Deconstruction, Literature* (Ithaca: Cornell University Press, 1981), pp. 3–11; Gerald Graff, *Literature against Itself: Literary Ideas in Modern Society* (Chicago: University of Chicago Press, 1979), pp. 5–7, 129–149.

7. See, for example, Richard Levin, *New Readings vs. Old Plays: Recent Trends in the Reinterpretation of English Renaissance Drama* (Chicago: University of Chicago Press, 1979); Grant Webster, *The Republic of Letters: A History of Postwar American Literary Opinion* (Baltimore: Johns Hopkins University Press, 1979); William E. Cain, *The Crisis in Criticism: Theory, Literature, and Reform in English Studies* (Baltimore: Johns Hopkins University Press, 1984); Gerald Graff and Reginald Gibbons, eds., *Criticism in the University* (Evanston, Ill.: Northwestern University Press, 1985); Gerald Graff, *Professing Literature: An Institutional History* (Chicago: University of Chicago Press, 1987).

8. These tenets are drawn, selectively, from Levin, *New Readings*, pp. 2–5.

9. See Cain, *Crisis in Criticism*, p. 106.

10. Douglas, *How Institutions Think*, p. 112.

11. Ibid., p. 48.
12. On the development of aesthetic criticism out of biblical criticism, see Stephen Prickett, *Words and the Word: Language, Poetics, and Biblical Interpretation* (Cambridge: Cambridge University Press, 1986).
13. Barry Barnes, *Scientific Knowledge and Sociological Theory* (London: Routledge and Kegan Paul, 1974), pp. 87–97.
14. See Barry Barnes, *T. S. Kuhn and Social Science* (New York: Columbia University Press, 1982), pp. 45–46.
15. Cain, *Crisis in Criticism*, p. 101.
16. Cleanth Brooks and Robert Penn Warren, *Understanding Fiction* (New York: Appleton-Century-Crofts, 1959), p. 28.
17. The theory and ideology of literary education have been studied in France for several years. For an overview and bibliography, see Clément Moisson, *Qu'est-ce que l'histoire littéraire?* (Paris: Presses universitaires de France, 1987), pp. 96–154, 242–265.
18. Barnes, *Scientific Knowledge*, p. 21.
19. John Crowe Ransom, *The World's Body* (New York: Scribner's, 1938), p. 327.
20. Barnes, *Scientific Knowledge*, pp. 39, 62.
21. Barnes, *T. S. Kuhn*, p. 104.
22. Bruno Latour and Steve Woolgar, *Laboratory Life: The Construction of Scientific Facts* (Princeton: Princeton University Press, 1986), pp. 194–207.
23. Bruno Latour discusses this dissemination of "soft facts" in *Science in Action: How to Follow Scientists and Engineers through Society* (Cambridge: Harvard University Press, 1987), p. 208.
24. See Sergei Eisenstein, *Film Form*, ed. and trans. Jay Leyda (New York: World, 1957), pp. 98–101; Vladimir Nizhny, *Lessons with Eisenstein*, trans. and ed. Ivor Montagu and Jay Leyda (New York: Hill and Wang, 1962), pp. 15–17; Sergei Eisenstein, *The Film Sense*, trans. Jay Leyda (New York: World, 1957), p. 151.
25. Sergei Eisenstein, *Film Essays and a Lecture*, ed. and trans. Jay Leyda (New York: Praeger, 1970), pp. 122–123; Eisenstein, *Film Form*, pp. 234–235.
26. Jane Shapiro, "Stranger in Paradise," *Village Voice*, 16 September 1986, 20–21.
27. Barry W. Holtz, "Midrash," in Holtz, ed., *Back to the Sources: Reading the Classic Jewish Texts* (New York: Summit, 1984), p. 189.
28. See Sigmund Freud, *The Complete Introductory Lectures on Psychoanalysis*, trans. and ed. James Strachey (New York: Norton, 1966), pp. 482–483.
29. See Sylvia Scribner, "Thinking in Action: Some Characteristics of Practical Thought," in Robert J. Sternberg and Richard K. Wagner, eds., *Practical Intelligence: Nature and Origins of Competence in the Everyday World* (Cambridge: Cambridge University Press, 1986), p. 21.
30. Current positions are well developed in Dan Sperber and Deirdre Wilson, *Relevance: Communication and Cognition* (Cambridge: Harvard University

Press, 1986), and John H. Holland, Keith J. Holyoak, Richard E. Nisbett, and Paul R. Thagard, *Induction: Processes of Inference, Learning, and Discovery* (Cambridge: MIT Press, 1986).

31. Anomaly as a trigger to interpretation may underlie Dudley Andrew's claim that certain moments "block" our movement through a film and elicit "our active interpretation." See his *Concepts in Film Theory* (New York: Oxford University Press, 1984), p. 168.

32. Theorists of literary criticism have outlined conventions similar to the ones adduced here. See Jonathan Culler, *Structuralist Poetics: Structuralism, Linguistics, and the Study of Literature* (Ithaca: Cornell University Press, 1975), chaps. 6–9; Ellen Schauber and Ellen Spolsky, *The Bounds of Interpretation: Linguistic Theory and Literary Texts* (Stanford: Stanford University Press, 1986), chaps. 6 and 7; Peter J. Rabinowitz, *Before Reading: Narrative Conventions and the Politics of Interpretation* (Ithaca: Cornell University Press, 1987), chaps. 2–5.

33. Holland et al., *Induction*, p. 7.

34. Ibid., p. 279.

35. Ibid.

36. This tendency is especially strong in cases where the perceiver generates his or her own hypothesis. See K. J. Gilhooly, *Thinking: Directed, Undirected, and Creative* (New York: Academic Press, 1982), pp. 86–90.

37. See P. N. Johnson-Laird, *Mental Models: Towards a Cognitive Science of Language, Inference, and Consciousness* (Cambridge: Cambridge University Press, 1983), pp. 10–12; K. J. Holyoak, "An Analogical Framework for Literary Interpretation," *Poetics* 11 (1982): 110–113.

38. For a general overview of schema theory, see Ronald W. Casson, "Schemata in Cognitive Anthropology," *Annual Review of Anthropology* 12 (1983): 429–462. The three types of schemata to which I refer are drawn from Reid Hastie, "Schematic Principles in Human Memory," in E. T. Higgins et al., eds., *Social Cognition: The Ontario Symposium*, vol. 1 (Hillsdale, N. J.: Erlbaum, 1981), pp. 39–88.

39. Richard Nisbett and Lee Ross, *Human Inference: Strategies and Shortcomings of Social Judgment* (Englewood Cliffs, N. J.: Prentice-Hall, 1980), pp. 7–8.

40. Barnes, *T. S. Kuhn*, p. 10.

41. Michał Głowinski, "Reading, Interpretation, Reception," *New Literary History* 11 (1979): 78.

42. This position, in many variants, is presented in the anthology *The Rhetoric of the Human Sciences: Language and Argument in Scholarship and Public Affairs,* ed. John S. Nelson, Allan Megill, and Donald N. McCloskey (Madison: University of Wisconsin Press, 1987).

43. For an analysis of reviewing style, see D. Edelstein's hilarious article "The Poetics of Affirmation: Signification and Mimesis in the Works of Lyons, Siegel, and Shalit," *Village Voice,* 12 January 1988, 70.

44. Donald N. McCloskey, *The Rhetoric of Economics* (Madison: University of Wisconsin Press, 1985), p. 124.

45. Susan Sontag, "Against Interpretation," in *Against Interpretation and Other Essays* (New York: Delta, 1966), pp. 7, 9.

46. Kermode, *Genesis,* p. 145.

3. Interpretation as Explication

1. Andrew Sarris, *The Primal Screen: Essays on Film and Related Subjects* (New York: Simon and Schuster, 1973), p. 37.

2. The most entertaining summary is that of Raymond Durgnat, *Films and Feelings* (Cambridge: MIT Press, 1967), pp. 61–75.

3. Parker Tyler, "*Rashomon* as Modern Art," in *The Three Faces of Film,* rev. ed. (South Brunswick, N. J.: A. S. Barnes, 1967), p. 37.

4. Peter Wollen, *Signs and Meanings in the Cinema,* 2d ed. (Bloomington: Indiana University Press, 1972), p. 77.

5. André Bazin, *French Cinema of the Occupation and Resistance: Birth of a Critical Esthetic,* trans. Stanley Hochman (New York: Ungar, 1981), p. 63.

6. Ibid., p. 139.

7. Alexandre Astruc, "The Birth of a New Avant-Garde: La Caméra-stylo," in Peter Graham, ed., *The New Wave* (Garden City, N.Y.: Doubleday, 1968), pp. 17–23. The essay originally appeared in the weekly *L'Ecran français* in 1948.

8. For a discussion of the social background of this work, see Dudley Andrew, *André Bazin* (New York: Oxford University Press, 1978), pp. 82–131; Dudley Andrew, "Bazin before *Cahiers:* Cinematic Politics in Postwar France," *Cineaste* 12, 1 (1982): 12–16.

9. André Bazin, *Orson Welles* (Paris: Chavane, 1950), p. 59.

10. Ibid., p. 44.

11. André Bazin, "Pour en finir avec la profondeur du champ," *Cahiers du cinéma* 1 (April 1951): 17–23.

12. Alexandre Astruc, "Au-dessous du volcan," *Cahiers du cinéma* 1 (April 1951): 29–33.

13. See André Bazin, "On the *Politique des auteurs,*" in Jim Hillier, ed., *Cahiers du cinéma: The 1950s: Neo-Realism, Hollywood, New Wave* (Cambridge: Harvard University Press, 1985), pp. 257–258.

14. Eric Rohmer, "Leçon d'un échec: A propos de *Moby Dick,*" *Cahiers du cinéma* 67 (January 1957): 23.

15. See Thomas Elsaesser, "Two Decades in Another Country: Hollywood and the Cinephiles," in C. W. E. Bigsby, ed., *Superculture: American Popular Culture and Europe* (Bowling Green, Ohio: Bowling Green Popular Press, 1975), pp. 198–216.

16. See Bernard Chardère, "Ouverture pour un index," *Positif* 50/51/52 (March 1963): 219–220.

17. Jean-Paul Torok and Jacques Quincey, "Vincente Minnelli ou le peintre de la vie rêvée," *Positif* 50/51/52 (March 1963): 57.

18. Gerard Legrand, "Maîtrise de Losey," *Positif* 61/62/63 (June-July-August 1963): 148, 150.

19. Andrew Sarris, "*Citizen Kane*—The American Baroque," *Film Culture* 9 (1956): 14.
20. Ibid.
21. Ibid., p. 16.
22. Andrew Sarris, *Confessions of a Cultist: On the Cinema 1955–1969* (New York: Simon and Schuster, 1971), p. 11.
23. Andrew Sarris, "*The Seventh Seal,*" *Film Culture* 19 (1959): 51–61; Sarris, "*A Man Escaped,*" *Film Culture* 14 (November 1957): 6, 16; Eugene Archer, "The Rack of Life," *Film Quarterly* 12, 4 (Summer 1959): 3.
24. Sarris, *Confessions*, p. 13.
25. Sarris, "Notes on the Auteur Theory in 1962," *Film Culture* 27 (Winter 1962–63): 7.
26. This was the prototype for such works as Richard Roud, ed., *Cinema: A Critical Dictionary: The Major Film-Makers* (New York: Viking, 1980); Jean-Pierre Coursodon, Pierre Sauvage, et al., *American Directors* (New York: McGraw-Hill, 1983); and Christopher Lyon, ed., *The International Dictionary of Films and Filmmakers,* vol. 2, *Directors/Filmmakers* (Chicago: St. James Press, 1984).
27. Andrew Sarris, ed., *Interviews with Film Directors* (Indianapolis: Bobbs-Merrill, 1967).
28. Lindsay Anderson, "French Critical Writing," *Sight and Sound* 24, 2 (October-December 1954): 105.
29. The last two impulses owed a good deal to *Sequence* (1945–1952), in some ways the English *Revue du cinéma.*
30. Penelope Houston, "The Critical Question," *Sight and Sound* 29, 4 (Autumn 1960): 163.
31. V. F. Perkins, "The British Cinema," *Movie* 1 (June 1962): 7. See also Charles Barr, "*Le Film maudit,*" *Motion* 3 (Spring 1962): 39–40.
32. William Empson, *Seven Types of Ambiguity* (New York: Meridian, 1955), p. 5.
33. Ian Cameron and Richard Jeffrey, "The Universal Hitchcock," *Movie* 12 (Spring 1965): 23.
34. See "Movie Differences," *Movie* 8 (1963): 34.
35. Jonas Mekas, "The Cinema of the New Generation," *Film Culture* 21 (Summer 1960): 1–6.
36. See Annette Michelson, "Film and the Radical Aspiration," in P. Adams Sitney, ed., *The Film Culture Reader* (New York: Praeger, 1970), pp. 404–421. This is the 1966 version of an essay which Michelson was to publish in revised form in 1974.
37. David Curtis, *Experimental Cinema: A Fifty-Year Evolution* (New York: Delta, 1971), p. 161.
38. Carl I. Beltz, "Three Films by Bruce Conner," *Film Culture* 44 (Spring 1967): 58–59.
39. For an informative history of avant-garde debates, see Phillip Drummond, ed., *Film as Film: Formal Experiment in Film, 1910–1975* (London: Hayward Gallery, 1979), and especially Drummond, "Notions of Avant-Garde Cinema," pp. 9–16.

40. Tyler, *Three Faces,* 63–64.
41. Parker Tyler, *Underground Film: A Critical History* (New York: Grove Press, 1969), p. 8.
42. Ibid., p. 145.
43. P. Adams Sitney, "Imagism in Four Avant-Garde Films," in Sitney, *Film Culture Reader,* pp. 195–199; Sitney, *"Anticipation of the Night* and *Prelude," Film Culture* 26 (Winter 1962): 55.
44. For discussions of the institutional development of the American avant-garde, see J. Hoberman and Jonathan Rosenbaum, *Midnight Movies* (New York: Harper and Row, 1983), pp. 39–76, and Dominique Noguez, *Une Renaissance du cinéma: Le Cinéma "underground" américain* (Paris: Klinck-sieck, 1985), pp. 13–45, 75–236.
45. My schemata differ from those laid out in James Peterson, "In Warhol's Wake: Minimalism and Pop in the American Avant-Garde Film" (Ph.D. diss., University of Wisconsin, 1986), but I am indebted to his pioneering attempt to delineate the logic underlying the critical literature of Pop and minimalist cinema.
46. Gregory Battcock, "Four Films by Andy Warhol," in Battcock, ed., *The New American Cinema* (New York: Dutton, 1967), p. 251.
47. Lee Heflin, "Notes on Seeing the Films of Andy Warhol," *Afterimage* 2 (Autumn 1970): 31.
48. Battcock, "Four Films," p. 223.
49. Sam Hunter, "New Directions in American Painting," in Gregory Battcock, ed., *The New Art* (New York: Dutton, 1966), p. 60.
50. Clement Greenberg, "Modernist Painting," *Arts Yearbook* 4 (1961): 101.
51. See Battcock, "Four Films," pp. 234–237.
52. Ibid., p. 238.
53. Greenberg, "Modernist Painting," p. 101.
54. Peter Gidal, *Andy Warhol: Films and Paintings* (London: Studio Vista, 1971), pp. 126–134.
55. Battcock, "Four Films," pp. 240–242.
56. Greenberg, "Modernist Painting," p. 104.
57. See Sitney, "Imagism," p. 199.
58. P. Adams Sitney, "Structual Film," in Sitney, *Film Culture Reader,* p. 338.
59. Ibid., p. 339.
60. Ibid., p. 341.
61. Beltz, "Three Films," p. 57.
62. Annette Michelson, "Toward Snow," in P. Adams Sitney, ed., *The Avant-Garde Film: A Reader of Theory and Criticism* (New York: New York University Press, 1978), p. 177.
63. "Sixth Independent Film Award," *Film Culture* 33 (Summer 1964): 1.
64. Battcock, "Four Films," pp. 237, 244.
65. Annette Michelson, "Bodies in Space: Film as Carnal Knowledge," *Artforum* 7, 6 (February 1969): 57.
66. Michelson, "Toward Snow," p. 172.
67. Ibid., p. 174.
68. Ibid., p. 175.

69. Wanda Bershen, "*Zorns Lemma*," *Artforum* 10, 1 (September 1971): 42–45.

70. Lois Mendelson and Bill Simon, "*Tom, Tom, the Piper's Son*," *Artforum* 10, 1 (September 1971): 53.

71. Phoebe Cohen, "*Scenes from under Childhood*," *Artforum* 11, 5 (January 1973): 51.

72. Stephen Koch, "*The Chelsea Girls*," *Artforum* 10, 1 (September 1971): 85.

73. Rosalind Krauss, "Montage *October:* Dialectic of the Shot," *Artforum* 11, 5 (January 1973): 61, 64; Annette Michelson, "From Magician to Epistemologist: Vertov's *The Man with a Movie Camera*," in P. Adams Sitney, ed., *The Essential Cinema: Essays on the Films in the Collection of Anthology Film Archives* (New York: New York University Press, 1975), pp. 95–111.

74. For a brief survey, see P. Adams Sitney, "The Idea of Morphology," *Film Culture* 53/54/55 (Spring 1972): 1–24.

75. Mention should also be made of Standish Lawder, whose close analysis and painstaking historical research also attracted art historians to the study of avant-garde film. See his "Structuralism and Movement in Experimental Film and Modern Art, 1896–1925" (Ph.D. diss., Yale University, 1967), and *The Cubist Cinema* (New York: New York University Press, 1975).

76. For a discussion, see Paul Arthur, "The Last of the Last Machine? Avant-Garde Film Since 1966," *Millennium Film Journal* 16/17/18 (Fall–Winter 1986–1987): 74, 78–79.

77. *Cinim,* founded in 1966, folded in 1969; *Cinemantics, Independent Cinema,* and *Cinema Rising* each lasted only a year. Over the long term, *Afterimage,* founded in 1970, has survived, but with an erratic publication schedule.

78. See David Curtis, "English Avant-Garde Film: An Early Chronology," in David Curtis and Deke Dusinberre, eds., *A Perspective on English Avant-Garde Film* (London: Arts Council of Great Britain, 1978), pp. 9–18, and Steve Dwoskin, *Film Is: The International Free Cinema* (Woodstock, N.Y.: Overlook Press, 1975), pp. 61–71.

79. For a detailed discussion of the debates on experimental cinema, see David Rodowick, *The Crisis of Political Modernism: Criticism and Ideology in Contemporary Film Theory* (Urbana: University of Illinois Press, 1988).

80. Peter Sainsbury, "Editorial 2," *Afterimage* 2 (Autumn 1970): 4.

81. "Foreword in Three Letters," *Artforum* 10, 1 (September 1971): 9.

82. Sainsbury, "Editorial 2," p. 7.

83. Sainsbury, "Editorial," *Afterimage* 4 (1972): 5; Simon Field, "The Light of the Eye," *Art and Artists* 7, 9 (December 1972): 36.

84. Malcolm Le Grice, "Real Time/Space," *Art and Artists* 7, 9 (December 1972): 39; Le Grice, "Thoughts on Recent 'Underground' Films," *Afterimage* 4 (Autumn 1972): 80–82.

85. Malcolm Le Grice, "Kurt Kren," *Studio International* 973 (November–December 1975): 184–188.

86. Deke Dusinberre, "On Expanding Cinema," *Studio International* 978 (November–December 1975): 224.

87. Sainsbury, "Editorial" (1972), p. 3.
88. Peter Gidal, "Notes on *La Région centrale*," in Gidal, ed., *Structural Film Anthology* (London: British Film Institute, 1976), p. 52.
89. Malcolm Le Grice, *Abstract Film and Beyond* (Cambridge: MIT Press, 1977), p. 120.
90. Peter Gidal, "Theory and Definition of Structural/Materialist Film," in Gidal, *Structural Film Anthology*, pp. 2–3.
91. Deke Dusinberre, "St George in the Forest: The English Avant-Garde," *Afterimage* 6 (Summer 1976): 6.
92. Peter Gidal, "Beckett & Others & Art: A System," *Studio International* 971 (November 1974): 186–187; Peter Gidal, *"Back and Forth,"* in Gidal, *Structural Film Anthology*, p. 47.
93. Peter Gidal, "Notes on *Zorns Lemma*," in Gidal, *Structural Film Anthology*, p. 73.
94. Gidal, "Film as Film," in Curtis and Dusinberre, *Perspective on English Avant-Garde Film*, p. 23.
95. Mike Dunford, "Experimental/Avant-Garde/Revolutionary/Film Practice," *Afterimage* 6 (Summer 1976): 109.
96. Peter Wollen, "The Avant-Gardes: Europe and America," *Framework* 14 (1981): 9.
97. This draws on R. S. Crane, *The Languages of Criticism and the Structure of Poetry* (Toronto: University of Toronto Press, 1953), p. 117.
98. For this distinction, see ibid., pp. 119–122.
99. See, for a survey of the issues involved, Stephen C. Levinson, *Pragmatics* (Cambridge: Cambridge University Press, 1983), and also Dan Sperber and Deirdre Wilson, *Relevance: Communication and Cognition* (Cambridge: Harvard University Press, 1986).
100. Astruc, "Birth of Avant-Garde," p. 20.
101. See, for example, John Russell Taylor, *Cinema Eye, Cinema Ear: Some Key Film-Makers of the Sixties* (New York: Hill and Wang, 1964), p. 11.
102. Jacques Rivette, "The Essential," in Hillier, *Cahiers: The 1950s,* p. 133.
103. Ian Cameron and Robin Wood, *Antonioni* (New York: Praeger, 1968), p. 8.
104. See, for instance, I. A. Richards, *Principles of Literary Criticism* (New York: Harcourt, Brace, 1928), pp. 180–185; William Empson, *Seven Types of Ambiguity: A Study of Its Effects in English Verse* (Cleveland: Meridian, 1955), pp. 95–99; and F. R. Leavis, *New Bearings in English Poetry* (Ann Arbor: University of Michigan Press, 1960), p. 25.
105. See Edward Buscombe, "Ideas of Authorship," *Screen* 14, 3 (Autumn 1973): 77–78.
106. See Benedict de Spinoza, *A Theologico-Political Treatise and a Political Treatise,* trans. R. H. M. Elwes (New York: Dover, 1951), p. 103.
107. Steve Dwoskin, *"Mare's Tail," Afterimage* 2 (Autumn 1970): 41.
108. See, for example, Mark Segal, "Hollis Frampton/*Zorns Lemma*," *Film Culture* 52 (Spring 1971): 88–89.
109. Battcock, "Four Films," p. 240.
110. Michelson, "Bodies in Space," p. 59.

111. See Gregg Toland, "L'Opérateur de prise de vues," *Revue du cinéma* 4 (1 January 1947): 22–23.

112. Peter Bogdanovich, *The Cinema of Howard Hawks* (New York: Museum of Modern Art Film Library, 1962), p. 8.

113. Michael Snow, "Letter from Michael Snow to P. Adams Sitney and Jonas Mekas," *Film Culture* 46 (1967): 4–5.

114. Sitney, "Imagism," p. 197.

115. Regina Cornwell, "Paul Sharits: Image and Object," *Artforum* 10, 1 (September 1971): 56–57.

116. Paul Sharits, "Hearing: Seeing," *Film Culture* 65–66 (1978): 69.

117. Tim Bruce, quoted in Curtis and Dusinberre, *Perspective on English Avant-Garde Film*, p. 51.

118. Murray Krieger, *The New Apologists for Poetry* (Bloomington: Indiana University Press, 1963), p. 128. See Gerald Graff, *Professing Literature: An Institutional History* (Chicago: University of Chicago Press, 1987), for an account of how New Criticism, which started as a cultural critique, became a practice of "explicating texts in a vacuum" (p. 146).

119. Annette Michelson, "*What Is Cinema?*" *Artforum* 6, 10 (Summer 1968): 70.

120. Jonathan Rosenbaum, *Film: The Front Line 1983* (Denver: Arden Press, 1983), p. 138.

121. Sarris, *Interviews*, p. viii.

122. See Ian Cameron, "Films, Directors, and Critics," *Movie* 2 (September 1962): 4–7, and "*Movie* Differences," *Movie* 8 (1963): 34.

123. V. F. Perkins, *Film as Film* (New York: Penguin, 1972), p. 173.

124. Fereydoun Hoveyda, "Sunspots," in Jim Hillier, ed., *Cahiers du Cinéma: The 1960s: New Wave, New Cinema, Reevaluating Hollywood* (Cambridge: Harvard University Press, 1986), p. 143.

125. Jonas Mekas, *Movie Journal: The Rise of a New American Cinema, 1959–1971* (New York: Collier, 1972), p. 316.

126. Quoted in Jim Hillier, "Introduction," in *Cahiers: The 1960s*, p. 3.

127. Andrew Sarris, *The American Cinema: Directors and Directions, 1929–1968* (New York: Dutton, 1968), p. 30.

128. "*Barabbas:* A Discussion," *Movie* 1 (June 1962): 26.

129. See Perkins, *Film as Film*, p. 131; cf. David Robey, "Anglo-American New Criticism," in Ann Jefferson and David Robey, eds., *Modern Literary Theory: A Comparative Introduction* (London: Batsford, 1982), p. 75.

4. Symptomatic Interpretation

1. Quoted in Pierre Macherey, *A Theory of Literary Production*, trans. Geoffrey Wall (London: Routledge and Kegan Paul, 1978), p. 8.

2. Immanuel Kant, *Critique of Pure Reason*, trans. Norman Kemp Smith (London: Macmillan, 1983), p. 310.

3. Sigmund Freud, *Leonardo da Vinci and a Memory of His Childhood*, trans. Alan Tyson (New York: Norton, 1964), pp. 32–37.

4. Ernest Jones, *Hamlet and Oedipus* (1949; reprint, Garden City, N.Y.: Doubleday Anchor, n.d.), pp. 59, 75.

5. Ibid., p. 114.

6. Marie Bonaparte, *The Life and Works of Edgar Allan Poe: A Psycho-Analytic Interpretation,* trans. John Rodker (London: Imago, 1949), pp. 641–664.

7. So tight is the weave of influences that we could speak of an "invisible college." Kracauer studied with Adorno and was for some time affiliated with the Frankfurt School group. Deming acknowledged her debt to Kracauer. Kracauer and Bateson allude to each other. Wolfenstein and Leites worked at Columbia's Center for Research in Contemporary Cultures; their book thanks Mead, Bateson, and Riesman. In his turn, Riesman modeled his work on the anthropological studies of Mead and Benedict; he acknowledged his debt to his teacher, Erich Fromm, once affiliated with the Frankfurt School; and he admiringly cited Warshow's work. Tyler, for reasons that should become apparent, has no particular reason to cite anyone.

8. Martha Wolfenstein and Nathan Leites, "Two Social Scientists View *No Way Out*: The Unconscious vs. the 'Message' in an Anti-Bias Film," *Commentary* 10 (1950): 388–389.

9. Ibid., p. 391.

10. In this they were following a trail blazed by Kenneth Burke and Erik Erikson. See Burke, "The Rhetoric of Hitler's 'Battle,'" in *The Philosophy of Literary Form: Studies in Symbolic Action,* rev. ed. (New York: Vintage, 1957), pp. 164–189; and Erik Homburger Erikson, "Hitler's Imagery and German Youth," *Psychiatry* 5, 4 (November 1942): 475–493.

11. Gregory Bateson, "An Analysis of the Nazi Film *Hitlerjunge Quex,*" in Margaret Mead and Rhoda Métraux, eds., *The Study of Culture at a Distance* (Chicago: The University of Chicago Press, 1953), p. 305; Bateson, "Cultural and Thematic Analysis of Fictional Films," in Douglas G. Haring, ed., *Personal Character and Cultural Milieu,* 3d ed. (Syracuse: Syracuse University Press, 1956), pp. 138, 142.

12. Siegfried Kracauer, *From Caligari to Hitler: A Psychological Study of the German Film* (New York: Noonday, 1958), p. 162.

13. Robert Warshow, *The Immediate Experience: Movies, Comics, Theatre, and Other Aspects of Popular Culture* (New York: Atheneum, 1970), p. 133.

14. Kracauer, *From Caligari to Hitler,* p. 159.

15. Barbara Deming, "The Library of Congress Film Project: Exposition of a Method," *Library of Congress Quarterly Journal of Current Acquisitions* 2, 1 (1944): 11.

16. Ibid., pp. 21–22.

17. Barbara Deming, *Running Away from Myself: A Dream Portrait of America Drawn from the Films of the Forties* (New York: Grossman, 1969), p. 21.

18. Warshow, *Immediate Experience,* pp. 128–129.

19. Martha Wolfenstein and Nathan Leites, *Movies: A Psychological Study* (New York: Atheneum, 1970), pp. 12–13.

20. Bateson, "Analysis," p. 303.

21. Parker Tyler, *Magic and Myth of the Movies* (New York: Simon and Schuster, 1947), p. 115.
22. Parker Tyler, *The Hollywood Hallucination* (New York: Simon and Schuster, 1944), pp. 37–73.
23. Tyler, *Magic and Myth,* pp. 176–182, 126.
24. Tyler, *Hollywood Hallucination,* pp. 179–181.
25. D. Mosdell, *Canadian Forum* 27 (August 1947): 118.
26. Tyler, *Magic and Myth,* p. 23.
27. Ibid., p. 26.
28. Tyler, *Hollywood Hallucination,* p. 204.
29. Tyler, *Magic and Myth,* pp. 1–30.
30. Parker Tyler, *The Three Faces of the Film,* rev. ed. (South Brunswick, N.J.: A. S. Barnes, 1967), p. 11.
31. Tyler, *Hollywood Hallucination,* p. 2.
32. The notion of structuralism is itself elusive; a harsh but enlightening survey of the problem is Marc Angenot, "Structuralism as Syncretism: Institutional Distortions of Saussure," in John Fekete, ed., *The Structural Allegory: Reconstructive Encounters with the New French Thought* (Minneapolis: University of Minnesota Press, 1984), pp. 154–158.
33. See, for example, Lee Russell, "Roberto Rossellini," *New Left Review* 42 (March-April 1967): 69.
34. Geoffrey Nowell-Smith, *Visconti* (Garden City, N.Y.: Doubleday, 1968), p. 9.
35. Ibid., p. 10.
36. Ibid., pp. 127–131.
37. Ibid., p. 119.
38. "Le Western" (1961), *Etudes cinématographiques* 12–13 (1969); Jean-Louis Rieupeyrout, *La Grande Aventure du western: Du Far West à Hollywood (1894–1963)* (Paris: Cerf, 1964); Raymond Bellour, ed., *Le Western: Approches, mythologies, auteurs-acteurs, filmographies* (1966; reprint, Paris: 10/18, 1968).
39. Alan Lovell, "The Western," British Film Institute/Education Department seminar, March 1967.
40. Lovell, "The Western," p. 12.
41. Peter Wollen, *Signs and Meaning in the Cinema,* 3d ed. (Bloomington: Indiana University Press, 1972), p. 93.
42. Ibid., pp. 81–91.
43. Ibid., p. 96.
44. Jim Kitses, *Horizons West: Anthony Mann, Budd Boetticher, Sam Peckinpah: Studies of Authorship within the Western* (Bloomington: Indiana University Press, 1970), p. 12.
45. Colin McArthur, "The Roots of the Western," *Cinema* (U.K.) 4 (October 1969): 12–13; Edward Buscombe, "The Idea of Genre in the American Cinema," *Screen* 11, 2 (March–April 1970): 38.
46. Ibid., pp. 41–42; John G. Cawelti, "The Concept of Formula in the Study of Popular Literature," *Journal of Popular Culture* 3, 3 (Winter 1969): 386.

47. Colin McArthur, *Underworld USA* (New York: Viking, 1972), p. 17.
48. For a broad and polemical account, see Tony Dunn, "The Evolution of Cultural Studies," in David Punter, ed., *Introduction to Contemporary Cultural Studies* (London: Longman, 1986), pp. 71–91.
49. See Claude Lévi-Strauss, "The Structural Study of Myth," in *Structural Anthropology,* trans. Claire Jacobson and Brooke Grundfest Schoepf (Garden City, N.Y.: Doubleday, 1967), p. 226.
50. Edmund Leach discusses this issue in *Claude Lévi-Strauss* (New York: Viking, 1970), pp. 56–57, 72.
51. See John Caughie, "Auteur-Structuralism: Introduction," in Caughie, ed., *Theories of Authorship* (London: Routledge and Kegan Paul, 1981), p. 124.
52. For an example, see Sam Rohdie, "A Structural Analysis of *Mr. Deeds Goes to Town,*" *Cinema* (U.K.) 5 (February 1970): 29–30.
53. Geoffrey Nowell-Smith, "Cinema and Structuralism," *Twentieth-Century Studies* 3 (May 1970): 134.
54. Charles Eckert, "The English Cine-Structuralists," in Caughie, ed., *Theories of Authorship,* pp. 158–164.
55. Wollen, *Signs and Meaning,* p. 78.
56. Ibid., p. 80.
57. Ibid., p. 105.
58. Alan Lovell, "Robin Wood—A Dissenting View," *Screen* 10, 2 (March–April 1969): 42–55; Robin Wood, "Ghostly Paradigm and H. C. F.: An Answer to Alan Lovell," *Screen* 10, 3 (May–June 1969): 35–48; Alan Lovell, "The Common Pursuit of True Judgment," *Screen* 11, 4/5 (August–September 1970): 76–88.
59. Lee Russell, "Samuel Fuller," *New Left Review* 23 (January-February 1964): 87. See also Russell, "John Ford," *New Left Review* 29 (January-February 1965): 72–73.
60. Nowell-Smith, *Visconti,* p. 62.
61. Ibid., p. 178.
62. Wollen, *Signs and Meaning,* p. 113.
63. McArthur, "Roots of the Western," p. 13.
64. Louis Althusser and Etienne Balibar, *Reading Capital,* trans. Ben Brewster (London: New Left Books, 1970), p. 28.
65. Jacques Derrida, *Writing and Difference,* trans. Alan Bass (Chicago: University of Chicago Press, 1978), pp. 192–196.
66. Foucault's more recent "antirepression" hypothesis does not, it seems to me, represent a rejection of the concept of interpretation or of that of symptomatic meaning. To put it too briefly, his "genealogical" analysis of Western sexuality suggests that the concept of sexual repression has itself masked (that is, repressed) the real forces at stake—power relations.
67. Macherey, *Theory of Literary Production,* p. 122.
68. The sole exception to the rule of applied exegesis would seem to be programmatic statements like Althusser's article "Ideology and Ideological State Apparatuses" or Lacan's influential "Mirror Stage" article; practicing

critics seem to use such works as condensed versions of more lengthy theoretical arguments. See Louis Althusser, *Lenin and Philosophy and Other Essays,* trans. Ben Brewster (New York: Monthly Review Press, 1971), pp. 127–186, and Jacques Lacan, "The Mirror Stage as Formative of the Function of the I," in *Ecrits: A Selection,* trans. Alan Sheridan (New York: Norton, 1977), pp. 1–7.

69. As early as 1963, in an interview with Barthes, Lacanian issues were broached. See Roland Barthes, "Towards a Semiotics of Cinema," in Jim Hillier, ed., *Cahiers du Cinéma: The 1960s: New Wave, New Cinema, Reevaluating Hollywood* (Cambridge: Harvard University Press, 1986), pp. 276–285. A year later, in an interview Lévi-Strauss hinted at a nature/culture interpretation of *The Birds;* Michel Delahaye and Eric Rohmer, "Entretien avec Claude Lévi-Strauss," *Cahiers du cinéma* 156 (June 1964): 26–27). In 1965 *Cahiers* published a roundtable in which its critics dourly observed the schematic qualities of theme-centered criticism; Jean-Louis Comolli et al., "Twenty Years On: A Discussion about the American Cinema and the *Politique des Auteurs,*" in Hillier, *Cahiers: The 1960s,* pp. 196–209. *Cahiers* also forged an alliance with the literary avant-garde, featuring several *Tel quel* writers in its special number on problems of narrative (no. 185, Christmas 1966) and running texts by *Tel quel* authors discussing Pollet's *Méditerranée; Cahiers* 187 (February 1967): 34–39.

70. Robert Benayoun, "Les Enfants du paradigme," *Positif* 122 (December 1970): 7–26.

71. Jean-Louis Comolli and Jean Narboni, "Cinema/Ideology/Criticism (1)," in *Screen Reader 1: Cinema/Ideology/Politics* (London: SEFT, 1977), p. 7.

72. Jean-Pierre Oudart, "Le Mythe et l'utopie," *Cahiers du cinéma* 212 (May 1969): 35.

73. Jean Narboni, "A-propos," *Cahiers du cinéma* 216 (October 1969): 39. Bellour's article "'Les Oiseaux': Analyse d'une séquence," is on pp. 24–38.

74. See the following articles in *Cahiers du cinéma: La Vie est à nous,* film militant," 218 (March 1970): 44–51; "*Young Mr. Lincoln* de John Ford," 223 (August 1970): 29–47; "*Josef von Sternberg et Morocco,*" 225 (November–December 1970): 6–13; "La Métaphore 'commune,'" 230 (July 1971): 15–21; "La Guerre civile en France," 202 (October 1971): 43–51.

75. Editors of *Cahiers du cinéma,* "John Ford's *Young Mr. Lincoln,*" in *Screen Reader 1,* p. 139.

76. Ibid., p. 121.

77. Ibid., p. 150.

78. There is, Bellour has pointed out, an important precedent in the collective volume *Tu n'as rien vu à Hiroshima!* (Brussels: Editions de l'Institut de Sociologie, 1962). See Bellour, *L'Analyse du film* (Paris: Albatros, 1980), pp. 15–16. A useful bibliography of the trend is R. Odin, "Dix années d'analyses textuelles de films: Bibliographie analytique," *Linguistique et sémiologique* 3 (1977).

79. See Paul Willemen, "Editorial," *Screen* 14, 1/2 (Spring–Summer 1973): 5; Stephen Heath, "Introduction: Questions of Emphasis," ibid., pp. 9–12.

80. Sam Rohdie, "Review: *Movie Reader, Film as Film*," *Screen* 13, 4 (Winter 1972–73): 138–143.

81. Wollen, *Signs and Meaning*, p. 167.

82. Ibid., p. 162.

83. Geoffrey Nowell-Smith, "I Was a Star-Struck Structuralist," *Screen* 14, 3 (Autumn 1973): 96–99. See also Alan Lovell, *Don Siegel: American Cinema* (London: British Film Institute, 1975), p. 11.

84. Frederick Engels, letter to Margaret Harkness, April 1888, in *Marx and Engels on Literature and Art: A Selection of Writings*, ed. Lee Baxandall and Stefan Morawski (St. Louis: Telos, 1973), pp. 115–116.

85. Charles W. Eckert, "The Anatomy of a Proletarian Film: Warner's *Marked Woman*," *Film Quarterly* 17, 2 (Winter 1973–74): 11.

86. Toril Moi, *Sexual/Textual Politics: Feminist Literary Theory* (New York: Methuen, 1985), pp. 44–49.

87. Susan Elizabeth Dalton, "Women at Work: Warners in the 1930s," in Karyn Kay and Gerald Peary, eds., *Women and the Cinema: A Critical Anthology* (New York: Dutton, 1977), pp. 267–282; Diane Giddis, "The Divided Woman: Bree Daniels in *Klute*," *Women and Film* 3–4 (1973): 57.

88. Mary Ann Doane, Patricia Mellencamp, and Linda Williams, "Feminist Film Criticism: An Introduction," in Doane, Mellencamp, and Williams, eds., *Re-Vision: Essays in Feminist Film Criticism* (Frederick, Md.: University Publications of America, 1984), p. 8.

89. Molly Haskell, *From Reverence to Rape: The Treatment of Women in the Movies* (New York: Holt, Rinehart, and Winston, 1974), p. 2.

90. Ibid., pp. 105–106.

91. Claire Johnston, *Notes on Women's Cinema* (London: British Film Institute, 1973), pp. 2–3.

92. Claire Johnston, "Women's Cinema as Counter-Cinema," ibid., pp. 24–26.

93. Ibid., p. 37.

94. Claire Johnston and Pam Cook, "The Place of Woman in the Cinema of Raoul Walsh," in Phil Hardy, ed., *Raoul Walsh* (London: Edinburgh Film Festival, 1974), p. 100.

95. Ibid., p. 107.

96. Like most exemplars, it came under assault. See Elisabeth Lyon, "Discourse and Difference," *Camera Obscura* 3–4 (1979): 14–20, and Janet Bergstrom, "Rereading the Work of Claire Johnston," ibid., pp. 21–31.

97. Laura Mulvey, "Visual Pleasure and Narrative Cinema," *Screen* 16, 3 (Autumn 1975): 6–18.

98. It is possible that the discourse of the Women's Liberation Movement during the late 1960s enabled critics to take the act of looking as a significant textual cue. For example, Naomi Jaffe and Bernadine Dohrn's article "The Look Is You" (1968) emphasizes the extent to which women

are forced to define themselves through consumption and thereby to become commodities. The dualities of object/subject, looked at/looker, and passive/active are tacitly aligned with the female/male one. Subsequent work was able to flesh out this conceptual grid by reference to psychoanalytic theory and to features of the film medium (for example, camera as "looker"). The Jaffe-Dohrn article is reprinted in Massimo Teodori, ed., *The New Left: A Documentary History* (Indianapolis: Bobbs-Merrill, 1970), pp. 355–358.

99. For more recent discussions of her aims in the essay, see Laura Mulvey, "Feminism, Film, and the Avant-Garde," *Framework* 10 (Spring 1979): 3–10, and "Afterthoughts on 'Visual Pleasure and Narrative Cinema' Inspired by *Duel in the Sun* (King Vidor, 1946)," *Framework* 15/16/17 (1981): 12–15.

100. Stephen Heath, "Film and System, Terms of Analysis, Part I," *Screen* 16, 1 (Spring 1975): 49.

101. Ibid., p. 74.

102. Ibid., p. 76.

103. Stephen Heath, "Film and System, Terms of Analysis, Part II," *Screen* 16, 2 (Summer 1975): 107.

104. *Ekran* 9, 10 (1985): 59.

105. See, for example, Richard Abel, "Paradigmatic Structures in *Young Mr. Lincoln*," *Wide Angle* 2, 4 (1978): 20–26; J. A. Place, "*Young Mr. Lincoln*, 1939," ibid., pp. 28–35; Ron Abramson and Rick Thompson, "*Young Mr. Lincoln* Reconsidered: An Essay on the Theory and Practice of Film Criticism," *Ciné-Tracts* 2, 1 (Fall 1976): 42–62.

106. See Robert B. Ray, *A Certain Tendency of the Hollywood Film, 1930–1980* (Princeton: Princeton University Press, 1985), pp. 153–174; Robin Wood, *Hollywood from Vietnam to Reagan* (New York: Columbia University Press, 1986), pp. 46–68.

107. Paul Willemen, "For Information: Cinéaction," *Framework* 32/33 (1986): 227.

108. See Jim Hopkins, "Epistemology and Depth Psychology: Critical Notes on *The Foundations of Psychoanalysis*," in Peter Clark and Crispin Wright, eds., *Mind, Psychoanalysis, and Science* (Oxford: Blackwell, 1988), pp. 33–60.

109. Mary Douglas, *How Institutions Think* (Syracuse: Syracuse University Press, 1986), p. 76.

110. Raymond Boudon, "The Freudian-Marxian-Structuralist (FMS) Movement in France: Variations on a Theme by Sherry Turkle," *The Tocqueville Review* 2, 1 (Winter 1980): 6–16.

111. See Gerald Graff, *Professing Literature: An Institutional History* (Chicago: University of Chicago Press, 1987), pp. 6–7.

112. See Vincent B. Leitch, *American Literary Criticism from the Thirties to the Eighties* (New York: Columbia University Press, 1988), pp. 180, 320, 383–384.

113. Warshow, *Immediate Experience*, pp. 158–159.

114. Deming, *Running Away*, p. 25.

115. Tyler, *Magic and Myth,* p. xxiii.
116. Warshow, *Immediate Experience,* p. 161.
117. Wolfenstein and Leites, *Movies,* pp. 25–47.
118. Tyler, *Hollywood Hallucination,* p. 177.
119. David Reisman, *The Lonely Crowd: A Study of the Changing American Character* (New Haven: Yale University Press, 1965), p. 351.
120. Warshow, *Immediate Experience,* pp. 128–129.
121. Tyler, *Hollywood Hallucination,* p. 246.
122. Elisabeth Lyon, *"La Passion, c'est pas ça," Camera Obscura* 8/9/10 (1982): 9; Constance Penley, "Pornography, Eroticism," ibid., p. 15; Janet Bergstrom, "Violence and Enunciation," ibid., pp. 25–26.
123. Editors of *Cahiers du cinéma,* "Morocco," in Peter Baxter, ed., *Sternberg* (London: British Film Institute, 1980), pp. 81–94; Jean-Louis Comolli and François Géré, "Two Fictions Concerning Hate," in Stephen Jenkins, ed., *Fritz Lang: The Image and the Look* (London: British Film Institute, 1981), pp. 125–146.
124. Wollen, *Signs and Meaning,* pp. 113, 167.
125. Quoted in E. Ann Kaplan, "Interview with British Cine-Feminists," in Kay and Peary, eds., *Women and the Cinema,* p. 402.
126. In addition to Jon Halliday's *Sirk on Sirk* (New York: Viking, 1972), which documents Sirk's self-awareness, *Screen* once published a letter in which Sirk congratulated the critics on their ability to "think in contradictions" and quoted Mao on the need to reconcile theory and practice; *Screen* 12, 3 (Summer 1971): 98.
127. Comolli and Narboni, "Cinema/Ideology/Criticism," p. 7.
128. Colin MacArthur, "Counter-Introduction: Limits of Auteurism," in Wayne Drew, ed., *David Cronenberg* (London: British Film Institute, 1984), p. 2.
129. Wood, *Hollywood from Vietnam to Reagan,* p. 48.
130. Ibid.
131. Ibid., p. 298.
132. Ibid., p. 304.
133. See Raymond Durgnat, *Films and Feelings* (Cambridge: MIT Press, 1967); *Luis Buñuel* (Berkeley: University of California Press, 1968); *Franju* (Berkeley: University of California Press, 1968); *The Crazy Mirror: Hollywood Comedy and the American Image* (New York: Horizon, 1970); *A Mirror for England: British Movies from Austerity to Influence* (New York: Praeger, 1971); *The Strange Case of Alfred Hitchcock* (Cambridge: MIT Press, 1974); *Jean Renoir* (Berkeley: University of California Press, 1974).
134. Dudley Andrew, *Film in the Aura of Art* (Princeton: Princeton University Press, 1984), pp. 193, 97.
135. Ibid., p. 68.
136. E. Ann Kaplan, *Women and Film: Both Sides of the Camera* (New York: Methuen, 1983), p. 10.
137. Ibid., p. 155.
138. There is, for instance, Sitney's remark that Jack Smith's *Flaming Creatures* "brings to the fore what has been latent" in the films of von Sternberg

and Maria Montez; *Visionary Film* (New York: Oxford University Press, 1974), p. 391.

139. Stephen Heath, "Repetition Time: Notes around 'Structural/Materialist' Film," in *Questions of Cinema* (London: Macmillan, 1981), p. 167.

140. Felix Thompson, "Notes on Reading of Avant-Garde Films—*Trapline, Syntax*," *Screen* 20, 2 (Summer 1979): 105.

141. Anonymous, "Le 'Groupe Dziga-Vertov' (2)," *Cahiers du cinéma* 240 (July-August 1972): 5.

142. Paul Willemen, "Voyeurism, the Look and Dwoskin," *Afterimage* 6 (Summer 1976): 49.

143. Carola Klein, "On Making *Mirror Phase*," in Elizabeth Cowie, ed., *Catalogue: British Film Institute Productions 1977–1978* (London: British Film Institute, 1978), p. 63; Pam Cook, "Views: 1," ibid., p. 61; Kari Hanet, "Views: 2," ibid., p. 62.

144. Nicky Hamlyn, "*Dora*, a Suitable Case for Treatment," *Undercut* 3/4 (March 1982): 53. See also Keith Kelly, "*Riddles of the Sphinx:* One or Two Things about Her," *Millennium Film Journal* 2 (Spring-Summer 1978): 95–100.

145. Peter Gidal, "On *Finnegan's Chin*," *Undercut* 5 (July 1982): 22.

146. On art cinema, see for example Sylvie Pierre, "L'Homme aux clowns," *Cahiers du cinéma* 229 (May-June 1971): 48–51; Serge Daney and Jean-Pierre Oudart, "A propos de la 'place' de *Mort à Venise*," *Cahiers du cinéma* 234–235 (December 1971, January–February 1972): 79–93; Jean-Pierre Oudart, "Le Hors-champ de l'auteur (*Quatre nuits d'un rêveur*)," *Cahiers du cinéma* 236/237 (March-April 1972): 86–89. See also the essays on Miklós Jancsó in *Cahiers du cinéma* 219 (April 1970): 30–45; the essays on *The New Babylon* in *Cahiers* 230 (July 1971): 15–21 and 202 (October 1971): 43–51; and, for a symptomatic account of Godard's work, Gérard Leblanc, "Sur trois films du Groupe Dziga Vertov," *VH101* 6 (1972): 20–36. A scathing symptomatic analysis of avant-garde cinema is in Parker Tyler, *Underground Film: A Critical History* (New York: Grove, 1969), pp. 9–82.

147. See Constance Penley and Janet Bergstrom, "The Avant-Garde—Histories and Theories," *Screen* 19, 3 (Autumn 1978): 113–127; Mick Eaton, "The Avant-Garde and Narrative: Two SEFT/London Film-Makers Co-op Day Schools," *Screen* 19, 2 (Summer 1978): 129–134.

148. As for symptomatic reading in particular, it is not clear that the theory is comprehensive and coherent; nor are the ideas drawn from Lacan, Althusser, Macherey, Freud, and Marx that back up critical inferences always applied systematically and cogently. Recent critiques may be found in J. G. Merquior, *From Prague to Paris: A Critique of Structuralist and Post-Structuralist Thought* (London: Verso, 1966), and Noël Carroll, *Mystifying Movies: Fads and Fallacies of Contemporary Film Theory* (New York: Columbia University Press, 1988).

149. There is an enlightening discussion of this problem in Ellen Schauber and Ellen Spolsky, *The Bounds of Interpretation: Linguistic Theory and Literary Text* (Stanford: Stanford University Press, 1986), pp. 161–178.

150. Thus it may well be that Stanley Fish's assertion that critical theories are inevitably self-confirming constitutes an accurate description of current critical practice—not because of any intrinsic logic of interpretation, but because the competition of discrete schools and the doctrinal nature of their assumptions perpetuate a productivity tailored to the host institution's demands. See Fish, *Is There a Text in This Class? The Authority of Interpretive Communities* (Cambridge: Harvard University Press, 1980), pp. 268–371.

5. Semantic Fields

1. Thus, although the term *semantic field* is central to one particular semantic theory—see John Lyons, *Semantics,* vol. 1 (Cambridge: Cambridge University Press, 1977), pp. 220–269—I use it in its broader, more customary sense.

2. Recent theorists of criticism seem to have agreed that the most basic interpretive convention is the assumption that the work harbors *significance*. See Jonathan Culler, *Structuralist Poetics: Structuralism, Linguistics, and the Study of Literature* (Ithaca: Cornell University Press, 1975), pp. 114–115; Ellen Schauber and Ellen Spolsky, *The Bounds of Interpretation: Linguistic Theory and Literary Text* (Stanford: Stanford University Press, 1986), pp. 87–89. I take it that significance implies both the assumption that the work harbors implicit or symptomatic meanings and the assumption that those meanings can be constructed only through positing one or more semantic fields.

3. See Richard Levin, *New Readings vs. Old Plays: Recent Trends in the Reinterpretation of English Renaissance Drama* (Chicago: University of Chicago Press, 1979), p. 11.

4. See, for example, Lubomír Doležel, "Le Triangle du double: Un Champ thématique," *Poétique* 64 (November 1985): 463.

5. Gerald Prince, "Thématiser," *Poétique* 64 (November 1985): 430.

6. Jean Domarchi, "Les Secrètes d'Eisenstein," *Cahiers du cinéma* 96 (June 1959): 1–7; Jean-Pierre Oudart, "Sur *Ivan le Terrible*," *Cahiers du cinéma* 218 (March 1970): 15–19.

7. Cleanth Brooks and Robert Penn Warren, *Understanding Poetry,* 3d ed. (New York: Holt, Rinehart, and Winston, 1960), p. 342.

8. R. S. Crane, *The Languages of Criticism and the Structure of Poetry* (Toronto: University of Toronto Press, 1953), pp. 123–124.

9. Eric Rohmer, "Rediscovering America," in Jim Hillier, ed., *Cahiers du cinéma: The 1950s: Neo-Realism, Hollywood, New Wave* (Cambridge: Harvard University Press, 1985), p. 90.

10. See *Godard on Godard,* trans. Tom Milne (New York: Viking, 1972), pp. 23, 38; Eric Rohmer, "Ajax ou Le Cid? (*Rebel without a Cause*)," *Cahiers du cinéma* 59 (May 1956): 35.

11. Fereydoun Hoveyda, "Sunspots," in Jim Hillier, ed., *Cahiers du cinéma:*

The 1960s: New Wave, New Cinema, Reevaluating Hollywood (Cambridge: Harvard University Press, 1986), p. 142.

12. I discuss art-cinema thematics in *Narration in the Fiction Film* (Madison: University of Wisconsin Press, 1985), pp. 205–233.

13. V. F. Perkins, *"King of Kings," Movie* 1 (June 1962): 29.

14. David Thomson, *Movie Man* (New York: Stein and Day, 1967), p. 74.

15. Seymour Chatman, *Antonioni, or The Surface of the World* (Berkeley: University of California Press, 1985), p. 60.

16. Jane Shapiro, "Stranger in Paradise," *Village Voice,* 16 September 1986, 20.

17. "Godard's *Passion," Framework* 21 (1983): 4–7.

18. See, for instance, Tag Gallagher, *John Ford: The Man and His Films* (Berkeley: University of California Press, 1986), p. 476.

19. See, for example, Gerald Mast, *Howard Hawks, Storyteller* (New York: Oxford University Press, 1982), p. 139.

20. Sandy Flitterman, *"Guest in the House:* Rupture and Reconstitution of the Bourgeois Nuclear Family," *Wide Angle* 4, 2 (1980): 18.

21. Jean-Louis Comolli, "The Curtain Lifted, Fallen Again," *Cahiers du cinéma in English* 10 (May 1967): 52.

22. Leland Poague, in Poague and William Cadbury, *Film Criticism: A Counter Theory* (Ames: Iowa State University Press, 1982), pp. 93–97.

23. Dudley Andrew, *Film in the Aura of Art* (Princeton: Princeton University Press, 1984), pp. 174–176.

24. Parker Tyler, *The Hollywood Hallucination* (New York: Simon and Schuster, 1944), pp. 135–136, 200; *The Magic and Myth of the Movies* (New York: Simon and Schuster, 1947), p. 124.

25. Leo Steinberg, *Other Criteria: Confrontations with Twentieth-Century Art* (New York: Oxford University Press, 1972), p. 76.

26. Henry Geldzahler, "Some Notes on *Sleep,"* in P. Adams Sitney, ed., *Film Culture Reader* (New York: Praeger, 1970), pp. 300–301.

27. Paul Mayersberg, "The Testament of Vincente Minnelli," *Movie* 3 (October 1962): 10.

28. Jonathan Culler, *The Pursuit of Signs: Semiotics, Literature, Deconstruction* (Ithaca: Cornell University Press, 1981), p. 36.

29. For an attempt to clarify the problems of reflexivity as a concept, see Don Fredericksen, "Modes of Reflexive Film," *Quarterly Review of Film Studies* 4, 3 (Summer 1979): 299–320.

30. Alan C. Purves and Victoria Rippere, *Elements of Writing about a Literary Work: A Study of Responses to Literature* (Champaign, Ill.: National Council of Teachers of English, 1968), pp. 37–41.

31. Fred Camper, "The Films of Douglas Sirk," *Screen* 12, 2 (Summer 1971): 61; Jean Narboni, "Vers l'impertinence," *Cahiers du cinéma* 196 (December 1967): 4.

32. Jean Douchet, "La Troisième clé d'Hitchcock (II)," *Cahiers du cinéma* 102 (December 1959): 34–35; George M. Wilson, *Narration in Light: Studies in Cinematic Point of View* (Baltimore: Johns Hopkins University Press, 1986), pp. 64–66.

33. Nick Browne, "Deflections of Desire in *The Rules of the Game:* Reflections on the Theater of History," *Quarterly Review of Film Studies* 7, 3 (Summer 1982): 253–254.

34. Catherine Johnson, "The Imaginary and *The Bitter Tears of Petra von Kant*," *Wide Angle* 3, 4 (1980): 21.

35. Stanley Cavell, "*North by Northwest*," in Marshall Deutelbaum and Leland Poague, eds., *A Hitchcock Reader* (Ames: Iowa State University Press, 1986), pp. 250–260.

36. Thomson, *Movie Man,* pp. 114–115. As I have laid it out, the chain of inference is formally invalid.

37. Emile Vuillermoz, "Un Film d'Abel Gance: *La Roue*," *Cinémagazine,* 23 February 1923, 329.

38. J. P. Telotte, "Film Noir and the Dangers of Discourse," *Quarterly Review of Film Studies* 9, 2 (Spring 1984): 107.

39. Toby Mussmann, "*The Chelsea Girls*," *Film Culture* 46 (Summer 1967): 43.

40. Epi Weise, "The Shape of Music in *The Rules of the Game*," *Quarterly Review of Film Studies* 7, 3 (Summer 1982): 201.

41. David Bordwell, "*Citizen Kane*," in Bill Nichols, ed., *Movies and Methods* (Berkeley: University of California Press, 1976), pp. 275–276.

42. Jane Feuer, *The Hollywood Musical* (London: British Film Institute, 1982), p. 107.

43. Jean Douchet, "Dix-sept plans," in Raymond Bellour, ed., *Le Cinéma américain: Analyses de films,* vol. 1 (Paris: Flammarion, 1980), p. 232.

44. Annette Michelson, "About Snow," *October* 8 (Spring 1979): 118.

45. Mast, *Howard Hawks,* pp. 18, 207.

46. Thomson, *Movie Man,* p. 146.

47. Jean Douchet, "Hitch and His Audience," in Hillier, *Cahiers: The 1960s,* pp. 150–151.

48. Stanley Cavell, *Pursuits of Happiness: The Hollywood Comedy of Remarriage* (Cambridge: Harvard University Press, 1981), pp. 213–214.

49. Stephen Heath, "*Jaws,* Ideology, and Film Theory," in Bill Nichols, ed., *Movies and Methods,* vol. 2 (Berkeley: University of California Press, 1985), p. 514.

50. Jean-Louis Comolli and François Géré, "Two Fictions Concerning Hate," in Stephen Jenkins, ed., *Fritz Lang: The Image and the Look* (London: British Film Institute, 1981), p. 142.

51. Robert Cohen, "Mizoguchi and Modernism: Structure, Culture, Point of View," *Sight and Sound* 47, 2 (Spring 1978): 113.

52. Parker Tyler, *Sex Psyche Etcetera in the Film* (Harmondsworth: Penguin, 1969), pp. 120–133.

53. Stephen Z. Levine, "Structures of Sound and Image in *The Rules of the Game*," *Quarterly Review of Film Studies* 7, 3 (Summer 1982): 217–218.

54. Levin, *New Readings,* pp. 42–49; Culler, *Structuralist Poetics,* p. 174.

55. D. A. Cruse, *Lexical Semantics* (Cambridge: Cambridge University Press, 1986).

56. Jean Aitchison, *Words in the Mind: An Introduction to the Mental Lexicon* (Oxford: Blackwell, 1987), pp. 74–85.

57. Cruse, *Lexical Semantics,* p. 206.
58. P. Adams Sitney, "Autobiography in Avant-Garde Film," in Sitney, ed. *The Avant-Garde Film: A Reader of Theory and Criticism* (New York: New York University Press, 1978), p. 200.
59. Ibid., pp. 201–209.
60. Chatman, *Antonioni,* p. 54.
61. Ibid., pp. 56–64.
62. Eric Rentschler, *West German Film in the Course of Time* (Bedford Hills, N.Y.: Redgrave, 1984), pp. 168–171.
63. Eric Rohmer and Claude Chabrol, *Hitchcock: The First Forty-Four Films,* trans. Stanley Hochman (New York: Ungar, 1979), p. 98.
64. Andrew Sarris, *"The Seventh Seal," Film Culture* 19 (1959): 51–56.
65. Tania Modleski, "Time and Desire in the Woman's Film," in Virginia Wright Wexman, ed., *Letter from an Unknown Woman* (New Brunswick, N.J.: Rutgers University Press, 1986), pp. 250–262.
66. Tony Bennett and Janet Woollacott, *Bond and Beyond: The Political Career of a Popular Hero* (New York: Methuen, 1987), p. 98.
67. Fredric Jameson, "Postmodernism and Consumer Society," in Hal Foster, ed., *The Anti-Aesthetic: Essays on Postmodern Culture* (Port Townsend, Wash.: Bay Press, 1983), pp. 113–123.
68. Vivian Sobchak, *Screening Space: The American Science Fiction Film* (New York: Ungar, 1987), pp. 228–234.
69. E. H. Gombrich, *Art and Illusion: A Study in the Psychology of Pictorial Representation* (Princeton: Princeton University Press, 1972), pp. 370–371.
70. Schauber and Spolsky, *Bounds of Interpretation,* p. 126.
71. Dan Sperber, *Rethinking Symbolism* (Cambridge: Cambridge University Press, 1975), p. 64.
72. Andrew Sarris, *The American Cinema: Directors and Directions 1929–1968* (New York: Dutton, 1968), p. 125; Jim Kitses, *Horizons West: Anthony Mann, Budd Boetticher, Sam Peckinpah: Studies of Authorship within the Western* (Bloomington: Indiana University Press, 1970), p. 91.
73. Bill Nichols, *Ideology and the Image* (Bloomington: Indiana University Press, 1981), pp. 140–153.
74. Fredric Jameson, "Class and Allegory in Contemporary Mass Culture: *Dog Day Afternoon,*" in Nichols, ed., *Movies and Methods,* vol. 2, p. 732.
75. Siegfried Kracauer, *From Caligari to Hitler: A Psychological Study of the German Film* (New York: Noonday, 1959), pp. 61–76.
76. Jacques Rivette, "L'Art de la fugue (*I Confess*)," *Cahiers du cinéma* 26 (August-September 1953): 50.
77. Paul Mayersberg, *"The Miracle Worker* and *The Left-Handed Gun,"* Movie 3 (October 1962): 27–28.
78. A. J. Greimas and J. Courtés, *Semiotics and Language: An Analytical Dictionary,* trans. Larry Crist, Daniel Patte, et al. (Bloomington: Indiana University Press, 1982), pp. 308–309.
79. James H. Kavanaugh,"'Son of a Bitch': Feminism, Humanism, and Science in *Alien," October* 13 (Summer 1980): 91–100.
80. Culler, *Structuralist Poetics,* pp. 225–226.

81. Jean Sémolué, *Dreyer* (Paris: Editions universitaires, 1962), pp. 98–99.

82. Peter Wollen, *"Naked Kiss,"* in David Will and Peter Wollen, eds., *Samuel Fuller* (Edinburgh: Edinburgh Film Festival, 1969), p. 86.

83. Mast, *Howard Hawks,* pp. 138–142.

84. Pam Cook, "Duplicity in *Mildred Pierce,"* in E. Ann Kaplan, ed., *Women in Film Noir* (London: British Film Institute, 1978), p. 73.

85. Teresa de Lauretis, *Alice Doesn't: Feminism, Semiotics, Cinema* (Bloomington: Indiana University Press, 1984), pp. 88–101. Unlike Cook, de Lauretis does not present the oppositions in tabular form; but I believe that my list is faithful to the proportional series she discusses.

86. See, for example, ibid., pp. 97–98.

87. Cruse, *Lexical Semantics,* p. 137.

88. Bill Simon, "'Reading' *Zorns Lemma,"* *Millennium Film Journal* 1, 2 (1978): 39.

89. Maurice Schérer, "Génie du Christianisme (*Europe 51*)," *Cahiers du cinéma* 25 (July 1953): 45.

90. Raymond Bellour, *L'Analyse de film* (Paris: Albatros, 1980), pp. 137–159.

91. Martha Wolfenstein and Nathan Leites, *Movies: A Psychological Study* (New York: Atheneum, 1970), pp. 149–174.

92. R. A. Randall, "How Tall Is a Taxonomic Tree? Some Evidence for Dwarfism," *American Ethnologist* 3, 3 (1976): 544–552.

93. See, for example, Claire Johnston, *"Double Indemnity,"* in Kaplan, *Women in Film Noir,* pp. 102–103.

94. Robin Wood, *"Alphaville,"* in Charles Barr et al., *The Films of Jean-Luc Godard* (New York: Praeger, 1969), p. 85.

95. Barbara Deming, *Running away from Myself: A Dream Portrait of America Drawn from the Films of the Forties* (New York: Grossman, 1969), pp. 8–38, 172–186; Tyler, *Hollywood Hallucination,* pp. 100–136; Wolfenstein and Leites, *Movies,* p. 27.

96. Robin Wood, *Hollywood from Vietnam to Reagan* (New York: Columbia University Press, 1985), p. 150.

97. Janet Bergstrom, "Sexuality at a Loss: The Films of F. W. Murnau," in Susan Rubin Suleiman, ed., *The Female Body in Western Culture: Contemporary Perspectives* (Cambridge: Harvard University Press, 1986), p. 258.

98. Ibid., p. 260.

99. Cruse, *Lexical Semantics,* p. 189.

100. Jacques Rivette, "L'Ame au ventre (*Sommarlek*)," *Cahiers du cinéma* 84 (June 1958): 47.

101. David Ehrenstein, *Film: The Front Line 1984* (Denver: Arden Press, 1984), p. 103.

102. Annette Kuhn, *Women's Pictures: Feminism and Cinema* (London: Routledge and Kegan Paul, 1982), pp. 34–35.

103. Rick Altman, *The American Film Musical* (Bloomington: Indiana University Press, 1987), pp. 138–142.

104. Kavanaugh, "'Son of a Bitch,'" p. 98.

105. Johnston, *"Double Indemnity,"* p. 101.

106. Peter Lehman and William Luhr, *Blake Edwards* (Athens: Ohio University Press, 1981), p. 226.
107. Ibid., pp. 223–231.
108. Thierry Kuntzel, "The Film-Work, 2," *Camera Obscura* 5 (1980): 14–17.
109. See, for example, Miriam Hansen, "Pleasure, Ambivalence, Identification: Valentino and Female Spectatorship," *Cinema Journal* 24, 4 (Summer 1986): 6–32. Here Valentino is interpreted as an erotic object of the look, and he thus becomes "feminized" in ways that "theatricalize" voyeurism and create an oscillation between sadistic and masochistic positions.
110. Crane, *Languages of Criticism,* p. 124.
111. Levin, *New Readings,* pp. 15–16.
112. On cross-cultural categorization systems, see George Lakoff, *Women, Fire, and Dangerous Things: What Categories Reveal about the Mind* (Cambridge: Harvard University Press, 1987), especially p. 99.

6. Schemata and Heuristics

1. E. H. Gombrich, *Art and Illusion: A Study in the Psychology of Pictorial Representation* (Princeton: Princeton University Press, 1972), p. 29.
2. John H. Holland, Keith J. Holyoak, Richard E. Nisbett, and Paul R. Thagard, *Induction: Processes of Inference, Learning, and Discovery* (Cambridge: MIT Press, 1986), p. 38.
3. Northrop Frye, *Anatomy of Criticism: Four Essays* (Princeton: Princeton University Press, 1957), p. 77.
4. See on this point John Reichert, *Making Sense of Literature* (Chicago: University of Chicago Press, 1977), pp. 100–101.
5. Pam Cook, "Approaching the World of Dorothy Arzner," in Claire Johnston, ed., *The Work of Dorothy Arzner: Towards a Feminist Cinema* (London: British Film Institute, 1975), pp. 9–18.
6. Stein Haugom Olsen has a detailed discussion of this matter in *The Structure of Literary Understanding* (Cambridge: Cambridge University Press, 1978), pp. 94–117. There he emphasizes that ordinary experience largely informs the noncontroversial "denotative" redescriptions of the text's world, while high-level interpretations, having greater indeterminacy, also call upon knowledge of literary and critical conventions.
7. See Jonathan Culler, *Structuralist Poetics: Structuralism, Linguistics, and the Study of Literature* (Ithaca: Cornell University Press, 1975), pp. 140–160; Christopher Butler, *Interpretation, Deconstruction, and Ideology* (London: Oxford University Press, 1984), pp. 4, 99.
8. For a pertinent discussion of the Kantian notion of regulative ideas, see Jon Elster, *Ulysses and the Sirens: Studies in Rationality and Irrationality* (Cambridge: Cambridge University Press, 1984), pp. 2–3, 33–35; on the informativeness of *ceteris paribus* conditions, see Jerry A. Fodor, *Psychosemantics: The Problem of Meaning in the Philosophy of Mind* (Cambridge: MIT Press, 1987), pp. 4–6.

9. See on this point Noël Carroll, *Mystifying Movies: Fads and Fallacies of Contemporary Film Theory* (New York: Columbia University Press, 1988), especially chap. 3.

10. My example is drawn from Ronald W. Casson, "Schemata in Cognitive Anthropology," *Annual Review of Anthropology* (1983): 431–432.

11. There are various conceptions of schemata in the cognitive theory literature. Good introductions can be found in John R. Anderson, *Cognitive Psychology and Its Implications* (New York: Freeman, 1985), pp. 124–133, and Neil A. Stillings et al., *Cognitive Science: An Introduction* (Cambridge: MIT Press, 1987), pp. 30–36, 65–73, 150–156. More advanced discussions pertinent to arguments in this book are in Mark Johnson, *The Body in the Mind: The Bodily Basis of Meaning, Imagination, and Reason* (Chicago: University of Chicago Press, 1987), pp. 18–40, and George Lakoff, *Women, Fire, and Dangerous Things* (Cambridge: Harvard University Press, 1987), pp. 68–135, 269–303.

12. The relevant argument is in Immanuel Kant, *Critique of Pure Reason*, trans. Norman Kemp Smith (London: Macmillan, 1983), A137-B176–A147-B187. Important discussions are Robert Paul Wolff, *Kant's Theory of Mental Activity: A Commentary on the Transcendental Analytic of the "Critique of Pure Reason"* (Cambridge: Harvard University Press, 1963), pp. 70, 206, 210–218; W. H. Walsh, "Schematism," in *Kant: A Collection of Critical Essays*, ed. Robert Paul Wolff (Garden City, N.Y.: Doubleday, 1967), pp. 71–87; Donald W. Crawford, "Kant's Theory of Creative Imagination," in *Essays in Kant's Aesthetics*, ed. Ted Cohen and Paul Guyer (Chicago: University of Chicago Press, 1982), p. 162; and Gordon Nagel, *The Structure of Experience: Kant's System of Principles* (Chicago: University of Chicago Press, 1983), pp. 67–81.

13. Johnson, *Body in the Mind*, pp. 117–119; Lakoff, *Women, Fire*, p. 274.

14. Lakoff, *Women, Fire*, pp. 79–90.

15. Quoted in Beryl Smalley, *The Study of the Bible in the Middle Ages* (Oxford: Blackwell, 1952), p. 23.

16. Linda Williams, "When the Woman Looks," in Mary Ann Doane, Patricia Mellencamp, and Linda Williams, eds., *Re-Vision: Essays in Feminist Film Criticism* (Frederick, Md.: University Publications of America, 1984), p. 83.

17. Dietrich Dörner, "Heuristics and Cognition in Complex Systems," in Rudolf Gröner, Marina Gröner, and Walter F. Bischof, eds., *Methods of Heuristics* (Hillsdale, N.J.: Erlbaum, 1983), pp. 89–91. The "rules" for reading literature proposed in Peter J. Rabinowitz, *Before Reading: Narrative Conventions and the Politics of Interpretation* (Ithaca: Cornell University Press, 1987), are thus "heuristics" in my terms here.

18. Richard Nisbett and Lee Ross, *Human Inference: Strategies and Shortcomings of Social Judgment* (Englewood Cliffs, N.J.: Prentice-Hall, 1980), pp. 7–8.

19. See Neil A. Stillings et al., *Cognitive Science: An Introduction* (Cambridge: MIT Press, 1987), pp. 88–92. This adds support to the argument that critical reasoning is nondeductive.

20. Donald Spoto, *The Art of Alfred Hitchcock: Fifty Years of His Motion Pictures* (Garden City, N.Y.: Doubleday, 1979), p. 206.

21. Kathe Geist, "Yasujiro Ozu: Notes on a Retrospective," *Film Quarterly* 37, 1 (Fall 1983): 6.

22. Andrew Sarris, "Random Reflections—II," *Film Culture* 40 (Spring 1966): 21.

23. Mark Nash, *Dreyer* (London: British Film Institute, 1977), p. 13.

24. See Alain Le Boulluec, "L'Allégorie chez les Stoiciens," *Poétique* 23 (1975): 312–317; Robert M. Grant with David Tracy, *A Short History of the Interpretation of the Bible,* rev. ed. (London: SCM Press, 1984), pp. 24–25, 28–31. A general discussion is in Tzvetan Todorov, *Symbolism and Interpretation,* trans. Catherine Porter (Ithaca: Cornell University Press, 1982), pp. 101–104.

25. Sigmund Freud and Josef Breuer, *Studies on Hysteria* (New York: Avon, 1966), p. 252.

26. Sigmund Freud, *Collected Papers,* vol. 3: *Case Histories,* trans. Alix and James Strachey (London: The Hogarth Press, 1956), pp. 123–126. For a thorough discussion of Freud's use of puns and his general debt to philological techniques of interpretation, see John Forrester, *Language and the Origins of Psychoanalysis* (London: Macmillan, 1980), pp. 63–70, 166–180.

27. Sigmund Freud, *The Interpretation of Dreams,* trans. and ed. James Strachey (New York: Basic Books, 1960), pp. 408–409. Elsewhere Freud comments that dream displacement often creates punning allusions that appear to be bad jokes. See Freud, *The Complete Introductory Lectures on Psychoanalysis,* trans. and ed. James Strachey (New York: Norton, 1966), pp. 174, 236.

28. Jonathan Culler, *The Pursuit of Signs: Semiotics, Literature, Deconstruction* (Ithaca: Cornell University Press, 1981), p. 72. A more extended discussion is Culler, "The Call of the Phoneme: Introduction," in Culler, ed., *On Puns: The Foundation of Letters* (Oxford: Blackwell, 1988), pp. 1–16.

29. Todorov calls this the "paronymic detour"—passing not directly from signifier to signified but in roundabout fashion, through another signifier. Todorov, *Symbolism,* p. 76.

30. As one might expect, *Rules of the Game* solicits such punning: see George A. Wood, "Game Theory and *The Rules of the Game,*" *Cinema Journal* 13, 1 (Fall 1973): 33, and Nick Browne, "Deflections of Desire in *The Rules of the Game:* Reflections on the Theater of History," *Quarterly Review of Film Studies* 7, 3 (Summer 1982): 253–254.

31. David Thomson, *Movie Man* (New York: Stein and Day, 1967), p. 151.

32. Stephen Jenkins, "Lang: Fear and Desire," in Jenkins, ed., *Fritz Lang: The Image and the Look* (London: British Film Institute, 1981), p. 120.

33. George Lakoff and Mark Johnson, *Metaphors We Live By* (Chicago: University of Chicago Press, 1980).

34. Jean Aitchison, *Words in the Mind: An Introduction to the Mental Lexicon* (Oxford: Blackwell, 1987), pp. 116–126; Ray Jackendoff, *Consciousness*

and the Computational Mind (Cambridge: MIT Press, 1987), pp. 290–291.

35. See Paul Willemen, "Cinematic Discourse—The Problem of Inner Speech," *Screen* 22, 3 (1981): 63–93.

36. Paul Willemen, "The Ophuls Text: A Thesis," in Willemen, ed., *Ophuls* (London: British Film Institute, 1978), pp. 70–71.

37. Ella Shochat and Robert Stam, "The Cinema after Babel: Language, Difference, Power," *Screen* 26, 3/4 (May–August 1985): 38.

38. Ibid.

39. Latt. [sic], "*The Street,*" *Variety,* 7 September 1927, 21.

40. Indeed, semantic fields, by virtue of their internal structure, can be considered "semantic" or "substantive" schemata in their own right. Most of the schemata examined in the following chapters are by contrast "hollow" structures, operating independently of particular semantic features.

41. Lynne Kirby, "Temporality, Sexuality, and Narrative in *The General,*" *Wide Angle* 9, 1 (1987): 32–33.

42. See, for example, Jacqueline Rose, "Paranoia and the Film System," *Screen* 17, 4 (Winter 1976–77): 85–104; Raymond Bellour, "Psychosis, Neurosis, Perversion," *Camera Obscura* 3/4 (Summer 1979): 105–132.

43. See Tony Augarde, *The Oxford Guide to Word Games* (New York: Oxford University Press, 1986), p. 166.

44. See P. N. Johnson-Laird, *Mental Models: Towards a Cognitive Science of Language, Inference, and Consciousness* (Cambridge: Cambridge University Press, 1983), for what has become the principal line of argument. In a different sense, Lakoff's *Women, Fire, and Dangerous Things* uses the concept of mental models to incorporate schema theory.

45. Holland et al., *Induction,* p. 14.

7. Two Basic Schemata

1. For a classic experiment involving string and pliers, see John Anderson, *Cognitive Psychology and Its Implications,* 2d ed. (New York: Freeman, 1985), pp. 224–225.

2. See Ellen Schauber and Ellen Spolsky, "Stalking a Generative Poetics," *New Literary History* 12 (1981): 402.

3. Boris Tomashevsky, "Literary Genres," *Russian Poetics in Translation* 5 (1978): 55.

4. A sensitive and sensible discussion of the problem can be found in Rick Altman, *The American Film Musical* (Bloomington: Indiana University Press, 1987), pp. 4–15.

5. Ludwig Wittgenstein, *Philosophical Investigations,* trans. G. E. M. Anscombe (New York: Macmillan, 1953), pp. 31e–32e.

6. Alistair Fowler, *Kinds of Literature: An Introduction to the Theory of Genres and Modes* (Cambridge: Harvard University Press, 1982), p. 38.

7. Some such process may be at work in legal interpretation as well. "Constructive interpretation," writes Ronald Dworkin, "is a matter of imposing purpose on an object or practice in order to make of it the best possible

example of the form or genre to which it is taken to belong." See *Law's Empire* (Cambridge: Harvard University Press, 1986), p. 52.

8. Constance Penley, "Time Travel, Primal Scene, and the Critical Dystopia," *Camera Obscura* 15 (1987): 67–72.

9. Andrew Britton et al., "*The Reckless Moment*," *Framework* 4 (Autumn 1976): 21.

10. Stephen Heath, "Film and System: Terms of Analysis," *Screen* 16, 1 (Spring 1975): 11.

11. See, for example, Raymond Borde and Etienne Chaumeton, *Panorama du film noir américain* (Paris: Minuit, 1953); cf. E. Ann Kaplan, ed., *Women in Film Noir* (London: British Film Institute, 1978).

12. Robin Wood, *Hollywood from Vietnam to Reagan* (New York: Columbia University Press, 1986), pp. 17–25.

13. See James Donald Peterson, "In Warhol's Wake: Minimalism and Pop in the American Avant-Garde Film" (Ph.D. diss., University of Wisconsin-Madison, 1986), pp. 52–53.

14. A well-developed example is Martin Walsh, *The Brechtian Aspect of Radical Cinema* (London: British Film Institute, 1981).

15. See Stanley Cavell, *Pursuits of Happiness: The Hollywood Comedy of Remarriage* (Cambridge: Harvard University Press, 1981), and Jean-Louis Comolli and Jean Narboni, "Cinema/Ideology/Criticism (1)," in John Ellis, ed., *Screen Reader 1: Cinema/Ideology/Politics* (London: SEFT, 1977), pp. 2–11.

16. See, for example, James Collins, "Postmodernism and Cultural Practice: Redefining the Parameters," *Screen* 28, 2 (Spring 1987): 22.

17. Robert Stam, "Jean-Luc Godard's *Sauve qui peut (la vie)*," *Millennium Film Journal* 10/11 (1981): 194–198.

18. Roswitha Mueller, "The Mirror and the Vamp," *New German Critique* 34 (Winter 1985): 176–193.

19. Ellen Schauber and Ellen Spolsky point out that "even if the only *relevant* units are the units seen within an interpretation, that is, are already understood as relevant, the units that do not fit into the hypothetical interpretation may also be noticed." *The Boundaries of Interpretation: Linguistic Theory and Literary Text* (Stanford: Stanford University Press, 1986), p. 27.

20. Wittgenstein, *Philosophical Investigations*, p. 32e.

21. The example comes from Daniel Dennett, *Brainstorms: Philosophical Essays on Mind and Psychology* (Cambridge: MIT Press, 1981), p. 107.

22. See Jerry Fodor, *Psychosemantics: The Problem of Meaning in the Philosophy of Mind* (Cambridge: MIT Press, 1987), for an argument that ascribing beliefs and desires to humans and animals is one of the triumphs of folk psychology.

23. See on this point Christopher Butler, *Interpretation, Deconstruction, and Ideology* (London: Oxford University Press, 1984), p. 73.

24. For philosophical discussions, see P. F. Strawson, *Individuals: An Essay in Descriptive Metaphysics* (Garden City, N.Y.: Anchor, 1963), pp. 81–113; Steven Lukes, "Conclusion," in Michael Carrithers, Steven Collins,

and Steven Lukes, eds., *The Category of the Person: Anthropology, Philosophy, History* (Cambridge: Cambridge University Press, 1985), pp. 282–301. From a historical perspective, Jon Whitman suggests that the original threefold scheme of Christian exegesis (historical, moral, and spiritual meanings) arose from the Stoic division of man into body, soul, and spirit. *Allegory: The Dynamics of an Ancient and Medieval Technique* (Cambridge: Harvard University Press, 1987), pp. 62–63.

25. For a different discussion of the person schema, see Amelie Oksenberg Rorty, "A Literary Postscript: Characters, Persons, Selves, Individuals," in Rorty, ed., *The Identities of Persons* (Berkeley: University of California Press, 1976), pp. 301–323.

26. E. H. Gombrich provides a useful history of such personification techniques in Western art in "*Icones Symbolicae:* Philosophies of Symbolism and Their Bearing on Art," in *Symbolic Images* (Chicago: University of Chicago Press, 1972), pp. 123–191.

27. See *ibid.*, p. 269.

28. This is not to say that there are not significant cultural or historical differences in the ways "character" is made. Indeed, my folk-psychological schema may point at once to certain contingent universals of person-ascription that are necessary for social interaction of any type, and to those dimensions along which epochs and societies may vary the concept of the person.

29. "John Ford's *Young Mr. Lincoln:* A Collective Text by the Editors of *Cahiers du cinéma,*" in John Ellis, ed., *Screen Reader,* vol. 1 (London: SEFT, 1977), p. 29.

30. Jacques Rivette, "Letter on Rossellini," in Jim Hillier, ed., *Cahiers du cinéma: The 1950s: Neo-Realism, Hollywood, New Wave* (Cambridge: Harvard University Press, 1985), p. 202.

31. Teresa de Lauretis, *Alice Doesn't: Feminism, Semiotics, Cinema* (Bloomington: Indiana University Press, 1984), p. 98.

32. Jean-Pierre Oudart, "Sur *Ivan le Terrible,*" *Cahiers du cinéma* 218 (March 1970): 16.

33. A discussion of how literary education trains people to interpret character in this fashion can be found in François Rastier, "Un Concept dans le discours des études littéraires," *Littérature* 7 (October 1972): 87–101.

34. V. F. Perkins, "*River of No Return,*" *Movie* 2 (September 1962): 18–19.

35. Robin Wood, *Ingmar Bergman* (New York: Praeger, 1969), pp. 147–149.

36. Janet Bergstrom, "Sexuality at a Loss: The Films of F. W. Murnau," in Susan Rubin Suleiman, ed., *The Female Body in Western Culture: Contemporary Perspectives* (Cambridge: Harvard University Press, 1986), pp. 251–257.

37. Eugene Archer, "*I Vitelloni,*" *Film Culture* 10 (1956): 24.

38. Collins, "Postmodernism," pp. 13–14.

39. Martha Wolfenstein and Nathan Leites, *The Movies: A Psychological Study* (New York: Atheneum, 1970), p. 245.

40. James Monaco, *The New Wave: Truffaut, Godard, Chabrol, Rohmer, Rivette* (New York: Oxford University Press, 1976), p. 31.

41. Laurence Wylie, "La Vérité derrière les masques," *Quarterly Review of Film Studies* 7, 3 (Summer 1982): 243.

42. David Curtis, *Experimental Cinema: A Fifty-Year Evolution* (New York: Delta, 1971), p. 179.

43. Brian O'Doherty, "Bruce Conner and His Films," in Gregory Battcock, ed., *The New American Cinema: A Critical Anthology* (New York: Dutton, 1967), p. 196.

44. The most powerful theoretical alternative to a schema account has been Barthes's discussion, in *S/Z* and elsewhere, of the "semic code." The code assigns connotative attributes to places, objects, and persons. According to the code, a character can be designated as reckless or impious. In fact, Barthes claims, the character's identity is nothing but a collection of semes. What creates the illusion of the character's individuality? "The proper name enables the person to exist outside the semes, whose sum nonetheless constitutes it entirely." Roland Barthes, *S/Z*, trans. Richard Miller (New York: Hill and Wang, 1974), p. 191. At the theoretical level, there would be much to say about Barthes's position. He assumes that we have no prior and extraliterary assumptions about the person's continuing unity; he considers only persisting traits, not occasion-specific emotions, goals, and so on; and his account may not apply easily to the cinema, where we see those bodies we must imagine in reading most books. In any event, film critics have on the whole ignored Barthes's theory. For an example of an application of it, see Julia Lesage, "*S/Z* and *Rules of the Game*," *Jump Cut* 12/13 (1976): 45–51, which by and large translates traditional description of character into Barthes's terms: for example, "Here Genevieve's and Octave's costumes both connote their personalities—burly, awkward, unpolished and maladroit Octave and jaded, sophisticated and brittle Genevieve" (p. 48).

45. Marvin D'Lugo, "Historical Reflexivity: Saura's Anti-*Carmen*," *Wide Angle* 9, 3 (1987): 56, 59.

46. Ibid., pp. 55–56.

47. Ibid., p. 56.

48. Ibid., p. 58.

49. André Bazin, "On the Politique des Auteurs," in Hillier, *Cahiers du cinéma: The 1950s*, p. 256.

50. Paul Willemen, "Distanciation and Douglas Sirk," in Laura Mulvey and Jon Halliday, *Douglas Sirk* (Edinburgh: Edinburgh Film Festival, 1972), p. 24.

51. Alfred Guzzetti, *Two or Three Things I Know about Her: Analysis of a Film by Godard* (Cambridge: Harvard University Press, 1981), p. 219.

52. Simon Watney, "Gardens of Speculation: Landscape in *The Draughtsman's Contract*," *Undercut* 7/8 (Spring 1983): 4, 7.

53. D'Lugo, "Historical Reflexivity," p. 57.

54. E. Ann Kaplan, *Women and Film: Both Sides of the Camera* (London: Methuen, 1983), p. 167.

55. Mary Ann Doane, "The Retreat of Signs and the Failure of Words: Leslie Thornton's *Adynata*," *Millennium Film Journal* 16/17/18 (Fall–Winter 1986–87): 151–157.

56. See Michel Charles, *L'Arbre et la source* (Paris: Seuil, 1985), p. 134.

57. Jacques Doniol-Valcroze, "Un Homme marche dans la trahison (*High Noon*)," *Cahiers du cinéma* 16 (October 1952): 59.

58. See Richard Levin, *New Readings vs. Old Plays: Recent Trends in the Reinterpretation of English Renaissance Drama* (Chicago: University of Chicago Press, 1979), p. 13.

59. Monaco, *New Wave*, p. 154.

60. Colin MacCabe, "*Slow Motion*," *Screen* 21, 3 (1980): 114.

61. Eugene Archer, "*A King in New York*," *Film Culture* 16 (January 1958): 4–5.

62. Annette Michelson, "Film and the Radical Aspiration," in P. Adams Sitney, ed., *The Film Culture Reader* (New York: Praeger, 1970), p. 414.

63. Jean Domarchi, "Le Chef-d'oeuvre inconnu," *Cahiers du cinéma* 39 (October 1954): 34.

64. Andrew Sarris, *The Primal Screen: Essays on Film and Related Subjects* (New York: Simon and Schuster, 1973), p. 50.

65. Luc Moullet, "Ré-création par la recréation (*Tarnished Angels*)," *Cahiers du cinéma* 87 (September 1958): 55–56.

66. P. Adams Sitney, *Visionary Film: The American Avant-Garde* (New York: Oxford University Press, 1974), p. 188.

67. Patricia Erens, "The Galler Home Movies: A Case Study," *Journal of Film and Video* 38 (Summer–Fall 1986): 22.

68. Stephen Jenkins, "Lang: Fear and Desire," in Jenkins, ed., *Fritz Lang: The Image and the Look* (London: British Film Institute, 1981), p. 123.

69. Jacques Rivette, "L'Art de la fugue (*I Confess*)," *Cahiers du cinéma* 26 (August-September 1953): 50.

70. Donald Spoto, *The Art of Alfred Hitchcock: Fifty Years of His Motion Pictures* (Garden City, N.Y.: Doubleday, 1979), p. 277.

71. William Rothman, "The Filmmaker within the Film," *Quarterly Review of Film Studies* 7, 3 (Summer 1982): 226–227.

72. For a philosophical discussion of this process, see Steven Collins, "Categories, Concepts, or Predicaments? Remarks on Mauss's Use of Philosophical Terminology," in Carrithers, Collins, and Lukes, *Category of the Person,* pp. 73–74.

73. Isadore of Seville, quoted in Whitman, *Allegory,* p. 270. See also Paolo Valesio, "Esquisse pour une étude des personifications," *Lingua e stile* 4 (1969): 1–8; Morton Bloomfield, "A Grammatical Approach to Personification Allegory," *Modern Philology* 60 (February 1963): 163–168.

74. Fereydoun Hoveyda, "Sunspots," in Jim Hillier, ed., *Cahiers du cinéma: The 1960s: New Wave, New Cinema, Reevaluating Hollywood* (Cambridge: Harvard University Press, 1986), p. 143.

75. Bazin, "On the Politique des Auteurs," p. 255.

76. Eric Rohmer and Claude Chabrol, *Hitchcock: The First Forty-Four Films,* trans. Stanley Hochman (New York: Ungar, 1979), p. 67.

77. Tag Gallagher, *John Ford: The Man and His Films* (Berkeley: University of California Press, 1986), p. 159.

78. Bill Nichols, *Ideology and the Image* (Bloomington: Indiana University Press, 1981), p. 137.
79. Nick Browne, *The Rhetoric of Filmic Narration* (Ann Arbor: UMI Research Press, 1982), p. 11.
80. André S. Labarthe, "My Name Is Orson Welles," *Cahiers du cinéma* 117 (March 1961): 24.
81. Raymond Bellour, "Hitchcock the Enunciator," *Camera Obscura* 2 (Fall 1977): 68.
82. Beverle Houston, "Missing in Action: Notes on Dorothy Arzner," *Wide Angle* 6, 3 (1984): 31.
83. Philip Rosen, "Difference and Displacement in *Seventh Heaven*," *Screen* 18, 2 (Summer 1977): 100.
84. Bruce F. Kawin, *Mindscreen: Bergman, Godard, and First-Person Film* (Princeton: Princeton University Press, 1978), p. 106.
85. André Gaudreault, *Du littéraire au filmique: Système du récit* (Paris: Méridiens Klincksieck, 1988), pp. 117–131.
86. V. F. Perkins, *Film as Film: Understanding and Judging Movies* (Harmondsworth: Penguin, 1972), p. 134.
87. Edward Branigan calls it a "reading hypothesis"; see "What Is a Camera?" in Patricia Mellencamp and Philip Rosen, eds., *Cinema Histories, Cinema Practices* (Frederick, Md.: University Publications of America, 1984), pp. 87–107. See also David Bordwell, *Narration in the Fiction Film* (Madison: University of Wisconsin Press, 1985), pp. 119–120.
88. Raymond Bellour, "Hitchcock the Enunciator," *Camera Obscura* 2 (Fall 1977): 85. For a discussion of how enunciation theories of narration make appeal to the camera as invisible observer, see Bordwell, *Narration*, pp. 24–25.
89. Michael Renov, "Re-Thinking Documentary: Toward a Taxonomy of Mediations," *Wide Angle* 8, 3 and 4 (1986): 74–75.
90. Annette Kuhn, *Women's Pictures: Feminism and Cinema* (London: Routledge and Kegan Paul, 1982), p. 174.
91. Parker Tyler, *Magic and Myth of the Movies* (New York: Simon and Schuster, 1947), p. 212.
92. Peter Wollen, "*Passion* 1," *Framework* 21 (1983): 4.
93. See François Jost, *L'Oeil-caméra: Entre film et roman* (Lyon: Presses universitaires de Lyon, 1987), pp. 30–35; André Gaudreault, "Narration et monstration au cinéma," *Hors cadre* 2 (Spring 1984): 87–98; André Gardiès, "Le Su et le vu," *Hors cadre* 2 (Spring 1984): 45–65; Jean-Paul Simon, "Enonciation et narration: Gnarus, auctor et Protée," *Communications* 38 (1983): 155–191.
94. Andrew Sarris, "Rossellini Rediscovered," *Film Culture* 32 (Spring 1964): 61–62.
95. Andrew Sarris, "Introduction: The Fall and Rise of the Film Director," in Sarris, ed., *Interviews with Film Directors* (Indianapolis: Bobbs-Merrill, 1967), p. iii.
96. See, for example, Stephen Koch, *Star-Gazer: Andy Warhol's World and His Films* (New York: Praeger, 1973), p. 77.

97. Tim Hunter, *"Summer Storm,"* in Mulvey and Halliday, *Douglas Sirk,* p. 34.

98. Laura Mulvey, "Visual Pleasure and Narrative Cinema," *Screen* 16, 3 (Autumn 1975): 17.

99. Ibid., p. 18.

100. Geoffrey Nowell-Smith, "Minnelli and Melodrama," *Screen* 18, 2 (Summer 1977): 117.

101. Mark Nash, *Dreyer* (London: British Film Institute, 1977), p. 25.

102. Ian Cameron, "Hitchcock I: The Mechanics of Suspense," *Movie* 3 (October 1962): 6.

103. V. F. Perkins, *"Rope," Movie* 7 (1963): 12.

104. Anonymous, "Why Preminger?" *Movie* 2 (1962): 11.

105. Perkins, *Film as Film;* see especially pp. 139–157.

106. Laura Mulvey, "Afterthoughts on 'Visual Pleasure and Narrative Cinema' Inspired by *Duel in the Sun* (King Vidor, 1946)," *Framework* 15/16/17 (1981): 15.

107. David Thomson, *Movie Man* (New York: Stein and Day, 1967), p. 189.

108. P. Adams Sitney, *Visionary Film: The American Avant-Garde* (New York: Oxford University Press, 1974), p. 349.

109. Mary Ann Doane, *The Desire to Desire: The Woman's Film of the 1940s* (Bloomington: Indiana University Press, 1987), p. 79.

110. Annette Michelson, "About Snow," *October* 8 (Spring 1979): 121.

111. Donald Richie, *Ozu* (Berkeley: University of California Press, 1974), pp. 153–155.

112. Kaplan, *Women and Film,* p. 184.

113. Christian Metz, *The Imaginary Signifier,* trans. Celia Britton et al. (Bloomington: Indiana University Press, 1981), pp. 49–51.

114. Katherine Dieckmann, "Neil Jimenez: On the Cutting Edge," *Village Voice,* 12 May 1987, 66.

115. See Ian Cameron and Robin Wood, *Antonioni* (New York: Praeger, 1968), pp. 10–13; Robin Wood, *"Tokyo Story," Movie* 13 (Summer 1965): 32.

116. Sam Rohdie, *"House of Bamboo,"* in David Will and Peter Wollen, eds., *Samuel Fuller* (Edinburgh: Edinburgh Film Festival, 1969), pp. 38–39.

8. Text Schemata

1. See Robert M. Grant with David Tracy, *A Short History of the Interpretation of the Bible,* rev. ed. (London: SCM Press, 1984), pp. 14–15; Edward L. Greenstein, "Medieval Bible Commentaries," in Barry W. Holtz, ed., *Back to the Sources: Reading the Classic Jewish Texts* (New York: Summit Books, 1984), pp. 207–221; Tzvetan Todorov, *Symbolism and Interpretation,* trans. Catherine Porter (Ithaca: Cornell University Press, 1982), pp. 140–142, 155–162; Michel Charles, "La Lecture critique," *Poétique* 34 (April 1978): 147.

2. A detailed exposition of the "contextualism" of New Criticism can be

found in Murray Krieger, *The New Apologists for Poetry* (Bloomington: Indiana University Press, 1963).

3. Susan Sontag, "Against Interpretation," in *Against Interpretation and Other Essays* (New York: Delta, 1966), pp. 9–10.

4. See George Lakoff, *Women, Fire, and Dangerous Things: What Categories Reveal about the Mind* (Cambridge: Harvard University Press, 1987), pp. 271–275.

5. Cleanth Brooks and Robert Penn Warren, *Understanding Fiction* (New York: Appleton-Century-Crofts, 1943), p. 171.

6. Bill Nichols, *Ideology and the Image* (Bloomington: Indiana University Press, 1981), p. 113.

7. Robert C. Pooley et al., *Exploring Life through Literature* (Glenview, Ill.: Scott, Foresman, 1968), p. 36.

8. Pascal Bonitzer, "Système de *La Grève*," *Cahiers du cinéma* 226/227 (January-February 1981): 44.

9. Lucy Fischer, "*Meshes of the Afternoon*," in John G. Hanhardt, ed., *A History of the American Avant-Garde Cinema* (New York: American Federation of the Arts, 1976), pp. 69–70.

10. Annette Kuhn, *The Power of the Image: Essays on Representation and Sexuality* (London: Routledge and Kegan Paul, 1985), p. 91.

11. Paul Mayersberg, "*The Trial of Joan of Arc*," *Movie* 7 (1963): 30.

12. Kuhn, *Power of the Image*, p. 93.

13. Jacques Aumont, *Montage Eisenstein*, trans. Lee Hildreth, Constance Penley, and Andrew Ross (Bloomington: Indiana University Press, 1987), p. 89.

14. Peter Brunette, "Toward a Deconstructive Theory of Film," *Studies in the Literary Imagination* 19, 2 (Spring 1986): 65.

15. Andrew Britton, "Sexuality and Power, or the Two Others," *Framework* 6 (Autumn 1977): 10.

16. Jean-Louis Comolli and François Géré, "Two Fictions Concerning Hate," in Stephen Jenkins, ed., *Fritz Lang: The Image and the Look* (London: British Film Institute, 1981), p. 141.

17. Alfred Guzzetti, *Two or Three Things I Know about Her: Analysis of a Film by Godard* (Cambridge: Harvard University Press, 1981), p. 165.

18. Nick Browne, "Deflections of Desire in *The Rules of the Game*: Reflections on the Theater of History," *Quarterly Review of Film Studies* 7, 3 (Summer 1982): 254.

19. Alexandre Astruc, "The Birth of a New Avant-Garde: La Caméra-Stylo," in Peter Graham, ed., *The New Wave* (Garden City, N.Y.: Doubleday, 1968), p. 20.

20. V. F. Perkins, "The British Cinema," *Movie* 1 (June 1962): 6.

21. Fred Camper, "*A Geisha (Gion Festival Music)*," *Film Center Program Notes*, School of the Art Institute of Chicago, 8–9 June 1978, p. 4.

22. John Belton, *The Hollywood Professionals: Howard Hawks, Frank Borzage, Edgar G. Ulmer* (London: Tantivy, 1974), p. 16.

23. Brian Henderson, "Harvard Film Studies: A Review," *Film Quarterly* 35, 4 (Summer 1982): 33.

24. Nick Browne, *The Rhetoric of Filmic Narration* (Ann Arbor: UMI Research Press, 1982), pp. 38–39.
25. Pam Cook, "Duplicity in *Mildred Pierce*," in E. Ann Kaplan, ed., *Women in Film Noir* (London: British Film Institute, 1978), p. 81.
26. V. F. Perkins, *Film as Film: Understanding and Judging Movies* (Harmondsworth: Penguin, 1972), p. 80; Michael Walsh, "*Out of the Past:* The History of the Subject," *Enclitic* 5, 2; 6, 1 (Fall 1981–Spring 1982): 13.
27. Andrew Sarris, *The American Cinema: Directors and Directions 1929–1968* (New York: Dutton, 1968), p. 72.
28. Dana Polan, *The Political Language of Film and the Avant-Garde* (Ann Arbor: UMI Research Press, 1985), p. 107.
29. Tania Modleski, "'Never to Be Thirty-Six Years Old': *Rebecca* as Female Oedipal Drama," *Wide Angle* 5, 1 (1982): 41. See also Modleski, *The Women Who Knew Too Much: Hitchcock and Feminist Theory* (New York: Methuen, 1988), p. 53, where the same claims appear in slightly altered form, and p. 130, n. 20, where Modleski differentiates her interpretation from Mary Ann Doane's.
30. Mary Ann Doane, *The Desire to Desire: The Woman's Film of the 1940s* (Bloomington: Indiana University Press, 1987), p. 170.
31. Ibid., p. 171.
32. Vlada Petrić, "From Mise-en-Scène to Mise-en-Shot: Analysis of a Sequence," *Quarterly Review of Film Studies* 7, 3 (Summer 1982): 275.
33. [Andrew Britton?], "*Pursued:* A Reply to Paul Willemen," *Framework* 4 (Autumn 1976): 13.
34. Stephen Jenkins, "Lang: Fear and Desire," in Jenkins, ed., *Fritz Lang: The Image and the Look* (London: British Film Institute, 1981), p. 93.
35. Mark Nash, *Dreyer* (London: British Film Institute, 1977), p. 31.
36. Philip Rosen, "Difference and Displacement in *Seventh Heaven*," *Screen* 18, 2 (Summer 1977): 95–101.
37. Lea Jacobs, "*Now Voyager:* Some Problems of Enunciation and Sexual Difference," *Camera Obscura* 7 (1981): 99.
38. Sarris, *The American Cinema*, p. 118.
39. Donald Spoto, *The Art of Alfred Hitchcock: Fifty Years of His Motion Pictures* (Garden City, N.Y.: Doubleday, 1979), p. 276.
40. Richard Thompson, "Pronoun Trouble," in Gerald Peary and Danny Peary, eds., *The American Animated Cartoon: A Critical Anthology* (New York: Dutton, 1980), p. 228.
41. William Paul, *Ernst Lubitsch's American Comedy* (New York: Columbia University Press, 1983), p. 85.
42. Jean Narboni and Jean-Pierre Oudart, "*La Nouvelle Babylone* (la métaphor 'commune,' 2)," *Cahiers du cinéma* 232 (October 1971): 49.
43. Deborah Linderman, "Uncoded Images in the Heterogeneous Text," *Wide Angle* 3, 3 (1979): 37.
44. E. Ann Kaplan, *Women and Film: Both Sides of the Camera* (London: Methuen, 1983), p. 66.
45. Michel Chion, *La Voix au cinéma* (Paris: Etoile, 1982), p. 109.
46. Graham Bruce, *Bernard Herrmann: Film Music and Narrative* (Ann Arbor:

UMI Research Press, 1985), p. 178; Royal S. Brown, "Herrmann, Hitchcock, and the Music of the Irrational," *Cinema Journal* 21, 2 (Spring 1982): 31–33.

47. P. Adams Sitney, *Visionary Film: The American Avant-Garde 1943–1978*, 2d ed. (New York: Oxford University Press, 1978), p. 181.

48. Ibid., p. 424.

49. Toby Mussman, "Marcel Duchamp's *Anemic Cinema*," in Gregory Battcock, ed., *The New American Cinema* (New York: Dutton, 1967), p. 153.

50. See, for a general overview, Tzvetan Todorov, *Theories of the Symbol*, trans. Catherine Porter (Ithaca: Cornell University Press, 1982).

51. Laura Mulvey, quoted in Lester D. Friedman, "An Interview with Peter Wollen and Laura Mulvey on *Riddles of the Sphinx*," *Millennium Film Journal* 4/5 (1979): 16.

52. David Edelstein, "NYU Rushes the Tinsel Leagues," *Village Voice*, 3 December 1985, supplement, "Filmmaking in New York," p. 4.

53. Robert B. Ray, *A Certain Tendency of the Hollywood Cinema, 1930–1980* (Princeton: Princeton University Press, 1985), p. 286.

54. André Bazin, "William Wyler, or the Jansenist of Mise-en-Scène," in Christopher Williams, ed., *Realism and the Cinema* (London: Routledge and Kegan Paul, 1980), p. 52.

55. See Jacques Rivette, "Rédécouvrir l'Amérique," *Cahiers du cinéma* 54 (Christmas 1955): 12.

56. On Hawks, see for example Jean-Luc Comolli, "La Grandeur du simple," *Cahiers du cinéma* 135 (September 1962): 56. On DeMille, see Michel Mourlet, "Sur un art ignoré," *Cahiers du cinéma* 98 (August 1959): 32.

57. V. F. Perkins, "The Cinema of Nicholas Ray," *Movie* 9 (1963): 7.

58. For a discussion of Perkins' "expressive realism," see Noël Carroll, *Philosophical Problems of Classical Film Theory* (Princeton: Princeton University Press, 1988), pp. 187, 236.

59. John Russell Taylor, *Cinema Eye, Cinema Ear: Some Key Film-Makers of the Sixties* (New York: Hill and Wang, 1964), p. 18.

60. Parker Tyler, *Sex Psyche Etcetera in the Film* (Harmondsworth: Penguin, 1969), p. 126.

61. John Mraz, "*Lucia*: Visual Style and Historical Portrayal," *Jump Cut* 19 (December 1978): 21.

62. Gillian Swanson, "Psychoanalysis and Cultural Practice," *Undercut* 1 (March-April 1981): 40.

63. Michael Stern, *Douglas Sirk* (Boston: Twayne, 1979), p. 101.

64. Ibid.

65. Paul, *Lubitsch's American Comedy*, p. 265.

66. Nichols, *Ideology and the Image*, p. 186.

67. Peter Wollen, "*Passion* 1," *Framework* 21 (1983): 4.

68. Robin Wood, *Personal Views: Explorations in Film* (London: Gordon Fraser, 1976), p. 100.

69. Richard Abel, *French Cinema: The First Wave, 1915–1929* (Princeton: Princeton University Press, 1984), p. 495.

70. For a discussion, see Richard Levin, *New Readings vs. Old Plays: Recent*

Trends in the Reinterpretation of English Renaissance Drama (Chicago: University of Chicago Press, 1979), pp. 78–145.

71. Nichols, *Ideology and the Image,* p. 151.

72. Claire Johnston, "Dorothy Arzner: Critical Strategies," in Johnston, ed., *The Work of Dorothy Arzner: Towards a Feminist Cinema* (London: British Film Institute, 1975), pp. 6–7.

73. Martin Walsh, *The Brechtian Aspect of Radical Cinema* (London: British Film Institute, 1981), pp. 64–65.

74. Paul Vecchiali, "Les Cinq fils Hammond (*Guns in the Afternoon*)," *Cahiers du cinéma* 140 (February 1963): 48.

75. Paul Mayersberg, "Carmen and Bess," *Movie* 4 (November 1962): 23; Ian Cameron, "Hitchcock I: The Mechanics of Suspense," *Movie* 3 (October 1962): 5.

76. Ian Cameron and Richard Jeffrey, "The Universal Hitchcock," *Movie* 12 (Spring 1965): 23.

77. Tag Gallagher, *John Ford: The Man and His Films* (Berkeley: University of California Press, 1986), p. 195.

78. Kaja Silverman, "A Voice to Match: The Female Voice in Classic Cinema," *Iris* 3, 1 (1985): 57–70.

79. See Ellen Schauber and Ellen Spolsky, *The Bounds of Interpretation: Linguistic Theory and Literary Text* (Stanford: Stanford University Press, 1986), pp. 99, 120–122; Stein Haugom Olsen, *The End of Literary Theory* (Cambridge: Cambridge University Press, 1987), p. 42.

80. "The goals toward which one moves in synthesizing a plot are, of course, notions of thematic structure." Jonathan Culler, *Structuralist Poetics: Structuralism, Linguistics, and the Study of Literature* (Ithaca: Cornell University Press, 1975), p. 221.

81. Eric Rohmer, "Les Lecteurs des *Cahiers* et la politique des auteurs," *Cahiers du cinéma* 63 (October 1956): 55.

82. Lakoff, *Women, Fire, and Dangerous Things,* p. 275.

83. Culler, *Structuralist Poetics,* p. 222.

84. Eugene Archer, "The Rack of Life," *Film Quarterly* 12, 4 (Summer 1959): 3; Robert Burgoyne, "Narrative and Sexual Excess," *October* 21 (Summer 1982): 58.

85. Ibid., p. 59.

86. Doane, *The Desire to Desire,* p. 102.

87. See, for example, Cameron, "Hitchcock I," pp. 4–7; "Hitchcock 2: Suspense and Meaning," *Movie* 6 (1963): 8–12; Mark Shivas, "*Anatomy of a Murder,*" *Movie* 2 (September 1962): 23.

88. See, respectively, Wanda Bershen, "*Zorns Lemma,*" *Artforum* 10, 1 (September 1971): 45; Peter Sainsbury, "Editorial," *Afterimage* 4 (Autumn 1972): 4–5; Bill Simon, "'Reading' *Zorns Lemma,*" *Millennium Film Journal* 1, 2 (1978): 42, 48; Noël Carroll, "Film," in Stanley Trachtenberg, ed., *The Postmodern Moment* (Westport, Conn.: Greenwood, 1986), pp. 107–108.

89. Stein Haugom Olsen, *The Structure of Literary Understanding* (Cambridge: Cambridge University Press, 1978), p. 89.

90. Frank Kermode, *The Genesis of Secrecy: On the Interpretation of Narrative* (Cambridge: Harvard University Press, 1979), p. 53.

91. See Bordwell, Janet Staiger, and Kristin Thompson, *The Classical Hollywood Cinema: Film Style and Mode of Production to 1960* (New York: Columbia University Press, 1985), pp. 25–29; Bordwell, *Narration in the Fiction Film* (Madison: University of Wisconsin Press, 1985), pp. 38, 56–57.

92. Cited in Richard Mayer, *Thinking, Problem-Solving, Cognition* (New York: Freeman, 1983), p. 67.

93. Walsh, *Brechtian Aspect,* pp. 61–65.

94. P. Adams Sitney, *Visionary Film: The American Avant-Garde, 1943–1978,* 2d ed. (New York: Oxford University Press, 1978), p. 331.

95. Chris Berry, "Sexual Difference and the Viewing Subject in *Li Shuang-shuang* and *The In-Laws*," in Berry, ed., *Perspectives on Chinese Cinema,* Cornell University East Asia Papers no. 39 (Ithaca: Cornell China-Japan Program, 1985), p. 41.

96. David Bordwell, *The Films of Carl-Theodor Dreyer* (Berkeley: University of California Press, 1981), p. 90.

97. Frank P. Tomasulo, "*Bicycle Thieves:* A Re-Reading," *Cinema Journal* 21, 2 (Spring 1982): 2.

98. Pam Cook, "Duplicity in *Mildred Pierce*," in Kaplan, *Women in Film Noir,* pp. 71–74.

99. Ibid., p. 71.

100. Marc Vernet, "Le Personnage de film," *Iris* 7 (1986): 103–105.

101. Barry Boys, "*The Courtship of Eddie's Father,*" *Movie* 10 (June 1963): 31–32.

102. Pierre Leprohon, *Michelangelo Antonioni: An Introduction,* trans. Scott Sullivan (New York: Simon and Schuster, 1963), p. 59.

103. Richard Abel, *French Cinema: The First Wave, 1915–1929* (Princeton: Princeton University Press, 1984), p. 462.

104. André Bazin, *What Is Cinema?,* vol. 2, trans. and ed. Hugh Gray (Berkeley: University of California Press, 1971), p. 54.

105. Marsha Kinder, "Antonioni in Transit," in Roy Huss, ed., *Focus on Blow-Up* (Englewood Cliffs, N.J.: Prentice-Hall, 1971), pp. 87–88.

106. Edward Branigan, *Point of View in the Cinema: A Theory of Narration and Subjectivity in Classical Film* (Berlin: Mouton, 1984), pp. 161–163.

107. Levin, *New Readings,* p. 113.

108. Archer, "Rack of Life," pp. 11–12.

109. Thomas Schatz, *Hollywood Genres* (New York: Random House, 1981), p. 249.

110. Ruth McCormick, "Ritual, the Family, and the State: A Critique of Nagisa Oshima's *The Ceremony*," *Cineaste* 6, 2 (1974): 26.

111. For example, Judith Williamson notes of Mulvey and Wollen's *Riddles of the Sphinx:* "The film undercuts its own strategy, by not recognizing that the power of an image of Female Mystery is so strong that it functions in the most traditional way and is *too strong to be undercut by anything later in the film.*" *Consuming Passions: The Dynamics of Popular Culture* (London: Boyars, 1986), p. 132, italics added. Stephen Heath faults the

film for not opening the unconscious and the symbolic onto "historical determinations"; this would be "a fully political task." "Difference," *Screen* 19, 3 (Autumn 1978): 73–74.

112. Modleski, "'Never to Be Thirty-Six,'" p. 40.

113. Cook, "Duplicity," p. 81.

114. See Grant and Tracy, *Interpretation of the Bible,* pp. 19–21.

115. Quoted in Angus Fletcher, *Allegory: The Theory of a Symbolic Mode* (Ithaca: Cornell University Press, 1964), p. 237n.

116. For a thorough discussion of classical and medieval allegorical procedures, see Jon Whitman, *Allegory: The Dynamics of an Ancient and Medieval Technique* (Cambridge: Harvard University Press, 1987). On rabbinical allegory, see Gerald L. Bruns, "Midrash and Allegory: The Beginnings of Scriptural Interpretation," in Robert Alter and Frank Kermode, eds., *The Literary Guide to the Bible* (Cambridge: Harvard University Press, 1987), pp. 637–644. See also Sigmund Freud, *The Interpretation of Dreams,* trans. James Strachey (New York: Basic Books, 1960), pp. 261–264.

117. See Erwin Panofsky, *Meaning in the Visual Arts: Papers in and on Art History* (Garden City, N.Y.: Doubleday, 1955), p. 36; Walter Benjamin, *The Origin of German Tragic Drama,* trans. John Osborne (London: New Left Books, 1977), pp. 163–188.

118. Myth critics' inclination toward allegory is discussed in Vincent B. Leitch, *American Literary Criticism from the Thirties to the Eighties* (New York: Columbia University Press, 1988), pp. 128–129, 142–144.

119. See Jean-Yves Tadié, *La Critique littéraire au XXᵉ siècle* (Paris: Belfond, 1987), pp. 119–124.

120. See for example Craig Owens, "The Allegorical Impulse: Toward a Theory of Postmodernism," *October* 12 (Spring 1980): 67–86; 13 (Summer 1980): 59–80.

121. Jacques Lacan, "Seminar on 'The Purloined Letter,'" in John P. Mueller and William J. Richardson, eds., *The Purloined Poe: Lacan, Derrida, and Psychoanalytic Reading* (Baltimore: Johns Hopkins University Press, 1988), pp. 28–55.

122. Elizabeth Wright, "Modern Psychoanalytic Criticism," in Ann Jefferson and David Robey, eds., *Modern Literary Theory: A Comparative Introduction* (London: Batsford, 1982), pp. 128–129.

123. Stephen Heath, *Questions of Cinema* (London: Macmillan, 1981), p. 142.

124. Kaja Silverman, "Kaspar Hauser's 'Terrible Fall' into Narrative," *New German Critique* 24/25 (Fall–Winter 1981–82): 75, 74.

125. Vladimir Propp, *Morphology of the Folktale,* 2d ed., trans. Svata Pirkova-Jakobson (Austin: University of Texas Press, 1968).

126. Roland Barthes, "The Struggle with the Angel: Textual Analysis of Genesis 32: 22–32," in *Image Music Text,* trans. and ed. Stephen Heath (New York: Hill and Wang, 1977), pp. 138–141.

127. Peter Wollen, *Readings and Writings: Semiotic Counter-Strategies* (London: New Left Books, 1982), pp. 31–32.

128. Ibid., p. 24.

129. See, for example, Kuhn, *Power of the Image,* pp. 77–81, 86.

130. Stephen Jenkins, "Lang: Fear and Desire," in Jenkins, ed., *Fritz Lang: The Image and the Look* (London: British Film Institute, 1981), pp. 84–87.

131. Elizabeth Cowie, "Fantasia," *m/f* 9 (1984): 90–91.

132. This is one part of a larger tendency toward the epiphanic structure of that "boundary situation" story that Horst Ruthrof has found in this century's fiction: plays, novels, and short stories have long been organized around "pointed situations in which a presented persona, a narrator, or the implied reader in a flash of insight becomes aware of meaningful as against meaningless existence." *The Reader's Construction of Narrative* (London: Routledge and Kegan Paul, 1981), p. 102.

133. See, for examples, Brooks and Warren, *Understanding Fiction*, p. 87; Northrop Frye, *A Natural Perspective: The Development of Shakespearean Comedy and Romance* (New York: Harcourt, Brace and World, 1965), pp. 73–87; Simon O. Lesser, *Fiction and the Unconscious* (New York: Vintage, 1957), pp. 222–224, 233–234.

134. Kaplan, *Women and Film,* p. 158.

135. Ibid., p. 161.

136. Northrop Frye, *Anatomy of Criticism: Four Essays* (Princeton: Princeton University Press, 1957), p. 90.

137. Jacqueline Suter and Sandy Flitterman, "Textual Riddles: Woman as Enigma or Site of Social Meanings? An Interview with Laura Mulvey," *Discourse* 1 (Fall 1979): 95.

138. See, for an extended instance, Eugene R. Kintgen, *The Perception of Poetry* (Bloomington: Indiana University Press, 1983). The book's treatment of "preaesthetic" interpretation as problem-solving complements several points I have sought to make here.

9. Interpretation as Rhetoric

1. See, for example, Hayden White, *Metahistory: The Historical Imagination in Nineteenth-Century Europe* (Baltimore: Johns Hopkins University Press, 1973). For a critique, see Maria Ruegg, "Metaphor and Metonymy: The Logic of Structuralist Rhetoric," *Glyph* 6 (1979): 141–157.

2. See, for an attempt to integrate these within a structuralist framework, Tzvetan Todorov, *Symbolism and Interpretation,* trans. Catherine Porter (Ithaca: Cornell University Press, 1982), p. 75.

3. Attentive readers will have noticed my own rhetorical tactics showing here. For the technique-minded, the category is epideictic, the device is the artifice of praising associated qualities. See Aristotle, *The Rhetoric,* trans. W. Rhys Roberts, in Jonathan Barnes, ed., *The Complete Works of Aristotle,* vol. 2 (Princeton: Princeton University Press, 1984), p. 2176.

4. Ibid., pp. 2224–2225.

5. See Donald McCloskey, *The Rhetoric of Economics* (Madison: University of Wisconsin Press, 1985), p. 121.

6. "Hiroshima, notre amour," in Jim Hillier, ed., *Cahiers du cinéma: The*

1950s: Neo-Realism, Hollywood, New Wave (Cambridge: Harvard University Press, 1985), p. 66.

7. Dudley Andrew, *Film in the Aura of Art* (Princeton: Princeton University Press, 1984), p. 65.

8. Laura Mulvey, "Visual Pleasure and Narrative Cinema," *Screen* 16, 3 (Autumn 1975): 18.

9. Andrew, *Film in the Aura of Art,* pp. 76–77.

10. Michel Charles, *L'Arbre et la source* (Paris: Seuil, 1985), pp. 278–289.

11. Frank Kermode, *The Genesis of Secrecy: On the Interpretation of Narrative* (Cambridge: Harvard University Press, 1979), p. 16.

12. Chaim Perlman, *The Realm of Rhetoric,* trans. William Klubeck (Notre Dame: University of Notre Dame Press, 1982), p. 35.

13. Lloyd F. Bitzer, "Aristotle's Enthymeme Revisited," *Quarterly Journal of Speech* 45, 4 (December 1959): 407–408.

14. Chaim Perlman asserts: "In a controversy it is most often not the *argument* from authority which is questioned but the *authority* who is called upon." *Realm of Rhetoric,* p. 94.

15. Robert B. Ray, *A Certain Tendency of the Hollywood Cinema, 1930–1980* (Princeton: Princeton University Press, 1985), p. 173; Fred Camper, "The Films of Douglas Sirk," *Screen* 12, 2 (Summer 1971): 44.

16. Raymond Bellour, "Hitchcock the Enunciator," *Camera Obscura* 2 (Fall 1977): 72.

17. Tony Safford, "Riddles of the Political Unconscious," *On Film* 7 (Winter 1977–78): 41.

18. Ian Cameron and Richard Jeffrey, "The Universal Hitchcock," *Movie* 12 (Spring 1965): 21.

19. Teresa de Lauretis, *Alice Doesn't: Feminism, Semiotics, Cinema* (Bloomington: Indiana University Press, 1984), p. 76.

20. Immanuel Kant, *The Critique of Pure Reason,* trans. Norman Kemp Smith (London: Macmillan, 1983), p. 310; Rudolf A. Makkreel, *Dilthey: Philosopher of the Human Sciences* (Princeton: Princeton University Press, 1975), p. 266.

21. See Don Ranvaud, "Laura Mulvey/Peter Wollen: An Interview," *Framework* 9 (1979): 31; Safford, "Riddles of the Political Unconscious," p. 41; Elizabeth Cowie, *"Riddles of the Sphinx;* Views: 1," in Cowie, ed., *Catalogue: British Film Institute Productions, 1977–1978* (London: British Film Institute, 1978), p. 49.

22. See Stuart Gilbert, *James Joyce's Ulysses: A Study* (New York: Vintage, 1958), pp. vi–ix; Sylvia Beach, "Introduction (1961)," in Samuel Beckett et al., *Our Exagmination Round His Factification for Incamination of Work in Progress* (New York: New Directions, 1972), pp. vii–viii.

23. Adriana Aprà et al., "Interview with Nicholas Ray," *Movie* 9 (1963): 14.

24. Tim Lucas, "The Image as Virus: The Filming of *Videodrome,*" in Piers Handling, ed., *The Shape of Rage: The Films of David Cronenberg* (Toronto: General, 1983), p. 157.

25. "Chabrol Talks to Rui Nogueira and Nicoletta Zalaffi," *Sight and Sound* 40, 1 (Winter 1970–71): 6.

26. See Kristin Thompson, *Breaking the Glass Armor: Neoformalist Film Analysis* (Princeton: Princeton University Press, 1988), chap. 11, for a discussion of how Godard employed such a strategy with respect to *Sauve qui peut (la vie)*.

27. Stephen Heath, "Difference," *Screen* 19, 3 (Autumn 1978): 72; André Bazin, *Orson Welles* (Paris: Chavane, 1950), p. 30.

28. Aristotle, *Rhetoric,* pp. 2223–2224.

29. Richard Levin, *New Readings vs. Old Plays: Recent Trends in the Reinterpretation of English Renaissance Drama* (Chicago: University of Chicago Press, 1979), pp. 28–41.

30. Jon Whitman, *Allegory: The Dynamics of an Ancient and Medieval Technique* (Cambridge: Harvard University Press, 1987), p. 61.

31. See James L. Kinneavy, *A Theory of Discourse* (New York: Norton, 1971), pp. 264–272.

32. See, for example, Stephen Heath, *Questions of Cinema* (London: Macmillan, 1981), pp. 19–75, 145–164.

33. Levin, *New Readings,* p. 4.

34. Adriana Aprà, quoted in Peter Brunette, *Roberto Rossellini* (New York: Oxford University Press, 1987), p. 148.

35. Christine Gledhill, "Feminism and *Klute,*" in E. Ann Kaplan, ed., *Women in Film Noir* (London: British Film Institute, 1978), p. 128.

36. David Stern, "Midrash and the Language of Exegesis: A Study of Vayika Rabbah, Chapter 1," in Geoffrey H. Hartman and Sanford Budick, eds., *Midrash and Literature* (New Haven: Yale University Press, 1986), p. 107; T.-M. Charland, *Arts praecandi: Contribution à l'histoire de la rhétorique au Moyen Age* (Paris: Vrin, 1936), pp. 135–218; Charles, *L'Arbre et la source,* pp. 139–141.

37. William Rothman, *Hitchcock—The Murderous Gaze* (Cambridge: Harvard University Press, 1982), p. 294.

38. Tania Modleski, "'Never to Be Thirty-Six Years Old': *Rebecca* as Female Oedipal Drama," *Wide Angle* 5, 1 (1982): 41.

39. Heath, *Questions of Cinema,* p. 159.

40. Linda Williams, "When the Woman Looks," in Mary Ann Doane, Patricia Mellencamp, and Linda Williams, eds., *Re-Vision: Essays in Feminist Film Criticism* (Frederick, Md.: University Publications of America, 1984), p. 87.

41. Seymour Chatman, *Antonioni, or The Surface of the World* (Berkeley: University of California Press, 1985), p. 121.

42. Ian Cameron and Robin Wood, *Antonioni* (New York: Praeger, 1968), p. 72.

43. Steve Neale, *Genre* (London: British Film Institute, 1980), p. 43.

44. Jacques Rivette, "The Hand," in Hillier, *Cahiers: The 1950s,* p. 143.

45. It resembles what Kenneth Burke calls "amplification by extension." *A Rhetoric of Motives* (New York: World, 1962), p. 593.

46. Williams, "When the Woman Looks," p. 87.

47. Donald Spoto, *The Art of Alfred Hitchcock: Fifty Years of His Motion Pictures* (Garden City, N.Y.: Doubleday, 1979), p. 216.

48. Ibid., p. 217.
49. A start is Linda Brodkey, *Academic Writing as Social Practice* (Philadelphia: Temple University Press, 1987).
50. C. J. van Rees, "How a Literary Work Becomes a Masterpiece: On the Threefold Selection Practised by Literary Criticism," *Poetics* 12 (1983): 408.
51. Dana Polan, *Power and Paranoia: History, Narrative, and the American Cinema, 1940–1950* (New York: Columbia University Press, 1986), pp. 147–148.
52. Bernard Dupriez calls the device *double lecture* and can find no examples of it outside recent French theory. See *Gradus: Les procédés littéraires (dictionnaire)* (Paris: Bourgeois, 1980), p. 167.
53. *The Oxford Universal Dictionary on Historical Principles,* 3d ed. (Oxford: Clarendon Press, 1955), p. 1872.
54. Roland Barthes, *The Grain of the Voice: Interviews, 1962–1980,* trans. Linda Coverdale (New York: Hill and Wang, 1985), p. 241.
55. Mary Ann Doane, *The Desire to Desire: The Woman's Film of the 1940s* (Bloomington: Indiana University Press, 1987), p. 183.
56. R. Barton Palmer, "Editor's Introduction," *Studies in the Literary Imagination* 19, 1 (Spring 1986): 1–2.
57. Bruno Latour, *Science in Action: How to Follow Scientists and Engineers through Society* (Cambridge: Harvard University Press, 1987), p. 232.
58. Russell Jacoby, *The Last Intellectuals: American Culture in the Age of Academe* (New York: Basic Books, 1987); William E. Cain, *The Crisis in Criticism: Theory, Literature, and Reform in English Studies* (Baltimore: Johns Hopkins University Press, 1984); Régis Debray, *Teachers, Writers, Celebrities: The Intellectuals of Modern France* (London: New Left Books, 1981).
59. Jean-Louis Comolli and Jean Narboni, "Cinema/Ideology/Criticism (1)," in John Ellis, ed., *Screen Reader 1: Cinema/Ideology/Politics* (London: SEFT, 1977), p. 9.
60. Sam Rohdie, "Editorial," *Screen* 13, 3 (Autumn 1972): 3.
61. Constance Penley, "The Avant-Garde and Its Imaginary," *Camera Obscura* 2 (Fall 1977): 11.
62. Stephen Heath, "Film and System: Terms of Analysis, Part 2," *Screen* 16, 2 (Summer 1975): 98–99.
63. Ben Brewster et al., "Reply," *Screen* 17, 2 (Summer 1976): 114.
64. E. Ann Kaplan, *Women and Film: Both Sides of the Camera* (London: Methuen, 1983), p. 16.
65. The *Camera Obscura* Collective, "Feminism and Film: Critical Approaches," *Camera Obscura* 1 (Fall 1976): 10.
66. Rosalind Coward, "Class, 'Culture,' and the Social Formation," *Screen* 18, 1 (Spring 1977): 102.
67. Paul Willemen, "Notes on Subjectivity: On Reading Edward Branigan's 'Subjectivity under Siege,'" *Screen* 19, 1 (Spring 1978): 49.
68. Comolli and Narboni, "Cinema/Ideology/Criticism," p. 9.
69. Robin Wood, "Male Desire, Male Anxiety: The Essential Hitchcock," in

Marshall Deutelbaum and Leland Poague, eds., *A Hitchcock Reader* (Ames: Iowa State University Press, 1986), pp. 221–222.

70. Geoffrey Nowell-Smith, "I Was a Star-Struck Structuralist," *Screen* 14, 3 (Autumn 1973): 98.
71. Charles Eckert, "Shall We Deport Lévi-Strauss?" *Film Quarterly* 27, 3 (Spring 1974): 64.
72. Ibid., p. 65.
73. David Bordwell, "Addendum, 1975," to *"Citizen Kane,"* in Bill Nichols, ed., *Movies and Methods,* vol. 1 (Berkeley: University of California Press, 1976), pp. 288–289.

10. Rhetoric in Action

1. From *Cahiers du cinéma* 113 (1960); translated in Jim Hillier, ed., *Cahiers du cinéma: The 1960s: New Wave, New Cinema, Reevaluating Hollywood* (Cambridge: Harvard University Press, 1986), pp. 150–157. Page numbers in parentheses refer to this version.
2. *Hitchcock's Films* (South Brunswick, N.J.: A. S. Barnes, 1977). All parenthetical page numbers cite this edition.
3. David Thomson's interpretation of the film in *Movie Man* (New York: Stein and Day, 1967), pp. 196–201; James Naremore's dissection of it in his monograph *Filmguide to Psycho* (Bloomington: Indiana University Press, 1973); and Donald Spoto's discussion in *The Art of Alfred Hitchcock: Fifty Years of His Motion Pictures* (Garden City, N.Y.: Doubleday, 1979) all take Wood's interpretation as a point of departure.
4. All parenthetical references are to *Films and Feelings* (Cambridge: MIT Press, 1967), pp. 209–220.
5. *Film as Film* (Harmondsworth: Penguin, 1972), pp. 107–115. Page references in parentheses are to this edition.
6. As a contrast, see Perkins' much earlier essay on *Psycho,* "Charm and Blood," *Oxford Opinion,* 25 October 1960, 34–35.
7. The term is used by Charles L. Stevenson in "On the 'Analysis' of a Work of Art," in Francis J. Coleman, ed., *Contemporary Studies in Aesthetics* (New York: McGraw-Hill, 1968), p. 71.
8. See Noël Carroll, "The Future of Allusion: Hollywood and the Seventies (and Beyond)," *October* 20 (Spring 1982): 54–56, 65.
9. Royal S. Brown, "Herrmann, Hitchcock, and the Music of the Irrational," *Cinema Journal* 21, 2 (Spring 1982): 14–49; Graham Bruce, *Bernard Herrmann: Film Music and Narrative* (Ann Arbor: UMI Research Press, 1985), pp. 183–213.
10. Pages cited in parentheses refer to the version reprinted in Marshall Deutelbaum and Leland Poague, eds., *A Hitchcock Reader* (Ames: Iowa State University Press, 1986), pp. 311–331.
11. William Rothman, *Hitchcock—The Murderous Gaze* (Cambridge: Harvard University Press, 1982), pp. 245–341. This book was completed in 1980 and does not cite Bellour, so it seems likely that Rothman arrived at his reflexive interpretation independently.

12. Kaja Silverman, *The Subject of Semiotics* (New York: Oxford University Press, 1983), p. 211.
13. R. Barton Palmer, "The Metafictional Hitchcock: The Experience of Viewing and the Viewing of Experience in *Rear Window* and *Psycho*," *Cinema Journal* 25, 2 (Winter 1986): 4–19.
14. Larry Crawford, "Subsegmenting the Filmic Text: The Bakersfield Car Lot Scene in *Psycho*," *Enclitic* 5, 2; 6, 1 (Fall 1981–Spring 1982): 35–43.
15. The essay was first published in *Wide Angle;* citations are to the version published in Deutelbaum and Poague, *A Hitchcock Reader,* pp. 332–339.
16. Bruno Latour, *Science in Action: How to Follow Scientists and Engineers through Society* (Cambridge: Harvard University Press, 1987), p. 44.
17. Page citations in parentheses refer to Deutelbaum and Poague, *A Hitchcock Reader,* pp. 340–349.
18. Cf. Gerald Prince, "Thématiser," *Poétique* 64 (November 1985): 428–429.
19. The term is Robert de Beaugrande's; see "Surprised by Syncretism: Cognition and Literary Criticism Exemplified by E. D. Hirsch, Stanley Fish, and J. Hillis Miller," *Poetics* 12 (1983): 89.
20. Quoted in René Wellek, *A History of Modern Criticism 1750–1950,* vol. 5, *English Criticism, 1900–1950* (New Haven: Yale University Press, 1986), p. 275.
21. Robin Wood, *Hollywood from Vietnam to Reagan* (New York: Columbia University Press, 1986), p. 49.

11. Why Not to Read a Film

1. This is not to say, though, that theoretical reflection is any less amenable to the sort of analysis I have proposed here. "Doing theory" operates with respect to cognitive and rhetorical norms within an institutional framework, and it ought thereby to consist of shared hypotheses, assumptions, schemata, and heuristics. For example, one might attribute the influence of the Lacanian mirror-stage parable to the fact that it is vivid and representative, thus memorable and capable of habitual application. A brief analysis of the rhetoric of contemporary theory can be found in Raymond Tallis, *Not Saussure: A Critique of Post-Saussurean Literary Theory* (London: Macmillan, 1988), pp. 18–26.
2. For a discussion, see David Bordwell, "ApProppriations and ImProprieties: Problems in the Morphology of Film Narrative," *Cinema Journal* 27, 3 (Spring 1988): 5–20.
3. Dudley Andrew, quoted on the back cover of Philip Rosen, ed., *Narrative, Apparatus, Ideology: A Film Theory Reader* (New York: Columbia University Press, 1986).
4. J. Hillis Miller, quoted in Imre Saluszinsky, *Criticism in Society: Interviews with Jacques Derrida, Northrop Frye, Harold Bloom, Geoffrey Hartman, Frank Kermode, Edward Said, Barbara Johnson, Frank Lentricchia, and J. Hillis Miller* (New York: Methuen, 1987), p. 221. Elsewhere, Miller

frankly adopts the mercantile metaphor I have been using when he describes the expanding market for theory: "Although literary theory may have its origin in Europe, we export it in a new form, along with other American 'products,' all over the world—as we do many of our scientific and technological inventions, for example, the atom bomb." J. Hillis Miller, "Presidential Address 1986: The Triumph of Theory, the Resistance to Reading, and the Question of the Material Base," *PMLA* 102, 3 (May 1987): 287. The particular parallel remains puzzling, since the "atom bomb" is one of the few things that the United States is notably reluctant to export.

5. Roland Barthes, *Criticism and Truth,* trans. Katherine Pilcher Keuneman (Minneapolis: University of Minnesota Press, 1987), pp. 73, 86.

6. Roland Barthes, *The Grain of the Voice: Interviews, 1962–1980,* trans. Linda Coverdale (New York: Hill and Wang, 1985), p. 76. Here Barthes uses the term *symbolic* to refer to what I have been calling implicit or symptomatic meaning. See also Frank Kermode, *The Art of Telling: Essays on Fiction* (Cambridge: Harvard University Press, 1983), p. 74.

7. Jacques Derrida, "The Purveyor of Truth," in John P. Muller and William J. Richardson, eds., *The Purloined Poe: Lacan, Derrida, and Psychoanalytic Reading* (Baltimore: Johns Hopkins University Press, 1988), pp. 198–199.

8. Barbara Johnson, *The Critical Difference: Essays in the Contemporary Rhetoric of Reading* (Baltimore: Johns Hopkins University Press, 1980), pp. 97–102.

9. Tony Bennett and Janet Woollacott, *Bond and Beyond: The Political Career of a Popular Hero* (New York: Methuen, 1987), p. 153.

10. William Cadbury and Leland Poague, *Film Criticism: A Counter Theory* (Ames: Iowa State University Press, 1982); Dudley Andrew, *Concepts in Film Theory* (New York: Oxford University Press, 1984).

11. Barthes, *Grain of the Voice,* p. 138.

12. Dan Sperber, *Rethinking Symbolism,* trans. Alice L. Morton (Cambridge: Cambridge University Press, 1975), pp. 83–84; Stephen Prickett, *Words and the Word: Language, Poetics, and Biblical Interpretation* (Cambridge: Cambridge University Press, 1986), p. 200.

13. Susan Sontag, "Against Interpretation," in *Against Interpretation and Other Essays* (New York: Delta, 1966), p. 6.

14. Erich Auerbach, *Mimesis: The Representation of Reality in Western Literature,* trans. Willard R. Trask (Princeton: Princeton University Press, 1953), pp. 48–49.

15. Tzvetan Todorov, *Theories of the Symbol,* trans. Catherine Porter (Ithaca: Cornell University Press, 1982), p. 254.

16. Roland Barthes, *The Pleasure of the Text,* trans. Richard Miller (New York: Hill and Wang, 1975), pp. 27–28, 42–43.

17. Colin McCabe now finds the very word disturbing. See his *Tracking the Signifier: Theoretical Essays: Film, Linguistics, Literature* (Minneapolis: University of Minnesota Press, 1985), pp. 132–133.

18. Michel Charles, *L'Arbre et la source* (Paris: Seuil, 1985), p. 126.

19. See Ian Jarvie, "Toward an Objective Film Criticism," *Film Quarterly* 14, 3 (Spring 1961): 21–22; and David Lodge, "After Bakhtin," in Nigel Fabb, Derek Attridge, Alan Durant, and Colin MacCabe, eds., *The Linguistics of Writing: Arguments between Language and Literature* (Manchester: Manchester University Press, 1987), pp. 95–96.

20. I am assuming that lapsing into silence is out of the question. In a more just society, though, no teacher would be compelled to write academic prose merely to hold a job.

21. While this book was in final draft, I discovered that Paisley Livingston's stimulating *Literary Knowledge: Humanistic Inquiry and the Philosophy of Science* (Ithaca: Cornell University Press, 1988), chaps. 6 and 7, proposes that somewhat comparable questions might be put at the center of literary research.

22. Sontag, "Against Interpretation," p. 13.

23. Manny Farber, *Negative Space* (London: Studio Vista, 1971), p. 25.

24. One journalist carrying on Farber's tradition is J. Hoberman of the *Village Voice*.

25. Vance Kepley, *In the Service of the State: The Cinema of Alexander Dovzhenko* (Madison: University of Wisconsin Press, 1986).

26. Donald Crafton, *Before Mickey: The Animated Film, 1898–1928* (Cambridge: MIT Press, 1982), pp. 35–57, and *Emile Cohl* (Princeton: Princeton University Press, 1989); André Gaudreault, "Detours in Film Narrative: The Development of Cross-Cutting," *Cinema Journal* 19, 1 (Fall 1979): 39–59; Tom Gunning, "De la fumérie d'opium au théâtre de la moralité: Discours moral et conception du septième art dans le cinéma primitif américain," in Jean Mottet, ed., *David Wark Griffith: Etudes sous la direction de Jean Mottet* (Paris: L'Harmattan, 1984), pp. 72–90; Charles Musser, "The Early Cinema of Edwin Porter," *Cinema Journal* 19, 1 (Fall 1979): 1–38; Janet Staiger, "'The Handmaiden of Villainy': Methods and Problems in Studying the Historical Reception of a Film," *Wide Angle* 8, 1 (1986): 19–27; Kristin Thompson, *Breaking the Glass Armor: Neoformalist Film Analysis* (Princeton: Princeton University Press, 1988), pp. 218–244; Charles Wolfe, "The Return of Jimmy Stewart: The Publicity Photograph as Text," *Wide Angle* 6, 4 (1985): 44–52. These works are only a sampling of what contemporary historical research has contributed to contextualizing films' referential and explicit meanings.

27. Lea Jacobs, *Reforming Women: Censorship and the Feminine Ideal in Hollywood, 1928–1942* (Madison: University of Wisconsin Press, forthcoming); Richard Maltby, "*Baby Face* or How Joe Breen Made Barbara Stanwyck Atone for Causing the Wall Street Crash," *Screen* 27, 2 (March-April 1986): 22–45.

28. For a sampling, see John Fell, ed., *Film before Griffith* (Berkeley: University of California Press, 1983).

29. André Bazin, "Evolution of the Language of Cinema," *What Is Cinema?*, trans. and ed. Hugh Gray (Berkeley: University of California Press, 1967), pp. 23–40.

30. Noël Burch, *To the Distant Observer: Form and Meaning in the Japanese Cinema* (Berkeley: University of California Press, 1979).

31. See, for example, Thomas Elsaesser, "Why Hollywood," *Monogram* 1 (April 1971): 4–10; "Tales of Sound and Fury," *Monogram* 4 (1972): 2–15.

32. See Raymond Bellour, *L'Analyse du film* (Paris: Albatros, 1979); Thierry Kuntzel, "The Film-Work, 2," *Camera Obscura* 5 (1980): 7–68; Marie-Claire Ropars, "The Overture of *October*," *Enclitic* 2, 2 (Fall 1978): 50–72; 3, 1 (Spring 1979): 35–47; Ropars, *Le Texte divisé: Essai sur l'écriture filmique* (Paris: Presses universitaires de France, 1981).

33. Christian Metz, *Film Language: A Semiotics of the Cinema,* trans. Michael Taylor (New York: Oxford University Press, 1974), pp. 108–146; Peter Wollen, *Readings and Writings: Semiotic Counter-Strategies* (London: Verso, 1982), pp. 79–91.

34. Mary Ann Doane, *The Desire to Desire: The Woman's Film of the 1940s* (Bloomington: Indiana University Press, 1987), pp. 102–103.

35. Geoff Pevere, "Cronenberg Tackles Dominant Videology," in Piers Handling, ed., *The Shape of Rage: The Films of David Cronenberg* (Toronto: General, 1983), pp. 137–146.

36. Teresa de Lauretis, *Alice Doesn't: Feminism, Semiotics, Cinema* (Bloomington: Indiana University Press, 1984), p. 88.

37. I try to isolate some conventions of this mode of narration in *Narration in the Fiction Film* (Madison: University of Wisconsin Press, 1985), pp. 205–233.

38. See David Bordwell, "Historical Poetics of Cinema," in R. Barton Palmer, ed., *The Cinematic Text: Methods and Approaches* (New York: AMS Press, forthcoming); Bordwell, *Ozu and the Poetics of Cinema* (Princeton: Princeton University Press, 1988); Noël Carroll, "Trois propositions pour une critique de la danse contemporaine," in Chantal Pontbriand, ed., *La Danse au défi* (Montréal: Parachute, 1987), pp. 177–188.

39. For a recent sampling of work on early cinema, see Paolo Cherchi Usai, ed., *Vitagraph Co. of America: Il Cinema prima di Hollywood* (Pordenone: Studio Tesi, 1987); on genre, see Rick Altman, *The American Film Musical* (Bloomington: Indiana University Press, 1987); on style and narrative, see David Bordwell, Janet Staiger, and Kristin Thompson, *The Classical Hollywood Cinema: Film Style and Mode of Production to 1960* (New York: Columbia University Press, 1985).

40. Aristotle, *Poetics,* trans. Gerald F. Else (Ann Arbor: University of Michigan Press, 1967), pp. 37–42.

41. Michael Reddy, "The Conduit Metaphor—A Case of Frame Conflict in Our Language about Language," in Andrew Ortony, ed., *Metaphor and Thought* (Cambridge: Cambridge University Press, 1979), pp. 284–324.

42. See, for an analogous discussion of literature, Paul Kiparsky, "On Theory and Interpretation," in Fabb et al., *Linguistics of Writing,* pp. 184–198.

43. See Bordwell, *Ozu and the Poetics of Cinema,* chap. 8, for further discussion.

44. A recent example is Michèle Lagny, Marie-Claire Ropars, and Pierre Sorlin, *Générique des années 30* (Paris: Presses universitaires de Vincenne, 1986).

45. Stuart Liebman, "Apparent Motion and Film Structure: Paul Sharits'

Shutter Interface," *Millennium Film Journal* 2 (Spring-Summer 1978): 101–109.

46. Kristin Thompson, *Eisenstein's "Ivan the Terrible": A Neoformalist Analysis* (Princeton: Princeton University Press, 1981), pp. 287–302.

47. David Bordwell, *Narration in the Fiction Film* (Madison: University of Wisconsin Press, 1985), pp. 274–310.

48. Bordwell, *Ozu and the Poetics of Cinema,* chaps. 5 and 6; E. H. Gombrich, *The Sense of Order: A Study in the Psychology of Decorative Art* (Ithaca: Cornell University Press, 1979).

49. A more detailed discussion of these possibilities is offered in Kristin Thompson, *Breaking the Glass Armor,* chap. 1.

50. Cf. Jonathan Culler's suggestion that a poetics could seek to show "why we interpret literary works as we do" in *The Pursuit of Signs: Semiotics, Literature, Deconstruction* (Ithaca: Cornell University Press, 1981), p. 9.

51. In this respect they resemble the "models" discussed by Ian Hacking in scientific practice; see *Representing and Intervening: Introductory Topics in the Philosophy of Natural Science* (Cambridge: Cambridge University Press, 1983), pp. 216–219.

Index